Brandeis University

A Host at Last

Brandeis University
Alumni Association

Congratulations
on your graduation

BRANDEIS UNIVERSITY

A Host at Last

REVISED EDITION

❖⇒◉⇐❖

Abram L. Sachar

BRANDEIS UNIVERSITY PRESS

Distributed by University Press of New England
Hanover and London

Brandeis University Press
Distributed by University Press of New England,
Hanover, NH 03755
© 1995 by the Trustees of Brandeis University
Printed in the United States of America   5   4   3   2   1
CIP data appear at the end of the book

To the students of the first twenty years,
who helped give Brandeis its image of
intellectual vitality and passionate concern for
the underprivileged and disinherited

Contents

Contents

Illustrations follow page 104.

Foreword to the Revised and Expanded Edition

About two weeks before his death in July 1993, Dr. Abram Sachar asked me to visit him at his home in Newton, Massachusetts. Although his health was declining, he remained in high spirits. As usual, he had many anecdotes to share about Brandeis and the people he had known during his extraordinary career. In the course of this, our last, conversation, he asked me to supervise the publication of the expanded edition of *A Host at Last,* his lively personal account of the founding of Brandeis in 1948 and its early years, which was first published in March 1976. Dr. Sachar had nearly completed the task himself, but understood that he would not live long enough to see it through to publication. I assured him that I would fulfill his wish.

Two years earlier, while I was serving as the faculty editorial representative for the Brandeis University Press, Abram Sachar had asked me if the Press would be interested in bringing out a revised and expanded edition of *A Host at Last.* By then the author had become a legendary figure who had helped found the only Jewish-sponsored, nonsectarian university in the United States and had served as the university's first president from 1948 to 1968. The title phrase, *A Host at Last,* reflected Dr. Sachar's pride in the mission of Brandeis University, namely, to welcome students of all backgrounds and beliefs. The Jewish community would be "a host at last" in the tradition of other denominational groups responsible for the founding of some of the finest colleges and universities in the United States.

A Host at Last was distilled from a much longer manuscript that Dr. Sachar had written earlier. Many passages—and in some cases entire chapters of the manuscript—were deleted, primarily in the interest of economy. Unfortunately, the excised material contained information and anecdotes that could be found nowhere else. To preserve the historical record of the institution, in September 1976 the university printed about one hundred copies of the full text. Distribution of this limited, nonsaleable edition was restricted to libraries and a handful of individuals.

After stepping down as president, Dr. Sachar remained active in Brandeis University affairs, first as chancellor and later as chancellor emeritus. He maintained an office in the international center on campus that bears his name, and, until he died on July 24, 1993, at the age of 94, he reported to work regularly and toiled tirelessly for the university.

One of Dr. Sachar's final tasks on behalf of the university he cherished was to prepare the revised book that follows. Now titled *Brandeis University: A Host at Last,* it incorporates all of the significant material contained in the first edition and restores the most significant material deleted from the original manuscript. Moreover, it contains new information about events since 1976 and reflects the further insights Dr. Sachar gleaned with the passage of time.

Brandeis University   Jehuda Reinharz
Waltham, Massachusetts   President
October 1994

Preface to the First Edition

Launching a privately sponsored university in the mid-twentieth century, without an initial capital endowment and without hope of alumni support for at least a generation, presented many problems that earlier universities did not have to face. I have attempted here, after a twenty-year incumbency as the first president, to select the highlights in the story of the unusual means that were attempted to fulfill the high hopes of the founders. Of course, not every contribution in academic planning and in crucial resources could be detailed. The narrative is highly selective, but I hope enough is included to explain how this little Benjamin in the clan won its place in the fellowship of quality universities and is likely to retain it.

I am beholden to many good friends, loyal staff, and faculty colleagues for their help with the manuscript that improved its accuracy and perspective. There is room here only for general thanks to them, no less sincere, however, when it is not individually identified. But there is a very special debt to Natalie Greenberg, my editor at the Atlantic Monthly Press; to my former research assistant, Marylou Buckley, now with Boston College; and to my son Howard, professor of history at George Washington University, all of whom scrutinized the entire text and were affectionately ruthless in modifying judgments that were inevitably subjective when they were offered by one who had the responsibility for two decades of day-by-day activities. Above all, there is an inexpressible debt to my wife. In the preparation of my other volumes I could count on her sacrificial patience and good critical judgment. Here I was writing the story of a university in whose building she was an invaluable collaborator: it is her story as much as mine.

Brandeis University   A.L.S.
Waltham, Massachusetts
March 1976

Preface to the
Revised Edition

More than fifteen years have passed since this "autobiography" of the university first appeared in 1976. Five successors have followed my incumbency, during which period, at the request of the Board of Trustees, I have served in the specially created role of Chancellor. I have continued no duties in academic affairs or administration. I have interpreted my role as "a counselor, when asked." This function is defined, in the words of the university catalogue, as "Founding President, Abram L. Sachar, whose 20 years of experience is now utilized for the welfare of the University." I have tried to be a good predecessor.

This revision only selectively covers the years beyond my presidency. In it I offer no evaluation of the administrations that followed mine except to express gratitude to the board and to my successors that there has been sustained commitment to the pledges that were made when the university was founded. These pledges targeted high quality in teaching and research, recruitment of faculty on the basis of capacity, and providing opportunity for enrollment and employment to all, never compromised by ethnic, religious, or economic considerations.

With the benefit of hindsight, I have, however, reviewed the pioneering years of the university so as to place them in the perspective of achievement. Many of our faculty and students who came to Brandeis in the pioneering years have fashioned distinguished careers, especially in community service, higher education, the media, government and diplomacy, business and allied callings.

As I worked on this revision, the task sent me down memory lane and offered the opportunity to review the challenges that we faced in our pioneering years. I consulted the influential *Comparative Guide to American*

Colleges in its edition of the mid-sixties, when our pioneering effort had come of age. In the Guide there was a listing, in four groupings, assessing the quality of the colleges: several hundred "selective," another few hundred "very selective," a third numbering about sixty "highly selective," and, in the top rank of thirty-five, "the most selective in the country." This banner group included Harvard, Yale, Mt. Holyoke, Dartmouth, Carleton, Princeton, Wellesley, and two score others mainly founded in the eighteenth and nineteenth centuries. Brandeis, not yet in its twentieth year, was in this peer listing. There is natural pride in the salute at the Harvard commencement during the fortieth year of Brandeis: "A fresh venture in independent higher education, now entering its fifth decade, . . . stands sturdy and full of vigor."

A.L.S.

Brandeis University
A Host at Last

CHAPTER ONE

The American Tradition of Privately Sponsored Colleges

From the earliest days of American history, higher education was considered the special province and responsibility of denominational groups. The founding fathers looked to the clergy and their parishioners to teach the young, guide their elders, and convert the Indians. In 1636, a young Puritan minister, John Harvard, who had been educated at Emmanuel College in Cambridge, England, bequeathed his little library and a few hundred pounds to help establish a college on the Charles River in the Massachusetts Bay Colony. He hoped that it would train "a learned clergy and a lettered people." The General Court of the colony was so impressed by the gift that it ordered the new Cambridge school to henceforth be called "Harvard College."

The founders spelled out their objectives. Their expectations, as Sir Walter Scott would say, had less of earth in them than heaven. John Harvard's generosity was not enough to ensure the school's survival. It quickly fell upon hard times and had to suspend operations. Studies were not resumed until Henry Dunster, an English curate, became president in 1640. He was the sole faculty member, and four students were enrolled in his classes. Dunster proved to be a good administrator, but, in 1653, he dismayed the colony by turning Baptist. He was retired as president, publicly admonished, and placed under bond "to keep the peace."

Lack of funds continued to plague the college until a group of Congregationalist ministers, the Harvard Corporation of the time, hesitantly petitioned the General Court to use some of the principal of the college's first substantial money gift, the one hundred pounds sterling that Ann Radcliffe, Lady Mowlson, had contributed to form the nucleus of a scholarship fund. The court, aghast at the attempt to encroach upon a trust, refused and instead assigned the tolls and rentals from the Charlestown ferry to tide Harvard over its difficulties. Of course, since nothing is as permanent as what is enacted as temporary, the tolls continued to be paid to Harvard for two hundred years. During this same period, the towns and villages of the colony assessed themselves voluntarily—so many bushels of grain, cords of wood, and like provender—to keep the college alive. This forerunner of annual giving, known as "the college corn," enabled Harvard to function precariously until hard cash became more available in the new world.

The base of Harvard's support ultimately came from those who were urged by the clergy "to protect a beleaguered faith from the erosion of the irresponsibles." Solicitation for contributions remained primary in the tasks of the president and the Corporation, so as to save the faith as well as to make sure that a little of England was preserved and sustained on the banks of the Charles.

William and Mary, founded in 1693 and named for the reigning British sovereigns, was linked from the outset with the Episcopal tradition dominant in Virginia. Its charter obligated the college to educate youth piously "in good letters and manners" and to "propagate the Episcopal faith among the Indians." A duty on exports of tobacco was assigned to supplement its perpetually insecure budget. It took strenuous debate to enact the tax; the attorney general was not overly impressed by the claim that the college would help save souls. He interrupted the initial debates with the shout: "Souls! Damn your souls! Raise tobacco." Financial problems continued to threaten the existence of the college, and it was necessary to persuade the legislature to preempt the taxes on peddlers and export duties on skins and furs. But the financial bind remained, and the college closed twice, for years at a time, during both the Revolution and the Civil War. Ultimately it became a unit of the Virginia public educational system.

In 1701, Yale was launched by Congregationalist clergy, themselves Harvardians, who were determined to counteract the softening of the Puritan tradition at Harvard, which was beginning to earn the label of "godless." One group of frustrated hard-liners among the pioneering trustees pleaded their case with a metaphor. "The affair of our school," they wrote, "hath been in a Condition of Pregnancy: Painful with a witness have been the Throwes thereof in this General Assembly; But we just now hear, that after the violent pangs threatening the very life of the babe, divine providence as a kind of obstetrix hath mercifully brought the babe into the world, and behold a man-child is born, wherefore we all rejoice." Perhaps it was the uniqueness of the metaphor that helped win the support of an American-born English merchant, Elihu Yale, who had amassed a fortune as a director of the East India Company. The appeal by Cotton Mather, who became president of Yale, offered a brand of immortality that proved irresistible. "Sir, though you may have your felicities in your family, . . . yet certainly if what is forming at New Haven might bear the name of Yale College, it would be better than an Egyptian pyramid." Elihu's contribution took the form of nine bales of merchandise, mainly dry goods, valued at about $550. The gift was considered critical enough to redeem Cotton Mather's incentive. Old Elihu protested that what he was doing was little enough and did not deserve such acclaim. But he accepted the honor and was proud of it. As a good Congregationalist, he knew his Book of Proverbs: "It is naught, it is naught, saith the buyer: but when he is gone his way, then he boasteth."

Disciples of the "new light," in the revival of Presbyterianism, broke away from Yale to found Princeton in 1746, Timothy Dwight and the senior Aaron Burr being among its first presidents. Princeton had to cope with physical as well as fiscal problems in its early years. Its presidents almost invariably succumbed to fever soon after they assumed office. It became necessary for its representatives to travel to Scotland, preaching and begging funds from Scottish Presbyterian congregations, themselves very much down at the heel too. Not until a sturdier Scotsman, John Witherspoon, was induced to migrate to New Jersey in 1768 did Princeton begin to enjoy relative stability. Witherspoon was to gain the additional distinction of being the only clergyman to sign the Declaration of Independence. The practice of raiding congregations to acquire presidents never ceased, and every head of Princeton, including Woodrow Wilson, was a Presbyterian minister or the son of one. Since the college so often deprived congregations of their ministers to serve as faculty, it tried to make up for its pure-hearted pilferage through consolation payments to the bereft churches, a kind of academic alimony.

Columbia, established in 1754 as King's College, was funded by the contributions of Episcopalians, supplemented by the proceeds of a lottery. When strident objections were raised, the college relinquished half of the lottery revenue so that New York could build a jail and a pesthouse. Having yielded income for such a purpose, there was little problem when the campus was moved in 1897 from its original site to the grounds of an insane asylum on Morningside Heights; mischievous alumni liked to jibe that the acquisition of the site did not call for change in the activities of the new residents. The president was invariably a communicant of the faith, and far into the twentieth century it required a special revision in the bylaws of Columbia to name Dwight Eisenhower president, since he belonged to a small Kansas sect, the Church of the Brethren.

Brown University was founded in 1764 as a Baptist bailiwick, at first under the name Rhode Island College. It was a continuous struggle to keep its doors open, and the word went out from the Corporation "that if any person would, previous to the next Commencement, give to the college six thousand dollars, he would have the right to name it." Similar philanthropic bargains were offered by other struggling colleges, and as they received the stipulated sum, they accepted the names of their benefactors—James Bowdoin, William Denison, Henry Rutgers, William Carleton. Nicholas Brown got an even better deal: Rhode Island became Brown at a discount, with only a five thousand-dollar contribution. But the patron soon found that he was on a treadmill, and his initial down payment ultimately expanded to $160,000. In his instance, there was no regret. Brown was genuinely interested in the university, and his gifts, especially for an endowed chair in belles lettres and the humanities, came with a whole heart.

In all, very few of the newly established colleges could escape the hazards of precarious support. Pioneering a college was rarely related to peace of mind. But neither was insecurity a deterrent. Ingenious methods were often devised to supplement resources. In the 1820s, a network of local sewing clubs was organized whose members undertook the support of Kenyon College. Ministers rounded out paltry salaries by soliciting subscriptions, taking a percentage so that they and their families could survive. If all such strenuous efforts still left the colleges financially vulnerable, this was to be expected. After all, the faculty and administrators were doing God's work, and they had no right to expect assured security. As late as 1869 when Charles Eliot was inaugurated as president of Harvard, he hailed the impecunious status of the faculty as an inspiring example of self-sacrifice in a materialist society. He noted: "The poverty of scholars is of inestimable worth in this money-getting nation. It maintains the true standards of virtue and honor. The poor friars, not the bishops, saved the Church. The poor scholars and preachers of duty defend the modern community against its own material prosperity. Luxury and learning are ill bed-fellows."

In the thirteen colonies, Catholics were few in number and as little welcome as Jews and Quakers. In the infant republic, the Catholic haven, such as it was, centered around Baltimore and southern Maryland. The colony had been founded by wealthy English Catholics. Among these were Roman Catholic priests who had been members of the Society of Jesus until the order was suppressed throughout the world in 1773 by Pope Clement XIV, himself under pressure from various governments that felt threatened.

In 1789 Bishop John Carroll of Baltimore, a relative of the more famous Charles, one of the signers of the Declaration of Independence, was eager to launch a Catholic college. Unless this was done, he worried, there would be few opportunities for Catholics to obtain a higher education in their own country and an even gloomier prospect for a native-born clergy. Carroll, educated by Jesuits in Europe, obtained a charter for a college at

Georgetown and requested the twice exiled Jesuits to serve as its faculty. They were reluctant. The reestablishment of their order depended upon keeping a low profile; besides, many of them feared they had been too long away from teaching and scholarship. Even after 1806, when permission was granted to reestablish the Society of Jesus in the United States and Georgetown became an acknowledged Jesuit institution, the faculty continued to refer to itself simply as "the Gentlemen of Maryland," so tenuous was their hope of complete acceptance. Georgetown was no more secure than any of the other young denominational colleges, but it possessed, as would other Catholic colleges and universities, a "living endowment" in the unpaid services of celibate members of its religious orders.

The growth of Catholic-founded colleges and universities in the United States in the nineteenth century to more than two hundred by 1900 was made possible by two providential developments. First came the acquisition, through the Louisiana Purchase, of former French and Spanish territories, where French Jesuits had laid the foundations for what would become St. Louis University and other colleges. Inadvertently, the French Jesuits helped pave the way for the collegiate instruction of women in the new world. Many had kinfolk, sisters, cousins, aunts, who were members of French religious orders for women, including the prestigious Madames of the Sacred Heart. These intrepid ladies followed in their brothers' footsteps, establishing academies for young ladies near the edges of the frontier. In due time, some of these academies became accredited, degree-granting colleges. Maryville in St. Louis is only two years younger than Wellesley College and one year younger than Smith.

In the later 1840s came a tidal wave of immigration set off by the famines and crop failures that swept northern Europe from westernmost Ireland to East Poland, what John Kennedy referred to as "the great bloodletting." Catholics gravitated in large numbers to the big cities, and it was primarily in such centers that the Catholic-sponsored colleges were established and grew to impressive influence; Georgetown and St. Louis were followed by the various Loyolas, Notre Dame, and many others.

The Quakers fostered a constellation of colleges that began in Pennsylvania and then fanned out to many parts of the country. A highly unpopular sect, the Quakers had a special interest in the founding of such colleges. As pacifists, they had opposed fighting in the American Revolution and had been equated with the Loyalists, most of whom had fled to Canada in the bitter quarrels of the War for Independence. To be sure, those who remained were model citizens, evincing a rare talent for success without resorting to "sinful" but lucrative trading in slaves and rum. Their philanthropy, often unidentified publicly, worked its beneficence quietly and modestly. Yet nothing they did—or did not do—could live down the opprobrium that had been generated when the colonies were fighting the British for survival.

In the mid-nineteenth century, some of their leaders expressed the conviction that the establishment of colleges and preparatory schools dedicated to the highest standards would be an appealing and practical way to create a new image. Virtually every religious denomination had been making superb contributions to American higher education. Why not the Quakers? Such an approach might very well overcome the blemishing misconception of untrustworthiness. The counsel was followed, and soon a network of choice colleges came into being—Haverford, Swarthmore, Bryn Mawr, Earlham, and others. Within a generation, the Quaker name had been completely rehabilitated. Quaker incentive also extended to medical education for women, and many of the first American women physicians were Quakers.

As Americans moved west, church and college moved with them and were among the earliest concerns of the pioneers. New England Congregationalists opened up the Northwest Territory, and such colleges as Oberlin in Ohio almost immediately came into being. The founding principal of Oberlin, John H. Shepherd, took it as his mission in the territory of 1833 to save its people from "rum, brandy, gin, whiskey" and the church from "Romanists, Atheists, Deists, Universalists, and all classes of God's enemies." Within a few years, the objectives of Oberlin had been sufficiently liberalized for the college to become the first institution to admit women students on an even footing with men. From the outset, it had placed no bar on the basis of color, and it played a vanguard role in the antislavery movement by sacrificial cooperation with the Underground Railroad that sent fleeing blacks onward to freedom. And it offered a special welcome for "wayward girls" from New York City who were to be rehabilitated.

It was clear then, before the explosive expansion of land-grant colleges in the nineteenth century and the establishment of state universities and municipal colleges supported by taxation, that the denominationally founded college was the norm in American education. Of the approximately two hundred colleges and universities founded before Horace Mann began his crusade for public education in the mid-nineteenth century, all but twenty-five had a denominational base. This was understandable as a response to the unique pragmatism of the American spirit. Religious expression was increasingly linked to practical social effort. It was no coincidence that the first private hospitals of the country also came into being through denominational initiative.

By the time of World War II, the residuum of denominational origins had all but disappeared in most of the earlier colleges. The curriculum became militantly secular, the courses unrelated to theological orthodoxy. It was rare to impose compulsory attendance at religious services. Religious studies, theology, and philosophy became electives rather than requirements. The Catholic institutions had to wait until Pope John XXIII and Vatican II to eliminate the required four years of religious studies for undergraduates. To their surprise, many theology courses became popular electives. But there remained the pride of sponsorship, the comfort of playing host, the satisfaction of fulfilling a religious mission in modern, practical terms of service to the common good. Every denominational group could point to colleges it had founded and sustained, most with scores of institutions to their credit.

Astonishingly enough, the Jews, the People of the Book, whose sons and daughters sought opportunities in higher education in greater proportion than did any other group, had never pioneered a college for whose viability they were responsible and where they could play host. The phenomenon bears exploration and understanding.

Although there were Jewish settlements in the United States well before the Revolution, they were not large enough in numbers, affluent enough, or concentrated substantially enough in a locality for cohesive community action. Major Mordecai Noah, a visionary of the early nineteenth century, was apparently the first American Jew known to have broached the suggestion that Jews establish a college or university in the tradition of the other sectarian groups. Noah was a colorful character who had dabbled in newspaper ventures as a publisher and editor; he had written popular plays and had been a theatrical impresario. He was an early young hawk who advocated defiance of Britain before the War of 1812. He became sheriff of New York City and encountered some of the prejudice that made it difficult for Jews, even when insignificant in numbers, to advance on their merits. "What a pity," an outraged citizen wrote, "that Christians are to be hanged by a Jew." Noah responded, "What a pity that Christians should have to be hanged."

In 1825 Noah announced a bizarre scheme to organize a Jewish training settlement from which Jews could go to Palestine to reestablish a homeland there. Of course, Palestine would first have to be wrested from the Turks, but the irrepressible Noah was quite sanguine that this could be accomplished. Meanwhile, he purchased several thousand acres of land in Grand Island, northwest of Buffalo, and named it Ararat to recall the spot where another Noah landed his Ark after the great flood. Among those who participated in the flamboyant ceremonies was an Indian chieftain in full regalia, for Noah believed ardently that the Indians were descended from the lost ten tribes of Israel.

From the fertile imagination of this restless character, labeled "Major Bombastes Furioso" by the *New York Post,* came the proposal that the

Jews of America establish a college in the tradition of other denominational groups. In 1843 and 1844, showing understandable anxiety that Jewish young people, including his own children, could not observe their religious traditions in colleges founded by his Christian neighbors, Noah sponsored the establishment of a college where, "while obtaining a classical education, they could acquire a liberal knowledge of the principles of their religion." He was echoing the clarion to action that had brought into being Harvard, Yale, Princeton, and the other institutions that Christian zeal had fathered. Noah's concern was so compelling that he was ready to found the college himself and share substantially in its financial burdens. But the call fell on ears that were as skeptical as they had been when they heard of the proposed utopia on Grand Island. Like so many similar attempts to found a university in the century that followed, fulfillment required much more than grandiloquent announcements or even the acquisition of site and charter.

It should be noted that, though overwhelming obstacles stood in the way of establishing a Jewish-sponsored college, Jewish families were not remiss in their support of higher education. Major private gifts to already existing universities were not exceptional. Julius Rosenwald, Lucius Littauer, Felix Warburg, Jacob Schiff, James Loeb, and Herbert Lehman represented scores of Jewish philanthropists who were exemplary benefactors. But a family gift to a college that had already endured its pioneering travail could not be compared with the corporate contribution of a denominational group ready to assume responsibility for the ongoing life of a university.

The basic problem for the Jewish community was not financial, though that task loomed large, as it did for all denominational groups involved in the sponsorship of universities. The primary difficulty was that the time never seemed propitious to move ahead with such proposals. American Jews, with intimate, compelling ancestral ties abroad, constantly had to respond to emergency situations that demanded priority. As immigrants poured in during the final decades of the nineteenth century—at first thousands, then hundreds of thousands, even millions prodded by persecution and economic and social discrimination in eastern European countries— the major public service resources of the Jewish community were pre-empted to cope with new eruptive exigencies. World War I brought misery to the millions who were trapped in the war-torn areas, and massive relief programs had to be mounted that were unparalleled in the history of philanthropy. The rise of Hitler, the expulsion of Jews from Nazi-dominated lands, the Holocaust, the Displaced Persons' camps, the daring expedients to salvage the survivors, the desperate plans to smuggle a fraction of them into Palestine—all these tragic needs placed enormous burdens on the American Jewish community. When the claims upon Jewish compassion were so urgent, how could one press for support to launch a university, however strong the moral obligation?

To compound the problem, the founding resources now necessary were discouragingly oppressive. The hundreds of institutions that were created before the twentieth century could begin modestly and grow slowly. But a university born in the postwar world required millions to launch and additional millions to operate. The curriculum now covered a vast academic range; facilities, especially for modern science, called for ever more generous support. Unless adequate resources were assured, only such faculty as could not obtain positions elsewhere would be attracted. So the concept of a Jewish-founded university, appealing as it was to a proud and sensitive Jewish community, had to be assigned a very low priority.

Yet the proposals continued to be advanced, stimulated primarily because of the restrictions that kept the denominationally founded colleges limited largely to white Christian enrollment. Even when these exclusive policies eased somewhat after World War I, only a small number of Jews found it possible to gain admission. A brilliant Louis Brandeis, with a background that seemed to fit the gentleman's lineage, could pass muster at Harvard and could achieve a record in the law school that remained unmatched for decades. But a Jewish applicant had to be gold to pass for silver, and with the increase in numbers of native-born American Jews and the inevitable increased desire for college opportunities, the discrimination became a galling outrage. President Lowell of Harvard, who was troubled by the disproportionate increase of applications for admission from Jewish students, attempted to impose a quota. In the professional schools, the admissions difficulties for Jews were even more serious. Medical schools drew the line sharply. For those who survived the battle to achieve a degree in medicine, one of the most favored fields of endeavor among Jews since long before Maimonides, there were heartbreaking disappointments ahead, since the denominationally sponsored hospitals offered few internships and even fewer staff places for the Jewish physicians.

Of course, there was very little expectation that the establishment of a college under Jewish auspices could have more than the slightest influence upon the problems of discriminatory practices. What could one or two or even scores of Jewish-founded colleges do to open college opportunities for Jewish students who sought them? Most Jewish leaders, too, realized that quotas must be fought where they existed and that it would be abandoning principle to establish a university as a refuge. Nevertheless, the discriminatory practices of many of the most desirable colleges kept alive the issue of a Jewish-sponsored university. In the early 1940s, Henry Monsky, president of B'nai B'rith, the largest mass organization in Jewish life, revived the project and appointed a national committee, on which I served, to seek a campus in the Middle West. But all the eloquent arguments that were marshalled in support could not counteract the anxieties of the Nazi terror and the disasters that engulfed Jewish life abroad.

Then, in 1946, there was a totally unexpected turn. A New England medical and veterinary campus, on the brink of bankruptcy, suddenly became available, and the aspirations of a century beckoned fulfillment.

CHAPTER TWO

Birth Pangs

Middlesex University in Waltham, Massachusetts, a suburb of Boston, was a small, privately owned and supported institution, primarily a medical and veterinary school though it was also empowered to confer degrees in the liberal arts. It had been founded in 1926 by a Boston surgeon, Dr. John Hall Smith, who had committed his personal resources to the venture. Though he was part of the Protestant elite of Massachusetts, Dr. Smith had heretical convictions about medical school admissions. He steadfastly refused to set up restrictions on the basis of race or creed, and Middlesex increasingly became a refuge for Jews who were discriminated against elsewhere and for whom Middlesex was almost a last, desperate measure. The university was in endless trouble with the Medical Association, which questioned its standards and constantly threatened to revoke its accreditation. Dr. Smith insisted that such problems arose because the association was determined to prevent Middlesex from graduating large numbers of Jewish doctors and veterinarians into a tightly held Protestant monopoly. The authorities denied the charge, insisting that the facilities of Middlesex were hopelessly inadequate, its academic standards abysmally low, and its apparent "liberal" admissions policy merely a dodge to extract as much tuition income as possible. Dr. Smith had heard these charges through all the years that accreditation was challenged. He exploded in angry rejoinder that the pious disclaimers of its approving authorities covered a blatant antisemitism. He marshalled the record of Middlesex graduates who, though plagued by onerous restrictions and obstructions in taking qualifying examinations to earn licenses to practice, managed nevertheless to achieve distinction in their specializations.

Dr. Smith died in 1944, fighting to the end and, in the process, exhausting virtually all of his life's savings. His son, C. Ruggles Smith, an alumnus of Harvard and the Harvard Law School, abandoned his practice and took over the university presidency. For two years after his father's death, he struggled to keep Middlesex open. Parts of the campus's acreage were sold off to meet faculty salaries and other current obligations. Maintenance was curtailed, and the plant began to fall apart. The Massachusetts legislature then suspended the first three years of the medical program, permitting a year of grace for the senior class to graduate. Only the veterinary school remained, but with very little hope that it could be salvaged.

As bankruptcy loomed, a most unlikely intermediary emerged, Dr. Joseph Cheskis, who had been serving as the dean of liberal arts. Cheskis was a Jewish immigrant from Lithuania who had come to the United States by way of a number of teaching posts in France. He had developed an uncanny linguistic skill, and it was a quaint experience to hear his French and Spanish spoken with a Litvak accent. He had joined the Middlesex faculty as the underpaid head of its humanities division and had become its dean. One of his most heartwarming duties was to recruit scholars who were in flight from Hitler-dominated Europe. They were a harried lot, low-salaried, unprotected, but grateful for an academic berth when none others had been available. Now Middlesex too was about to go under. Cheskis had lived with adversity too long to be overwhelmed by it. He had established valuable relationships with national Jewish organizations during his negotiations to relocate refugee academicians. He determined to revive these relationships in the hope that, through them, something might still be salvaged from the impending wreckage. After all, Middlesex had been a friend in need to Jewish students and faculty. Were there not some resources in the Jewish community that might now be marshalled?

Cheskis's inquiries vindicated his intuition. One of his close friends in the labor movement informed him that there was a committee of public spirited Jews in New York who were seeking a campus on which to establish a Jewish-founded university. The committee was headed by Dr. Israel Goldstein, the rabbi of one of the country's most influential Conservative congregations. Dr. Goldstein, unlike so many of the men who had dreamed of such a venture, was not a visionary. He had had long experience in organizing projects, in his own synagogue, in the councils of Conservative Judaism, in the Zionist movement, and in such communal agencies as the Board of Conciliation, which he founded. In the mid-1940s, outraged by the unfair practices of many of the medical schools, he began exploring, with the cooperation of a small group of New Yorkers, the possibility of developing a Jewish-sponsored college that could cope with the problem of discrimination as well as offer a climate hospitable to positive Jewish values.

Dr. Cheskis strongly urged Ruggles Smith to negotiate for the pooling of resources—Middlesex to offer its campus and existing facilities, the New York committee to assume responsibility for the survival and ongoing support of the medical and veterinary school. He pointed out to Smith and the beleaguered trustees that only a quick transfer could save the medical school from collapse. The budget was not a large one, but the treasury was empty, the unpaid creditors had raucous voices, and, though the institution was in suspense, the overhead was mounting. What was to happen to the teaching staff, most of whom were defenseless refugees who could not obtain other academic positions? There were also pension obligations for some of the already retired faculty.

Smith acted promptly and on January 7, 1946, dispatched a letter to Dr. Goldstein suggesting that Middlesex University might offer a practical possibility for his committee's objectives. He described the campus in rather enthusiastic terms. "It represents an investment of more than a million dollars, with a plant admirably designed for its needs, with a good library." Unfortunately, Smith added, the university had been locked in a hopeless struggle with the authorities in the medical establishment, and it could not survive without an assured constituency and an endowment. Smith said he would recommend the transfer of the campus and its charter if Goldstein's group demonstrated it had the capacity to "re-establish the School of Medicine." The condition was added, apparently in deference to Dr. John Hall Smith's long battle for principle, that when the university passed to its new sponsors there would never be discrimination on the basis of creed or ethnic origin!

Dr. Goldstein responded cordially and visited Middlesex soon afterward. Even allowing for the ravages of a severe New England winter, it was disappointingly clear that Smith had vastly exaggerated the Middlesex assets. The buildings were in deplorable condition; the grounds were unkempt and needed complete rehabilitation. Dr. Goldstein and his committee were not discouraged. The ninety acres of Middlesex campus were favorably located on the Charles River, close to Boston and yet far enough away to offer a college-town atmosphere. With adequate funding, Dr. Goldstein hoped the landscaping could be brought to its potential and the buildings, however neglected and dilapidated, reconstructed and expanded. But over and above the physical factors was the undoubted psychological stimulus the acquisition of an actual campus would create.

With both parties eager for the transfer, negotiations began at once to convert Middlesex into the as yet unnamed Jewish-sponsored university. Within a few weeks the deal was completed. The campus and the charter passed to the Jewish committee with no purchase investment, a better bargain therefore than the acquisition of Manhattan from the Indians for twenty-four dollars in beads. The committee undertook to assume many of the outstanding obligations, primarily the pensions for retired faculty and for the widow of John Hall Smith. But the committee had no money, no constituency, and no educational objectives except the conviction that the school would represent a corporate gift of the Jews to American higher education.

Dr. Goldstein first sought a letterhead committee of outstanding public figures whose names would give prestige to the undertaking. First he turned to Dr. Albert Einstein, whose cooperation, he was hopeful, would assure endorsement from the academic and financial world. Ever since Dr. Einstein's flight from Nazi Germany, the world famous scientist had been living in Princeton at the Institute for Advanced Studies where his research was supplemented by an active interest in the promotion of world peace. In association with scientists and scholars, he had become increasingly concerned about antisemitic discrimination in American colleges. When Dr. Goldstein approached him about sponsorship of a Jewish-founded university, the aspect most appealing to him was the broadened opportunity it would offer for students and faculty to whom other doors were closed. He realized that a single university could offer very little quantitative amelioration, but it could become an important visible symbol of protest and achievement. He wrote to Dr. Goldstein on January 22, 1946, that he would lend his name to the venture. "Such an institution, provided it is of a high standard, will improve our situation a good deal and will satisfy a real need. As is well known, under present circumstances, many of our gifted youth see themselves denied the cultural and professional education they are longing for. . . ." A fortnight later, he consented to give his name to the Foundation for Higher Learning that was to be the fund-raising vehicle. With the Einstein name on the masthead of the Foundation, Dr. Goldstein quickly obtained the endorsement of scores of other nationally prominent personalities—Jewish community leaders, churchmen, political figures, college presidents, educators, and publishers.

When the negotiations were completed to transfer title, it was deemed important to shed quickly the identification with Middlesex. Initially there was some sentiment to adopt the name of Albert Einstein, but the idea evoked little enthusiasm. It was argued that an American university should bear the name of a native American who symbolized the best traditions of American life. The discussion was academic, however, since Dr. Einstein himself neither sought the identification nor encouraged it. Dr. Goldstein then canvassed the list of those who had endorsed the project, and there was an almost unanimous judgment that the university be named for Louis Dembitz Brandeis, the late justice of the United States Supreme Court.

The name was an inspiration. Brandeis had died in October 1941 after one of the most influential careers in American history. He had earned the reputation of "the people's lawyer" because of his long years of gallant fighting for social causes before World War I. He had become an ardent Zionist and had considerable influence on President Wilson in persuading him to endorse the Balfour Declaration in 1917, which validated the right of the Jews to establish a homeland in Palestine. He was the first Jew to sit on the Supreme Court. With Oliver Wendell Holmes, he had consistently supported the liberal position in a Court dominated by conservatives. The name Brandeis, therefore, seemed to combine most felicitously the prophetic ideal of moral principle and the American tradition of political and economic liberalism. The choice of name was universally applauded, but it carried with it a sobering responsibility. The new university would have to live up to the symbol it represented. Einstein wrote, "Brandeis is a name that cannot be merely adopted. It is one that must be achieved."

It was necessary to make a survey of immediate needs in preparation for the opening of the new university year. Dr. Paul Klapper, president of Queens College in New York, had taken the responsibility for evaluation, and he assigned Dr. Roland Whittaker, a member of his chemistry faculty, to survey the Waltham campus and to offer his recommendation. Whittaker's report, submitted in mid-August 1946, was devastating, and it cast doubt on the viability of the entire venture. The ninety-acre campus, he noted, was so badly run down that, without extensive renovation, it could not continue to function as a medical and veterinary school. The grounds were in deplorable condition. The fields were choked by undergrowth, with poison ivy everywhere. The walks were eroded, and the roads were poor, with little exterior lighting to make them safe when darkness fell. The existing library space could accommodate only a few thousand volumes and seating for about seventy. The decrepit old building, originally a stable, could not be expanded. Only one section had a basement. There was a "Castle" that Dr. Smith had constructed without an architect. It might still serve the medical school if its primitive laboratories were reconstructed and if modern equipment became available; but its ventilation was inadequate, and it would be dangerous to conduct chemistry or other life science programs there. There were no dormitories, no dining halls, no recreational facilities. Whittaker wondered what students, unless desperate for admission somewhere, would wish to apply, and what faculty of standing would be willing to cast their destiny there.

In summary, Whittaker concluded that the expenditures to convert the existing facilities and the construction of the required new buildings would approach a million dollars and that, over the first four years, an additional outlay of two million would barely meet minimal needs. Whittaker added that since it was already mid-August, no program of reconstruction could be completed by the target date, only six weeks away. "It will take months, possibly a year, for the architects to prepare plans for such a project. Even if the plans were ready today it is highly unlikely that enough construction could be completed to take care of the first class by September of 1946."

Whittaker therefore recommended that the board limit itself to the existing medical and veterinary school, utilizing whatever new funds it could gather to bring it up to the standards demanded by the accreditation authorities. The plan for a liberal arts college required a campus development quite apart from the medical school area, and, since it was clearly impossible to undertake in the foreseeable future, it had better be indefinitely postponed.

While Whittaker was conducting his survey and writing the report, the campus was inspected by another nationally renowned New York rabbi, Louis I. Newman, who had advocated the creation of a Jewish-founded university in 1923 and who had welcomed the initiative of Dr. Goldstein and the New York group in reviving the project. But he was so discouraged by what he saw that he repudiated the entire enterprise.

Dr. Goldstein was an inveterate optimist, but even he was chastened by the Whittaker report and by Newman's reactions. He forwarded the rabbi's letter to Ruggles Smith, adding a gloomy postscript. "Rabbi Louis I. Newman, who has been one of our strongest supporters, visited the campus recently. He is withdrawing from our ranks because he does not feel that this campus is worthy of the project which we have announced."

When the Whittaker report reached President Klapper, he too had second thoughts about the practicality of opening a liberal arts college on the Middlesex site. He wondered whether it would not be wiser to do whatever patchwork job was necessary for the medical and veterinary facilities and to plan for a liberal arts college later, perhaps at another site. He wrote on August 14, 1946, "In the light of these primary needs (listed in the Whittaker report), and the large amount that will be necessary to provide minimum physical equipment for effective work, it may be well to reconsider the project of setting up a liberal arts college as the initial step in the reorganization."

Meantime, Goldstein had recovered his fighting morale. He insisted that, having gone this far, one more supreme effort was justified to fulfill a historic objective with a campus that, despite its disadvantages, was already in hand and still protected with degree-granting authority. He pledged that he would concentrate most of his community activities to achieve this objective. The trustees decided to give him his way. Goldstein went to work at once to supplement his letterhead names by enlisting families that could go beyond endorsement and offer financial backing. As soon as the transfer of title had been effected, he brought together a development and public relations staff, and preparations began for a series of fund-raising functions. Dr. Goldstein made sure that no doubts were reflected in any of the publicity releases, which announced that two million dollars would soon be in hand. These releases were followed by the announcement of a projected six million-dollar campaign. On March 19, a month after the acquisition of the campus, the *New York Times* carried a story that a fund of ten million dollars was close to assurance.

Before the venture could prove its viability, however, a series of violent quarrels erupted among the sponsors that precipitated Dr. Einstein's resignation and threatened to destroy the projected school even before it was launched. The Einstein name was a magnetic asset; but the old man had rather austere views of what such a university should be, and there were serious clashes with Dr. Goldstein almost from the outset. When he had been approached to lend his name as a sponsor of the university, Dr. Einstein took it for granted that he was to be more than a public relations gimmick. He assumed that matters of academic policy would be discussed with him and that he would have a role in reaching decisions. He was especially concerned that Dr. Goldstein might take it upon himself to make commitments that would influence academic orientation in ways he could not countenance. Einstein's old friend, Dr. Stephen Wise, a dominant force in American Jewish life who knew Dr. Goldstein well and was critical of his flair for press releases, cautioned Dr. Einstein to insist upon safeguards to hold him in check. In a letter of June 28, 1946, Dr. Wise said: "You write to me in confidence. I answer you in the same spirit. As a friend, I say to you, you ought not tie yourself up with the Foundation bearing your name, unless there be some completely trustworthy person, like our friend Otto Nathan [a member of the faculty of the Jewish Institute of Religion], standing at the side of Dr. Israel Goldstein, to give him the benefit of his own wise judgment and your judgment, and thus ensure for him at once a place in relation to the proposed university. . . . You must have someone at the side of Dr. Goldstein whom you can trust."

Dr. Einstein was clearly approaching the same conclusion. Only a few days before, Dr. Goldstein had circulated a letter in which he announced that he had appointed an advisory committee to help in the selection of faculty for the still not organized school. Dr. Einstein's letter of July 1 to Dr. Goldstein was quite blunt. "I am seriously perturbed about the preparation of the academic institutions of the College. When you visited me last, on May 30th, I made it clear that I attach greatest importance to the selection of the men who are to organize the academic life of the new institution. . . . I was greatly surprised to learn from Rabbi Wise (who had written about his probable acceptance of a place among the sponsors) that according to your letter of June 25th, an advisory committee has already been appointed and 'is beginning to give some thought to the selection of the faculty.' When I allowed my name to be used in connection with the establishment of a Jewish sponsored university, an undertaking of tremendous significance, I took it for granted that no important step would be taken concerning the organization without my consent, because without such consideration I feel unable to assume responsibility in the matter. In the present case I do not approve the step mentioned in your letter to Dr. Wise and I regret this procedure as a breach of confidence toward me."

The next day, Dr. Einstein dispatched a letter to the fund-raising director in which he suspended the use of his name for any further promotion until his misgivings were allayed. "I received today the third batch of invitations to be signed and mailed by me," he wrote. "For the time being, however, I am not able to sign them as my further cooperation in the whole enterprise has become doubtful. As soon as things will be cleared up you will hear from me again." Dr. Goldstein smoothed over what he termed a misunderstanding and quickly accepted Einstein's condition that thereafter all such academic matters be left to a small, specially appointed advisory committee responsible to the board and that Dr. Otto Nathan serve as Dr. Einstein's representative. The committee personnel was discussed in a meeting with Dr. Einstein at his Princeton home. Dr. Goldstein and Ralph Lazrus, head of the nationally respected Benrus Watch Company, became the representatives of the board. It was agreed that invitations to serve be sent to Frank Graham, president of the University of North Carolina, to David Lilienthal, head of the Atomic Energy Commission, and to Paul Klapper. Dr. Klapper, who was already deeply involved, accepted the assignment; the others did not reply to the invitation.

For the next six weeks, relationships with Einstein were clouded by an uneasy wariness. Einstein refused to appear personally at a function planned for October, unwilling to be "the big elephant that was to be on display." Einstein's name was undoubtedly a major asset in enhancing the prestige of the venture and soliciting help for it, but Goldstein and his colleagues were learning that he had strong independent views and that the continuous threat of resignation was a seriously complicating factor in planning ahead.

On September 2, 1946, the truce blew up, and Einstein resigned from all association with the project. He wrote that his confidence had been so severely breached that he refused to accept any further responsibility for a university where Goldstein would continue to play an important part. He cited two climactic actions that had forced his decision: Goldstein's alleged negotiations, without prior consultation with him, "for submission of Dr. Abram Sachar's name as the first president of the University," and his invitation to Cardinal Spellman of New York to participate in a major interpretive function that was scheduled for November. He wrote: "From a letter by Mr. Young to my secretary I have learned that Cardinal Spellman has been invited to deliver the invocation at the forthcoming dinner. I have also learned that you have discussed with Dr. Sachar the possibility of his appointment as chancellor and organizer of the University and faculty without the authorization or even knowledge of the Advisory Committee. These two facts represent two new breaches of confidence from your side. I have decided, therefore, not to cooperate any longer with you and I will have to make it clear that from now on I cannot take any more responsibility for any of your acts concerning the planned university. I also cannot permit that my name be used for fund raising in behalf of an enterprise in which you play an important part. Finally, I must request that my name be removed entirely from the name of your foundation and I expect to be notified as soon as this has been done."

Dr. Goldstein did not seek a conference with Dr. Einstein to discuss the alleged "breaches of confidence." The tone of the letter of disavowal made it clear that Einstein would probably refuse to receive him. He wrote at once to deny that he "had made any commitment to Dr. Sachar about the Presidency of Brandeis" and to express bewilderment that Einstein would make an issue of the invitation to Cardinal Spellman. It had never occurred to him, he protested, that Einstein "would be concerned about the participants in a fund raising dinner."

In his denial of any commitment to me about the presidency, Dr. Goldstein was entirely accurate. Dr. Einstein had apparently been the victim of irresponsible gossip. There had indeed been a conference in Miami with me several months before in which Dr. Goldstein had sounded out my interest in a Jewish-founded university, and he had asked if I would be willing to join the panel of national sponsors he was recruiting. In our meeting, I expressed warm approbation of the Brandeis project and indicated my willingness to serve on a national council of about a hundred public figures. But no word of presidency was sounded or even intimated, and later, when Dr. Einstein again withdrew and Dr. Goldstein offered to return to the Brandeis Board of Trustees, he suggested no names for the Brandeis presidency except his own.

Moving ahead of chronology, I should note here that about eighteen months later, in April 1948, Dr. Goldstein curiously reversed himself about his quarrel with Einstein over the presidency. In a letter to me after I had become president, he offered congratulations and then added: "It was, as you know, my judgment, shortly after I launched the enterprise more than two years ago, that you should be its president. Now it can be told,—that my conversation with you regarding that subject was the main cause of Professor Einstein's rift with me." I could not permit this self-serving distortion to remain unchallenged. I was astonished when the issue of the presidency had been resolved that Dr. Goldstein attributed his final break with Einstein as a result of his recommendation of me. In acknowledging Dr. Goldstein's congratulations on May 13, 1948, I added: "I cannot permit one brief statement in your letter to pass without comment. So far as I could learn, Dr. Einstein did not object to the possibility of my coming in as president. He objected to your exploration without consultation with him. He would have objected to anybody, if he were not brought into the discussions before the negotiations opened."

The other "breach of confidence" referred to by Dr. Einstein related to the invitation extended by Dr. Goldstein to Cardinal Spellman. In a short volume on the origins of Brandeis University published a few years later, Dr. Goldstein dismissed the serious import of his action and referred to the invitee, without naming him, only as "an eminent Christian Churchman." Dr. Einstein is made out to be capriciously sensitive. Dr. Goldstein omits to mention that Cardinal Spellman had only recently returned from a visit to Spain where he publicly expressed extravagant admiration for Generalissimo Franco. Dr. Einstein could not condone this salute to the collaborator of Hitler, and the episode must have been especially painful for one whose dearest associates had been victims of the Holocaust. One of our trustees, Adele Rosenwald Deutsch, who lived in Princeton and enjoyed Dr. Einstein's friendship, repeated to me a conversation in which he had said to her, "How was it to be expected that I could have any further confidence in the sensitive discretion of Dr. Goldstein who recognized no outrage nor even indignity in an invitation to the Cardinal at the public launching of the Jewish-founded university?"

When the resignation arrived, Dr. Goldstein realized at once that the hostile withdrawal of a man of Dr. Einstein's prestige would be ruinous to the entire venture. His own association had been a matter of great pride: He had obtained title to a potentially valuable campus and a charter that protected its degree-granting power. It was heartbreaking for him to leave at such a juncture. But the decisive tasks that would bring a functioning university into being still lay ahead—to win the substantial support such an enterprise demanded and to induce the participation and enrollment of a quality faculty and student body. He was realistic enough to admit that, if it became known that Dr. Einstein had withdrawn after a quarrel with him, he would make no headway in generating support. He decided to eliminate himself, with no strictures and no recriminations. Dr. Einstein promptly withdrew his resignation and appealed to a number of close friends to help him in the tasks of reorganization, naming Dr. Otto Nathan as his liaison. Leadership then passed to a New England committee headed by George Alpert, a gifted Boston lawyer, who had served most resourcefully as legal counsel in the negotiations that transferred the campus and charter of the Middlesex Veterinary and Medical College to the Jewish committee.

During the next nine months, until June 1947 when another disastrous internal crisis erupted, the conviction gradually emerged that the university would have to become a totally new venture. The Massachusetts medical establishment had, indeed, been thwarted in its attempt to get the Middlesex charter revoked, but it had become clear that, even with more encouraging results in funding, the medical and veterinary programs could never be more than third rate. Would it not be tragic if, after so many decades of aspiration and hope, the contribution of the proud and sensitive American Jewish community would be identified merely as a precariously sustained institution that functioned ineffectually and without dignity? Would it not be wiser to cut loose from the past and concentrate on the creation of a liberal arts college, born of confidence, uninhibited by any legacy of frustration?

Hence, abandoning the pledges made in all good faith to Ruggles Smith and the Middlesex trustees that the transfer of campus and charter to the new group would save Middlesex as a medical and veterinary school, the decision to start anew prevailed. The official announcement to suspend the medical school operation was released immediately after the small group of seniors were awarded their degrees at the 1947 commencement. A face-saving effort was half-heartedly made to continue the veterinary school, but the accreditation authorities intervened and permitted only a preveterinary enrollment for one year, a final probationary period. Yet here, too, it was considered irresponsible to struggle on when there was so little expectation that guarantees to entering students could be fulfilled. Hence, despite indignant and well-publicized protests and demonstrations by the disappointed students and their parents, the veterinary school also terminated operations in June 1947. It was announced that Brandeis University, retaining only the physical campus of Middlesex, would be launched as a liberal arts university. The target date for its opening was postponed for another year until the fall of 1948.

Meanwhile, Dr. Einstein was becoming as uneasy with the procedures of the Boston leadership as he had been with Dr. Goldstein's. A high-powered public relations and development staff had been employed, which, like Dr. Goldstein's, operated on the promotional strategy that frequent announcements of imposing goals would create an aura of success and increase confidence in the viability of the troubled enterprise. Hence there were constant references, in interviews and press conferences, to totals obtained that equated hopes with confirmed pledges, and a figure of over two million dollars crept into the releases. The three or four larger commitments were reannounced at each affair, though the largest of them, $100,000, had to be quietly canceled when the donor's wife threatened to have him committed for an act that she labeled insane. Undiscouraged, the staff steadily escalated the goals; by the end of 1946 they became $5 million, by March of 1947 the Boston press referred to them as $15 million.

It was a brave ploy at a time when the payment of minor bills was ignored and when the attenuated monthly payroll of the medical school loomed as a continuous frustration. Dr. Einstein became increasingly alarmed by the irresponsible fund-raising strategy. It would have been difficult for any prudent businessman to remain comfortable in such a promotional climate. For Dr. Einstein, the world's most meticulous scientist, it became intolerable. In June 1947, the gathering crisis exploded when Dr. Einstein announced that he was again withdrawing from the Brandeis sponsorship, this time with finality, and he prohibited any further use of his name.

In his statement, Dr. Einstein offered no reason for the irretrievable break. But Alpert explained publicly that Dr. Einstein had wished to offer the presidency of Brandeis to Harold J. Laski, a British intellectual who had played a major role in fashioning the ideology of the Labour party. He had been a visiting professor at Harvard, where he had been continuously identified with left-wing movements. After a visit to Russia when he had sympathetically interpreted the Communist revolution, he had been accused by a British newspaper of following the Communist line. He had sued for libel and lost. Alpert claimed he had to resist Einstein where the future of the university was at stake. "I had no intention of identifying Laski with communism," he declared, "but, having filed suit and having a British court throw out his suit, Laski projected an image that would hopelessly complicate the problem of a university that was seeking to establish itself. . . . I can compromise upon any subject but one," he added. "That one is Americanism. So far as I am concerned, there cannot be now, nor can there ever be, the slightest compromise concerning that."

Alpert's statements, widely reported, drew an angry response from one of the New York trustees, Ralph Lazrus. He accused Alpert of interjecting the Laski issue as a means of diverting attention from basic differences with Einstein. He declared that Einstein had long been troubled by the exaggerated rhetoric Alpert was using in announcing academic plans for the future. He added, "Dr. Einstein believed firmly that the purple announcements about expansion were premature and unwarranted and could well wait until a firm foundation had been established for a quality curriculum and instruction." Alpert returned to his charge that the break came about because there had been an attempt "to foist on the university a thoroughly unacceptable choice as president, a man utterly alien to American principles of democracy, tarred with the Communist brush. This would have condemned the University to impotence from the start."

The charges and countercharges in the public press continued for a full week, during which Dr. Einstein remained silent. Then, on June 28, he issued a statement that explained his withdrawal. He accused Alpert of lying about the whole issue. He had indeed, with the board's authorization, felt out Laski about his interest in the university and had been told at once that he, Laski, was not temperamentally fitted for such an executive post and that he did not wish to leave England. Dr. Einstein had assumed that the issue was closed, and he was astonished when Alpert suddenly reopened the whole matter. "Alpert's charges," he said, convinced him "that the proposed University could not become the type of institution that he and his colleagues had in mind under the existing circumstances and the present leadership, and he was convinced anew that it was none too early to sever the connection."

This was the last public statement on the issue by Dr. Einstein. He would make no further comments to the press that would dignify what his associates excoriated as Alpert's "demagoguery." But in private conversations and in correspondence currently in the university's archives, he amplified his reactions to Alpert's interjection of the Laski issue and its implied aspersion that he and his associates were determined to build a left-wing oriented university. Back in March, three months earlier, he had thought of Laski, among others, as the type of solidly rooted academician, progressive and innovative, that the university needed. His suggestion to sound out Laski as a possible president of Brandeis had been discussed with members of the board. Alpert was present when the suggestion was made, and he had approved it.

According to Dr. Nathan in a later discussion with me, the Laski issue had been closed long before. It was only when other misunderstandings and disputes arose between the two men that Alpert, realizing that in any controversy with Einstein he would have little credibility with the public, reached back to the Laski matter, made it the central issue of the controversy, and released a lurid story to the press about his unwillingness to "compromise his Americanism." It was this "cheap demagoguery," said Nathan, that had so alienated Einstein.

Einstein's withdrawal carried with it not only the resignation of the New York trustees but the cancellation of most of the support that had been pledged at the fund-raising meetings. The financial loss was negligible since the response to all the frenetic campaigning in New York had been less than indifferent. The outraged reaction to the public recriminations and name-calling was more devastating, however. Alpert had to build afresh, and, at this point, he was limited to whatever he could salvage in the Boston area. The Jewish community leadership resisted his appeals for cooperation, some because they had no confidence in him and his reputation as a difficult collaborator, some because they feared the venture would become an almost exclusive Boston responsibility, threatening the financial resources of the established institutions.

Alpert also had to contend with the heavy undercurrent of resentment against him for having demeaned a man whom many regarded as the greatest living Jew, besmirching his name by identifying him with Communist fellow-travelers. They could not forgive the long interview he had given to Bill Cunningham, the influential *Boston Herald* correspondent and national radio commentator, who had elaborated on the contrast between Albert Einstein and the left-wingers "who had tried to capture the university" and George Alpert who had patriotically announced that "he would never compromise on his Americanism."

Rebuffed by the first- and even the second-line leadership, Alpert turned now to men who were not as well known but who were attracted to the university's concept and had already pledged financial support. I do not suppose any university ever had a more unlikely group of founding fathers. With Alpert they numbered eight, although Dudley Kimball, the eighth, had come over from the Middlesex board and can perhaps be described more as a founding uncle than a founding father. Kimball came from an old New England family; one of his ancestors had been a seventeenth-century Harvard trustee. He liked to jest that he was the nonsectarian member of the board. Besides Alpert and Kimball only Norman Rabb, the youngest of the founders, was college educated. Rabb's parents had been Russian immigrants, and had started humbly in Boston with a little grocery business. The patriarch of the family, Joseph Rabinovitz, saw exceptional opportunities in the supermarket development that was beginning to transform food distribution, and he applied his talents to them with remarkable native acumen. His children were given every advantage; the three boys went to Harvard, and the daughter, Jeannette, received her degree from Radcliffe, later marrying a department store executive in New York. The oldest, Sidney, was an authentic business genius and, once he took executive responsibility for the food distribution enterprise, he developed it into Stop and Shop, one of the largest and most powerful supermarket chains in New England. Just as there was a division of responsibility for the management of the food empire, so there was in the family philanthropy which operated as a unit. Sidney concentrated on domestic causes and identifications—the Beth Israel Hospital, the Combined Jewish Appeal, the Symphony, the Art Museum, the Public Library, relations with the Christian community. Irving, the youngest, was mainly identified with Israeli needs;

he headed many of the local campaigns and joined the national strategy bodies that wrestled with the financial crises of the successive wars for Israeli survival. Norman took the assignment for Brandeis. In 1947 it had very little status but Norman had confidence in its potential and his family encouraged his commitment.

Morris Shapiro, also a Russian immigrant, began his business career in Boston as a raincoat cementer, and he learned his English by attending night classes in a YMCA school. When some modest savings had been accumulated, he joined his brothers in a clothing venture that grew into a substantial manufacturing company, the Trimount Company. He was one of the most generous contributors to the Combined Jewish Philanthropies and, in the Israeli campaigns, he usually headed the apparel division.

Meyer Jaffe had migrated from Russia when he was fifteen and had settled in Fall River, Mass., where he began his way up as an errand boy. He too had no formal schooling, but apparently this was no obstacle since he built a major corrugated shipping box company that became one of the largest in New England. In the charities of Fall River he usually set the pattern of generous giving. Since he had considerable experience in the planning and construction of his manufacturing plants, he was named chairman of the building committee of the University, with the responsibility to achieve renovation and reconstruction with virtually no cash resources. He often remarked wryly that it was much easier to maneuver in the jungle of the business world.

James Axelrod was a native of Boston whose parents had migrated from Russia and had established a small woolen manufacturing concern. Axelrod went further in his formal education than most of the other founding trustees, completing two years in the old English High School. But he was soon drawn into the family business and, when his father retired, Jimmy took over full responsibility. He quickly expanded its narrow base and the Wamsutta Mills became a national enterprise. In the emergency campaigns of 1947 and 1948, when the fate of Israel hung upon financial and diplomatic support from the United States, Jimmy's gifts were the largest in all of New England. He accepted the bid to help in the launching of Brandeis and was one of the "sleepers" who turned out to be a major asset. Many a prospect, invited for a day of relaxation in the sun in the Axelrod summer home in "Kochloeffel Alley" in Nantasket, could not resist his Etta's culinary artistry and his own low-keyed, non-intellectual, teasing persuasion.

It was the two remaining members of the founding group who continue to fascinate those who explore the origins of Brandeis. Of the group, perhaps Abraham Shapiro provided the widest contrast to the Nicholas Boylstons, the Lady Ann Radcliffes, and the royal or would-be royal patrons of other American universities. He was born in Lithuania and had reached the United States by way of South Africa. He had built a small shoe manufacturing business in Worcester. Along the way, he acquired considerable Boston real estate of great value. Among his many philanthropies, he created an emergency fund, The Two Ten Associates, for assistance to those in the shoe business who fell upon hard times. The fund has become a major self-help resource. It was Shapiro who subscribed the first fifty thousand dollars for Brandeis as soon as the Boston group assumed responsibility for the university. His Catholic friends, who were legion, never forgot the experience of some Boston pilgrims who wished to climax their visit to Rome by receiving a Papal blessing but were not able to break through the overcrowded Vatican schedule. Shapiro happened to be staying in their hotel and learned of their disappointment. He immediately called one of the American dignitaries on the Papal staff whose college education he had financed, and the pilgrims, to their astonishment, were in the Papal presence early the next day. Among my deep regrets is that Abraham Shapiro died in the first year of the university and thus did not share in the pride of its later achievements.

Finally, there was Joseph Ford, "Uncle Joe" even to those who knew him slightly. He had hoped as a boy in Russia to become an engineer, but the obstacles for a Jew in search of a university education were too formidable. He migrated before he was twenty and first worked as a cutter of women's nightgowns. He attended evening school for a time, mainly to learn some serviceable English. His simple, modest style, in thought and action, was often mistaken for gullibility and naivete and was most misleading. It covered ingenious business acumen and brought him success as a leading soft goods manufacturer. Like Abe Shapiro's, Ford's philanthropies were legion, but because of his own early denial of opportunity, he had a particular, if quiet, passion for giving to schools and colleges. Not that he left out hospitals, temples, homes for the elderly, and the whole network of Jewish and civic causes. Every stray dog or cat could be sure of shelter in the Ford menage. Who but Joe would spend the interval between the trustees' breakfast and the trustees' meeting by scooping up a handful of Danish pastries and feeding whatever campus dog was in mooching attendance?

These were the men who joined Alpert to help create a modern university in the heart of the world's most distinguished center of learning. They were modestly successful in business and their professions, but they had almost no experience in the management of educational institutions. As they turned to tasks whose risks they probably never realized, there was little cheering from the sidelines.

Beset on every side, Alpert received a telephone call from Dr. Goldstein, who indicated that he was now ready to return to the leadership of the project. The Boston group went in a body to New York, and in a conference at the Waldorf-Astoria, they explored with Dr. Goldstein the meaning of his proffered availability. There was no mention of a search for a president; Dr. Goldstein indicated that he himself was ready to assume the responsibility. But he added quite candidly that he would have to impose some conditions. He was unwilling at this time to bring in as members of the Board of Trustees any of the Boston group except the two college men, George Alpert and Norman Rabb. He wished to use the next few months to seek out "men and women of eminence in academic and cultural fields." He assured the men who had refused to give up after he and Dr. Einstein had resigned that he would be glad to have them remain with the fundraising Foundation. But, as trustees of the university, they would have to wait until the climate of the board had been set by other appointees; then, "in due course and in due proportion, the members of the Boston group would be added."

Alpert and his colleagues were deeply affronted. They felt that Dr. Goldstein had not earned the right to set conditions that excluded the men who had become the sole beachhead of support for the university. Virtually all the impressive letterhead supporters had vanished. The main pledges, made during Dr. Goldstein's brief incumbency, had evaporated after his resignation. In the months that followed, until Dr. Einstein, too, had resigned, it was the loyalty and tenacity of the Boston group that had kept the project breathing. Yet, here was Dr. Goldstein snubbing these men, intimating that they were not of sufficient caliber and prestige to serve on the board. They were the first to realize that informed judgment was indispensable in creating a university of quality, and they were prepared to welcome counselors, as trustees, from the academic world. But such new recruits, they said, should be invited as collaborators and not as substitutes.

In a second conference the next day with just Alpert and Axelrod in his synagogue study, Dr. Goldstein insisted upon his conditions. The Boston group caucused briefly in another room and then, mincing no words, informed Dr. Goldstein that, though most of them were only humble businessmen, they would try to make the venture succeed without his help. Thus ended Dr. Goldstein's identification with the project. The remaining New York trustees resigned, and the university became the sole responsibility of George Alpert as chairman of the Board of Trustees, Morris Shapiro as president of the Brandeis Foundation, and their six New England colleagues.

Alpert and his fellow trustees had put on a bold front with Dr. Goldstein during their humiliating experience with him, and they felt cornered, indeed, trapped. They had legal title to a campus and a charter but almost no resources with which to convert technical control into practical reality, and they were facing the hostility of powerful elements in the Greater Boston community. They determined to make one last attempt for support by presenting the case for Brandeis at a special meeting of key Boston families. It was planned for December 26, 1947. Even Alpert and Abe Shapiro, who were the most determined, went into the session with more gloom than confidence. "If we make no headway there," Alpert told Shapiro grimly, "we'll just have to call it quits."

About fifty men gathered for the showdown. Only a few were really committed to the venture; the rest were either skeptical or indifferent, present because friends whom they could not refuse had asked them to attend. One of them, Yoland Markson, a respected community leader, probably voiced the sentiment of all the doubters. He noted that the little bastion in Palestine was at that moment battling desperately to stay alive, that the Displaced Persons' camps were crowded with the survivors of the Holocaust, that inevitably the university would become a Boston responsibility, and that limited resources ought not to be depleted at such a time to the detriment of prior causes.

Thus far, Markson probably was expressing the sentiment of the majority. Then he added a gratuitous note, insisting that college education unrelated to the professions was a very much overrated need, that those who had practical common sense and stamina, the main ingredients for success, would usually come through without ornamental degrees. Joe Ford had been sitting quietly, already determined that his contribution would be influenced by the reaction of the other community leaders. But Markson's comment touched a raw nerve. He rose in anger, scolded Markson for denigrating one of the great privileges of American freedom, and then announced that he would pledge $25,000. His statement transformed the mood of the audience. Within a few minutes, more than a quarter million dollars had been pledged, including a major gift from Markson himself. Alpert and his colleagues had not only their mandate but a new reserve of courage with which to go ahead. Later, as they looked back upon the many dispiriting vicissitudes that the venture had undergone, they counted the Somerset Hotel meeting and Ford's response as the turning point in giving reality to the dream of a Jewish-founded university.

CHAPTER THREE

"We Knew We Were Pilgrims"

Now the search for a president began in earnest so that the university could open in the fall of 1948 with a faculty and student body under assured leadership. The trustees sought the advice of the two men they most respected: Dr. Paul Klapper, president of Queens College, and David K. Niles, who had served as administrative assistant to President Roosevelt and had continued in the post under President Truman.

Dr. Klapper had been chairman of the academic advisory committee and had supervised the survey of campus needs. The presidency of Brandeis had been offered to him after Dr. Goldstein's contretemps, but he quickly begged off. He did not believe that he could undertake such pioneering hazards in his middle sixties, especially since, as he put it, "he was a member of the coronary club." He suggested that the trustees invite me to the campus to explore my availability.

David Niles was based at the White House, but he returned regularly to Boston for weekends. There he directed the nationally famous Ford Hall Forum and held court for the young New England leaders in far-into-the-night discussions on the issues of the day. My friendship with Niles went back many years to when I was on the faculty of the University of Illinois and had been invited several times to speak at Ford Hall. When consulted by the Brandeis trustees, Niles joined in Dr. Klapper's recommendation that I be promptly approached. The next day, Niles called me (we had moved to Sherman Oaks, California, in 1947) to say that he had proposed me for the presidency of Brandeis, and he urged that I come to Boston to be interviewed by the trustees. I had just begun to unwind after retiring from twenty years of administration, travel, and fund-raising as national director of the Hillel Foundations, and I was also quite aware of the troubles that had beset the Brandeis project. I asked for some time to think out the implications of the invitation, for I was not sure that even a trip was warranted. In the meantime, I wrote to Dr. Stephen Wise, a devoted friend. His reply was a devastating appraisal of the entire Brandeis project, citing the stigma that it bore after the resignation of Dr. Einstein.

"I have rarely had a letter that troubles me more than your own. If I were not an old warm friend of yours, who believed enough in you to ask you to be my successor some years ago as President of the Jewish Institute of Religion, I would not write to you as I am about to write to you. I want you and Thelma to know that I cannot think of a greater disaster that could befall you than to tie yourself up with Brandeis University. . . . I close by saying to you, dear Abe, I covet service and honor for you. You still have, under fifty, something to contribute, much to contribute, to Jewish life, to Jewish learning, to the Jewish university life of our country. Beware of this! You will be enmeshed in something which will bring you nothing but pain and hurt and shame if you associate yourself with Brandeis University."

While my wife, Thelma, and I were weighing the significance of another transcontinental uprooting, David Niles called again, and I shared with him the alarming admonitions of the Wise letter. Dr. Wise was one of his intimate friends, and he made no attempt to refute his advice. But he insisted that, however great my misgivings, I owed it to the validity of the concept at least to come for the interview. I agreed to make the trip east, planning to stop in Washington for a preliminary discussion with Niles and then to fly on to Boston.

I met with Niles in his White House office. He reminded me that the issue was not whether there should be a Jewish-founded university, for that issue had been settled; the commitment had been made. The only remaining question was whether the university would be a pedestrian undertaking, embarrassing the American Jewish community, or a high-quality institution that would meet the hopes of generations who had so long waited for fulfillment. He paid me the compliment of expressing confidence that I would have sufficient prestige and leverage in the American Jewish community and in academic circles to counteract the wrangles of the past. But he urged me to be firm with the trustees, insisting that there must be sufficient independence in the presidency to make sure that the highest academic standards would be met and that internal bickering be contained. I then flew on to Boston.

The trustees had apparently called me in not to look me over, nor to determine whether I was their man. Undoubtedly they had, in advance, done considerable checking of my background and national experience. The conference turned into an undisguised appeal for me to take over the Brandeis presidency. As each one spoke, he emphasized different aspects of the projected university, but all of them revealed how deeply committed they were to the venture. America had been good to them, immigrants or the sons of immigrants, and because they remembered the restrictions and humiliations of their people in eastern Europe, they could not take for granted what they had been free to achieve in their adopted land. The Lowells, the Cabots, the Eliots, the Coolidges, the Saltonstalls—they were secure in their status; there was no call upon them to demonstrate gratitude. But an Abraham Shapiro, whose accent was pure Slobodka, felt impelled to express appreciation for the freedom and dignity of American life. How better to do so than by becoming the host in a great academic enterprise, open to all, in the fellowship of the best universities. As I listened to them, they reinforced the conviction that there was enormous power in the constituency that they represented, a power that had been generally misunderstood and overlooked by those who glamorized letterhead names. These remarkable men all had the traditional Jewish awe of education and the educated man. Most of them had no university of their own. Here they found an ideal identification, and they were determined to fashion it into the proudest of symbols, regardless of what it required in energy and resources. In their appeal to me to head up the university, they were seeking not only an interpreter and an executive officer whose competence they had appraised in technical administrative terms; they were seeking an ally for the fulfillment of a visceral commitment.

I made no decision that night, asking for a quiet week of reflection at home. To this day, my wife contends she knew when I alighted from the returning plane and she saw the look in my eyes that I had made up my mind to enlist in the venture (even though I didn't realize it then). Within the week, I concluded that, however serious the public relations damage of the two acrimonious years of prehistory, the concept of the university had sufficient inner power to overcome the basic obstacles. I decided to accept the offer of the presidency, but there were several conditions that had to be met, which I outlined in a letter to George Alpert before returning to Boston to complete the negotiations.

First, the trustees would have to pledge to underwrite whatever deficit might develop in the initial four years of the university's existence. There had to be protection for the precarious beginning years, and this could be provided only by the founding trustees. If there were such a guarantee, it would take Brandeis at once from the realm of hope and promise and establish it as a solvent, confident enterprise.

A second condition had to do with the pledge of a free hand for the president and the administration in the academic affairs of the university—curriculum, degrees, admissions, honors. "I am sure," I added, "that you and the trustees would not want it any other way. You indicated that you envisaged the task of the trustees to conduct the business affairs of the University and were very ready to give complete freedom to the president and the proper faculty representatives in all matters that concern educational policy." This point had to be validated in the light of the recent public experience where lay boards and their leadership had often moved into the functional aspects of communal institutions. It would be safer to have this jurisdiction clarified from the outset.

The third condition related to the expansion of the board so that it would become nationally representative. "At present," I wrote, "Brandeis is virtually a Boston project and even in Boston much of the 'official' leadership is either skeptical or downright opposed. For a while it may be possible to push the project in the face of such opposition, or in spite of the limitation of support to Boston. But the project must soon burst out of such confining limits. It must be developed into a national enterprise with a flooring of national support, with the sustained interest of national leadership."

The final condition had to do with the responsibility for fund-raising. In my conference with the trustees, I had been assured that this essential task would be "a very minor part" of my duties, that the trustees would do most of the cultivation and legwork. I was realistic enough to know that a president of a modern, privately sponsored university could not avoid the tasks of interpretation and fund-raising. But I dutifully noted the promise of the trustees, knowing that this pledge was an illusion and knowing that they knew it too. I must confess that I set down this understanding with tongue in cheek.

After dispatching the letter to Alpert, I wrote to Dr. Wise to tell him that, if the conditions I had outlined were fully met, I planned to accept the presidency of Brandeis. The letter was as much a summary for me of my approach to an awesome new responsibility as it was a report for him.

"I waited to write you again until I had the opportunity to visit the proposed Brandeis University campus and to confer with the present leadership of the project. Your letter had made a very deep impression on me. You must know how grateful I am that you wrote to me like a father to a son, deeply interested in the effect of any decisive action on our family destiny. I have spoken to David Niles at great length and to others whose judgment I cherish. It seems to me now that a distinction must be drawn between the concept of Brandeis and the way it has been handled in the past couple of years. No one has doubted that the concept is sound, that the University sponsored by Jews, but open to all groups, which is a gift of the American Jewish community to American education, is a valuable project."

Dr. Wise responded at once, quite disappointed, but wishing me the best of good fortune. "I have your letter. I am sorry to say to you that I must predict, as your old friend, that if you accept the post of President of Brandeis University, you will, in time, have every reason to regret it. I wish you the best of good fortune, but just put this letter in your files—I warn you, I warn you! . . ."

After dispatching my letter to Alpert, I wrote to Niles to inform him of the conditions I had set for acceptance of the presidency and to ask for his continued collaboration. I expected that he would be among the first new members of an enlarged Board of Trustees. I concluded, "I need not add that one of the strongest inducements to consider this whole project affirmatively has been the assurance that you believe in it, and that we could always count upon your tremendous store of experience. . . ."

A few days later, I flew east again for the definitive interview. The trustees gladly accepted all the conditions I had set forth. I was not surprised by their ready acquiescence to respect the administration's complete freedom of action in academic matters. But I was surprised by the alacrity with which they agreed to underwrite the deficits that might develop over the next four years of inevitable expansion. None of the trustees were men of limitless wealth, yet they were undertaking a guarantee that might call for substantial personal sacrifice. Though they were never called upon to meet that guarantee, it was a magnificent act of faith that, in my judgment, entitled them to be designated as the founding trustees who turned rhetoric and aspiration into responsible commitment.

On May 1, I moved into the Parker House in Boston, which became my residence for the next few months. My family remained in California so that the younger children, Edward and David, could finish their year's schooling. Howard, our oldest son, was studying and traveling in Europe after graduating from Swarthmore. I commuted to California every fortnight until the entire family could be reunited in the fall, settling into a Brookline apartment hotel while the search for a president's house was under way. An old New England home in Newton was located, but it took many months to renovate and redecorate it. The furnishing became a cooperative effort, a special committee undertaking the responsibility to solicit contributions from selected firms. The living room was equipped by one firm, the dining room by another, the study by a third. Individual articles came in for an enlarged institutional kitchen, the bedrooms, the sunroom, the garden. At the end, the president's house had become a lovely center not only for personal living but for major university entertainment, and all virtually without cost.

On June 14, I was introduced to the Boston Jewish community at a general rally in the Statler Hotel, where about a thousand people gathered to meet the new president and to hear his conception of the university and plans for the future. I had two objectives in the scheduled address: first, an affirmative interpretation of the university and the rationale for its support; second, an attempt to dissipate what I considered misunderstandings about its objectives that had been put forward by some of its earlier sponsors. The affirmative theme, a quality university underwritten for the first time by American Jews, needed little further buttressing; it had already been widely publicized. Only one point that had first attracted Dr. Einstein seemed to me to need rebuttal. He had worried a great deal about discrimination in many of America's best institutions. In his telephoned address to the New York meeting, when he still headed the Foundation, he had noted that Brandeis would be a moral response to the quota system. "Effective remedy can get secured only through self help," he said. "We must attempt to create opportunities for higher intellectual education at least for a part of our young people. In this way the number of youngsters seeking admission to existing universities will decline which will improve our moral situation there." Such reasoning had never seemed to me to be valid or appropriate. It was not valid because a small university, or even a very large one, could not possibly draw off more than an infinitesimally small number of Jewish applicants. And surely, it was unwise for a Jewish-founded university to become a ghetto for Jews who were excluded by the discriminatory practices of other universities. Quotas must be fought where they existed, and not by flight.

I then turned to the distinction between a Jewish-founded university and a Jewish university. Some of the early sponsors leaned toward the concept of a university that, while offering general studies, concentrated on Jewish values and was intended to train students for Jewish leadership. After his resignation, Dr. Goldstein published a volume in which he expressed the hope that the administration would be concerned with the university as "the inculcator of uniquely Jewish values, an intellectual and cultural center of Jewish import, and the training ground for American Jewish leaders of tomorrow."

I pledged, of course, that Brandeis would be vitally concerned with Jewish studies, that there would be a close relationship to the educational institutions of Israel, and that there would be proper respect for the Jewish tradition. But there was no expectation that the university would become a parochial school on a university level. The model was to be not the Yeshiva or Catholic University of America or Baylor, but rather Harvard or Princeton or Swarthmore. At no point in my address did I directly refute the earlier sponsors of the university, but I made it clear that I would always keep in mind that Brandeis was not intended to be a refuge for students who fled from discrimination elsewhere and that, while the temper and climate of the university would reflect the traditions of the host group, there would be no attempt at indoctrination of any kind. The enthusiastic response of the audience, and afterward of the press and other media, made me feel that these expressed purposes struck a responsive chord in a proud and sensitive constituency whose support we hoped to enlist.

Perhaps our objective was best expressed in the seal that was soon afterwards devised for the university. The heraldry was assigned to Kenneth Conant, an erudite Harvard professor who developed a design that included the three hills of Boston, beacons flaring from them, within which he centered the Hebrew word for truth—Emet. Harvard's seal also focused on truth, but had expressed it in the Latin word, Veritas. I added the framework verse from the Psalms, "the search for truth even unto its innermost parts."

Meantime, renewal work on the campus that had been going forward all through the spring and summer of 1948 to prepare for the opening of the school year was accelerated. The small, white stone house, once the private residence of Dr. John Hall Smith, was converted into an administration center and, inevitably, was dubbed the White House. The architects struggled with the other facilities that had been meant for a medical and veterinary school. There was the Castle, a series of interconnected buildings that had been constructed by Dr. Smith without an architect. He had received his inspiration from an old volume that contained a picture of the Cavendish Castle in Ireland. Many paradoxes were concentrated in the refashioning of the campus; but they were climaxed when the main facility of the first Jewish-founded university turned out to be modeled on a medieval Irish castle!

Some of the laboratories were made over to provide a university cafeteria. Classrooms were combined for a makeshift gymnasium and rumpus room. All other spaces, down to the last nooks and crannies, were transformed into dormitory facilities for approximately 150 students. As the Castle was steadily surrounded by modern buildings, it became a passionately protected symbol for student dissentients who were in revolt against the pragmatic spirit of their world. It was quaint and perhaps even bizarre; it boasted none of the modern conveniences that their parents had in their bourgeois, middle-class homes. But exactly because of this, the antiestablishmentarians fought for the privilege of being assigned there. They brought their friends out to be photographed in a courtyard that made them feel that they were transported to the nonindustrial middle ages. They exulted when the federal government gave permanent status to the Castle by naming it a national treasure!

The one general classroom building of old Middlesex was remodeled to include several science laboratories, and its open inner court was roofed over to house a lecture hall with a capacity of about 500; later, as Nathan

Siefer Hall, it became the school auditorium. There was an apple orchard and a wishing well that the first students vowed must never disappear. Later, when nostalgia had to be sacrificed to the relentless pressure of the needs of a modern university and sophisticated science laboratories displaced both orchard and well, there were anguished letters of protest to *Justice,* the school newspaper.

As with the president's house in Newton, the call went out for assistance in renovating the campus. Gifts in kind poured in—carpeting, linoleum, draperies, kitchenware, kegs of nails, bundles of plywood, desks, chairs, beds, mattresses, lamps, microscopes, Bunsen burners—equipment that was indispensable and equipment that was useful but that could not usually be refused. Of course, it did become necessary occasionally to decline gifts, though with tact and finesse. One tender-hearted nature lover offered to purchase 150 birdhouses so that Brandeis could become a major sanctuary for the birds of New England. I asked for the counsel of the Audubon Society and was advised to be cautious about "gifts that eat." Bird feed would be quite a drain on the narrow resources of a young school, and, within an hour after ingestion, there would be problems for the maintenance staff and for the more idyllically inclined students lounging under the trees. The donor's well-intentioned offer was gently declined. But the generous impulses of the university's patrons were, on the whole, more utilitarian, and the campus began to take on attractive form and operating effectiveness for the assignments that lay ahead.

Now applications for admissions began to trickle in. We had decided to enroll only freshmen, taking no transfers in the first years so as to create our own tradition. With this plan, it would take four years to complete a full undergraduate cycle, giving us welcome leeway to stagger the development of the curriculum, the appointment of the faculty, and the investment for the physical facilities. We had no way of knowing whether there would be enough applicants to form even a very small freshman class, so each day's mail was an adventure. Ruggles Smith, who had been named director of admissions and registrar and who maintained his office on the campus, kept me informed after the daily morning and afternoon mail deliveries. Sometimes the message would be, "Not much this morning, one applicant," or, "Good word today, four inquiries and three matriculations." It was an anxious count, for we were fully aware that only a very special type of student would be attracted to a college that was not accredited and could not be for at least the six qualifying years and whose degree, if we ever reached the point of granting degrees, might not have any academic value. Those who applied obviously had diverse motives. Some intrepid souls were intrigued by the prospect of becoming part of a pioneering class in a pioneering school. Some expected to find a comforting, compatible climate in a Jewish-founded university. Some may not have been accepted in the schools of their first choice. Ultimately, 107 enrolled, and in later years, when they became respected alumni, many of them leaders in their professions, they took pleasure in referring to their youthful selves as "kooks with a passion for adventure."

The inauguration of the university and the installation of the first president was scheduled for October 8, 1948, in Symphony Hall in Boston. The invitation was sent to university presidents and the heads of learned societies around the world. There was a cordial response, and we were gratified to be host to one of the largest university convocations of the twentieth century. The unusually large representation that came for the installation was, of course, not a tribute to anything that had yet been accomplished. The campus had barely been settled, and a small freshman class prayerfully enrolled. There was no certainty about the monthly payroll for even modest expenditures. We had to conclude that participation by representatives of the oldest universities was obviously a tribute to an assured potential. The academic world knew the Jewish community and had deep respect for its generosity in every communal undertaking. The president of Brown University, Henry Wriston, perhaps spoke for all his colleagues when he called me aside at the reception that followed the convocation. He wished me well and then added: "How fortunate you are. Just think of being president of a university that will never have any financial problems!" I was startled, for taken by itself, the comment seemed to be repeating the old canard that Jews are affluent enough to undertake anything. Wriston caught himself, for he had not meant this at all. He added that it was his experience, over a long lifetime, that Jews had an unusual sense of communal dedication. When they undertook anything, they could always be counted on to see their objective through. "Yes, Sachar, you are a lucky man."

But though, apparently, our Christian friends had undeviating confidence in the capacity of the Jewish community to meet its responsibilities, the Jewish establishment was not nearly so sure. Even our trustees still held their collective breath and were awed by the responsibility they had assumed. Most of them probably did not realize that Brandeis was located on Boston Rock, the highest point of land due west from the heart of the city on the perimeter of what is metropolitan Boston. It was from Boston Rock that Governor John Winthrop had surveyed the site of the future city more than three hundred years earlier. I could not help paraphrasing a sentence from Governor Winthrop's history of the Massachusetts Bay Colony, relating it to our situation as Brandeis began its academic journey: "We *knew* we were pilgrims."

Before completing the chronicle of the launching of Brandeis, a brief epilogue may be appropriate. It concerns the response to the later progress of the university by three of the men who were involved in the planning stages.

Albert Einstein's cold anger never thawed out. After my first year in the presidency, when I was beginning to recruit senior faculty members, I wrote to Dr. Einstein to ask for his recommendation for our physics department, hoping that the request, if granted, might open the door to reconciliation. Dr. Einstein refused to be drawn into any responsibility, even unofficially. On July 4, 1949, he wrote: "Thank you for your kind letter of June 26th. After my experiences with the distrust and the untruthfulness of certain members of the Board of Trustees, I do not feel justified to induce a younger colleague—even indirectly—to accept a position at Brandeis University. I feel therefore unable to propose somebody: I am, however, always ready to give you information about any prospective candidate."

In March 1952, as the university was completing the first four-year cycle, I tried again to effect a reconciliation. I knew the high regard Dr. Einstein had for David Niles, who was winding up his incumbency as administrative assistant to President Truman. I therefore wrote asking if Niles and I could call on him in Princeton to give him a report on what had happened in the four years since the university was launched. Dr. Einstein would not budge. He wrote back by return mail: "I was somewhat astonished by your letter of March 25th. The most concise answer to it has been formulated a hundred years ago by Schopenhauer who said: '*Erlitten Unbill vergessen, heisst mühsam erworbenes Gold zum Fenster hinaus werfen*'" (To forget injuries that we have suffered is equivalent to throwing well-earned money out of the window).

A year later, I made another attempt and, on May 20, 1953, transmitted the wish of the Board of Trustees for Dr. Einstein to receive one of the first honorary degrees the university now had the authority to confer. I expressed the hope that the period of misunderstanding could be permitted to merge into the trials and errors of pioneering. In reply, he sent a handwritten note in German declining the degree, though his personal references were cordial. He wrote: "It is a sorry thing not to be able to answer a friendly attitude in the same manner. But in this case, I can't help it. What happened in the stage of preparation of Brandeis University was not at all caused by a misunderstanding and cannot be made good any more. I therefore am unable to accept the doctorate honoris causa offered to me. . . ."

There was a final effort in 1954. As the faculty expanded, another appointment in the department of philosophy became urgent, and Dr. Rudolf Kayser, a son-in-law of Dr. Einstein who had won distinction with his studies in the philosophy of Spinoza, was warmly recommended. Knowing of the difficulties of the past years that had alienated his father-in-law, Dr. Kayser inquired of him whether he should be considered. Dr. Einstein had no quarrel with the quality of the university or with the standards that it maintained, and he encouraged Dr. Kayser to join the Brandeis faculty. I wondered whether this development had possibly changed Dr. Einstein's personal attitude, and in January 1954, I made a final effort. The old man was obdurately consistent. He wrote: "If you would be simply a private person who has written delightful books, I would gladly accept your kind offer to visit me. Under the prevailing circumstances, however, it is not possible for me to do so. As you are informed about the relevant past events you will easily understand." Soon after this exchange, Dr. Einstein died.

Dr. Goldstein's withdrawal from the project in 1947, a year before the university was launched, was apparently soon regretted by him when it became clear that the enterprise was to become an exciting American success story. He began then to press for recognition in the university literature and in public references as the "Founder of the University." In 1951 he published a volume in which he narrated the early events, glossing over many of the difficulties that had made his position untenable to Dr. Einstein and to the Boston group. The founding trustees deeply resented his self-advertising assumption of the role of founder. They remembered that he had twice withdrawn before the university had opened, the second time after a most insulting conference with the men who had saved the institution from collapse.

It was only when the passing years placed the early episodes in a calmer perspective that I was able to persuade the trustees, the number now substantially augmented, that perhaps the quarrels of the past could be laid to rest if Dr. Goldstein received the university's honorary degree. In 1958, in advance of the university's tenth anniversary, the founding group reluctantly acquiesced, though the citation that I wrote seemed to them overly magnanimous. It noted that Dr. Goldstein was being honored for having brought the university "to the threshold of fulfillment." Dr. Goldstein accepted the degree, but he remained dissatisfied. A few weeks after the exercise, he wrote to me to insist that the university literature refer to him as the "founder" of Brandeis, and he kept promoting the claim in periodic press conferences and interviews and in the biographical sketch that he thereafter regularly submitted to "Who's Who."

By 1963, it appeared that he had given up on the university. In an interview in the *Jerusalem Post* on December 13, he declared: "It could be said that my primary motivation in fathering Brandeis University was a Zionist one, that of creative Jewish survival, a Jewishly-sponsored seat of learning where Jewish youth primarily should receive not only a good general higher education but an opportunity for a higher Jewish education and the influence of a Jewish cultural environment and possible inspiration for careers of Jewish service. Brandeis University, with all its merits and

achievements, has not fulfilled these hopes. Since it is still a young institution, not yet tradition bound, it can still chart its course differently, if its
leadership so wishes. If not perhaps there is room in American Jewry for
a new effort in a more positive Jewish direction."

The interview made it clear that, had he taken over the Brandeis presidency and had the university survived, it would have become a Jewish parochial school on a university level, that the whole purpose of the effort
would have been diverted. In any case, as of December 1967, with the same
bluntness that he had used to tell the men who were desperately holding
the fort that they were unwanted as trustees, he was still vigorously pressing his claim as founder. This controversy, he wrote to me, "does not diminish my appreciation of the honorary degree awarded me by Brandeis
University on your recommendation. It was a gracious gesture, and was
appreciated by me as such. Yet it did not and does not cover the fundamental point of the foundership of this institution." Given the perspective
of a quarter century of steady university progress and a fuller knowledge
of the immense difficulties that had to be overcome, the words of the citation, that Dr. Goldstein had brought the concept of the university "to the
threshold of fulfillment," seemed to the founding trustees a more than
adequate summary of his contribution.

As for Stephen Wise, he was glad that his misgivings were likely to be
overcome. He had offered unequivocal advice to me not to accept the responsibility for the university as long as it was dominated by the chairman
of the board, and there was no question that he was disappointed when I
did not follow his advice. But our personal friendship had not been affected.
Three months after I was deep in my responsibilities, I sent him a report
of progress. In his reply, he still expressed misgivings, but he was now eager
to be kept informed. He wrote on August 2, 1948: "I am glad to have your
letter and it is good to know that you feel satisfied with the progress that
has been made. It will be good if in six months or a year you can write to
me that the University policy has been subject to none of the pressures
which I feared. . . . I want to hear about the progress that has been made.
I am glad to see that you are making a modest beginning, no full-fledged
university overnight, but a quiet, wholesome, modest beginning."

In March 1949, a dying man, Dr. Wise accepted the invitation of David
Niles to speak at the Ford Hall Forum, and he agreed to combine it with
a visit to the campus to see for himself what had been wrought in the six
months since the university had opened. He was mainly concerned to assure his protégé that there was no breach between us. He toured the campus
and was impressed with its transformation. Standing under the arch at the
entrance to the Castle, he posed for a photograph with me. He was large
enough of soul to say that "he had thought it could not be done, but that

it had been." Our luncheon with the family at the president's house was saddened by the thought that he could not long survive. That night he addressed a tearful overflow Ford Hall audience, to whom he had come to say goodbye. The next day, I wrote to thank him for the effort he had made and to ask for his blessing. "It is good to know that we have you now as a loyal warm friend of the University." I sent him the photograph that was taken under the Castle arch, and it was included as the last photograph of his life in the biography that his son, James, wrote. Within a few weeks he was dead.

Five years later when his daughter, Justine, a distinguished New York City judge, began to gather his papers, a record of more than fifty years of remarkable service on the world scene, they were all routed to Brandeis, housed there in the library archives for the use of historians who are concerned with the movers and shakers of the twentieth century. Some years later, they were transferred to the archives of the American Jewish Historical Society headquarters, which had been established on the Brandeis campus.

CHAPTER FOUR

Formulating Academic Aims and Gathering the First Faculty

I t was a challenging time to take over the presidency of a newly created national university. The country had been fundamentally transformed by World War II and its outcome, not only in its foreign and economic policies but in its social mores, its moral outlook, and its responsibility for citizens whose survival with minimal dignity demanded governmental concern. Transformed, too, was the whole field of education, its objectives as well as its techniques.

To begin with, the G.I. Bill of Rights, offering a college education to the returning veterans, fired millions of them with the determination to fulfill newly stirred ambitions. Most of them came from families who had never dreamed of the prospect of a college education. Now, earned in the crucibles of war, it was their right, perhaps the most precious of the fringe benefits that society could bestow. Every institution, Ivy League or what was quaintly called "freshwater college," was called upon to do its share to absorb the postwar armada. Many of them were completely unprepared, academically and physically, for their vastly expanded enrollment.

There was the predicament of housing. Single dormitory rooms became doubles, doubles became triples. The most selective colleges found themselves stringing hammocks in athletic facilities until priorities could be sorted out. What no one had really anticipated were the hundreds of married students who arrived, often with a child or two. Before the war, very few such undergraduates were enrolled, and they were excluded from campus accommodations. Nor had married graduate students been numerous in the depression years. Now, undaunted by dank, basement apartments and fifth-floor tenement walk ups, trailer camps, or cheap housing at a distance, they kept flooding in.

Among the returning veterans there were, of course, some good-time Charlies along for the ride, but for the most part, the new students were seriously motivated and more critical and demanding than their prewar counterparts. They were not to be fobbed off with lecture material that had been mechanically repeated through the years or with threadbare witticisms that no longer entertained or stimulated. Administrators, inured to students as inveterate shirkers, were astounded when they received petitions demanding longer library hours.

The college world was also dizzy with proposals for experimenting, for scrapping, if need be, much that went by the name of higher education. What, after all, was so sacrosanct about the time-honored curriculum that emphasized the classical humanist tradition? It came under heavy fire from those who now insisted upon preparation for "the world of reality." "Empty knowledge"—literature, the arts, philosophy, and "dead language" books that seemed unrelated to contemporary problems—was often disparaged as anachronistic.

The first decision to be made during the Brandeis launching period obviously had to do with the size and range of the university, for this determination would influence all other planning. We could opt for a large student body, ultimately many thousands, on the model of our neighbors, Boston University, Northeastern, the University of Massachusetts; or we could remain a small university, at first exclusively undergraduate, with a limited faculty. When we had earned accreditation, we could, in time, add graduate programs, avoiding undue enrollment expansion to guard against the loss of teaching intimacy.

We adopted the latter option. Indeed, the choice seemed inevitable. The academic world would be watching with more than perfunctory interest to see what the contribution of Jewish pride and sensitivity was to be. Some years later, I explained the Brandeis decision in a baccalaureate address that was published in the *Journal of Higher Education.* The case for expanded enrollment, enlarged classes, and what was virtually mass merchandising in higher education, had been eloquently presented by a highly successful business executive, Beardsley Ruml, in his volume *Memo to a College Trustee,* and my article served not only as a reply to his views but as the rationale for Brandeis's concept of its educational role.

Ruml had suggested that much more mileage could be obtained from a university faculty simply by doubling or tripling the size of its classes. He saw no magic in small, intimate groups; a faculty-student ratio in a college of quality could be raised, without jeopardy, from eight to one to twenty to one. Furthermore, too many colleges, in Ruml's opinion, were encumbered by superfluous courses that represented ever more recondite areas of research, which, in turn, siphoned off the teaching time of the faculty.

There should be drastic pruning in the number of such courses, he said, so that a smaller faculty could concentrate on a basic curriculum. Ruml noted that his suggested reforms would materially cut expenses and would make it possible to augment faculty salaries without the always painful recourse to increased tuition fees.

In my response, I acknowledged that there was considerable validity in much of what Ruml had written. There is, indeed, no special magic in small classes. I believe it was a president of Fisk who suggested that, unless there is really good teaching, a small class often merely assures the transmission of mediocrity in an intimate environment. I had no quarrel with Ruml's game of numbers. "It is indeed as easy to speak to two hundred as to fifty, but the essence of the educational experience is not the lecture; it is the faculty-student personal relationship. When the student body is materially increased at the same time that the faculty is decreased to achieve more economic operation, the personal relationship virtually disappears, except for an infrequent office appointment. For what is the most rewarding experience in the university?" I asked. "Is it not the association with a few exceptional spirits who have a decisive influence on thinking? What students recall of their college days is not fact and data but the rare incandescent teachers who profoundly affected their outlook."

I remembered that my own career was transformed because I came to know Roland Green Usher, who headed the history department at my alma mater, Washington University. It was his teaching of history, combining interpretative brilliance with dramatic presentation, that sent me into the field of history. When he burned Joan of Arc at the stake, I smelled the smoke in the room. If occasionally a member of his family could not use a symphony ticket, he would invite me to accompany him. I later became an assistant in his omnibus survey of western civilization, and I soon realized, if I were to concentrate on British history, that I must continue my graduate studies at Oxford or Cambridge. As it happened, I fetched up at Emmanuel College, Cambridge, on an 1851 Exhibition Fellowship set up by Queen Victoria in honor of her Prince Consort. There I encountered another great teacher, John Bury, the classical historian who edited Gibbon, who took me under his wing. Two such personalities, deeply interested in their students, patient with their questions, opened fascinating new worlds. Their views and their influence were vividly before me as I read Ruml's memo, and I was more than ever persuaded that his philosophy of education was misconceived when he advocated an economy program that would reach more with less. "A university is not a department store," I continued. "It is a fellowship of teachers and students in which the personal relationship must be maintained. For otherwise, the teacher is merely a voice on a platform, and the student is only a name in a roll book—or worse, a product to be merchandised as cheaply as possible. . . ."

When I turned to Ruml's recommendation to cut courses drastically in the interest of economy, I wondered whether he was not eliminating warts and blemishes by amputating limbs, thereby jeopardizing the whole educational organism. Of course, I agreed, not every piddling specialization should become an undergraduate course to satisfy the research program of a professor. Courses should be carefully screened to prevent sterility. But to reduce courses to meet an economic problem is rearranging a body of knowledge to gain maximum piece-goods efficiency. Some economies are counterproductive. There is an old Chinese proverb, "He who goes to bed early to save the expense of candles, often begets twins." We must think hard before eliminating a course that represents the thorough, disciplined mastery of a small, controlled academic field. It is one of the special glories of the educational process, fully as vital as the broad, synthesizing, general course that provides perspective. We need breadth, but we also need depth. This is what Thoreau probably meant when, hearing a friend boast of the many branches of knowledge taught in his college, he exclaimed, "Yes, indeed, all the branches but none of the roots." We have wrecked sensitivity and maturity in the cinema and in television by the obsessive stimulation of mass merchandising. The effectiveness of the Brandeis decision was perhaps best summed up by one of the students who was asked about the impact of her intimate course in politics. She spoke of her teacher in awe: "God, did he make us stretch!"

Although the temptation to follow Ruml's mass merchandising route was generally resisted, there was also little inclination to go the way of the experimental schools that caught many of the headlines of the day—Sarah Lawrence, Bennington, Reed, Antioch. Every part of the country had its laboratory of exciting educational experimentation, aimed at people who had special interests. They had many failures to discourage them and their eager sponsors, but also many exciting successes to give them fair visibility.

In the end, of course—or rather, in the beginning—we would imitate no single model. We would stand by the commitment to aim, in time, for a university with the very best graduate programs we could devise. In undergraduate education, we would strive for a college that would approximate the breadth of options offered by such schools as Swarthmore and Oberlin. We would not stake the entire destiny of our venture on the experimental projects that highly specialized schools offered.

Fortunately, there was ready access to a major report that Harvard had financed and sponsored over a two-year period. It had reviewed the whole educational scene, and it included recommendations that could be adapted to fit almost any college committed to the liberal arts and sciences tradition. A commission had been appointed in 1944 after many years of dissatisfaction with the elective system that President Charles Eliot, a revolutionary in his day, had introduced more than half a century before. Eliot had reacted sharply against the imported German university system, with its rigid curriculum. He had established an elective system that gave students wide latitude to select their courses, choosing what appealed to them, avoiding what seemed irrelevant or what they found too difficult. All that had been required was for them to amass the required number of official credits for classes attended.

The Harvard General Education Report, published in 1946, was the work of twelve outstanding senior professors who were released from formal teaching duties for two years. It unanimously recommended a core curriculum for the first two college years, about half of which would include basic courses that related to the humanities, the social sciences, and the natural sciences. Students would find sufficient leeway for specific subject choices in each discipline and even for one or two survey courses in history or literature or general science. After the studies in the core curriculum had been satisfactorily fulfilled, the student would then be free, with faculty advice and collaboration, to choose a concentration and devote the rest of the undergraduate career to it. The report frankly discussed the possible criticism of "superficiality" in an introductory curriculum that gave students considerable leeway. But it was agreed that a college career was a travesty when a student could receive a diploma without at least an introduction to the vocabulary and general concepts of basic western thought. In any case, the general education prelude was worth trying, since the last two years were planned as grueling ones, with a heavy load of demanding study in a chosen field.

The General Education Report was a formative influence in the development of the Brandeis curriculum, but, in a few instances, there was significant deviation. A fourth area was included in the core curriculum on the assumption that at least an overview was essential in music, theater, and the fine arts. We were one of the few colleges to include this area in its requirements. In most established universities, the creative arts were still struggling valiantly to attain respectability as an academic discipline.

Still another decision came early, the determination to make the university an instrument for whatever special services it had the resources and the capacity to perform. Its primary obligation as a quality teaching and research institution of course remained; but it was assumed that there was also an obligation to undertake projects that could be socially useful. This responsibility was not to be dismissed as "the service feature." Indeed, this course was followed by many of the scientists and social scientists who sought grants from national agencies to apply some of their basic research to the problems of health and social welfare or to develop methods to cope with the pathology of the cell, the diseases of the heart, or the riddles of aging in its medical and social consequences. Hence, from the beginning, the university gladly accepted such responsibilities if they could be fulfilled without depleting our general funds.

Some of them are described later—the Wien International Scholarship Program that welcomes gifted students to the campus from every part of the world, funded with generous scholarship grants; the Lemberg Center for the Study of Violence; institutes to sponsor research to take fullest advantage of television communication for educational purposes; special projects undertaken by the Florence Heller Graduate School for Advanced Studies in Social Welfare; semester seminars for specialists whose careers were related to civil rights and civil liberties; a tutoring program during a transitional year between the completion of high school and entry into college for students from economically depressed areas.

All efforts were now turned to the fulfillment of the ambitious academic plans. It was a frenetic experience to raise the immense extra funds to maintain a small faculty-student ratio, to meet the highest salary standards, to expand the curriculum so that there were sufficient offerings to maintain an effective balance between electives and required subjects, and to telescope into a few years acquisitions for the library that had taken other universities decades to achieve. Throughout the quest for support, the quality of the student body was vigilantly guarded. In 1953, when the application for accreditation was submitted, a study of the just admitted freshman class of three hundred noted that sixty-five, while in high school, were leaders of chamber music ensembles or members of orchestras or choruses, and that others in the class served on their high school papers, half of them as editors. Always an unusual proportion came from the New York School of Performing Arts, and many enrolled with special scholarships from the School of American Ballet, the Deerwood Adirondack Music Center, and the Jacob's Pillow Summer University of the Dance. The enrollment was studded with scores of high school valedictorians.

We set the end of the fifth year of Brandeis as the first academic deadline; the absolute minimum time required for accreditation by the New England authorities was the graduation of two classes. Our performance must have been adequate, because not only was the accreditation approved in this minimum span but the president of the accreditation body, Nils V. Wessel, then president of Tufts, accepted the invitation to be guest of honor at the celebration dinner. He congratulated Brandeis for an exemplary academic achievement "rare in academic annals," which made it an honor for the oldest schools of New England to welcome it into their fellowship.

Meantime, the task of organizing a quality faculty had begun, and it had called for unusual recruitment. If the university had been content to remain a local effort, offering a competent but undistinguished educational experience to run-of-the-mill students, it would not have been too difficult to enlist men and women to fulfill its goals. But we had undertaken a national responsibility that carried with it a very special symbolic significance. We therefore could not settle for mere adequacy. Yet what had we to offer to scholars of stature or young people of promise to induce them to cast their destinies with the beginning years of a precariously financed, unaccredited school that had emerged from a nightmare of raucous internal quarreling? I saw the task as twofold. Brandeis required a permanent nucleus of young and feisty faculty who had the courage to join our experiment early in their careers; and it needed a leaven of sagacious men and women whose scholarship had ripened, whose stature was national and international, and whose experience would give us balance.

The primary task was the most difficult, to seek out young people whose scholarly fulfillment, with time and perceptive encouragement, was likely. This search became a major challenge, and the counsel of friends and well-wishers in the academic world was crucial. In the main, we were fortunate. We had our share of falling stars, but a very high proportion of our risks turned out well. When Phi Beta Kappa accreditation was conferred in 1961, only thirteen years after the university's founding, the achievement in faculty recruiting was cited as outstanding. The report noted: "The pattern is clear: aggressive recruitment of younger men [and women] whose scholarship has been indicated but not fully demonstrated, and rapid advancement when they have produced as expected."

Perhaps nowhere was the value of investing in talented young people more completely vindicated than when Brandeis took calculated risks in accepting the recommendation of distinguished scientists that their protégés be given the encouragement of quick promotion. There was a ready answer to those who counseled caution when so much responsibility was shouldered by scholars in their twenties. We remembered that Johannes Kepler was twenty-four when he created modern optics and transformed astronomy, and Isaac Newton was twenty-four when he arrived by induction at the law of universal gravitation and observed wryly: "I was at the prime of my life." Einstein was twenty-six when he propounded the general theory of relativity and the proof of mass-energy equivalence. We did not hope to develop such authentic geniuses, but we were persuaded that to identify and encourage rare talent was worth any risk.

One of the most impressive examples was Saul Cohen, a scholar who had been trapped in the Tontine effect of the longer-established universities, which decrees that in the scramble to the top more will fall off than reach the summit. His sparkling originality in research, particularly in chemistry, remained unencouraged in his first university positions. When he did not rise beyond the rank of instructor or lecturer at Harvard, where he received his degree summa cum laude, nor later as a National Research Council fellow and lecturer at the University of California in Los Angeles, he turned away from an academic career to move into applied research with industrial corporations. These positions were apparently very lucrative, but the academic life was in his blood. When, ten years after his impressive doctorate at Harvard, he was offered an associate professorship at Brandeis, he welcomed the opportunity to return to campus life. He was promptly named head of the School of Science, and within two years, in 1952 when the first Brandeis class was graduating, he was appointed full professor. When the faculty had grown sufficiently to warrant its formal organization and the appointment of a dean, Cohen was the inevitable choice.

He was a hard driver, often seemingly abrasive, stern in his demands, but he asked for nothing from others that he did not ask of himself. He was single-minded in his devotion to the highest academic standards for the university, and he was generally perceived by his faculty colleagues as scrupulously fair and considerate. He supported me when there was criticism of the fast pace of construction, tens of millions poured into plant and facilities. He shared my view that modern teaching and research, especially in the sciences, was no longer a blackboard and chalk experience and could not function without adequate tools. Ours was never a docile faculty. Yet the policy of surrounding ourselves with strong and independent-minded men and women amply justified itself, and never more so than when Cohen gave farsighted leadership in structuring the expanded curriculum as the Brandeis graduate programs began to evolve. It was a thoroughly deserved tribute when he became the first faculty member named as University Professor. Though technically now retired, Cohen is to be found regularly in his laboratory, and he makes volunteer time also for gifted graduate students. He must have savored special satisfaction when Harvard named him in 1983 to its governing Board of Overseers and, in the next year, to its Joint Committee on Appointments.

Then there was Leonard Levy, a young instructor at Harvard, a protégé of Henry Steele Commager with whom he had taken his graduate work at Columbia. Upon Commager's recommendation, he was named in 1951 to the Brandeis faculty. He quickly demonstrated that the expectation of pre-eminent scholarship and painstaking teaching would not be disappointed. His promotion was rapid and, at thirty-four, the chair in constitutional studies that had been established as a tribute to Chief Justice Earl Warren was assigned to him. When his book *The Legacy of Suppression* appeared in 1960, Justice Frankfurter wrote to him that he would rather have been the author of the volume than to have been appointed to the Supreme Court. Levy startled the uncritical American public with his study of Thomas Jefferson when he countervailed the wisdom and usual exemplary statesmanship of the Monticello sage with his cavalier treatment of civil rights. The flow of learned articles and scholarly volumes never stopped. In 1969, Levy won a Pulitzer Prize for his *The Origins of the Fifth Amendment*. In the interim, he had served as dean of the Graduate School and then as dean of faculty. His administrative judgments, tough but always fair, matched his academic preeminence. Levy might have had the presidency of Brandeis after my retirement, but his wife, Elyse, was troubled with respiratory problems and required the drier climate of the West. The family therefore moved to California in 1970, and Levy joined the faculty of Claremont to head its graduate Department of History.

Now in his mid-seventies, he interprets retirement as retreading, and the flow of academic research remains animated. More than fifteen volumes dealing with aspects of constitutional history kept him moderately busy during the seventies and eighties. In between, perhaps for relaxation, he served as editor of the sixty-volume *Heritage Series* and the forty-volume *Harper Documentary History of Western Civilization,* and as editor-in-chief of the four-volume *Encyclopedia of the American Constitution.*

In contrast to Cohen's and Levy's tough academic and administrative stance, John Roche could be termed a Merry Andrew. Like them, he was uncompromising in the austerity of scholarly standards, but he was almost raffish in his unconventionality. He enjoyed working person to person, across the board, defying or ignoring the jurisdictional traffic signals. He came to Brandeis in 1956 from Haverford, where, though his classes must have often unsedated quiet Quakers, he was one of the most popular teachers. He had grown up in Brooklyn during the Great Depression, his neighborhood almost contiguous to the Jewish enclave. It was startling to have this Irish maverick suddenly light up a serious intellectual discussion with some juicy Yiddish phrases.

In those early days, with Brandeis but eight years old, the president's recommendations for faculty positions were still received with a modicum of respect. I had, however, some considerable difficulty with the Political Science Department where the redoubtable Herbert Marcuse exercised a certain *éminence grise*. Marcuse himself, of course, had been recruited on the strength of his undeniable scholarship at a time when many universities were cautious about employing committed and articulate Marxists. Roche, on the other hand, was an unabashed New Deal liberal. Indeed, within a few years, he had become the national president of Americans for Democratic Action. He also had directed the Fund for the Republic study of Communist infiltration into opinion-forming groups. Marcuse resisted Roche's appointment. He stormed, "I will not have this renegade . . . rammed down our throats." Roche would prove the more objective. Fifteen years or more later, he wrote in a *New York Times Sunday Magazine* article of his respect for Marcuse as a fellow faculty member, adding that the most radical action he had ever known Marcuse to take was to subscribe to *The Peking Review.*

Roche followed Cohen and became dean of the faculty. Inevitably he was dubbed "Abie's Irish Roche." He claimed never to have understood how a strong-willed president would run the risk of bringing in as dean one whose views would invite almost daily challenge. "Sachar," he wrote, "must sometimes have wondered why God had punished him with an Irish anarchist for a dean."

Roche wrote prolifically on American politics, the American presidency, and the Supreme Court, several volumes in collaboration with Leonard Levy. His volume on civil rights, where he discussed the Abrams case, the Gitlow case, and other Supreme Court landmark decisions, was widely acclaimed as a model of perceptive legal interpretation. Both Lyndon Johnson and Hubert Humphrey called upon him as a consultant. In 1966 he asked for and received a two-year leave of absence to become what was jocularly termed "intellectual-in-residence" at the White House. He served mainly as a speechwriter for the president and vice-president and as liaison to the academic community. The final years of the Johnson administration, ensnarled by the Vietnam War, were bitter ones, and they destroyed popular support. When the president announced he would not seek renomination, the loyal team around him began to send out feelers for new positions. Now their association with the Johnson administration became a major impediment. Many liberals who had insisted during the McCarthy years on drawing sharp distinctions between a scholar's academic competence and his political views began linking the two. Dean Rusk, longtime secretary of state in the Kennedy and Johnson administrations, knew that he would be harassed as a controversial figure if he accepted a faculty post in a major university, and he opted for a professorship in International Law at the University of Georgia in his native state. Walt Rostow found he could not return to MIT, where his former faculty colleagues had suddenly discovered, after his long tenure there, that he was not meeting the highest standards as a scholar. A weary John Roche called from the White House saying that he too wanted "to come home." Because he had been on official leave of absence, there was no need to clear his request with the faculty. I told him, "The key is under the mat, John, and you do not have to knock."

But the climate had changed. Most of the faculty respected his stature as a writer and teacher and his experience in the top advisory echelons of the government. He was deeply disappointed, however, by the way others who had been Americans for Democratic Action colleagues reappraised his scholarly credentials because of his views on international affairs and American foreign policy. Nor was it comfortable to teach a student body that had once loved him but among whom were now activists who could not forgive Vietnam. Roche struck back, especially in the syndicated articles he was writing regularly for the national press. He noted that the chief difference between doctrinaire liberals and cannibals was that cannibals ate only their enemies. In 1973 he accepted a call from the Fletcher School of Law and Diplomacy at Tufts to head its Department of International Politics.

No faculty member in our beginning years elicited more respect and affection from colleagues and students than Irving Fine. He had been a young instructor of music at Harvard, but although he had dazzled the faculty there, his promotion was blocked by the unavailability of tenured positions in a star-studded department. He came to Brandeis in 1950 and soon established a national reputation as a composer and musicologist. The memory of the encouragement given him by his mentors, Walter Piston, Serge Koussevitzky, and other titans in the world of music made him especially effective with students.

A problem with writing about Irving Fine is in finding a way to say, without causing pain to those who loved him most, that he was a driven young man—in the sense that Mozart and Schubert were driven. When he was in the heart of composition, he taxed himself relentlessly. The perfectionism that he expected from others was imposed as rigidly upon himself. One would have liked to put up a hand and say, "Irving, there is plenty of time." But for Irving there was never enough time—for teaching, composition, performance. He was ever worrying over curriculum and faculty, over festival and concert. His calls came through for more pianos, more classrooms, more secretarial assistance, and above all, for more funds to encourage graduate students, for more help to perform the compositions of gifted young people. He was most resourceful in his administrative battles, and when one door closed because of practical difficulties, he came in through another. He usually got what he wanted—rarely for himself, primarily for his colleagues and students.

Irving Fine died in 1962 in his forty-seventh year after presenting the latest of his works at Tanglewood. Mine was the grievous task of offering the eulogy at our Berlin Chapel, an assignment unmitigated by the presence of his parents, widow, and uncomprehending little daughters, with Leonard Bernstein and Aaron Copland among the pallbearers. Later, when Bernstein opened the season of the New York Philharmonic, he included in the program one of Fine's compositions. In his introduction he noted, "We are playing this adagio in Irving's memory, not only out of respect, or because he was my dear personal friend, but because his music is filled with his radiant goodness."

As more than a footnote, it should be added that Fine would have exulted at the establishment of an endowed chair in his name by his parents. The first incumbent was his colleague and fellow composer Arthur Berger, whose own distinction honored his choice. He had taught at Juilliard before coming to Brandeis and was also music critic for both the *New York Herald Tribune* and the *Saturday Review*. He had become the chief interpreter of Aaron Copland's work and later published the definitive biography of his old friend.

Although not a member of the early faculty, Jacob Cohen came to us only a decade after founding and is appropriately counted as one of our pioneering adventurers. He had chosen a university teaching career, and his first professional years, in his early twenties, were spent at Yale. He was caught up in the turbulence of the mid-century civil rights movements, and he took leave from Yale to add voice, pen, and political action to the evangelism of Martin Luther King. When he was called to Brandeis in 1960, he brought a reputation for scholarly activism. His courses on "The Sixties" and on "The Idea of Conspiracy in American Culture" so crowded his classroom that restriction on enrollment had to be set. In 1964 he took a two-year leave, and he joined the editorial staff of CORE, the Congress of Racial Equality.

The assassination of Dr. King deepened his interest in civil rights and led him to research the place of conspiracy in American politics. He wrote and lectured widely on cases that convulsed the McCarthy period in American life, the assassination of President Kennedy, the murder conviction of Sacco and Vanzetti (two Italian anarchists), treason charges against Alger Hiss and his alleged infiltration of the State Department in the Roosevelt administration, and the case of Julius and Ethel Rosenberg, also accused of passing national security secrets to the Soviet Union, a charge that sent them both to the electric chair.

He willingly accepted every offered university responsibility: chairman of the American Studies Department, chair of the Faculty Senate, and chairman of the University Social Science Council.

Cohen had trained as a classical singer, and he was often invited to participate in university musicales. His fine tenor voice and his familiarity with cantorial melody enriched many of the Jewish holiday services. He married a Soviet concert pianist, and their programs of lieder and operettas added elegance to informal university musicales. In a student poll, he was named as one of the most respected personalities on the campus.

A young physicist who came in the beginning years of the university was Jack Goldstein. After service in the army in the Pacific area in World War II, he had received his university training at Cornell, the Institute for Advanced Study at Princeton, MIT, and the Baird-Atomic, Inc., in Cambridge. He showed so much promise at Brandeis that within a few years he had earned a professorship in astrophysics. He was constantly called out to universities in the Third World for counsel in organizing science teaching. He was a model citizen in university governance, serving as dean of the Graduate School, dean of faculty, chairman of the Faculty Senate, chairman of the physics department, and one of the governors of the Brandeis Press.

After the science enclave had been completed and dedicated in 1965, I was visited by Goldstein, who wished to explore the possibility of expanding our offerings in astrophysics. There had been increasing interest in such courses, undoubtedly stimulated by the space program of the astronauts and by the promises evolving out of the development of solar energy. Obviously, if studies were to reach beyond the elementary level, it was essential to have access to an astronomical observatory. I shared his concern and promised that an observatory would go into the priority list for facilities. As it happened, the annual dinner of the Greater Boston Associates, which had become a reunion of our main local supporters, was scheduled for the following fortnight. In the course of my review of the year's progress, I decided "to go public" in an appeal for an expanded program in astrophysics. Having been conscientiously briefed by Goldstein, I probably astonished the audience with my sudden erudition in the field. If only Brandeis could construct a modest observatory, I implied, the heavens themselves would open. At the conclusion of the affair, Fritz Grunebaum, a leather goods importer whose plant was in Peabody, later a Fellow of the university, expressed great interest in the observatory. His father, a noted physician who had lived in Germany until the Nazi takeover, had died recently, and an observatory dedicated in his name might be just the memorial the family was seeking. The negotiations proceeded rapidly, and the coveted facility was underwritten. The construction crew was soon at work, and, within six months of Goldstein's visit, the astrophysics observatory named for Grunebaum's parents was dedicated.

Meantime, we had also turned for faculty members to the pool of exceedingly talented and capable people who had been retired by the then current tenure procedures. Some were victims of the political climate of the times, when even universities with a long tradition of academic freedom were not eager to venture into the eye of a hurricane. It seemed that precious talent was going to waste, and Brandeis, young and yearning, had need of it. Many in their late sixties and even in their seventies were in excellent health and at the peak of their effectiveness. They were becoming emeriti not because of decline or incapacity but to make room for younger scholars whose opportunities for promotion and tenure could not be foreclosed. But in a school where the entire early faculty could still be entertained in the living and dining rooms of the president's house, there was no problem of foreclosing early opportunities for younger members. Hence it seemed wise to offer key posts to a few distinguished scholars who had made their reputations elsewhere and who could offer not only their competence in special areas but also their mature judgment for the planning of the university's formative years. Furthermore, the students would be brought into personal relationships with personalities of great stature.

In the initial faculty of thirteen, one internationally eminent man of letters stood out, the novelist and critic, Ludwig Lewisohn. He had endured many years of torment in his native Germany and discrimination in American universities.

When just out of his teens, he had pursued his graduate studies at Columbia, whose master's degree he earned with highest honors. But his department chairman discouraged his expectation to teach English literature. Opportunities, he said, were foreclosed to Jews in fields unique to Anglo-Saxon ways of thinking. He lived precariously, supporting himself from the royalties of his novels and translations until a modest post as instructor in German literature became available at a state university in the Midwest. He was subject to more years of debilitating social and professional rejection, and then was terminated. During the next two decades, his literary reputation soared but still did not bring university employment. When he was invited to Brandeis as professor of comparative literature, he was already past the conventional retirement age. He welcomed the call not only for its guaranty of a sheltered base for his twilight years but for the restoration of dignity.

Lewisohn and his wife, Louise, and their cat, Cupcake, took up residence in the Castle dormitories as unofficial campus hosts. They lived close to their students, often ate with them in the dining hall, and entertained them in their remodeled apartment, usually in memorable bull sessions that lasted far into the night. Lewisohn was scintillating in discussing the works of Shakespeare, Goethe and other immortals, and he was incomparable as he ranged over his personal experiences with the giants of the contemporary world. When he spoke of Alexander Pope's "feast of reason and flow of soul," he could have been describing those evenings in the Castle with his fascinated student audience. Early on, the university library attained sufficient eminence to attract collections and documentation, and Lewisohn was named librarian and exercised his magisterial acumen in determining what would be enduringly valuable. When he died in 1952, his widow bequeathed to Brandeis his priceless collection of belles lettres.

Cupcake Lewisohn also deserves at least parenthetical recognition in any history of early Brandeis as the first in a long line of campus animal characters. One of the university guests was the publisher and commentator Bennett Cerf. In a hilarious article in the *Saturday Review,* he recalled his first stay at Brandeis, the high point of which was the co-rescue of Cupcake from one of the extremely tall campus trees. "Ludwig Lewisohn," wrote Cerf, "was in the middle of telling me how he had finished his two-volume biography of Goethe, when his wife, Louise, uttered a shrill cry of alarm. Cupcake, the Lewisohn's outrageously spoiled cat, had just knocked over a priceless Ming vase and escaped through the casement window. Ludwig was in hot pursuit before you could say Mister Crump. Around the campus at an ever madder pace sped Cupcake and her pursuer. Suddenly the playful feline shinnied up a Massachusetts variety of giant redwood tree. Ludwig went up after her, and captured her, too—on the highest branch, while students, faculty, and Cerf cheered a brilliant maneuver, faultlessly executed. Of course, there remained the minor formality of getting Ludwig and Cupcake down from the tree. The student body was equal to the emergency, producing the tallest ladder I ever saw to facilitate the descent. 'You handled that well,' I told the boy. 'We ought to by this time,' answered one. 'After all, this is the third time we've done it since Saturday.' "

Another felicitous addition in the first faculty choices was Paul Radin, who came to Brandeis in his seventy-fifth year after a long and fruitful career in teaching and research in anthropology. I had first met him in the early twenties when I was a student at Emmanuel College in Cambridge and he was completing a five-year lectureship at one of the other colleges there. Soon to appear were his landmark volumes, *Primitive Man as Philosopher* and the *Method and Theory of Ethnology,* and they marked him as one of the genuinely original minds of his generation. He had taught in many universities in Europe and in the United States. For such a man, Brandeis, with its small enrollment of highly motivated youngsters, had an irresistible appeal. In the foreword to the festschrift that was affectionately sponsored by his former students to salute his seventy-fifth year, I wrote, "It is further evidence of his still resilient and pioneering temperament that this eminent anthropologist should now bring his wisdom and his skills to the youngest of American universities. What Brandeis in its youth will give this veteran would be a little presumptuous to state. On the other hand, what he can offer us is clear. 'One who learns from the old,' said a Talmudic master, 'is like one who eats ripe grapes and drinks old wine.' I congratulate the new generation of Brandeis scholars who are privileged to take the cup of learning from his hand and in turn pass it on to their successors; for in it is the wine of life."

There was old wine, too, the rarest French vintage, represented by Albert Guerard. An expatriate from France, he had spent his teaching career in this country at Williams, Rice, the University of California, and, mainly, at Stanford. Upon statutory retirement, he gladly accepted the Brandeis bid. His son was professor of comparative literature at Harvard, and the senior Guerard welcomed the opportunity to be closer to his family. His classes in French literature and civilization, where his teaching was marked by his old world charm, went beyond fact and data. He was primarily concerned with interpreting the inner spirit of the humanities. "It is evident that in certain countries, knowledge had far outstripped wisdom; and the peril is with us too." He stressed the need to avoid glib judgments as true simply because they were wrapped in glittering prose. He encouraged dissent: "The curse of the moderates," he said, "has ever been their incurable timidity." He cautioned his students not to be overwhelmed by authority, not to admire ideas or policies simply because the pundits of the moment pronounced them wise or valid. "This," he said, "argues a servility which is demeaning. A man must have the courage of his own taste; or, in Blake's words, he must not allow himself to be connoisseured out of his senses." His counsel brought thoughtful appraisal to a highly cerebral student body that was often unduly fascinated by rhetoric, especially critical rhetoric. Many of his students went on into university careers in French cultural history with the indelible mark upon them of Guerard's training and perspective.

In a few instances, we agreed to make concessions to attract personalities whose career interests were not primarily university anchored. A new school, with no rigid institutional procedures, could easily cope with special arrangements. In our second year, we approached Max Lerner, who was successfully supplementing academic identification with sparkling journalism. When he was only twenty-five, he had been named assistant editor of the *Encyclopedia of Social Sciences* and then had become its managing editor. He had taught at Harvard, Williams, Sarah Lawrence, and the New School for Social Research. As an editor of *The Nation* and as a regular columnist for the *New York Post,* he had expertly interpreted the world's trouble spots. When he was approached in 1949 to accept a professorship in American civilization at Brandeis, he welcomed the offer but retained his New York base. His class schedule was telescoped into a day and a half so that he could fly from New York on the morning of one day and return by the evening of the next. He asked to be free every other semester for world travel. Thus we had only a part of his talents; beyond his teaching, the students could take advantage of only a fraction of his after-class time. But even a small piece of Lerner was manna for the university. He was an incisive teacher, lively and provocative, prodding the latent capacities of the very best students.

His temporary arrangement turned into one of the most permanent, and he remained a faculty member for nearly twenty-five years. He retired at seventy when he jauntily entered early middle age, determined to give more of his time to the twenty volumes he said he still had in his belly. At this writing, he had already completed and revised half a dozen.

Our relationship with Mrs. Franklin Roosevelt as a faculty member was a genuine love affair. When she joined the Board of Trustees and then served for three years as panelist director of a national television program on contemporary affairs, there may have been a general impression that she was merely lending her name for whatever prestige it would bring the university. But as it turned out, Mrs. Roosevelt took all of her duties quite seriously, and her identification, structured to meet her amazing schedule, was gratifyingly productive. She served as one of our most active trustees from 1950 until the day of her death in November 1962.

But it was when Mrs. Roosevelt joined the Brandeis faculty as a visiting lecturer that her capacity to communicate her passion for world peace and explore practical ways to achieve it was most clearly manifest. She agreed to offer a credit course that dealt with the many nonpolitical agencies of the United Nations—the Human Rights Commission, the Educational and Scientific Commission (UNESCO), the World Health Organization (WHO), and several others. The enrollment was limited to six American and seven foreign students who had come to Brandeis on Wien International Scholarships. Mrs. Roosevelt took personal interest in all the students, explored with them their career goals, and helped several of them with influential recommendations and contacts. She held a seminar several times a month, with related sessions directed by Lawrence Fuchs of the politics faculty. It was a rare experience to study the operations of the United Nations agencies and to have one of its most knowledgeable figures discuss its inner workings. When one of the Swedish students was asked about the class, he responded, with a measure of awe, "It was thrilling to have Mrs. Roosevelt talk casually about 'Franklin' and 'Winston' and their contemporaries, in the most intimate terms, and we felt that we were in a living room with the greats of our times, listening to a family discussion." Each year one of the seminars was conducted in the Roosevelt Hyde Park home, where the students moved among the memories of the great days of the Roosevelt incumbency.

None of us, of course, knew then of the heartbreak she lived with because of her strained domestic life. Perhaps the many responsibilities that she undertook—endless travel, lectures, assignments for public service, always as a nonprofessional volunteer—and the intensity with which she applied herself served as compensatory therapy. But there is no doubt that she treated most seriously her role as teacher. An editorial salute to Professor Roosevelt in the *New York Herald Tribune* when she began her Brandeis teaching duties was typical of the national reaction. "At the age of 75, which she will reach next Sunday, Mrs. Eleanor Roosevelt will be preparing to continue her course of lectures at Brandeis University on 'International Organization and Law.' Her personality and experience admirably fit her to work with undergraduates in this field. In war and peace she has traveled far on humanitarian errands. As the widow of a President who valiantly attempted to organize peace in the midst of war, she has been familiar with the spirit of the United Nations since its first faint stirrings; she has fought for the rights of women and children, the weak and the helpless, with her excellent mind as well as with her warm heart. Brandeis University is lucky to have her on the faculty, and fortunate indeed will be the students admitted to her classes. . . ."

Certainly no discussion of our unceasing effort to strengthen our academic structure should omit a unique piece of good fortune that came to us quite early in our quest. We could not hope to persuade many of the gifted men and women to leave permanent posts of established prestige and security. But some of them could be tempted to come to us for visiting periods of a semester or a year while they were on sabbatical or leave. At the outset, such appointments were only occasional, for their support had to be wrung out of extremely limited general funds.

In 1954, I approached the trustees of the Jacob Ziskind Foundation in the hope that its guidelines might permit a gift to support a visiting professorship program. The trustees were most favorably disposed. They allocated the sum of a half million dollars, whose income and portions of whose principal could fund the program. The Jacob Ziskind Visiting Professorship became one of the most productive developments in the academic life of the university. It not only fulfilled a vital curricular need but it brought fresh views and insights to the university. The roster of men and women who came included E. H. Carr of Cambridge, a former editor of the *London Times* and an authority on Soviet Russia; Pierre Emmanuel, the brilliant French poet and Resistance fighter; Erich Heller of the University of Wales, for German and comparative literature; Arnold Hauser of the University of Leeds, for the fine arts; Lewis Mumford, who was pioneering new concepts to protect our cities and our environment; Phillip Frank, professor of physics from the University of Vienna. One year we were graced by the presence of the novelist and short story writer, Hortense Calisher, as elegant in her person as in her prose. Some of those who came as visiting professors were sufficiently intrigued to wish to stay on, and several became permanent members of the Brandeis faculty, notably Alexander Altmann, professor of Judaic studies at the University of Manchester, and Cyrus Gordon of Dropsie College, professor of archeology and Mediterranean studies.

At first it was possible to invite only two or three visitors each year. Fortunately, the Ziskind Fund was most resourcefully invested, and its capital doubled within seven or eight years; hence, the number of visiting professors multiplied. Beyond 1968, as the endowment capital continued to grow, its impact on the curriculum deepened. I often referred to it as our academic Gulf Stream.

Special notice is warranted for another supportive teaching innovation that proved most productive in the beginning years of the university. Years after graduation and entrance into professional or business life, our earliest students kept recalling their experience in Education S., so called because it was a course that was originally designed for the seniors. It was an adaptation of the program that had long existed at All Souls College at Oxford, where statesmen, scholars, and professional people were invited as Fellows for various periods during a school year to discuss their views with those in residence.

About twelve or fifteen notable visitors were scheduled for each year, and they were chosen by senior students in collaboration with me. They were to discuss the turning points in their lives, their great decisions, why they made them, how they evaluated success or failure. We were gratified that no matter how high we reached we usually had a welcome, affirmative response.

The sessions were unstructured; the one requirement was an evaluation paper, based on discussions in the course and on reading from suggested lists that were distributed when the lecturers were announced. In the week following the visit, a faculty autobiography panel offered their reactions to the visitor's message. During the first few years, I presided over the sessions, acting as a moderator, keeping the discussions from trailing off. Afterward, Max Lerner, and then Milton Hindus, took over as moderators. The Commons Room in the Castle was invariably filled for the sessions that began at seven in the evening and often stretched beyond midnight. A student editor, reviewing one of the evenings, wrote that of the one hundred fifty seniors for whom the course was established, all four hundred turned up. The desire for attendance and participation was understandable, for the course featured a Who's Who of men and women of exceptional attainments. They included Indira Gandhi, Archibald MacLeish, Margaret Mead, Oscar Hammerstein, Alfred Kinsey, Aaron Copland, Harold Taylor, Alfred A. Knopf, Lewis Mumford, and scores of others.

A memorable evening was spent with Leo Szilard, the Hungarian scientist who had settled in the United States in 1937 and, two years later, had joined Albert Einstein in warning the American government that Hitler was well on the way to the completion of an atomic bomb. Szilard persuaded Albert Einstein to appeal to President Roosevelt to accelerate the research on nuclear power, for if Hitler won the race, the Nazis would control the world. Roosevelt authorized the Manhattan Project. This research involved America's leading scientists and such men as Einstein, Szilard, Oscar Levin, Fermi, Bohr, and others who had fled from Nazi Europe. The bomb was perfected, and the secret test at Alamogordo in July 1945 meant that America had control of the most destructive weapon in history. By then, the Nazis had surrendered, and Hitler had committed suicide; but the war against Japan was not yet over.

In his Brandeis appearance, Szilard described for his tensely listening audience his futile attempt to persuade the top American policymakers not to drop the bomb upon Japanese cities. Roosevelt had died a few months earlier, and the awesome responsibility for the decision rested with Harry Truman. Szilard could not reach him, but he did get to James Byrnes, then the assistant to the president. Byrnes told Szilard that it would be "political suicide" to have spent secretly more than two billion dollars on the bomb, without authorization, and then not to use it. Szilard commented acidly that President Truman's action was at least based on his grave concern over the heavy human cost of an invasion of Japan, the possible loss of half a million lives if the Japanese did not immediately surrender. But Byrnes was apparently more concerned with the political consequences of an immense expenditure for a weapon that was not used.

The discussion that followed centered on the rationale that justified Hiroshima, on the morality of saturation bombing, and on the judgment of Jean Rostand, who had written: "Science has made us gods before we are even worthy of being men." The evening with Szilard and the conversations with him became, for many of the students, their most vivid experience at Brandeis. Szilard, too, was immensely impressed with the student body, not as research experts, but as the vital, passionately concerned, intelligent representatives of the new generation upon whom the destiny of the world would depend. He returned later for a full semester as a visiting professor in the sciences.

When we asked Norbert Wiener, the father of cybernetics, to come to us, there was the liveliest curiosity in the expectation that we were to meet a *Wunderkind*. Wiener's childhood and boyhood had been a horror story. His father, a brilliant Russian immigrant who had become the first professor of Slavic languages and literature at Harvard, was an irascible perfectionist who had driven the precocious Norbert with a relentlessness that almost destroyed him. At seven he was performing advanced experiments in chemistry and physics in a home-built laboratory. He entered high school at nine and Tufts College at eleven. He received his undergraduate degree at fourteen and his Ph.D. from Harvard at eighteen. There were five prodigies at Harvard at the same time, and all of them lived in a blaze of cruel publicity. It took Wiener years to adjust to the realities of normal social life, and it was not until he was nearly thirty that he shed his other-worldly bewilderment to begin genuinely productive work as a professor of mathematics at MIT.

The audience of Education S. was introduced to a shy, unpretentious scholar, the prototype of the classic absentminded professor, ill at ease during the introduction and so hopelessly nearsighted that, while addressing the jam-packed Commons, he sometimes faced the wrong direction. When questions were asked, he would hurry up to the seats of the questioners to talk directly to them. But once he began speaking, completely uninhibited, all thought of his eccentricity disappeared. He was witty, self-deprecatory, and quite tolerant of the egomaniacal father who had pushed him so hard. As he outlined the problems of a prodigy who was advanced too fast intellectually in a rigidly conventional society, he was speaking to an audience whose collective I.Q. was also uncommonly high. There were many transfixed youngsters sitting before him who plainly identified with him.

Wiener had no quarrel with the early involvement of children in serious matters; there was no harm in introducing them to foreign languages, the discipline of mathematics, and the miracles of science. But he was envious of the gifted youngsters of the present generation who could enjoy the enlightened programs of an enriched curriculum with boys and girls of their own age instead of being propelled, usually by exhibitionist parents, into an environment where they were completely maladjusted, neither man nor boy.

Wiener devoted most of his discussion to the growing power of automation in our society and its likely impact upon the future. He described how far the world of applied science had already gone in the development of the mechanical brain. He had coined the name for the process, cybernetics, from the Greek root for steersman. Some of the products—the thermostat, the governor on engines, the computer—had already been integrated into daily living and were taken for granted. They had revolutionized not only procedures and techniques but the essence of research. They solved equations with lightning rapidity. They gathered information from more sensitive sources than man's own brainpower could by the use of strain gauges, voltmeters, photosensitive tubes. These never slept, became ill, nor tired, and, if properly designed, they never made mistakes. Wiener forecast expanded uses of the mechanical brain, not only for speed and accuracy but for the solution of problems of space and health and the production of food.

Of course, not all the guests who came for Education S. were received with enthusiasm, although all were given a courteous hearing. The purpose of the course was to present men and women who had unique outlooks on life and who had influenced their generation. Some of them represented values that were highly controversial. Their presentations and the questions and answers that they elicited made for dramatic confrontation, as when the head of the Central Intelligence Agency, Allen Dulles, came for a tough give-and-take evening. He had to move through the gauntlet of a picket line manned by students who were outraged by CIA operations.

Dulles noted that the CIA had originally been created as an information-gathering agency to guide top officials who conducted American foreign policy. But the realities of the Cold War had compelled the agency to go far beyond its original mandate. During the ten years under Dulles's direction, the United States had been locked in a struggle with the Soviet Union to prevent the engulfment of large parts of Europe and other combustible areas of the world. The Soviet secret service planned continuous infiltration and engineered government coups and kidnappings and assassinations. The CIA was therefore called upon to carry out missions that attempted to thwart and confound the secretive activities of America's enemies, and its move quite deliberately into espionage and counter-espionage.

Dulles did not look the cloak-and-dagger part. He was a quiet, restrained man who spoke temperately, unemotionally, as if he were analyzing a trade report. In the dinner hour preceding the Education S. session, he had told Thelma that his son had been desperately wounded in the Korean War and was living out his years as a vegetable in a veterans' hospital. Dulles presented the case for the CIA as an indispensable operation in a no-holds-barred world, where the very openness of a democracy compelled safeguards to protect its vulnerability against the machinations of totalitarian enemies. As he related little-known incidents, the listeners were taken through an Ian Fleming thriller. There was a barrage of questions, most of them pointedly critical, for this was an audience that could not easily square the methods of spying and subversion with the ideals of a democracy, even a democracy threatened and beleaguered. The questioners wondered how an agency that was virtually uncontrolled could protect itself against falling into the hands of unscrupulous politicians and demagogues who would use its power for personal or political purposes, how it could be insulated so that its techniques would not corrupt the routines of domestic life. These were troubling observations offered long before Watergate, when all such apprehensions came to tragic fulfillment. At the end of the evening, Dulles had won few converts, but the youthful audience must have been sobered by their introduction to the complexities that confront modern leadership as it wrestles with the problems of means and ends.

Of special interest to the student audience, which contained many budding authors who were certain that they were destined to create the great

American novel, was the visit of Alfred A. Knopf, the most respected of American publishers. Both as a commanding presence and as a perceptive entrepreneur, he was an exciting guest. His Borzoi colophon was to be found on hundreds of volumes that bore the most distinguished names in the literary world. The Knopf lists included more Nobel laureates than those of any other publishing house, and his Pulitzer Prize winners were legion.

Knopf fascinated his listeners with his adventures in the book world and his relationships with those who had become the classic names in the texts of the students. The foreign giants who passed in review were Knopf's personal friends—André Gide, Albert Camus, Joseph Conrad, D. H. Lawrence, E. M. Forster, Franz Kafka, Thomas Mann, T. S. Eliot, Julian Huxley. There were constellations of American names—Willa Cather, Elinor Wylie, Conrad Richter, John Hersey, Robert Hillyer, John Updike, Conrad Aiken, Edmund Wilson, Charles Beard. Knopf took his youthful audience through the corridors of half a century, stopping every few steps for a comment here, an evaluation there.

Under persistent questioning, he also talked about his own outlook, that of the hard-nosed business man to whom publishing was not an altruistic mission but who yet felt that he had an obligation, even when there was no adequate return, to encourage the best in belles lettres and the social sciences and to commission translations of the writings of first-rate minds of Europe, Latin America, and Asia, usually unknown in this country. Many of the volumes that his firm sponsored reflected Knopf's special interests: volumes on gastronomy and oenology, conservation, music and the arts. Clifton Fadiman, editing an anthology that brought together the best of the Knopf publications, said of him: "He takes for granted that life, whatever its meaning, is better enjoyed than suffered." Hence, Knopf lived well, dressed with superb taste, sought out the company of the most intelligent and well bred, "and cultivated without regard to the world's opinion, any private idiosyncrasies that caused no pain to others." He was a gourmet who appreciated the subtleties of perfectly prepared food, an authority on wines who insisted on the most exquisite vintages. Only the finest cigars would touch his lips. He told with relish the story of an early transcontinental trip when he met another world traveler in the Pullman smoking lounge and he offered him one of his cigars. The neighbor savored it and said admiringly that it was a magnificent choice. "It should be," said Knopf. "I have it made up for me by Upmann." "Oh really," was the reply, "what is your name?" "Knopf. Alfred Knopf. And what is yours?" "I am Upmann."

The discussion with the students went on for hours, and Knopf ranged over the whole field of publishing, its problems, its satisfactions, its precarious future in a world of paperbacks and mass merchandising. Long after the more formal session, there were still little knots of students gathered around him, asking about opportunities for the young in the world of letters and for advice about getting started. When he was finally released, the students knew that they had met an Olympian, and they understood better why he was so often called the aristocrat of publishers.

When Alexander Meiklejohn came for Education S., the students were introduced to one of the most amiably rambunctious of the educational mavericks of the century. Meiklejohn was already close to eighty (he lived into the nineties), but he stood well beyond six feet, straight as a ramrod, clear and sharp in speech, with an unmalicious irony, no spark of the rebel in him yet inert. He defended his unorthodox views in education, perhaps more roguishly before a sympathetic student audience but no less cogently than he always had when he began fifty years earlier to blast out at university systems that aimed to create "gentlemen" and "careerists" rather than people of intelligence who were to be called upon as the arbiters of destiny in a democracy.

As Meiklejohn reviewed the turning points in his long career, the barbed asides about his opponents still drew blood. He had been born in England but had migrated as a youngster of eight to the United States and was a product of the American school system, becoming a teacher of philosophy at Brown. Despite his unorthodox views, he was apparently an able administrator and served at Brown as dean for many years. Then, in 1912, at forty, he was called to the presidency at Amherst, a surprising choice, for the Amherst of that day was a staid, steadfast representative of the gentlemen's tradition, the antithesis of the concept that Meiklejohn had for students who were his charges. He stayed on at Amherst for twelve turbulent years during which he turned the college upside down. He was constantly at war with the senior faculty who took it as their duty to teach fact and data, and then expected that their teachings would be applied to the practical affairs of life. Apparently Meiklejohn was quite careless about personal expenses and bills, and when he was embroiled in unseemly quarrels with impatient creditors, the trustees and his opponents in the faculty seized upon plausible non-academic reasons to force him out. Obdurate to the last he refused to resign, and he had to be fired.

For a number of years the stormy petrel remained in public view through his critical articles that excoriated the objectives and techniques of higher education. In 1928, Glenn Frank, who had come to the presidency of the University of Wisconsin after a brilliant career as editor of the *Century*, and himself somewhat of a bold innovator, was intrigued, and he accepted Meiklejohn's plan to direct an experimental college within the framework of the University of Wisconsin. Meiklejohn invited specially selected students who would not be obliged to take any prescribed courses nor would be subject to regular university routine. Their faculty would set up their offices within the university dormitories and would be regularly available for consultation. In their first year the students would all concentrate on diverse aspects of the old Athenian culture and way of life, the civilization of Pericles and Plato. In their second year they would turn to modern America and explore its political and social facets in depth. The unstructured curriculum was based on the theory that concentration on one major theme would be infinitely more productive than the diffusion of time and effort over many unrelated subjects. If one civilization were studied in depth in this way and discussed with faculty and fellow students soberly and seriously, with no diversions, its lessons could be more intelligently applied to other cultures and ways of life.

The experiment received national attention and the Wisconsin campus drew reporters, commentators, and educators from every stratum. The publicity backfired, and the senior faculty grew angrier with each passing review of the announced results. The experimental college survived for only two years. Perhaps it was the fact that it attracted a disproportionate number of off-beat characters from everywhere, especially New York, who outraged the faculty and the God-fearing townspeople by the slovenly attire and the calculated rudeness of the newcomers. Or perhaps it was the revolutionary character of the novel curriculum, which moved from the extreme of rigidity to what the scoffing faculty termed "chaos." In any case, even the progressivism of La Follette's Wisconsin concluded that the college was too far out, and, when the legislature cut off funds, the experiment was suspended.

Meiklejohn was not discouraged. He turned up next in San Francisco where he opened a special experimental college, on the Wisconsin model, drawing mainly on working families. His faculty met weekly with selected adults to discuss the great books and ideas of the western heritage. The times were out of joint for him, for World War II soon engulfed all such experiments as seemingly irrelevant, and, as Meiklejohn put it gleefully, he had failed gloriously again. He was still as vigorous as ever, ready to fight at the drop of an educational cliche.

Very few of his audience, I believe, shared his animadversions. They themselves were brimming with ambition, and they hoped for successful careers in the areas of their competence. But they reveled vicariously in his trenchant criticism of the abuses of the Establishment and in his revolutionary evocations. I judge that there were very few adventurous souls who were ready to man the barricades with him, but they were probably glad that there were people like him around to serve as gadfly and conscience for the cocky and the overly smug. Ultimately this was the way American society judged his career. When he had reached the venerable nineties, the American Association of University Professors tendered him its award for service to academic freedom.

The inclusion of Education S. in the curriculum inevitably provoked intensive discussion among the faculty, and its academic validity was often challenged. There were many who held that the presentation and questioning of a succession of personalities, however interesting or influential, did not add up to a university course, and that it diluted rigid academic standards that called for structured learning and accompanying tests to maintain the discipline of study in depth. There were others who welcomed the course as a valuable supplement to the prescribed work of the curriculum. I shared their view that if 117 of 120 credits were assigned to conventional lectures and classes, term papers, and laboratory experiments, three could be spared to bring the students into close association with great personalities drawn from every area of national and international life.

After five years, Education S. was dropped as an accredited course, but not because of the criticism that it failed to meet curricular standards. A good number of clubs had been organized mainly to explore politics and social issues, and these also brought men and women of stature to the campus. Visiting lecturers also were now coming in such numbers—scientists, artists, statesmen, poets, social welfare technicians—that they made up a supplementary university experience in themselves. Above all, the growing sophistication of television and its documentaries and panel discussions with world figures fulfilled, with more ample resources, some of the original purposes of Education S. But in the beginning, the program helped to enrich the academic environment of a young university whose permanent faculty resources were still precarious.

After the university obtained full accreditation in 1954 and launched its graduate programs, we needed less reliance on the academic participation of retirees and visitors. Brandeis's reputation as a major institution of learning was sufficiently established to offer permanent appointment to scholars of national and international stature. The university had become an exciting intellectual center; its facilities, especially for the sciences and the creative arts, were exceptional, and its salary scale met the highest standards of the American Association of University Professors. There was an additional inducement to attract the most gifted faculty in its geographical location, where more than a score of colleges and universities were established within an area of less than a few hundred square miles. Here one's social life could be enjoyed with peers in one's field. As the funding for chairs proceeded at a gratifying pace, as graduate programs were added at the rate of one or two a year, faculty leaders were encouraged to recruit vigorously with no inhibiting expectation that a particular scholar "could not be moved." Within ten years, many of the departments of the university—biochemistry, chemistry, physics, mathematics, Judaic studies, music, psychology, and others—were given top rank by the American Council on Education.

CHAPTER FIVE

Completing a Campus in One Generation

In the past century, less than a dozen privately founded universities and colleges, including Brandeis, achieved almost immediate national stature. Among them were Johns Hopkins, the University of Chicago, Rice, Duke, Vanderbilt, and such women's colleges as Vassar, Smith, and Wellesley. All but Brandeis were launched with substantial endowments. Johns Hopkins, founded in 1876, was built on the $3.5 million of Baltimore and Ohio Railroad stock bequeathed by Hopkins. Chicago began in 1892 with a $35 million endowment in oil stock from John D. Rockefeller, who had dreamed of a Baptist-founded university. Within a few years, his gifts reached more than $80 million. The nest egg of Rice Institute was $10 million from the cotton fortune of William March Rice, although the school was not launched until 1912. The eccentric Rice had been murdered in 1900 by his valet, and litigation tied up the estate for years. When the sensational trials ended and the bequest was validated, Rice Institute was so substantially protected that until very recently it was not necessary to charge tuition at all. Stanford, in the beautiful Santa Clara Valley, near Palo Alto, was born of a $30 million endowment from the Central Pacific Railroad tycoon Leland Stanford. Organized almost as a personal fief, Stanford became the cautionary example of paternalistic control. The "impish delight" of Bierce in alluding to Leland Stanford was to turn the "L" into the English pound (£) and the "S" into the American dollar ($). Stanford's widow was vigilantly obsessive in her concentration on buildings, conceived as a memorial to his only son—to the exclusion of teaching and research. A faculty member remarked, as salary standards declined, "It's too bad men can't feed their families on buff sandstone; it seems to be the one plentiful thing."

The tobacco millions of James Buchanan Duke and his family persuaded

North Carolina to change the name of precariously financed Trinity College and move it to Durham, where, as Duke University and solidly reinforced, it began a new lease on life in 1924. Vanderbilt was incorporated in 1875 as a model university for the Southern Methodists. Its financial founder was the buccaneering Cornelius Vanderbilt, who relied upon his friend Andrew Carnegie's help and upon the General Education Board of the church for an additional $18 million. Vanderbilt's own share was so considerable that, at the inaugural services, the president turned without a qualm to the portrait of the old pirate and read for his invocation a text from the New Testament: "Cornelius, thy prayer is heard, and thine alms are in remembrance, in the sight of God."

Three women's colleges, Vassar, Smith, and Wellesley, received substantial seed money from farsighted individuals who defied the prevailing resistance to higher education for women. Matthew Vassar, a brewery magnate of Poughkeepsie, wished "to build and endow a college for young women which shall be to them what Yale and Harvard are to young men." Henry F. Durant, whose only child died when a boy, founded Wellesley as a memorial in 1875; he was confident that women were as capable of serious study as men in the Ivy League schools. Time would reward him with some of the first women astronomers, a pioneering aviatrix, and, among other influential alumnae, Madame Chiang Kai-shek. Smith also was inaugurated in 1875, almost by accident. Its female Maecenas, the spinster Sophia Smith, had written five wills, and on numerous occasions she nearly followed the advice of her pastor to bequeath her inherited wealth to Amherst.

Brandeis, as ambitious and aspiring as these older schools, began as poor as a church mouse or, rather, as a synagogue mouse. Justice Brandeis's name was a powerful moral asset, but no endowment came with it, nor was one expected. Support had to be won from a vastly dispersed constituency that in 1948 was almost unendurably overtaxed for philanthropic purposes. Yet Brandeis could not afford to grow slowly. It needed everything at once—faculty salaries, student scholarships, buildings, equipment, administrative and maintenance assurance. Tuition and room and board income provided only a fraction of its resources. Competition for philanthropic attention came not only from established schools but from the endless and urgent causes undertaken by American Jewry in the postwar period. Brandeis could not follow conventional fund-raising strategy. Its first graduates, barely more than a hundred, would celebrate their tenth reunion in 1962, when they would be still on the lower rungs of their professional and business careers and mostly in the midst of mortgage payments and pediatricians' bills.

Physical facilities at first offered the strongest appeal for major gifts, for they were immediately identifiable. The predominance of this type of gift giving was not unusual in the experience of universities. As far back as the twelfth century when the first colleges of Oxford were founded, the buildings, such as the dormitories and teaching facilities that served Balliol College, given by a Scot to afford the students a place of dignity and to rescue them from the hostels or inns, were the projects that held out the largest appeal.

A master plan for the physical growth of the university in its first ten years took early priority. We at first chose Eero Saarinen as architect, the brilliant Finn who had designed some of higher education's loveliest and most imaginative buildings. Saarinen died lamentably soon after taking the assignment. Only the dormitory quadrangle surrounding the old Middlesex ice pond is based on his master plan. The commission then went to the firm of Harrison and Abramovitz, a personal gratification for me since Max Abramovitz had been a gifted student in architecture at the University of Illinois during my Hillel days there.

Abramovitz revised the Saarinen plan not only to incorporate his own views but also to accommodate the tempo of construction that had accelerated to keep pace with academic needs. The bulldozer was rarely off the campus during our first twenty years. Since most donors could not redeem a large pledge all at once, we readily granted extended time schedules, and construction bills were covered by loans. Audacious as this policy may sound in the light of later economic developments, it proved prudent during the 1950s and 1960s when costs mounted much more sharply year by year than did interest rates on institutional loans. Had we deferred construction, academic progress would have been slowed, and the ultimate costs would have become prohibitive. By 1968 Brandeis had a $70 million investment in physical plant, connecting utilities, and landscaping—all entirely paid for or covered by valid pledges. Estimated replacement value by then was $200 million.

It would have been comforting had we been able also to build into our gift schedule for construction a sum to ensure maintenance. But a young university desperately in need of facilities could not prescribe total support conditions. Indeed, virtually no university could. Even Harvard was quite content to accept the pledge limited to the construction of its Widener Library, a memorial to the young heir who went down with the *Titanic* in 1912. When, after World War II, Thomas S. Lamont offered to underwrite a new undergraduate library facility, the need for a simultaneously established maintenance fund was better understood, and Lamont volunteered it.

During the pioneering period, our multitudinous needs dictated flexibility in negotiating for gifts. The first lecture auditorium constructed at Brandeis was assigned as a memorial to a family on the basis of a pledge that could not have been accepted for a minor seminar room ten years later. The first chairs at Brandeis were gladly named for families who could offer partial, often very partial, endowment.

The exigencies of pioneering were responsible also for the apparently capricious schedule of construction. Logically, the library would be given first priority, along with classrooms and laboratories. Accommodations for student living, office space, recreational facilities, student lounges—all necessary but not indispensable—would then wait their turn. Every effort was made to link a donor's gift with the facilities or the academic offerings most urgently needed, but often the donor, a modest contributor toward general funds, had a special interest that would result in a long-range, permanent identification on the campus for his family.

For these reasons, an athletic center was constructed years before an adequate library and major science facilities could be made available. Abraham Shapiro was the most generous of the first trustees. His zeal and tenacity were crucial during the controversies and dissensions that plagued the prefounding years. But his dream of Brandeis included a well-rounded student body, made possible by a diversified program where the American tradition of sports and competitive athletics could be pursued. He was convinced that the image of the university would be blemished if Brandeis attracted a student body that was overwhelmingly bookish. He feared classrooms filled with "grinds," all too often identified with Jewish intellectualism. Whenever the suggestion was made that it would not be fatal if all students were not well rounded—they did not have to roll—Shapiro would draw himself up to his full height of five feet five and insist that purely academic facilities had much more glamor for a Jewish constituency and that there would be little difficulty in obtaining them. He wanted the athletic center, and he wanted it not only for its functional service but because it would carry the message to the general public that Brandeis was a normal, wholesome American institution. And he was ready to provide the grant to bring this about. So an unpretentious but quite adequate athletic center facing the main roadway, bearing the name of Abraham Shapiro, was among the first new buildings to be dedicated, in the presence of the governor of the commonwealth, the secretary of labor, and the outstanding sports figures of New England.

In most instances it was possible to persuade donors to identify their gifts with the facilities that more immediately fulfilled our primary mission. It was determined from the outset that Brandeis was to be a dormitory school: we wanted our students to experience a complete campus environment. The old Castle, converted to house about 180 students, could provide living and dining space for only the first two years. Even as the first classes settled in, the planning went forward for the immediate construction of other dormitories. By the time of the first commencement, with approximately five hundred students enrolled, some modest cottages had been completed on the edge of the campus that became known as the

Ridgewood Quadrangle, the name taken from the street that it abutted. Five families joined in this project, and the donors' geographical locations indicated that the Brandeis supporting constituency was clearly becoming national. Each family took a unit, the Sidney Allens of Detroit, the Charles Fruchtmans of Toledo, the Arthur Rosens of Boston, the Dancigers of Dallas and Tucson, and the Louis Emermans of Chicago.

Despite all efforts to moderate the pace of enrollment, limiting acceptance to one of seven who applied, the demand for admission by highly qualified applicants expanded registration. Within a few years, the enrollment had reached a thousand, then fifteen hundred, on and on, until by 1968 the university had twenty-two hundred undergraduates. Brandeis would still be counted as a small university, but it needed to increase its dormitory space. A five-unit complex, with each unit housing approximately sixty students, was constructed in mid-campus, around a lovely reflecting pool, named for Anne J. Kane of Cleveland. The complex was designated as the Massell Court, honoring an Atlanta family that had opened out access for us to many southern communities. Each of the dormitories was named for its donor: Helen DeRoy of Detroit, the Irving Usens of Boston, a memorial to Anna Renfield of New York, and the Morris Shapiros of Boston (who underwrote two, identified as A and B). A student center that included a tastily furnished lounge, a major dining hall (including a supplementary kosher kitchen that non-Jewish students often patronized for its succulent special dishes), and a number of meeting and seminar rooms was named for George and Beatrice Sherman, also of Boston.

The need for still more dormitories remained a high priority right through the fifties and sixties. One large complex, around an attractive, elevated lawn area, was erected at the north end of the campus. The largest part of its cost was covered through a bizarre gift that perhaps best illustrated the totally unexpected routine of academic financing. During World War II, the Soviet Union had swept into the Baltic and the Balkan states and established puppet Communist regimes in each of them. The Red dictatorship in Rumania carried out not only a political purge but a complete economic reorganization. Foreign enterprises were nationalized, among them, all private oil interests. A substantial investment had been made in Rumania by American oil companies, and, in retaliation for the nationalization of their holdings, the American government froze the assets the Rumanian government had in the United States. Many of the private investors whose property had been confiscated in Rumania filed applications with the Treasury seeking reimbursement from these frozen Rumanian assets. One of these investors, the family of Adolf and Felicia Leon, approached the university with the suggestion that it would include in its application the pledge that, if there were reimbursements in whole or in part, the allocated sum would be contributed to the university for its construction needs. The Leon attorney was confident that the claim would receive special consideration if it were clear that, if granted, it would be used for a major educational contribution. The university gladly cooperated and, when the reimbursement bill finally surmounted all legislative hurdles, the proceeds were assigned to the university. A new complex of student dormitories were constructed at the north end of the campus, each dormitory underwritten by a separate family. The enclave became the Adolf and Felicia Leon Court, and the designation was so noted at the entrance to the area. There were thus many unique ways by which facilities were created on the Brandeis campus; one of the strangest was the underwriting of the attractive dormitory court as a result of investments in Rumanian oil that had been confiscated by a Communist government.

Four dormitories were built in this court, underwritten by the A. W. Link Scheffres of New York, the Frank Reitmans of Newark, and the Robert Cables and Maurice Gordons of Boston. It was here that the Milton and Hattie Kutz Student Center and dining hall was located and where many of the most important public functions of the university were held. Almost simultaneously another complex was built to house another three hundred students, in the east part of the campus close by the old Castle. The underwriting once again came from many parts of the country: the Henry Hassenfelds of Providence and Nashville, the large Shapiro family whose branches spread from one end of the country to the other, the Hyman Krivoffs of New Bedford, the Fred Pomerantzes of New York and Palm Beach, and the Lawrence Rubensteins of Newton, Massachusetts. It was here that Benjamin Swig of San Francisco, among his many other princely benefactions to the university, set up a student center and dining hall to serve this end of the campus, which he designated as a memorial to his wife, Mae.

Near the end of my incumbency, the construction of a fifth dormitory area, adjacent to Ridgewood, was received with mixed emotions by the sentimental inner family of Brandeis who clung to their dreams of a university in an intimate environment. They recognized the price of growth and accepted the need to meet the problem of ever-growing crowded living. But the site chosen for the David and Anne Rosenthal complex of three major buildings, accommodating about two hundred students and underwritten by a highly successful New York manufacturer, compelled the elimination of the little white house that had been the nerve center for the old Middlesex Medical School and the early administrative headquarters of the executive officers of Brandeis.

Each year, the university sponsored a gala dinner at one of the Boston hotels as a reunion for its New England donors. The great majority of attendees were part of what was called the Brandeis Associates, a loosely organized club whose membership consisted of those who made annual contributions of one hundred dollars or more. In regular attendance was a quiet, unassuming, shy little man, who would come up to the dais after the affair to shake hands with me and the special guests. I often wondered how he could afford even his modest contribution to the Brandeis Associates. I always greeted him and inquired about his welfare, and I always got the same answer, that he had "no complaints." No one seemed to know him. Apparently, the Brandeis gathering was the only public function he ever attended. In 1956 he died, and we learned that he had no family, no heirs, no friends, and that he had made the university his sole beneficiary. When his estate was appraised, it was revealed that he owned considerable real estate in Boston, and his ultimate bequest reached about $1.8 million. The first graduate programs were soon to be launched, and the most essential need was for a science research center. The decision was quickly made to build it with the proceeds of the bequest and to name the building, in his memory, the Julius Kalman Science Center. Often as I passed it, I could not help but think of this lonely man's tragedy. He never got the slightest satisfaction from any of his holdings. As long as he lived, despite his hidden paper wealth, he was Shakespeare's "O, without a figure." He came to life only after his death, through the invaluable facility that his resources made possible. I kept thinking also of what even the few words of greeting at an annual meeting must have meant to him if his response was to name the university his beneficiary.

At the 1953 Associates dinner, the dramatic announcement was made that Brandeis had earned accreditation by the New England Association of Colleges. The occasion was further highlighted by the announcement of a grant of half a million dollars from the Charles Hayden Foundation, the university's first major gift from a non-Jewish source. The gift had been carefully cultivated by one of the Brandeis Fellows, Sidney L. Kaye of Boston, a wholesale food distributor. He had won the personal friendship of J. Willard Hayden, the head of the foundation whose educational grants had, until then, been limited to the largest and most influential universities. Hayden was not an easy man to deal with. He was blunt and could be abrasive, and he knew very little about Jews. But he knew Sidney Kaye, and he admired his integrity and his thoughtfulness. When I accompanied him for several conferences with Hayden to place before him the needs of the university, it was clear that Hayden had only considered support for a new venture like Brandeis because it had elicited the loyalty and the commitment of Sidney Kaye. When the grant was announced, Hayden paid a glowing tribute to his old friend and then added a matching proviso for the contribution that was to generate exceptional stimulus in the fund-raising campaigns. His challenge launched a special appeal for life memberships in the Associates, pledges of two thousand dollars to be paid out over a two-year period. The campaign not only quickly achieved its goal, but it substantially broadened the supporting constituency of the university. The Hayden grant and the matching life membership proceeds provided the nucleus for an expanded science complex that was constructed over the next few years.

Thomas Gray and other poets invariably found inspiration in "the glimmering landscape" of the university grounds, but to university officials, its care and maintenance were a perennial financial problem. Where could the donor be found who was sufficiently perceptive to recognize that keeping the grounds trim and fresh, building and repairing the roads, and providing utilities were all an integral part of the imaginative landscaping that sustained the beauty of the campus? Until such a donor appeared, the expense would have to be borne from hard-to-obtain general funds.

I was hence much impressed when I learned how resourcefully Swarthmore College had coped with the problem. I was invited to Swarthmore to spend a few days with the students for a series of discussion groups and a wind-up convocation lecture, what the Quakers termed "The Collection." The campus was magnificent in its charm and grace, its natural advantages of location and terrain enhanced by meticulous care. I asked how priority had been given to landscaping and was informed that some years earlier one of the trustees, Arthur Hoyt of the Scott Tissue Company, had set up a landscape fund whose income was to provide for the beautification of the campus.

My search for a similar fund began as soon as I returned to Brandeis. Fortunately, through the intercession of one of our trustees, Lawrence Wien, we were able to interest a successful New York merchant, David Schwartz, the head of Jonathan Logan. He was a tough, blunt-spoken man, self-educated and an unlikely prospect for such a project. But in his business career, he had demonstrated a sure instinct for style, and he was the soul of generosity. His wife, Irene, was intrigued by the thought that the family could duplicate at Brandeis the role of the Hoyts at Swarthmore. It was especially important, she knew, for a new school like Brandeis, since without adequate landscaping, modern architecture can be stark and austere. The Schwartzes gave the university one of its most unusual gifts, a ten-year budget to cover the expenditures for initial landscaping during its most intensive building period. Each year some portion of the campus was chosen for beautification. Within a decade, the campus had been transformed.

Still another way of winning productive friendships was inaugurated in the mid-fifties through the initiative of Lawrence Wien. He began a series of "air safaries" to the campus. Every few weeks, he would personally lead a group, which ranged from about ten to more than two dozen people, in a one-day visit. He also recruited other "hosts" to round up their friends and business associates for such safaries. The party would gather at New York's La Guardia Airport early on a weekend morning, be met in Boston by a car caravan of well-briefed students, drive to the campus for a tour, lunch at the Faculty Center, where the university's high officials would speak informally about Brandeis's long-range objectives and answer questions, attend mini-seminars with distinguished faculty representing the areas that interested particular guests, and be driven back to the airport for the return flight. All the speeches, however eloquent, at affairs held in New York, all the promotional literature, however imaginative, could not compare with such visits to Brandeis, where the beauty of the campus could be seen and the departments' work could be interpreted by outstanding faculty. The New York weekend trips provided the model for those from other cities. Many important friendships were generated from such safaries, and they generated not only gifts and bequests but also the willingness to supply interpretive leadership in the home communities.

Since unrestricted funds were always a prime need, Brandeis very early adopted the fund-raising format of the plate dinner testimonial. This technique turned a public tribute to a devoted benefactor into a contribution to a cause close to the benefactor's interest. Invitations were sent to business associates and friends of the guest of honor. The dinner charge varied considerably, depending on the clientele. Once the dinner, drinks, and entertainment had been paid for, the rest was the net contribution to the cause. What could better represent American pragmatic ingenuity and the interests of sweet charity?

Brandeis did not hesitate to use this approach, concentrating upon guests of honor who were not merely successful in their industries or professions but who had also played a constructive role in community life. It was rarely difficult to find such guests, for from the very outset Brandeis had attracted men and women who had achieved public recognition. Once the pattern had been set, it was not difficult to sustain it. The dinners usually brought out large and well-disposed audiences. The charge ranged from about $100 to $500, and, when the special gifts of preliminary luncheons and parlor meetings were added, the affair rarely netted less than $250,000 in unencumbered funds. We were fortunate in having strong friendships in many of the basic industries, and it was therefore possible to arrange for about forty dinners a year—in some communities as annual affairs, in others in intervals of two or three years—ultimately building up a solid beachhead of support that could make up for the lack of endowment income on which the much older universities counted. After a few years, there were regular gatherings in such areas as beverages, shoes, food products, infant wear, jewelry, petrochemicals, cosmetics, electrical supplies, real estate, banking and finance, entertainment, publishing, and men's and ladies' clothing.

Through the intercession of Jack Poses, one of our trustees and the head of Parfums D'Orsay, we began invaluable relationships with the cosmetics industry. Some of the most successful houses were under Jewish ownership—Helena Rubenstein, Faberge, Charles of the Ritz, Revlon, and of course D'Orsay. For our first industry dinner, Poses obtained the cooperation of representatives from each of the major houses and many other firms. Leonard Bernstein, then a member of our faculty, was persuaded to serve as the guest of honor, and he was at his mischievous best. He felt very much at home with the purveyors of cosmetics. He revealed that he had almost been part of the industry, for his father had been a wigmaker in Boston long before the wig had become a fashion item. There was a small, struggling cosmetics house in New York that was eager to sell out, and Bernstein's father could have purchased the business for six hundred dollars. But he could see no future in a polish that turned women's nails a bloody red; it seemed so barbaric. So the offer was declined. The name of the firm was Revlon.

In the course of many trips to the West Coast, I established a good working relationship with popular figures in the entertainment world. The theater, the cinema, their actors, producers, writers, and investors included many of the most generous contributors to the causes of American Jewish life. I became almost a conversion favorite, for, when Jews married non-Jews, some of the rabbis would assign my volume *A History of the Jews* as a textbook for an introduction to the fate the convert was, for good or ill, to share. I was told by Danny Kaye that, on a plane one day, he was startled to find Carroll Baker deeply absorbed in the chapter on Judaism and Christianity. Elizabeth Taylor, in her flirtations with Judaism, made several attempts to master the intricacies of the section on prophetic Judaism. Sammy Davis, Jr., referred in his autobiography to "Dr. Abe," who reminded him of the common sorrow of the disinherited that was shared by Jews and blacks. Hence, when the guests at our plate dinners included these and other highly visible and popular personalities such as Joan Crawford, Lucille Ball, Jack Benny, Leo Jaffe, Eddie Cantor, Bess Meyerson, Sam Spiegel, Joe Levine, and Alan King, standing room attendance was always assured. Virtually all of these performers, whose services were often cheerfully donated to many good causes, were ideal interpreters for the university in their large circle of influence.

Danny Kaye appeared at several functions as guest of honor. He demonstrated his remarkable versatility when, at the end of the evening, he took the addresses of the participants who had preceded him and used them as texts for an extraordinary, spontaneous potpourri of wit, ridicule, schmaltz, and zany humor. One year, during the Passover holidays, Danny was filling an engagement in Boston at a benefit for the symphony orchestra, and we invited him, his wife, Sylvia, and their daughter to our family Seder. He had not attended one since his boyhood in his parents' home, and the nostalgic memories that were evoked apparently gave him so much joy that we were happily embarrassed to learn that he had invited his accompanist and all the Jewish members of his retinue to come to our home for the second night. He showed his appreciation by coming to the campus the next season to address a large, informal bull session, where one serious youngster refuted his inveterate optimism by quoting from Aristotle. Danny kept referring back to his questioner as Morris Aristotle, a name the young philosopher found difficult thereafter to shake off. Later, Danny Kaye received the university's honorary degree for his contributions to UNICEF, having brought laughter and good cheer to hundreds of millions of children when he traveled in their interest to the remotest parts of the world.

Perhaps the most dramatic example of princely generosity came out of the Palm Beach Country Club in Florida, one of the most luxurious resorts in the world, whose standards for membership include adequate community philanthropy. The rationale was simple. Any family that could afford the stiff fees of the club and the scale of living in Palm Beach was expected to meet its responsibilities to the community. The fulfillment of duty here was as much an indication of character as business or professional integrity or social grace. Such a constituency was a natural magnet for every important cause in Jewish life, and here the emergency appeals for Israel, hospitals, seminaries, rehabilitation centers, schools found exemplary support. Millions of dollars must have been contributed each year that came out of teasing conversations in a locker room, at a luncheon table, or between strokes on a golf course. These were much more effective sites for persuasion and fulfillment than formal, structured meetings or rallies. Indeed, the club frowned on fund-raising affairs. The members insisted that they had been endlessly involved in such functions at home, and, when they escaped routine for a well-earned holiday, they ought not to be diverted with the same round of pressures and appeals.

It was Morris Brown who first opened the club's cornucopia to Brandeis. Brown was a successful New York plastics manufacturer who, as president of the club, gave at least half of his full-time attention to its welfare. In supervising each detail of the club's administration, he came to know every member intimately. Genial, buoyant, and hospitable, he made it a personal concern to have the members enjoy every advantage the club offered. His solicitude was returned with affectionate goodwill, and no request of his could be easily denied. Old Joe Kennedy, who spent his winters in Palm Beach and held an honorary membership at the club, sensed this and asked Brown to lead the annual campaigns for St. Mary's, the community's Catholic hospital. The hospital's final affair was always held at one of the country clubs that excluded Jewish membership. An exception was regularly made for Brown, and the invitation was always pointedly declined, but the results of his quiet, personal campaign for hospital funds were always astonishingly successful.

Brown became a devoted supporter of the university in 1955 and was soon one of its most enthusiastic advocates. Later, having become a trustee, he was the co-chairman of the three-year campaign that raised sixty-five million dollars for the university. He readily agreed to invite the top leadership of the Palm Beach Country Club to a luncheon for me in his gracious home, and this informal function was the beginning of many years of productive parlor meetings in Palm Beach, where some of the most important gifts to the university were completed. It was at such a luncheon that the friendship with Nate and Frances Spingold developed. It led to a visit to the campus by the couple and to their decision to contribute five million dollars to construct the Theater Arts Center. It was also here that other necessary facilities and academic programs were underwritten. And it was this generous response to the university's needs that impelled the Board of Trustees to hold its February meetings in Palm Beach and to link them with a preliminary week of privately planned conferences and a Saturday night affair that became the social climax of the Palm Beach season.

Brown died suddenly in 1964 and was succeeded as president of the country club by a Boston shoe manufacturer, Louis Salvage, another university trustee. Salvage was held in the same high regard and affection by the country club membership, and his devotion to the university was equally unfaltering. He took pride in the cancer research laboratories that he underwrote for the university, and, since he set an example of generosity when he approached others, the response to his appeals did not waver. Toward the end of his life, his health failed rapidly, but he looked upon his chairmanship of the Brandeis weekend almost as a sacred responsibility, and, though it often meant getting out of a sickbed, he presided at the luncheon and the evening banquet. His staff would give him a prepared speech. Invariably, he would glance at it with cataract-ridden eyes, throw it away with a brusque "To hell with it," and talk in the plain homespun vernacular that his friends knew and loved.

Because so much depended on the results of the Palm Beach effort, the strategy for the week had to be planned far in advance. Trustees and Fellows who had winter homes in Palm Beach held their private sessions with selected prospects and, if help were needed in their interpretive tasks, university officials would join them. The Saturday luncheon would be the occasion for the announcement of such gifts as had been secured. There were usually about one hundred guests present, and the program for the afternoon would be planned for their benefit. I usually joined with Lawrence Wien in this appeal, and apparently we were an effective team. I would provide the prologue, half banter, half serious, interpreting the concept of the university and its most recent developments. Wien would then announce a special project that would become the Palm Beach designation. One season the objective was the purchase of highly valuable acreage contiguous to the campus, whose cost was divided into syndication units. In another season, plans were revealed to construct a social science center on the campus, and it was suggested that this would become a most appropriate tribute to Morris and Pearl Brown. In still another season, the appeal was linked to the vastly increased need for fellowships, since the university had launched several new graduate programs. Wien and a few trustees and Fellows set the level of pledges with their own generous commitments, and the bidding from the audience was fast and spirited. The average amount realized at such luncheons came to over a million dollars, and, when added to the commitments that were quietly secured beforehand, the Palm Beach week could realistically be listed with tuition and sponsored research as "assured income" for the university's general operating expenses.

CHAPTER SIX

The University Wins Itself Tenure

Before the sixteenth century, chairs, as we know them, were unusual articles of furniture. Common folk and even members of the rising merchant class rarely nurtured household expectations that went beyond the oaken fabric bench or stool. Gentlewomen enjoyed the luxury of silken cushions on the floor, and the principal room of a nobleman's castle contained but one recognizable chair, on which the lord of the manor sat to govern. Chairs also took the form of thrones, sometimes ornamented with a canopy or side curtains to shield a monarch or bishop from icy drafts. Thus, invariably, the chair betokened authority. The connotation has persisted into our own day, and the leader of a meeting "takes the chair" and is known as the chairman. Women's rights advocates have repudiated the exclusive male suffix, but they have not quarreled with the symbolism of the chair. By the time of the Renaissance, chairs, evolving into more utilitarian use, had become more common. But in the academic world, the term retained its magisterial connotation, and, equally significant, it represented the dignity and the prestige of a named professorship.

It was in 1502 that Lady Margaret Beaufort, the mother of King Henry VII, provided endowments at both Oxford and Cambridge to support eminent scholars. By her generosity, Lady Margaret changed the fiscal organization of the English universities and thus had a far-reaching effect on the colleges and universities of the new world, which owe their origins to English rather than to Continental models. In the medieval university a senior scholar was obliged to collect his fees individually from his students. Even the legendary Abelard, in the twelfth century, had to shoo away nonpayers and try to collect arrears from others. But scholars, then as now, were rarely favored with business acumen. Moreover, then as now, the popular lecturer or teacher drew the larger classes, while the equally gifted scholar whose subject was more demanding, or whose delivery was often somnolent, attracted fewer students and a smaller income. Endowed chairs allowed the incumbent to be evaluated by his peers rather than by the often fickle regard of those he taught. Thus, Erasmus, the first occupant of the Lady Margaret Chair in Divinity and Greek at Cambridge University, may well have been the first academician in the world of higher education who did not have to dun his students.

Lady Margaret's action left a more enduring legacy than her son's victory over the Plantagenets. Wealthy nobles and prelates followed her example, and the tradition was heartily endorsed in the new world, even when other trappings of royalty and nobility were eliminated. Thomas Hancock, a nephew of John who was one of the signers of the Declaration of Independence, founded a professorship at Harvard in Hebrew and theology. The will of Dr. Ezekiel Hersey provided for two chairs in medicine that have become coveted appointments. A wealthy merchant of Boston created Harvard's Nicholas Boylston Professorship of Rhetoric and Oratory, whose stipend was set at $1,500, a considerable sum in the eighteenth century. It carried the added privilege of allowing the incumbent to graze his cow in the Harvard Yard. The Boylston Chair was first held by John Quincy Adams, twenty years before he became president of the United States, and the chair sustained its tradition of prestige long after the liberal meaning of rhetoric and oratory had been transformed. Yet such endowed chairs were rare; there were only six in all of the colleges of the country before the American Revolution, and four of them were at Harvard.

In the four and a half centuries since a king's mother sought to release scholarship from mendicancy, the cathedral aspect of the endowed professorship has become purely symbolic, but the aura of distinction has never been lost. Every privately supported university reserves its named chairs for its outstanding tenured faculty, and scholars treat their appointment to endowed chairs as a high honor. From a practical point of view, the endowment that supports a chair guarantees that the salary of an incumbent will not be subject to the vagaries of university fund-raising income.

From the earliest days of Brandeis, the quest for the endowment of chairs was given high priority. But such gifts were very difficult to come by. It was much easier to interest even the most philanthropically motivated families in the underwriting of buildings, science laboratories, or centers for the humanities, the social sciences, and the creative arts. Fortunately, each year there were supporters who were sufficiently concerned about a particular academic field to channel their philanthropy, by outright grants or bequests, to express this interest. Endowments for chairs were also created through carefully planned testimonial affairs that saluted a national figure or a highly regarded community leader. Tribute gifts were encouraged for the endowment that was to bear the name of the honored guest.

The establishment of chairs could follow no master plan; fulfillment depended on unpredictable timing, when wills or bequests matured, or on the caprice of a particular testimonial opportunity. Nor could the amounts for the endowment be rigidly set. The Ivy League university could command a figure; Harvard now requires a capital fund of $2.5 million. Brandeis was too young, still at the threshold of national prestige, to set conditions. The acquisition of each chair, therefore, usually represented an adventure, often burdened with frustration, whose happy ending was by no means assured. How much depended upon factors extraneous to academic planning can best be demonstrated by describing how some of the earliest endowed chairs were funded.

In the late spring of 1948, before I was installed as president, I was on the scheduled program of the Town Hall of New York. I was introduced as president-elect of the newly launched university and, though my lecture topic related to European political developments, the open forum that followed elicited a number of questions about the concept of Brandeis and its projected orientation. When the program was over, a little old lady came up to me, introduced herself as Mrs. Max Richter, and expressed great interest in what the chairman of the forum had said when she introduced me. She hoped that I could spare the time on my next visit to New York to confer with her legal counsel.

Within a week, I was in touch with Charles Segal, Mrs. Richter's attorney, who was to become one of the university's first Fellows and a devoted friend through the next quarter century. He explained that Mrs. Richter had recently been widowed. Her husband had been a wealthy silk merchant and had left a substantial foundation whose income Segal was prepared to assign to colleges and universities that met high standards. Segal's main interest was Swarthmore College but he shared Mrs. Richter's enthusiasm for the concept of Brandeis, and he was prepared to explore with me how the Richter Foundation could be helpful. Our conference resulted in the establishment of the university's first assured professorial salary, an annual pledge to support a distinguished appointment, the actual endowment to become available after the passing of Mrs. Richter. The capital fund was received by the university some years later, one of the three or four largest in our portfolio. The immediate annual commitment enabled us to recruit an outstanding incumbent. The chair was offered to Max Lerner, who became a member of the faculty in our second year as the Max Richter Professor of American Studies.

Twenty-five years after the establishment of the chair, Charles Segal attended the commencement where his granddaughter graduated with high honors. In the intervening period, he had counseled many of his clients to include Brandeis when they planned testamentary gifts. Our long association was a happy and productive one. But the disquieting thought often occurred to me: What if I hadn't been booked for Town Hall, or had not been booked on that particular day, or what if Mrs. Richter had had a cold and decided not to attend. When I related to Max Lerner the capricious circumstances of the funding of the chair, he concluded that he became a professor at Brandeis because a little old lady did not have a cold on that fortunate Town Hall day.

The circumstances that resulted in the establishment of an endowed chair named for Harry Austryn Wolfson, the Harvard savant and one of the world's most respected philosophers, were light years away from the concerns of scholarship. The initial negotiations began with a real estate deal between one of our trustees, Lawrence Wien, and a highly successful New York realtor, Erwin Wolfson, who conceived, among other major enterprises, the Pan American Building project above Grand Central Station. The commission for the complicated transaction Wien had worked out would normally have amounted to approximately a quarter of a million dollars. Wien refused to accept any commission; Wolfson insisted that he had more than earned it. Wien then suggested that Wolfson make the sum available to Brandeis University, setting up an endowed chair in Wolfson's name. Wolfson demurred. "I am just a real estate operator," he said. "A chair bearing my name would carry little meaning except that money was contributed toward it, and not even my money, for the grant would really be your commission. But, if you want to go through with this, I would be glad to have the chair named for my cousin, Harry Wolfson, who is a famous professor of philosophy at Harvard."

In great glee, Wien called me. I shared his exultation, but cautioned him that a number of preliminary steps were required before the chair could be established and named. Certainly it was necessary to obtain Harry Wolfson's permission, and this might not be easy. Wolfson was the shyest and most self-effacing of scholars; there was no assurance that he could be persuaded to accept the designation. Besides, all of his half-century academic career had been spent at Harvard. How would he react if a chair in his honor went to another university, and how would the Harvard authorities react?

I called on Wolfson in the basement of Widener Library, where he had labored for a lifetime on his research and writings. He was a fragile-looking, gnomish man whose erudition was awesome, the authentic original of the scholar whose "mind is high in-starr'd in other spheres." His magnum opus was the twelve-volume *Structure and Growth of Philosophic Systems from Plato to Spinoza*. His *Philosophy of the Church Fathers*, a two-volume study of religious philosophers from Saint Paul to Saint Augustine, published when he was sixty-seven, had quickly become a scholarly classic.

When I found Wolfson's office, it was difficult to spot him quickly, for, as usual, he was almost buried under the helter-skelter of books and manuscripts. Once trapped by a tenacious visitor, he was always the soul of courtesy, although one sensed that he was anxious to get back to his research. I dispensed with amenities and apprised him of my purpose. I told him that his cousin Erwin was eager to establish a chair in philosophy at Brandeis, and we would be honored if it carried the name of Harry Wolfson. Wolfson blinked for a few moments and then remarked, "The chair should really be named for the person who most deserved it, our Uncle Mendel. It was Uncle Mendel who had the vision and the courage to pull up stakes in Lithuania at the turn of the century and to pioneer his way to the new world. It was Uncle Mendel who brought over Erwin's father and it was Uncle Mendel who brought me over. Yes, the chair should be named for him."

I agreed that Uncle Mendel deserved the love and gratitude of his family, but Erwin had been responsible for the gift that made the chair possible. Wolfson refused to be interrupted. I doubt that he had even heard me. He continued, "Uncle Mendel had the genius that was responsible for the business success of the other members of the family. Where would Erwin's father be without Uncle Mendel, and where would I be?" I still persisted. "The chair should have an illustrious incumbent," I pleaded. "Then surely," he argued, "his erudition would be unaffected by the name borne by the chair." How could I compete with the master in logic? In despair, I aimed a low blow. "Harry," I said, "Brandeis is a very young school. It would add immeasurably to its prestige if the chair honored the philosopher rather than the actual donor." Apparently I touched a vulnerable spot. "Well," he said, "if it would be more helpful for Brandeis, a school that I very much admire, then I withdraw my objection." But as I left, I could still hear him muttering that full justice was not being done to Uncle Mendel.

I then arranged to see federal Judge Charles E. Wyzanski, Jr., an old friend, who was serving as the chairman of the Overseers of Harvard. I wanted to sound him out on the possible reaction at Harvard if, after an incumbency of more than fifty years, Wolfson permitted his name to be linked with a chair at another university. Wyzanski quickly put me at ease. "Brandeis is not just another university," he reminded me. "It is Jewish-sponsored; it bears the name of one of Harvard's most illustrious sons. The gift has not been diverted from Harvard. If it did not go to Brandeis, it would not be made at all. The Harvard community would assuredly respond with admiration and would rejoice with the authorities at Brandeis that the chair strengthens the academic quality of the young university that bears such an honored Harvard name."

In 1968, I read an unusual story in the daily press that one of the publishing lords of West Germany, Axel Springer, had offered a million marks to Prime Minister David Ben-Gurion to help create an art museum in Israel. Springer was a devout Christian who had escaped the fate of dissidents in Nazi Germany during the Hitler regime because of what had been diagnosed by a cooperative physician as a terminal illness. He had not been involved in the Nazi apparatus, and when the regime collapsed in 1945, he was one of the men on whom Chancellor Adenauer counted for service in reorganizing Germany on a firm democratic base. He had inherited a modest newspaper and magazine chain and had built it into one of the major publishing empires of Europe. He shared Adenauer's deep sorrow and shame over the Holocaust and used the columns of his influential newspaper and magazines to advocate strong ties with Israel and just compensation for the victims of Hitlerism. There was considerable dispute in Israel over the acceptance of his proferred gift, just as there had been many emotional protests over the restitution funds West Germany had offered to Israel to help strengthen its economy. The latter funds had been accepted and had helped decisively to relieve the beleaguered little state. They were accepted not as compensation but as a gesture of national contrition, and the Springer gift was interpreted as having been offered in the same spirit and was also accepted.

When I read this story, I wrote to Axel Springer to explain the concept of Brandeis and the symbol that it represented in the American Jewish community. I expressed the hope that he would wish to extend his program of reconciliation to the Jews of America, where many survivors had settled. Such letters rarely get past a secretary's perfunctory processing. But in this instance, within a week, there was a transatlantic call from Ernst Cramer, special assistant to Springer, who indicated that his chief had been deeply impressed with my inquiry and that he, Cramer, was prepared to fly to the United States for a detailed exploration of what might be a practical action. Within a month, he was on the Brandeis campus, and I was negotiating with the affable, highly intelligent aide, one of the few Jews who had returned to Germany after the Nazis had been eliminated. Cramer readily agreed that such a project would most likely intrigue Springer, and he flew back with the assurance that he would warmly recommend it. Springer quickly accepted the recommendation and made available a million gold marks to endow the chair that was to be named for his mother, Ottilie

Springer. He understood fully that the gift carried with it no authority to influence either choice of the incumbent or the individual's freedom in teaching or research. Indeed, Springer would not have had it any other way.

When the gift and its purpose were announced, two small groups on campus vigorously dissented. One group was similar to the protesters in Israel who insisted that this endowment was "blood money" and should not be accepted no matter what rhetoric of reconciliation was used. The other group, mainly militant leftists on campus led by Herbert Marcuse, professor of politics, and Heinz Lubasz, assistant professor of history, also a German refugee, excoriated the administration for accepting such funds from the leading "reactionary" publisher in West Germany. Springer's politics, they declared, were a menace to the liberal socialist movement of the new world. These dissidents carried their opposition to extremes in the scurrility of their protest. I was saddened that there was no restraining counsel from either Marcuse or Lubasz, who had always been quick to attack censorship when it affected their views but who apparently believed that, because a donor represented a differing point of view, it was immoral to accept gifts from him, even though the project was fully protected in its freedom and objectivity.

The first incumbent of the Ottilie Springer Chair was Geoffrey Barraclough, who came to Brandeis from Oxford. He was one of the best respected historians of the contemporary world. He gladly accepted the assignment, noting that Springer had published the German translations of many of his writings. When the chair was officially installed, Axel Springer and members of his staff came to the campus for the occasion. Springer was delighted with Brandeis itself and was particularly moved by the creative way in which the memorial to his mother was to be established.

Springer came to Boston a few years later to receive an honorary degree from Boston University. I joined the dinner party where he was entertained by the president of the university. Springer welcomed me with an embrace and insisted upon revising upward the endowment that he had established so as to take inflation into account.

During the summer of 1964, Thelma and I were vacationing in a New Jersey spa, and there we met another guest, Miss Fannie Hurst, a novelist who had enjoyed considerable popularity in the pre–World War II period. She seemed very much alone, abstracted and uncommunicative. I remembered her well not only for her best-sellers, especially *Back Street,* but because she was a graduate of Washington University, Thelma's alma mater and mine. She had been quite a celebrity in her heyday. I approached her before dinner one evening and asked whether she would like to join us. Her face lit up, and she accepted with alacrity. During the few remaining days of our holiday, we looked forward to our evening meals together, when our conversation would touch upon matters of mutual interest—creative writing, education, travel, literary friendships—that brought her back to her great days. We parted the best of friends, though she, it seemed, rather sadly. Her marriage had been guided by the principle of "freedom from binding ties." She and her husband were in accord that they would lead completely independent lives, with meetings and associations for themselves only by appointment. The permissive marriage had not lasted; she had no family, she had built no intimate concerned friendships, and she knew her writing days were over. Apparently she knew also that she had not long to live. Now as a lonely, elderly lady, her reputation in eclipse, she spoke glumly of the time ahead, quoting at our parting from her favorite Tennyson: that the future meant only "to live forgotten and love forlorn."

A few months later, I received a call from her New York attorney who informed me that Fannie Hurst had died that morning. He transmitted her request that I deliver the memorial address at the funeral services. He also informed me that her rather substantial estate was to be divided between Washington University and Brandeis, which she had written into a revised will after our summer meeting. The very modest service was attended by a small group of old friends, mainly from the world of letters and the theater, by one of the Washington University representatives, and by Thelma and me.

When her estate had been probated, the Brandeis share was substantial. Her attorney accepted my suggestion that two endowed chairs be set up in Fannie Hurst's name and that each year two visiting professors be invited to join the faculty in creative writing. In the years that followed, the humanities and creative arts curricula were immeasurably enriched as these provisions were fulfilled. This form of enduring memorial seemed most appropriate for the strange, lonely, gifted woman who could write so eloquently of love but who somehow missed this kind of happiness for herself.

Sometimes inexplicable family tragedies follow the Biblical tradition of converting a "Valley of Weeping into a Place of Springs." Sidney Wien, Lawrence's younger brother, and his lovely wife, Ellen, of Atlanta, Georgia, had been prime benefactors of the university. They were deeply interested in its art program and, late in 1961, had set up a special fund that enabled the museum to acquire unusual paintings and sculpture. In December 1962, many of the art lovers and leading citizens of Atlanta organized a tour of the outstanding museum centers of Europe. The group's chartered plane caught fire on its return takeoff, and all perished in the flames and explosions. Sidney and Ellen Wien and one of their two daughters, Toni, were on the ill-fated plane. The other daughter, Claire (Mrs. Richard Morse), joined with her Uncle Lawrence in establishing, in their names, an endowed chair in the history of art.

In the spring of 1964, I received word of another plane crash that involved Richard Koret, a New York manufacturer who was one of the university's most devoted patrons. The call came to me from one of our trustees, Joseph Mailman, who was Koret's closest friend and one of the executors of his estate. Koret had no family. His whole life had been devoted to his business, in which he had been remarkably successful, building a famous fashion name for the beauty and originality of the Koret handbags. Mailman asked me to offer the funeral eulogy. Koret had left a sizable estate that was bequeathed to Brandeis, and after negotiations with the executors, it was determined that two fully endowed chairs would be established, one in Judaic studies, the other in the history of ideas, an experimental program the university was pioneering.

Though the university had established an influential center for Jewish studies, many of us felt that it was important to broaden our offerings to include Christian religious and philosophical thought. Our objective was not only to give fuller meaning to the nonsectarian image of the university; it was clear that there were so many Christian-Jewish interrelationships in religious philosophy that it was mutually advantageous to bring to the faculty some outstanding scholars in the field. After one of our staff strategy meetings, I was approached by a young assistant, Emmanuel Goldberg, who had come to Brandeis from the public relations department of neighboring Boston University. There he had worked closely with a Protestant board member, Albert V. Danielsen, a Wellesley realtor who had made large contributions to strengthen the Protestant service at Boston University and had helped to establish its Methodist chapel as a tribute to a former president, Daniel Marsh. The Danielsens had also been generous benefactors at a number of the Catholic-sponsored colleges and had provided financial assistance for several of the colleges for blacks in the South. Goldberg invited them to the campus to meet with me, and we spoke of the usefulness of adding a missing component in the Brandeis curriculum, a chair that would become the teaching center for a better understanding of Christian thought. They responded with enthusiasm; and they not only established the chair but gave an extra half million dollars to make possible the substantial strengthening of the offerings in philosophy and ethics. Danielsen was very proud to become a Fellow of the university, and thereafter hardly a public function took place on the Brandeis campus without his presence and the eloquent benediction he was often called upon to offer.

When I was succeeded in the presidency by Morris Abram, he learned that Danielsen, then in his late seventies, was still playing tennis regularly.

Abram, a tennis enthusiast, made an appointment for a match with him. Before the game, Abram asked my advice as to the kind of score he should permit this generous donor to run up. In the match that followed, President Abram, twenty-five years Danielsen's junior, had to play the game of his life to keep up with his septuagenarian opponent, who entered and completed each match with prayer. Danielsen was the only one who was startled by the ovation he received from the commencement audience of 1973, when he accepted the university's honorary degree that paid tribute to the catholicity of his religious and philanthropic interests.

One of our most effective patrons was Eleanor Roosevelt, especially when she joined our Board of Trustees and our part-time faculty. She willingly undertook special assignments either by addressing our functions or by conferring with families whose support we sought. One day, I learned from Oscar Kolin, the nephew of Helena Rubinstein, the queen of a vast cosmetics empire, that she was ready to endow a chair in chemistry at the university. She asked for one privilege, to make the pledge personally to Eleanor Roosevelt. I called Mrs. Roosevelt, explained that I would not ordinarily intrude on her crowded schedule, but that a visit to Helena Rubinstein's apartment to take tea with her would confirm a very generous endowment for the university. Mrs. Roosevelt's response was almost a reflex action: "I would go to China if it meant such a service to the university." At the appointed hour, Lawrence Wien and I called for her in his limousine. We drove to the sumptuous apartment of Helena Rubinstein, which was virtually an art gallery. En route, Mrs. Roosevelt asked innocently, "by the way, who *is* Helena Rubinstein?" The two ladies met and spent a delightful hour discussing their world travels, after which the commitment was made for the Helena Rubinstein Chair in Chemistry.

It seemed to us that many good purposes could be simultaneously served if we established the practice of creating endowed chairs not only through family benefactions or legacies but as enduring tributes to significant public figures. Chairs bearing revered names would honor the university; participation in the tribute, broadly distributed, with gifts ranging from the most modest to the most generous, would extend the supporting constituency. Every few years, therefore, a campaign would be mounted to honor an illustrious public figure—Earl Warren, Christian Herter, Harry Truman, Adlai Stevenson, and others.

It was after Chief Justice Warren had come to dedicate the statue of Justice Brandeis in 1956 that we began planning the strategy for setting up a chair in his name. Warren had consistently refused honors of any kind. He believed that, as chief justice of the United States, his position made it mandatory for him to avoid any identification that could be even remotely interpreted as becoming beholden. In addition, after a long political career, he had little concern for personal honors. But I remembered his warm, lifelong friendship with a West Coast trustee, Ben Swig, the owner of the Hotel Fairmont atop Nob Hill in San Francisco. Swig had always avoided calls upon the justice for any personal advantage or political purpose, but he agreed with us that the appeal to help a young university that bore the name of Louis Brandeis, who had been the inspiration for Warren's own outlook on the law, might break through Warren's resolve. Swig made the approach. From the lilt in Swig's voice when the long distance call came through to me, I knew that he had succeeded.

Inevitably, Swig became the chairman of the campaign, and at his side was Dan Koshland, head of the Levi Straus empire and one of San Francisco's most respected and beloved citizens. Swig later confided that, though he had raised millions for every variety of cause—other universities, hospitals and welfare funds, Israel—he had never experienced an occasion where funds were so readily subscribed. They came from the oldest friends of Warren's days as governor of California, when he had been nominated by both the Democratic and Republican parties—from those who had supported him in his race for the vice-presidency on the Republican ticket with Thomas Dewey (the famous kangaroo ticket where the back part was stronger than the fore), from loyal supporters of the university, from admirers of the crucial *Brown v. Board of Education of Topeka* decision of 1954.

A chair in the name of President Harry Truman was a natural. His most trusted presidential aide had been David Niles, who was the main architect of Truman's policy that placed the United States squarely behind the establishment of a sovereign Israel. Niles had been one of the founders of Brandeis and, in the earliest years, perhaps its most influential advocate. He died in 1953, but his chief never forgot his loyalty. When we invited Truman in 1957 to accept an honorary degree and reminded him of Nile's kith-and-kin relationship to the university, the former President promptly consented. It was at the commencement that I broached our wish to raise the endowment for a chair in history in his name. Truman had been an avid student of American history and had often surprised his advisers by his understanding of the forces that had shaped the national destiny.

Truman was clearly moved by our desire to establish a chair in his name, for no other university had offered him such an honor. I asked several of the national Democratic leaders to assume leadership: Jacob Arvey of Chicago, Sam Rayburn, Lyndon Johnson, Governor Harriman, and members of our own board, Senator Herbert Lehman and Mrs. Eleanor Roosevelt. All of them recognized, even before the longer-range verdict of history, Truman's unique qualities, which made him one of our strongest presidents. The gifts for the endowment, however, were not limited to Democratic supporters. Contributions came from all groups—from common folk whose response had affected the stunning political upset of 1948, from trade unions who remembered Truman's social welfare legislation, and from Jewish leaders who could never forget his aid in the creation of an independent Israel. Within a few months, the mission had been accomplished, and the endowment was in hand.

A cordial relationship had been established with Adlai Stevenson ever since Eleanor Roosevelt had invited him to participate in her program, *Prospects of Mankind,* which was regularly telecast from the Brandeis campus. He was delighted with the spirit of the university and became one of its warmest admirers. When, in 1961, Brandeis received Phi Beta Kappa accreditation, he readily consented to be the Convocation speaker and, as usual, charmed the audience who came to hear him at the informal breakfast and at the exercises themselves. When he died suddenly in 1961 on a London street, we all felt we had lost not only one of the most gifted of the world's statesmen but a devoted friend of the university. I asked one of our trustees, William Benton, former senator from Connecticut, publisher of the *Encyclopedia Britannica,* and one of Stevenson's closest friends, to help create an endowed chair in international politics in Stevenson's name. It was Benton who obtained the family consent for the campaign to establish the chair, and it was Benton, too, who gave us the leads to the special constituency that would most likely respond to the fulfillment of our objective. The chair was quickly subscribed and assigned to Ruth Morgenthau (daughter-in-law of the former Treasury Secretary), who came to Brandeis in 1963 and who was equally at home in political theory and in African anthropology. She later served as one of the American representatives to the United Nations and in other international organizations.

The ready willingness of the entire American diplomatic corps to help establish the Christian Herter Chair was a good example of the friendships the university could now command. Herter was a Republican Brahmin from one of the oldest Massachusetts families. He had served a long apprenticeship in diplomacy and government and had a brilliant incumbency as governor of Massachusetts. After the death of John Foster Dulles, President Eisenhower tapped Herter to become secretary of state, and few men in public affairs were more esteemed. The idea to honor him on his seventieth birthday through an endowed chair came from my assistant, Emmanuel Goldberg, who had initiated the campaign for the Danielsen Chair. Goldberg had been on Herter's staff in the governor's office and had won his chief's confidence. He approached Herter with the hope that, though an alumnus of Harvard, he would permit a campaign for a chair in international studies at Brandeis.

Goldberg then went directly to President Eisenhower and obtained his permission to use his name as the honorary chairman for the campaign. The sponsoring committee was enlarged to include many of the major officials in the state and federal governments. Then a strictly limited appeal, a model of sensitive understatement, was addressed to the men and women in the diplomatic services around the world. The response was gratifying. Contributions came from virtually every embassy and consulate, and they were usually accompanied by letters of affection that went far beyond the routine of acquiescence. Sadly, Christian Herter died in December 1966, at the very beginning of the solicitation. We were all deeply touched when the family's obituary notice indicated that memorial tributes in lieu of flowers could be made either to Johns Hopkins (Herter had endowed a department there for advanced studies in international relations) or to Brandeis University. The endowment fund was quickly completed. When the chair was dedicated, Governor Herter's oldest son spoke for the family, expressing appreciation that the memory of his father was to be perpetuated in this creative way.

There was special appropriateness in the decision to establish an endowed chair in legal institutions in the name of Judge Joseph Proskauer to honor his ninetieth birthday. Proskauer's brilliant legal career stretched back to the previous century. He had been a justice of the Superior Court of New York as well as an adviser to Governor Alfred Smith, many of whose most significant speeches he had written when Smith was the Democratic candidate for the presidency. He had given resourceful leadership to many major Jewish organizations, particularly to the American Jewish Committee.

Proskauer was one of the first national leaders I tried to reach for moral support when Brandeis was founded, but his excessively busy schedule prevented a conference until the university's tenth year. One day I broke through the battery of protective secretaries and got him on the telephone. I asked for just half an hour in his office, uninterrupted, and to this he yielded. It proved to be a significant thirty minutes for, at the end of it, he offered not only his blessing but the pledge to call his friends and colleagues to meet with me at the Lotos Club in New York. Out of that meeting came many new supporters for the university from a social group that had been extremely difficult to penetrate. Judge Proskauer joined our Board of Trustees soon afterward and became one of the most influential interpreters of the university. He remained remarkably active all through his eighties with little diminution of vitality. When called upon at any public gathering, his wit was keen and his observations pertinent. It was one of the board's most popular decisions to have a public celebration on his ninetieth birthday and to have the tribute take the form of an endowed chair in legal institutions.

We had a very knowledgeable committee to supervise the campaign, but it ran into an unusual obstacle. Proskauer, a nonagenarian, really belonged to a generation that was very much a part of the past. To members of his own firm and even to the senior partners who now managed exceptionally important litigation, the judge was a legend. The plate dinner attendance was much smaller than was expected for a man of Judge Proskauer's attainments. But in the long run, we accomplished our purpose. We turned to one of the judge's oldest friends and admirers, Dr. Maurice Hexter of our own board. Hexter had been the head of the Jewish Federation in New York for nearly half a century, and, quite apart from his profound understanding of changing social welfare currents, he had an encyclopedic knowledge of the hundreds of families who were the pillars of support for the agencies that served one of the largest Jewish communities in the world. He had known Proskauer for more than forty years, and his admiration for the judge bordered on reverence. He knew that the trustees of the Harry Kaufman Foundation were ready to follow any counsel Proskauer offered; and there was no more effective way to express appreciation for all the judge had meant to Kaufman in his philanthropies. Hexter suggested that I appeal to the foundation to complete the endowment for the Proskauer Chair. Indeed, he sent me a draft letter to write to the foundation, and, as I remember it, I changed only a "which" to a "that." The full amount needed was voted by the trustees.

Meantime, we enjoyed the gala testimonial evening, where the birthday program included a constellation of legal and governmental luminaries, including Justice Harlan who, between hearings at the Supreme Court, had made a special trip from Washington. I do not know how Judge Proskauer was impressed by all that was said about him; he was very busy making notes as each speaker detailed an illuminating episode. And, as usual, he stole the show. He revealed the secret of how, despite his habit of vigorous dissent and no-nonsense responses when he found himself in disagreement, no resentments or recriminations were uttered anywhere. "The reason is easy," the judged chuckled. "I outlived all the bastards."

One of our largest affairs was the testimonial for David Dubinsky, the ebullient head of the International Ladies' Garment Workers' Union (ILGWU), one of the nation's most powerful labor organizations. Dubinsky had been one of its founders and had served as its hard-hitting general secretary from the dark days of the depression of 1932 until his retirement in 1966. He converted the union into a model for labor management relations, winning a gratifying standard of living and progressive welfare benefits for his workers and playing, as well, an influential role in the liberal politics of New York and of the nation. He was a founder of the Americans for Democratic Action and of the Liberal party in New York, both often exercising decisive swing votes. As he approached the mandatory retirement age, he consented to be the guest of honor at a Brandeis function, the purpose of which was to create, in his name, a scholarship fund for students concentrating on labor economics. The attendance was a Who's Who of the political as well as of the mercantile and industrial world. Major contributions in his honor were made in advance of the plate dinner by outstanding manufacturers who had often been his toughest opponents in labor management confrontations. Dubinsky had already received almost every conceivable honor that his colleagues could conjure up. In his response to the recognition Brandeis was bestowing upon him, he said it was a paradox that a great university would name a scholarship fund for an immigrant boy who had landed on these shores with no assets and without even a rudimentary knowledge of the language, who could not afford a high school education. A few years later, he received the university's honorary degree.

There had been a longstanding university friendship with Jacob Potofsky, president of the Amalgamated Workers of America, the all-powerful union in men's clothing manufacturing plants. Potofsky had been attracted early to the university and was one of its first Fellows. He had succeeded the redoubtable Sidney Hillman, who had founded the union and had served as the right-hand man of Franklin Roosevelt in keeping labor relations on an even keel during the critical World War II years. Potofsky set up the Sidney Hillman Memorial Foundation and arranged for special lectures on labor themes to be given annually at Brandeis; the invitees were usually the most respected authorities in their field. He was one of the first to encourage the plate dinner routine, and he was often responsible for obtaining the guest of honor and the campaign chairman. A day came when he ran out of excuses to avoid serving as the guest of honor himself. No function of its kind ever gave the university staff so few problems in attendance or program. Potofsky, handsome and debonair, his face set off by an aristocratic little beard that made him look like a Viennese psychiatrist, captivated the audience with his first generation wit and his laudatory appraisal of the concept of the university. Later, when he received the university's honorary degree, his citation read: "An organizing strategist of the CIO through the bitterest years of labor conflict; friend and confidant of Presidents and the elect of the world, he is ever mindful that he came to high estate through Ellis Island and has eaten the bread of affliction."

Inasmuch as I had prevailed on so many devoted supporters to lend themselves to functions to advance the interest of the university, I could not very well object when my own name was requested for whatever leverage it could command when I reached my sixtieth birthday in 1959, especially when it was presented as an ideal occasion for raising a very substantial tribute fund. On February fifteenth, the birthday party was held in the crowded ballroom of the Waldorf Astoria in New York. Representatives of every segment of our diversified constituency participated— trustees, fellows, president's councillors, faculty and students, alumni, members of our National Women's Committee, and, of course, a large body of annual donors. Abraham Feinberg, chairman of the board, presided. Judge Proskauer, now well past eighty, sparkled as always. He could not understand what was so unique about a sixtieth birthday. "This is mere callow youth," he insisted. "Sachar is really just a child prodigy." Leonard Bernstein was in the full tide of his brilliant career as the director of the New York Philharmonic Orchestra. He reminisced with affection about his earliest years at Brandeis when he had served as a visiting faculty member in our Department of Music. He marveled at the *chutzpah* of a university president who, before even the first class had been graduated, did not hesitate to mount a music festival that featured the American premier of Kurt Weill's *Threepenny Opera*, arranged by Mark Blitzstein and starring the author's widow, Lotte Lenya. What he did not add was that the undoubted attraction for the huge audience at the festival was the announcement that he himself was to do the conducting.

There was one other surprise in the program. My mother, who had just passed her eightieth birthday and had flown in from St. Louis for the occasion, was asked to rise in her place to be greeted. She was surrounded by all of her children and most of her grandchildren. To me, the sustained standing ovation she received from the audience was no conventional amenity. There had been many dark moments since the days at the end of the last century when she arrived as an immigrant from Turkish-held Jerusalem, but, fully as much as my father who had died in the university's first year, she had held the family together and had never relinquished her ambitions for us.

I knew better than to go beyond the climactic moments of the evening. I contented myself with a look ahead to tasks that could be undertaken with renewed confidence, now that the foundation was set. The practical postscript to the evening was not inconsequential; more than $350,000 had been subscribed in advance. I asked that it be set up as a scholarship fund until my presidency had ended. It then became part of a five million-dollar tribute fund that made possible a fellowship program for study abroad for Brandeis students and faculty, the acquisition of valuable acreage for future expansion, and the erection of the International Center.

In 1962, the audacious decision was made to attempt an overall, three-year effort that would minimize the university's reliance on the caprice of annual public fund-raising. The goal was set at sixty-five million dollars, the most ambitious ever undertaken by the university. Twelve million would be assigned for the completion of construction still to be done under the master plan. Ten million would be used over the three-year period to cover the excess of expenditures over the assured income of tuition, room, and board. It was planned to allocate nearly three-quarters, about forty-three million, as endowment for faculty chairs, scholarships, and fellowships.

Our campaign was announced just as the Massachusetts Institute of Technology was launching one of its own with a goal set at sixty-six million. Brandeis was then fourteen years old, and its venture seemed more like quixotism than responsible resolve. But we pinned our faith on the leadership that gladly assumed responsibility: Joseph Linsey of Boston as general chairman; Morris Brown of Palm Beach, Ben Swig of San Francisco, and Sam Lemberg of New York as co-chairmen; Dr. Sidney Farber, the head of the Children's Cancer Fund, Eleanor Roosevelt, Senators Benton and Ribicoff, and other outstanding public figures who did not limit their service to letterhead identification. The planning took more than half a year and included the recruitment of committees in nearly a hundred cities. I flew thirty thousand miles in sixty flights to meet with those who were asked to accept responsibility for participation and, afterward, for the actual fund-raising drives. Most of our trustees, fellows, and president's councillors gave whatever time they could salvage from their own concerns. Apparently, through the years, we had built solid friendships in every section of the country, for within six months it was possible to announce that more than twenty million dollars had been committed. The pledges ranged from the modest amounts of young alumni to several million-dollar grants for specified designations. Then, about a third of the way into the campaign, came a providential development through two challenge grants from the Ford Foundation totaling twelve million dollars. If the required matching were met, it would successfully wind up the campaign, virtually complete the physical master plan, and add enough endowed chairs and scholarship support to lessen the vulnerability of the university's academic objectives.

The Ford Foundation had selected a limited number of universities who were quite clearly on their way to national eminence. It had undertaken to provide major grants that would permit such institutions to make commitments for academic programs, research, and construction that might otherwise have to wait for decades. The objective was further emphasized when the condition was attached that the universities were to generate matching gifts in cash, twice or three times the grant amounts, from private, nongovernmental sources. As the news of the Ford plan percolated through the educational world, there was a great stir among institutions eager to qualify for consideration. Brandeis, too, was determined to make its bid, although it seemed like a very remote hope. We had only just established a few graduate programs. Our alumni body was small, the oldest among them hardly out of their twenties. But the university had demonstrated spectacular progress; only thirteen years after its founding, it had achieved Phi Beta Kappa accreditation, and our master plan, physical and academic, betokened an ambition that had every possibility for early fulfillment if such a grant could be achieved. I therefore welcomed the appointment that was set with James Armsey, the Ford Foundation grants director.

It was a brisk autumn day in 1962 when I met with Armsey in New York. Though I came armed with a general proposal for expansion in many academic and physical areas, I expected that this visit would be preliminary, to be followed by the formal presentation of our plans. When I was ushered into the office, Armsey came forward to greet me most cordially. "Do you remember me?" he asked. Assuming I had never met him, I responded, "Should I have?" He then noted that he had been at the University of Illinois during the late 1920s when I was teaching in the history department. His roommate had been James Reston, who later went on to a distinguished career with the *New York Times*. Reston had taken my course in modern history and had often discussed my lectures when he returned to the dormitory quarters that he shared with Armsey. Armsey had not taken any of my courses, but Reston's complimentary evaluation had given him an introduction to my work that he had not forgotten. The exchange of Illinois reminiscences gave us an informal rapport that made it much easier for me to discuss my mission. Obviously the Brandeis proposal would have to make its own way, but it was no handicap that Armsey was so friendly and well disposed from the outset. Indeed, the meeting opened a personal friendship that included our wives and has been savored to the present.

The documentation required by the foundation gave us a superb opportunity to think through our plans for the next generation, for the requested funds were not meant to meet current expenditures nor to cover ongoing obligations. They were meant as seed money or, as the Ford prospectus put it, "to build on excellence and realistic aspirations for the future." The proposal thus outlined plans for a much-expanded undergraduate curriculum, a somewhat larger student body, resources for scholarship and fellowship aid that would attract ever better-qualified applicants, launching several new graduate departments, boosting salary levels for faculty to retain our best people and to recruit new faculty clearly on their way to distinguished careers, expanding the program of the Florence Heller Graduate School for Advanced Studies in Social Welfare, doubling the acquisitions for the university library, making available more generous subsidies for faculty research. All these objectives were in the master plan, but the pace of achievement had to be linked with funding.

We hoped the Ford grant and its matching inducements would bring these objectives to much earlier fulfillment.

The proposal was developed by a task force of sixty faculty and administrative staff members who spent many months gathering supporting data. What emerged was a volume of more than four hundred pages that included immediate projections and long-range objectives. When it reached Armsey, he noted that it was the best proposal of any that had been submitted. In November 1962, he called me personally to indicate that six million dollars had been assigned, with the proviso that eighteen million dollars was to be raised by us within a three-year period.

There was dramatic timing in the call, for it came just as the trustees were at their regular meeting on campus. I tried to be casual in making the announcement to them, but I failed completely. Meanwhile, the announcement had reached the Faculty Club, and the cheering was joined even by our foreign Ziskind visiting professors. Seven other universities were awarded grants in varying amounts and with different matching requirements; Notre Dame, Stanford, Johns Hopkins, Vanderbilt, the University of Southern California, Brown, and Denver. Brown was 198 years old, Stanford was 77. Brandeis was the youngest and the smallest. The criteria for the choice as detailed in the letter of transmission indicated where Brandeis had concentrated its strength. It had built "a solid structure of support in its unusual Jewish constituency"; it had developed "independent administrative and legal control, free of legislative and political influence"; it was favored by "resourceful and aggressive presidential leadership"; "its academic planning was in the best tradition of sound scholarship"; "the quality of its faculty and student body augured well for a future dedicated to the highest objectives of liberal education."

The Ford announcement was hailed as a major breakthrough for the young university. The *New York Herald Tribune* editorialized that it was the recognition of Brandeis's proven ability to create new outposts of excellence. "Brandeis University is marching toward a pinnacle of prestige in the academic world. Herein lies one of the educational stories of the century." The campaign that was mounted to raise the matching funds, with the slogan "three equals four," had a galvanic unifying effect on the entire Brandeis family. There were meetings in scores of cities—house parties, luncheons, telephone appeals. In the first year, three-fourths of the goal had been achieved; and then a major new incentive emerged. Apparently, Notre Dame and Stanford had achieved their goals very quickly and received a second grant. Of course, they had thousands of well-established alumni. But the university world took it for granted that, for Brandeis, miracles were commonplace. In any case, the very hope that a successful first campaign might lead to a second grant worked like a shot of adrenalin. Within eighteen months, the message went to the Ford Foundation that all conditions for its initial grant had been fulfilled.

In our second proposal, the commitment was undertaken to encourage matching contributions for academic purposes. Government agencies had frequently participated in underwriting physical facilities, usually health-oriented—science buildings, laboratory equipment—and Brandeis had received more than its proportionate share for such expanding needs. Why not extend this matching principle to academic designations to help endow chairs, fellowships, and scholarships? The university in its first sixteen years, up to 1964, had received contributions—primarily by bequest—for the endowment of fifteen chairs, mainly in scientific areas. The rate at which such chairs were being added, averaging one a year, represented a tolerable pace as long as we were not yet in the elite company of universities that were centuries old and had built impressive endowments. Was it too ambitious to aspire to add twenty-five new endowed chairs in a three-year period and to have them in the right balance so that the humanities, the creative arts, and the social sciences could also be materially strengthened? The proposal aimed to encourage the donor to contribute $250,000 for a chair designation, his gift to be supplemented by the Ford "bonus" of $150,000. If a total of $3.75 million were used for this purpose from the Ford funds, twenty-five endowed chairs could be established.

It was a Herculean undertaking since the campaign to match the first foundation grant had scarcely been completed. Thus, it was a proud moment when Brandeis again found itself in the select company of the few universities that, having successfully matched a first grant, entered the lists to aspire for a second. Armsey was the guest of honor at the function in December 1964 when the completion of the first grant and the challenge of the second were simultaneously celebrated. "The first Ford Foundation matching grant," he said, "was assigned to speed the growth of a great new educational enterprise. . . . Now, as you all know, we've done it again. And you have to do it again. But this time with a difference. This time Dr. Sachar is intent upon establishing a bevy of endowed chairs. He knows that people are more important than things and that, even though the things of education are necessary, the people of education, the first-rate students and a first-rate faculty, are absolutely essential. So with 'the things' a bit under control, he is now putting the big push on 'people' money." He added, "The fulfillment of this objective will enable Brandeis to take its place among the great universities of the nation and the world. There is no higher purpose to claim your allegiance and support." The *New York Times* editorial comment perhaps best summarized the significance of the successful double campaign: "The rationale of the Brandeis scheme is simply the inescapable fact that major donors more often like to attach their names to bricks-and-mortar monuments than to the more intangible support of faculty salaries. Yet only a well supported teaching faculty can assure an institution's excellence, and a sufficiency of highly paid professors constitutes a sizable item in each year's operation budget and in the annual drive for gifts. By making the endowment of professorial chairs as permanently and visibly identifiable as donations to a building fund and by being able to supplement the gift with a Ford Foundation 'bonus,' the university may well demonstrate that major donations can be channeled as readily into teaching as into construction. This is a sound merger of good fiscal sense and high educational purpose."

The new campaign went into high gear at once and was even more intensively conducted than the first one. Substantial fillip was provided when in the mid-sixties the influential *Comparative Guide to American Colleges,* noting the impact of the first grant, listed Brandeis among the twenty most selective colleges and universities in the United States. With the help of thousands of volunteers across the country, the second campaign was successfully completed in less than two years. Twenty-two chairs had been underwritten, and, by the end of the full three-year period, negotiations for several more were well under way. During the time span that had been set by the Ford Foundation, the original eighteen chairs had been expanded to more than forty. Four were in the field of science; the others righted the endowments' balance by seeding the humanities, the social sciences, and the creative arts. They included chairs in the arts of design, Judaic studies, economics, politics, social planning, history, legal institutions, behavioral science, theater arts, sociology, philosophy, and the fine arts.

The wisdom of the Ford grants was vindicated when the American Council on Education, in its 1968 report based on data gathered through 1966, ranked seven of the Brandeis departments among the top twenty graduate programs in the universities of the country. Equally gratifying, the campaign had secured many millions of dollars for scholarships and fellowship endowments. These took many forms, some sufficiently ample to see students through their entire university career, as in the case of the Chernis grant, which was first assigned to Gustav Ranis, a young German refugee who had been the valedictorian of our first commencement and who went on to a distinguished academic career at Yale and many years of service as a Brandeis trustee. Others were designated for special fields of concentration, such as the one set up by Harry and Mildred Remis of Boston that offered encouragement to young people of great promise in the creative arts, or the one by Mary and Abbey Hirschfield for graduate students in the humanities. Such grants were indispensable in a university where more than 30 percent of the student body required financial assistance.

Of course, such fulfillments carried sobering responsibilities. Armsey had warned that this would happen. "The grant," he said, when he announced the second Ford challenge, "may solve a few immediate problems, but it will create others. It won't make your life happier. The wholly new level of excellence the grants are designed to help you reach, while it is comforting to contemplate, is disturbing and disruptive to achieve."

I had no illusions about the burdens that the unending quest for excellence would impose. Brandeis, at least in its founding years when precedents were set, could not plan and function timidly with a bookkeeper's mentality. I was convinced, however, that the occasional risks were not irresponsible as long as we could rely upon a sensitive and generous constituency. This conviction was implicit in my reply to one of my friends, a midwestern college president. He asked me how our trustees and I could sleep nights when our obligations kept growing and there was no undergirding endowment to protect them. "Oh," I replied, "but we do have an endowment, and it is better than blue chip capital funds. Our endowment is people."

CHAPTER SEVEN

The Library:
Cherchez la Femme

If there was any one moment of doubt about the good sense of my decision to accept the presidency of Brandeis, it was when I had my first view of what passed for the library we had inherited from Middlesex University. It possessed approximately a thousand volumes, mainly medical and veterinary texts, most of them obsolete, that were housed in what had been the veterinary school stable. There were seats for about seventy-five readers. Even though our first class of little more than a hundred were only freshmen and it was planned to take four years to achieve the full undergraduate cycle, I wondered how the school could function, especially with our high-quality objectives. I remember the sinking feeling that came over me as I stood in front of the pathetic little structure, too incredulous to make any comment to the three trustees who had driven me to the campus to evaluate our assets and needs. One of my first actions when the shock of the visit wore off was to explore with some of our neighboring universities the possibility of using their facilities until we could create some of our own. The response was heartening. All who were approached welcomed the newcomer in their midst. They invited our faculty and students to use their stacks; they offered to supply occasional volumes on loan. But, of course, these could be no more than temporary courtesies, and it was painfully clear that a well-stocked library had to take priority over all other considerations.

It was a stroke of genius for the first chairman of the Board of Trustees, George Alpert, to conceive the plan of marshaling women's groups throughout the country and persuading them to adopt as their responsibility the Brandeis library and its maintenance. A few months before the first class was to be received on campus, in the summer of 1948, Alpert

1. The Castle, inherited from Middlesex Medical School.

2. Justice William O. Douglas meeting with student leaders in advance of the Education S. forum.

3. Leonard Bernstein rehearsing for the American premiere of *The Three Penny Opera*, 1950. 4. (*below*) The first enlargement of the Board of Trustees, 1951. New members include Adele Rosenwald Levy, Eleanor Roosevelt, and standing at the extreme right, David Niles, the administrative assistant to President Harry S Truman.

5. Inaugurating the Wien International Scholarship Program at a special convocation, October 1958. Lawrence Wien, who endowed the program, President Sachar, Senator John F. Kennedy, Wakako Kimoto Hironaka, M.A. '64, Senator Leverett Saltonstall, George Kennan, and Abraham Feinberg, chairman of the Board of Trustees. (Mrs. Hironaka, née Kimoto, is currently a member of the House of Councilors, the upper house in the Japanese Diet. In 1993–94 she served as director-general of the Environment Agency in the Cabinet of former Prime Minister Morihiro Hosokawa.)

6. Senator Kennedy and President Sachar with Eleanor Roosevelt at a 1960 filming of her program, "Prospects of Mankind." Senator Kennedy announced his intention to seek the Democratic nomination for president during this campus visit.

7. The three chapels.

8. Eleanor Roosevelt, President Sachar, and President Harry S Truman at a tribute dinner preceding the 1957 commencement at which President Truman received an honorary degree.

9. David and Paula Ben-Gurion arriving at Logan Airport for a campus visit. With them are Israeli Ambassador to the United States Avrahm Harmon and President Sachar.

10. Alumni Day 1974 at the Sachar International Center, now home to the Graduate School of International Economics and Finance. (Photograph by Ralph Norman)

11. Twenty-fifth reunion of members of the original Class of 1952.

12. Brandeis's first five presidents at the fortieth anniversary celebration in October 1988. From left to right: Marver Bernstein, Charles Schottland, Evelyn Handler, Morris Abram, and Abram Sachar. (Photograph by Julian Brown)

13. The newest addition to the science complex, the Benjamin and Mae Volen National Center for Complex Systems. (Photograph by Julian Brown)

14. Members of the Board of Trustees and honorary degree recipients at the 1992 commencement exercises. (Front row from left to right: Natan Sharansky, Founding Trustee Norman Rabb, Elena Bonner, Abram Sachar, President Samuel Thier, Chairman of the Board Louis Perlmutter '56, Quincy Jones, Board Vice Chairman Malcolm Sherman. Second row from left to right: Trustee and Congressman Stephen J. Solarz '62, Teddy Kollek, Robert McCormick Adams, Board Vice Chairman Barton J. Winokur, Charles Bronfman, Trustee Robert Shapiro '52, Trustee Henry L. Foster.)

15. Inside the Gosman Sports and Convocation Center, part of the Joseph F. and Clara Ford Athletic and Recreation Complex. (Photograph by Heather Pillar)

16. The new Carl and Ruth Shapiro Admissions Center at first light. (Photograph © 1994 Steve Rosenthal for Centerbrook Architects)

appealed to Edith Michaels of Boston to take the leadership in developing such auxiliary groups. Mrs. Michaels, a former president of the Boston chapter of Hadassah, with demonstrated organizational skills, had the time and energy to devote to the heavy tasks that would be required. In collaboration with another dynamic community leader, Hannah Abrams, a founding committee was selected whose members were drawn from special interest groups. It was hoped that each of the women would be able to muster recruits from their own constituencies for what would become the Brandeis University National Women's Committee.

The early months were critical, for there was almost instant resistance. Though the power structure in most of the larger communities did not oppose the concept of Brandeis, it was argued that the proliferation of membership chapters would inevitably siphon off support for budgets that were already strained to the limit. To counteract such opposition, it was necessary, before launching a chapter, to identify and make full use of personal friendships. Their advocacy would be indispensable to assure conciliatory persuasion in community councils. The initial strategic breakthrough would have to depend on *Who's Who* and, even more, on Who Knows Whom.

The women in Greater Boston who had been active in national organizations called upon their associates to take assignments for Brandeis. Even before the first students were enrolled, Mrs. Abrams secured an allocation from a local scholarship organization that made possible the purchase of the librarian's priority list of approximately a thousand volumes for the incoming freshman class. Memberships poured in, and the Boston chapter, headed by Mrs. Abrams, was soon followed by thriving chapters in Providence, New Bedford, Fall River, Springfield, and other New England communities, which, as expected, provided the momentum for expansion elsewhere.

During the many years of campaigning for the United Jewish Appeal, George Alpert had established relationships in many southern communities—Houston, Memphis, Louisville, and others. He appealed effectively to his many friends there to provide founding leadership for the women's chapters. I had been located for many years at the University of Illinois as a member of the history faculty and then as national Hillel director, and there were now hundreds of my former students in positions of responsibility in communities throughout the country, especially in the Middle West. Many of them had been welcomed into our home, some as babysitters for our children. The ties of affection that bound us were strong. When Brandeis came into being, some of my former students were among its most loyal allies. Initially, the Chicago chapter of the women's committee was virtually a Hillel alumnae group, and the affair was a sentimental reunion for Thelma and me and for our first members. In Cleveland, the dean of the Jewish community, Alfred Benesch, a Hillel commissioner and president of the Cleveland Board of Education, and his wife, Helen, offered help. They teamed up with Adeline Kane, whose husband Irving was a leader in national philanthropies, and with another community leader, Mrs. Leah Mellman, and this influential triumvirate soon built one of the largest chapters in the country.

In St. Louis, Rae Sachar, my sister-in-law, brought in a circle of socially prominent women, and around this nucleus several thousand women joined to make the chapter a major community force. Indianapolis, Kansas City, Milwaukee, Cincinnati, Columbus, Pittsburgh, Detroit, Minneapolis, and St. Paul were all early bastions in the Middle West. Chapters in Los Angeles, San Francisco, San Diego, and Denver soon opened up the West. And New York, Philadelphia, Baltimore, Washington, and Miami were beachheads for us up and down the Atlantic seaboard. Within a year, it was possible to convene a national conference in Boston with representatives from scores of cities across the country. As the years passed, the report of each national president, whose term was normally two years, glowed with the enthusiasm engendered by geographical expansion. The membership escalated rapidly from twenty-five thousand in fifty-two chapters in 1951 to seventy-two thousand in one hundred and twenty-five chapters in 1969.

Recognition that the Brandeis library was moving into the front ranks came in several ways: the speed of acquisition, mounting circulation figures, the use of research materials by increasing numbers of scholars. One of the most impressive acknowledgments of excellence was the invitation from the Association of Research Libraries for Brandeis to play a key role in the newly launched Farmington Plan, a cooperative effort among selected libraries to coordinate the acquisition of research materials from every part of the world, each institution to be assigned a specific area. Brandeis gladly joined and began to acquire materials from Egypt, Jordan, Iraq, Iran, Lebanon, Syria, the Arabian peninsula, and, of course, Israel. Later, the political tensions and the wars in the Near and Middle East made it difficult to sustain the flow of scholarly materials from the Arab states, but what did get through, directly or through intermediaries, was centered at Brandeis and was extensively used. With the remarkable advances in computer technology after the seventies, the Farmington Plan was superseded; but for a university library in its infancy, to be included in the innovative effort was a gratifying salute.

The pace of acquisition made it clear that an adequate library building could not be long postponed. By 1954, Brandeis had been accredited and had launched its first graduate programs, and the National Women's Committee sponsored a special campaign to add a wing to the converted stable. But thereafter, if the university was to rank as a first-class institution, no further temporary measures could suffice. A library that fitted the image Brandeis now projected would require an ultimate capacity of at least half a million volumes (soon the goal was expanded to a million), with reading and research space to accommodate the augmented student body and faculty of the future. There was no expectation that a donor would be found to parallel the munificence of a Widener, a Lamont, a Firestone, a Harkness, or a Rockefeller. But an adequate library for a mid-twentieth-century university would still call for many millions for construction and support. The attainment of full accreditation brought pride, but with it, the highest priority was given to the search for the indispensable library benefactor.

During the spring recess of 1956, I arranged for an appointment with a New York merchant, Jacob Goldfarb, whose reputation for enlightened philanthropy was legendary. I had established a warm relationship with him many years before through our mutual interest in the Hillel Foundations. He was already a generous patron of the university, but he had not identified any special area for long-range support. I was received most courteously and affectionately and was asked to outline the university's needs and the commitment they would require. I had no notion of what would appeal to him or how substantially he would wish to be involved. I therefore spoke of the priorities that had to be quickly met. They ranged from academic chairs and fellowships to major physical facilities, including the university library. He listened without interruption, a smile lighting up a cherubic face, but there was no immediate reaction to any specific proposal.

Apparently, however, a chord had been struck. Several days later, Goldfarb called me. He told me that at the Passover Seder the night before he had discussed a contemplated gift to the university with his wife, Bertha. Their first impulse had been to assign a million dollars in their wills. But, after sober second thought, they decided to make the money available at once to help underwrite the library. "So go ahead and don't delay further." I tried to cover my stunned delight by chiding Goldfarb for not at least reversing the telephone charges. When the decision was transmitted to the officers of the Women's Committee, they agreed that the best way they could make love to Goldfarb without creating connubial problems in the family was to pledge a matching sum. They already had raised half a million dollars, above their assigned budget in their first eight years, and it had been held for just such a possibility. They now were determined to double this zealously guarded amount quickly so that they could be appropriate partners with the Goldfarbs. At their National Conference in June, the delegates enthusiastically accepted the commitment, again beyond the regular budget, and it was fulfilled in a series of whirlwind life membership campaigns. Goldfarb insisted that he was infinitely better off than the Biblical Solomon, who had only a thousand women in his entourage.

We called in Harrison and Abramovitz and commissioned the firm to design a library whose scope was to remain undefined until we knew more clearly what other major donors would contribute. While the concept of the library was taking form, we continued to explore the interest of other families who might be induced to underwrite special areas, reference halls, reading rooms, carrels, and other major facilities. Samuel and Rieka Rapaporte, of Providence, underwrote a special wing as the Treasure Hall, fully equipped with temperature and humidity controlled vaults to house precious manuscripts, rare volumes, and other archival materials. Special support also came from Herman and Ethel Mintz of Boston; Alexander and Pauline Shapiro of Boston; Louis and Abraham Zimble of Boston; Ruth Samuels of Westport, Connecticut; Joseph Foster of Leominster, Massachusetts; Harold and Ellen Wald of Chestnut Hill, Massachusetts; and Francis Levien of Stamford, Connecticut. Other gifts paid honor to Edith Michaels, founder of the Women's Committee, and to the memory of Harry and Celia Meyers of Lawrence, Massachusetts.

When three million dollars had been pledged, the architects were authorized to turn their imaginative design into definite specifications. But before the building was halfway up, Goldfarb, while attending a trustees' meeting, called me aside and, almost shyly, noted that we must not modify any of the plans for the library simply to fit budgetary limits. He asked then that we put him down for another half million dollars. During the next year of construction, he quite spontaneously kept adding similar allocations, until his own contribution approached three million dollars. As the building neared completion, he said to me one day, "Bert and I are honored that the trustees plan to name the library for us. I want you to know, however, that if a major donor is obtained who is primarily concerned with the library, please give it to him. We have had our satisfaction in making our gift. The designation really is not personally important." This was not spoken with mock humility but was characteristic of an extraordinary couple. Obviously, it was the university that would be honored if the Goldfarb name were linked in perpetuity to its library. How completely it had entered the university vocabulary was made clear after the library had been completed. There was a reception for foreign students, and the Goldfarbs were in the receiving line. A youngster from Nigeria was introduced to them. "Goldfarb," he exclaimed excitedly. "Oh, you are the library!" The Goldfarbs beamed.

Because the plans for construction were constantly expanded, the dedication date had to be postponed several times. At each national conference of the Women's Committee, it required special ingenuity to devise ceremonies to contain the patience of the women and, incidentally but not too incidentally, to quicken the pace of pledge fulfillment. There was a groundbreaking in 1956 when the then national president, Esther Schneider, and Jacob Goldfarb and I wielded our shovels.

In 1958, there was a ceremony in the old library, and the names of all major contributors together with other memorabilia of the conference were sealed in an urn that was ultimately to be buried in the foundations of the new library. Now construction was underway, and, by 1959, the building had sufficiently advanced that it was possible to gather the elated delegates in a lower level that had already been completed. Advantage was taken of the presence at commencement of General Yigael Yadin, the world-famous archeologist who, with his father, had acquired and deciphered some of the Dead Sea Scrolls. This versatile soldier-scholar had demonstrated his uncanny military genius in the Israeli War of Liberation, when he had served as chief of staff. After he complimented the ladies on their choice of the library as their group commitment, he indicated how much at home he felt among the unfinished halls and rooms, still stark and unembellished as they were in his early days at the Hebrew University in Israel. He was certain that as each academic commitment was fulfilled, others would grow out of them and continue growing; a library, indeed a university, could not be a static resource, just as scholarship, learning, and research must always be self-regenerative. Mrs. David Rose, president at the time and official spokesman for the women, responded in an eloquent address in which she discussed the dream as if it were already a reality. "We sit here in an austere room, a room with blank walls and unfinished floor. Yet for all this, who among us is concerned with its bleakness; for we see it as it will be but a few months hence, lined with the books that will breathe spirit and life into it."

The library was completed in time for the opening of the school year in 1959, and the special convocation on November 8 brought thousands of friends and supporters to the campus. The special guests who received honorary degrees included the librarian emeritus of Harvard, Keyes DeWitt Metcalf, who had been an invaluable consultant during the planning stages, the sculptor Jacques Lipschitz, the historian Henry Steele Commager, and Julius Stratton, president of the Massachusetts Institute of Technology and later chairman of the executive committee of the Ford Foundation. The dedicatory address was given by Archibald MacLeish, the Pulitzer Prize poet and former head of the Library of Congress. He was especially eloquent as he defined and dramatized the place of libraries in a dangerously expanding technological world. Jacob Goldfarb was called upon, and his simple response was the most moving part of the occasion. In tears, he recalled that he had come to the United States as a penniless boy from Austria. His first jobs included messenger service for Western Union, receiving seven cents for each telegram delivered. He had worked his way up through the business world until he headed a great mercantile empire. It was a wondrous climax, he felt, to have been able to use the opportunities that his adopted land opened up to him so that he and his Bert could now make a library available to the university that had been fashioned by his people. These unadorned remarks, spoken with the inner passion of gratitude, were so moving that MacLeish, one of the most felicitous masters of the English language, asked the unpretentious merchant-donor for a copy of what he had said.

A word must be said here about Louis Schreiber, who served for nearly twenty years as the director of the library. He died in early middle age in a tragic automobile accident that also injured his wife. I write of him in the context of the library's creation to pay him the respect that he earned by his loyalty and conscientiousness but that was never really offered to him during his lifetime. Our original librarian had been a conscientious young man, William Leibovitz, whose ambitions were denied by fate. He died suddenly in our first year, and his duties fell on Schreiber, an assistant. Schreiber was virtually self-trained, with none of the academic credentials that the profession insisted upon for rank and status. Hence, although he carried heavy responsibilities for the physical needs of the library, working unconscionable hours, it was necessary to give the titles to academicians who ostensibly made judgments on acquisitions and library relationships. Everyone admired Schreiber for his ready accessibility and for his practical advice on problems of administration. The memorial collections that poured in after his death were sent with unabashed love for a man who found no task beneath his dignity if it served the university.

With the library completed, dedicated, and in full use, the Women's Committee had an alluring magnet to stimulate its efforts. Major drives continued, but they were now supplemented by intensive fund-raising campaigns that were essential to provide for substantially increased maintenance and acquisition costs.

One especially valuable and imaginative development was a project, mounted annually, to provide for subscriptions to learned journals. These had become a necessity since the launching of graduate departments. Major research developments, especially in the life sciences, were so quickly overtaking earlier studies that books were often obsolete by the time they were published. Even more highly specialized journals had multiplied at such a pace that there was already a digest devoted solely to abstracts and summaries of leading journal articles. Thousands of subscriptions would be needed to ensure full coverage, but at least hundreds were required to keep the faculty and graduate students current. Many of the journals were almost prohibitively expensive; the annual subscription for *Chemical Abstracts,* an indispensable tool for researchers in the life sciences, was five hundred dollars!

In 1962, soon after the Goldfarb Library was in full operation, it was decided to solicit special annual gifts to provide for the average cost of such subscriptions. The project was enthusiastically described at the women's national conference, and one hundred subscriptions were immediately announced. When the campaign was opened to the general membership, the response was equally gratifying. The subscription goal was set at 1,500 learned journals, and it was achieved within a few years. Many of the women went quite beyond individual subscriptions; they agreed to subsidize entire back files of the most important journals. By the end of the first year, there were already sixty-four complete files.

Capitalizing on this impetus, and with encouragement from the Ford Foundation, the women made a major effort in 1963 to complete whole centuries of documentation. In a remarkable spurt of acquisition, the library purchased microfilms of all periodicals published in England since the mid-eighteenth century, all American periodicals from 1800 (42,000 titles), printed materials such as broadsides, political lampoons in verse, playbills, poems, tracts, and pamphlets published in Britain back to the early nineteenth century (*125,000 titles*). It was a heartwarming climax to a banner year, in which the class of 1963 offered, as their class gift, all copies of American newspapers published in the eighteenth century.

Meanwhile, several years earlier, a "New Books for Old" campaign had been launched, which was especially effective in the larger cities. The idea came almost simultaneously from the leadership of the chapters in Boston and on the Chicago North Shore. Families were encouraged to give up volumes in their private libraries to be placed on sale at virtually giveaway prices. By the spring of 1964, the project had almost achieved the logistical efficiency of carefully planned military operations. The campaign of that year by the Chicago North Shore chapter was a prime example. Two hundred volunteers were marshaled for a Sunday afternoon canvass of listed homes. They were given eight thousand shopping bags and asked to fill them. In the first few hours, they had gathered twelve thousand volumes. The family of James L. Price contributed an entire library of four thousand volumes, which included many first editions, hand-tooled bindings, and the autographs of important authors. The volumes were taken to the parking lot of the Wilmette branch of Carson, Pirie, Scott, a leading Chicago department store. There, in a huge tent, sixty thousand volumes were laid out for mass disposal. Passersby goggled as they watched the fashionable suburbs' most elegant and best-groomed ladies, in smocks, ruining their manicures, as they dragged piles of dusty books to their assigned places, sifting, categorizing, pricing.

Before the sale began officially, access was given to specially invited booksellers, librarians, and connoisseurs. In the four-day sale period that followed, most of the volumes were sold. Those that remained were sent as gifts to libraries whose budgets did not permit adequate acquisition, as well as to institutions for the disadvantaged that had no library budgets. In 1965 there was a three-day sale in Dallas, attended by fifteen hundred, and the two thousand volumes that were not disposed of were sent to Vietnam for the American military. In succeeding years, thousands of volumes were sent by various chapters to Books for Equal Education, a nonprofit organization that distributed volumes to impecunious small rural areas and college libraries. The processing expenses were usually met by the donors. Within a few years, New Books for Old campaigns became annual events in sixty-five cities. When the twentieth anniversary of the Women's Committee was celebrated, it was announced that more than three million volumes had been thus "recycled."

The chapters kept vying with each other for ever more resourceful ways of reaching their communities. There were carefully planned and arranged luncheons that featured faculty speakers, tours of members' private art collections, international art exhibits and auctions. In May 1966, the Washington chapter took fullest advantage of its location and planned a three-day international art exhibit and auction co-sponsored with UNESCO. The preparations under the leadership of Mrs. Aaron Kimche and Mrs. Alfred Friendly took a full year and involved the active participation of more than two hundred members. The wife of the Venezuelan ambassador and Mrs. Arthur Goldberg, whose husband was chief of the United States delegation to the United Nations, headed the patrons' group. One or more paintings and other art works were sent on loan by each of fifty countries of the United Nations. Hundreds of other valuable paintings were donated for auction, including works by Renoir, Chagall, Dufy, and Henry Moore. The pre-auction buffet was held in the spacious halls of the World Bank. Among the hundreds of visitors were ambassadors, directors of museums and galleries, public officials, and artists. President and Mrs. Lyndon Johnson graced the occasion, and an internationally famous art auctioneer, Peter Wilson of Sotheby's, was introduced by Roger Stevens, chairman of the National Council on the Arts. More than one hundred and fifty art objects were sold, and the proceeds of the occasion, one of the most distinguished ever sponsored by the university, appreciably augmented the library budget.

One impressive function in Cleveland, where the Board of Trustees were guests, was held in the Museum of Natural History amidst the stuffed animals that represented the earliest historic eras. Dinner was served in one of the huge halls, and the dais for speaking was just under the dinosaur, whose long neck came quite close to the lectern. It cramped my style a little, for I was fearful that, when I told a story or two, the dinosaur might heckle, "Oh, I've heard that one before." The initiative of the women seemed to be inexhaustible. Hardly had one source of income been proposed when another was already on the agenda. Ever new categories were devised for those who were ready to expend more than the nominal dues.

Early in the development of the library, one of the national presidents, Mrs. Joseph Schneider, submitted a plan for the creation of an endowment fund that, however slowly built, would increasingly help to stabilize the supporting income. There were initial fears that emphasis on endowment, in a period when there were so many urgent needs, would become diversionary. Mrs. Schneider persisted. She noted that many of the women were in a financial position to render more than modest service to the university and that the completion of one specialized gift often stimulated the desire to move on to another. Many also would be encouraged by the availability of an endowment fund to remember the library in their wills. In the spring of 1957, the endowment program was officially accepted, with the understanding that gifts would be sought primarily from those who had already fulfilled responsibility for more basic priorities. Within a few years, the endowment had grown to more than a quarter-million dollars, and by the end of my incumbency as president in 1968, its income became a reliable factor in financing the library.

During the first years, the Women's Committee concentrated almost exclusively on the tasks of fund-raising. But since the chapter members were recruited primarily from families that were sensitive to educational objectives, they inevitably began reaching out for ways to serve the members themselves and their own communities. In 1956 study groups were launched that were open to members who were interested in specialized subjects. Begun modestly, these ultimately included discussion of the novel, poetry, drama, current educational issues, America in world affairs, contemporary history, Judaic studies, and the whole gamut of the humanities, the arts, and the social sciences. Syllabi were prepared by Brandeis faculty, with bibliographic references carefully selected to avoid either the superficiality of the dilettante or narrow specialization. Since participation was restricted to those who had a serious interest in the subject, the study groups were intimate enough to meet in private homes, and a gratifying esprit de corps was often developed. After ten years, it was reported that more than 125 study groups were functioning regularly. Virtually every group retained a constant core membership year after year, exploring diverse fields in a pattern of continuing education.

Many of the women found satisfaction in the study tours, which were based on extended trips to foreign countries. There was no originality in the project: Many organizations had been sponsoring such group tours, with chartered flights and all accommodations and sightseeing meticulously planned and supervised. But those under the auspices of the Brandeis women included distinguished faculty members who served as knowledgeable tutors. A three-week tour of the Mediterranean basin with Cyrus Gordon of our archeology faculty, following the route of the Phoenicians, was relaxing enough in itself, but it became a memorable experience as he described and evaluated the ancient civilizations of the Mediterranean and the Near East. A tour through the historic centers of England became especially significant when Oxford, Cambridge, Stratford on Avon, and the London theaters were explored under the guidance of Alan Levitan, a young professor of English literature and a gifted Shakespearean interpreter. Brandeis usually had access to outstanding figures who welcomed the groups and responded to their questions. In Israel, Ben Gurion, Golda Meir, Yigal Yadin, Yacov Dori, Yigal Allon, and other national leaders, remembering with appreciation their visits to Brandeis and the convocations where honorary degrees had been conferred upon them, were always eager to renew their friendships.

The existence of a major library facility inevitably stimulated interest in gifts and bequests of valuable book and documentary collections. In 1962, a dozen outstanding publishers and collectors met on campus. They validated their goodwill quite tangibly. Alfred Knopf, Ben Zevin, and Max Schuster not only offered counsel but arranged for gifts of hundreds of their firms' volumes. They also agreed to organize a bibliophile affiliate for the university to stimulate the acquisition of rare documentation and books and special collections. Leadership was also provided by several who, though businessmen, had a lifelong interest in the world of letters. There was Ralph Samuel, a New York banker who had been intrigued by nineteenth-century British history and had been collecting Disraeli letters, which he now began conveying to the university. There was Philip Sang, an ice cream manufacturer of Chicago, whose family and in-laws had already underwritten the impressive Olin-Sang American Civilization Center. He was an avid and extremely knowledgeable collector of American history documentation, with special interest in the colonial and revolutionary periods. Many of his most valuable items were given to the library. His catalogue, *The Genesis of American Freedom,* was the first volume published by the Brandeis Bibliophiles. It was listed by the American Institute of Graphic Arts as among the fifty best books of 1961 for its design and production.

Above all, there was Bern Dibner of Norwalk, Connecticut, who had developed a very successful engineering firm and had created the unique Burndy Library, which concentrated on the history of technology. He had not waited for a library building to offer his gifts. As early as 1957 he had sent us choice first editions of the writings of Galileo and Kepler, Darwin and Freud. He contributed a rare edition of the works of a little-known, medieval Jewish astronomer-physicist, Rafael Mirami, who had pioneered research on the optical properties of mirrors. This work was thought to have helped Pope Gregory regulate the Gregorian calendar of the sixteenth century. The optical properties of mirrors had great impact on the development of astronomy. Astronomy played a major role in the creation of the calendar, and Pope Gregory was a distinguished scientist. Dibner had new treasures for us almost every year, including choice items dealing with Leonardo da Vinci. A special Da Vinci hall was set apart in the library, underwritten by Dibner, to receive his gifts. He obtained from one of his friends, McKew Parr, the documentation that he had collected in his definitive volume, *So Noble a Captain,* on Magellan and the age of discovery. It brought to the library invaluable source material on exploration and discovery in the western hemisphere from the fifteenth to the eighteenth century.

Louise Lewisohn, proud of her late husband Ludwig's association with the first faculty of Brandeis, contributed his collection of belles lettres, especially rich in German and French literature. His correspondence, including letters from Thomas and Erica Mann, Stefan Zweig, and Edmond Fleg, also came to the library. One of the earliest treasures was the collection of volumes in economics that were part of the library of Morris Hillquit, who had played a decisive role in the New York labor movement early in the century. His daughter, Nina, delighted that the university was adhering faithfully to the tradition of liberalism that her father so much admired in Justice Brandeis, felt that our library was the ideal repository for his literary legacy.

In 1959, the library received from Dr. Oskar Samek, the literary executor of the Viennese publicist and poet Karl Kraus, a valuable collection of three thousand volumes on history and political science in German and English. The university also acquired the complete library of the Hebrew scholar-educator Leon Slommsky. Actor Joseph Schildkraut, the two-time Academy Award winner and the star of *The Diary of Anne Frank,* died at sixty-seven in 1963 in the midst of rehearsing a new Broadway musical. His will revealed that he had bequeathed to Brandeis his extensive library, mainly in German, and much of the valuable art collection that was begun by his father, who was a close friend of Justice Brandeis. Approximately 2,400 volumes from the estate of Perry Miller, the distinguished professor of American literature at Harvard, were acquired in 1964. They substantially strengthened our holdings in seventeenth- and eighteenth-century history and literature, with main focus on developments in New England.

A major treasure trove came to the university through the will of Arthur M. Schlesinger, Sr., a member of Harvard's history department for more than forty years, a Pulitzer Prize winner, and one-time president of the American Historical Society. He had revealed his intention to me at a dinner party in Boston that Alfred Knopf had arranged for some of "his authors." He had noted then that the Harvard library undoubtedly already had virtually all the volumes he had collected. When the bequest of the main part of his private library came to us, it included hundreds of out-of-print volumes and others often unobtainable through regular channels.

David Borowitz, a lamp manufacturer of Chicago, made available his rare collection of first editions of American and English literature. Leonard Simons, a Detroit public relations executive, had given many years to the gathering of important volumes in Judaica, which he had beautifully rebound. In 1961, he offered the collection to the university, and visitors to the library invariably stopped on the floor where they were shelved to admire the artistry of the bindings.

Of course, at the outset the library was still too young to identify any priorities for its collections. Hence the earliest gifts followed no identifiable pattern. A Shakespeare first folio was acquired, as was the first printed edition of the Zohar published in Mantua in the sixteenth century. In 1959, the library had begun to receive from Benjamin and Julia Trustman of Brookline the original prints of the nineteenth-century caricaturist Honore Daumier, whose biting satire on the French legal system had been expressed in thousands of delightful cartoons. After 1962, the Daumier gifts to the library became ever more extensive until four thousand items, easily the world's choicest collection, had been contributed. The main collection was housed in the library vaults, but selected items were rotated regularly for exhibition in the main lobby. Each year, prize items were organized for traveling exhibits that were sponsored by the Women's Committee in many cities.

Meantime, the library continued to acquire collections of historically significant letters. The family of Stephen Wise turned over many cartons of his correspondence. Since he played a dominant role in both American and Jewish life through the first half of the twentieth century, including the long Zionist struggle and relationships with Woodrow Wilson, Franklin Roosevelt, Albert Einstein, Felix Frankfurter, Louis Brandeis, and hundreds of other movers and shakers of the time, the gift provided invaluable source material. The papers were indexed and opened to scholars and researchers of twentieth-century Jewish life. From the Lasker family, we received the papers and letters of their distinguished forebear, Edward Lasker, the nineteenth-century German liberal leader whose political life was spent opposing the *Blut und Eisen* Prussianism of Bismarck. The collection was considered significant enough for the West German government to request its duplication for its official archives.

Another historically significant resource came to the library when David Niles died in 1953 and the family placed his papers in my custody. Reference to his association with Presidents Roosevelt and Truman were an important part of my volume, *The Redemption of the Unwanted*, which was published soon after I became chancellor. The papers were organized and indexed but remained restricted until they could be edited.

A collection of letters signed by some of the most famous literary names in modern history came to the library in 1958 from a New York patron and Brandeis friend, Milton I. D. Einstein. It included letters from Hans Christian Andersen, George Bernard Shaw, W. B. Yeats, D. H. Lawrence, Franz Liszt, Ambrose Bierce, Corot, Cabell, George Moore, Max Beerbohm, and many others. Einstein also presented a complete collection of eighteenth- and nineteenth-century graphic art books on etching, the history of the graphic arts, and specimens of the best engravings of these centuries. Ruth and Lester Glick of Cleveland, through the special interest of their son, Thomas, underwrote the acquisition of a collection of Spanish Civil War material, and the university became an important center for the study of one of the watersheds of modern history.

The negotiations for the acquisition from the Vatican of a world-famous collection of Hebrew codices turned out to be a fascinating adventure in both complicated funding and interfaith collaboration. In the fall of 1961, I was called by Father Paul Reinert, president of St. Louis University, an old, hometown friend, who outlined to me an enterprise that had excited his scholarly interest. He had received permission from Pope John XXIII to obtain a microfilm of the codices in the Vatican Library that represented nearly four hundred years of Hebrew writings in literature, history, philosophy, and religious thought, especially pertinent for the Spanish and Portuguese medieval Jewish experience. The collection comprised eight hundred codices, equivalent in bulk volume to twenty years of the *New York Times,* and it had been accumulated through the centuries mainly by confiscation during the dread periods of Jewish repression and expulsion. A microfilm, Father Reinert noted, deposited in the library of St. Louis University, would make it a precious reservoir of Jewish medieval learning and thought in the western hemisphere.

I congratulated Father Reinert on his resourcefulness and asked why he was calling me. He explained that, though he had the authorization to commission the microfilm, it would require a substantial budget, and he needed help to obtain it. "You have superb contacts," he said, "and surely in an enterprise of such scholarly promise you would be able to enlist their co-operation." He added, as a special inducement, that the Vatican authorities would undoubtedly release a second set of microfilm for our library if the funding were provided through us at Brandeis. Naturally the project intrigued me, and I promised to do all I could.

Within a fortnight, I called him back and told him that I had obtained the necessary funds. Apparently he had not expected such quick results, and he could not restrain a very un-Jesuitical exclamation: "The hell you say!" When he recovered, he asked, "Where did you get the funding?" "Oh, from Cardinal Cushing," I replied. Then I gave him the details. After Father Reinert's call, I consulted one of our trustees, Joseph Linsey, who had been very helpful to Cardinal Cushing in his fund-raising problems, and we both visited the cardinal in his mansion. I outlined the project that Father Reinert had in mind and suggested that, quite apart from making available the resource the Hebrew codices represented, there was an opportunity here, during the period of Pope John's appeal for an ecumenical climate, to provide a dramatic example of scholarly collaboration by two universities, one Catholic-founded and the other Jewish-founded. I suggested that the cardinal provide us with the names of half a dozen of his main supporters, with an introductory letter that would indicate his approval of the project. Cardinal Cushing had acute public relations antennae; he needed no persuasion to recognize the extraordinary symbolism of the effort. "No," he chuckled, "I shall not give you any names, nor introduce you to any of my contributors. However, I'll make the needed sum available from my own Cardinal's Fund."

Father Reinert rejoiced with me that the project had been so happily consummated. I did not learn for several weeks after our visit that Cardinal Cushing had approached several Jewish businessmen in Boston and had received from them very substantial contributions that went beyond the replenishment of the Cardinal's Fund. Providence, with a little help from His vigilant servants, may do His work circuitously, but often with remarkable effectiveness.

The microfilms were completed within a year and transferred to both universities. Father Lowrie J. Daly, S.J., who headed the Pope Pius XII Library of St. Louis University, on his return from the Ecumenical Council in Rome joined Professor Alexander Altmann of the Brandeis faculty, who was to be in charge of the codices, for the dedication. The guest of honor was, of course, Cardinal Cushing.

One of the most gratifying by-products of the activity of the women's groups was their ambassadorial role. When their members were bending every effort for the library, they were an ideal interpreter of the university concept for other members of the family. Mrs. Irving Crown of Chicago was a leader in the Chicago group. A succession of library gifts flowed from her; she rarely attended a conference without some exemplary announcement. The climax came when she and her husband, Irving, established an endowed graduate fellowship program in American civilization with a capital fund that yielded $75,000 annually, later increased to $100,000. Mrs. Samuel Spector, originally a New Englander, was a pioneer member of the Women's Committee. Early in our friendship, I noted the grace and modesty with which she and her husband functioned philanthropically. When a seminar room in music was set up by them in the library, they insisted that the name it bore be another's. When a crucially needed laboratory in science was underwritten, they wrote in the condition that the name upon it should be that of a distinguished physicist in whose research they took immense personal pride. Only a few months before Spector's death, I met with him, his wife, and their attorney to discuss procedures to create an endowed chair.

The reports that were delivered at the annual conferences noted the rapid growth of the women's chapters and their membership. They identified services of the library and the expanding activities that were sponsored in communities from Boston to San Francisco, from Minneapolis to New Orleans. Inevitably the question was asked, especially by the professional and lay leadership of other colleges, what were the forces that created this exceptional kind of loyalty? What motivated tens of thousands of women to give endless time and energy to planning and promoting immediate and long-range activities, all in the interest of a university that scarcely any of their families had attended? Undoubtedly, it had been an ingenious decision to assign the responsibility of the library to the women. A highly motivated group could thus concentrate on a special project that carried immense dignity and high quality, theirs to plan and achieve. Perhaps the indispensable place of the library was best summarized by Max Lerner, of our own faculty, at one of the national conferences that he addressed: "The educational process," he said, "is deeply conservative in the sense that it transmits the heritage. It is also deeply path breaking in the sense that the student learns to sift the heritage through his own mind and to take responsibility for his own formulations in his own conscience. Thus, a university library is a place to which neither the traditionalists nor the innovators can make an exclusive claim. It has a musty smell about it from the dust that has gathered on books and ideas over the centuries, but there is also in the air a slight smell of dynamite."

Each year, therefore, in good times or bad, during surges of national prosperity or periods of disruption and disenchantment, the reports of the women pointed to the consistency of growth and achievement. And when Father Hesburg of Notre Dame asked me, in awe, how all of this could have been done, my reply was entirely accurate: *"Cherchez la femme."*

CHAPTER EIGHT

The Sciences

Howard Mumford Jones, saddened by the gulf that seemed to be widening between the scientist and the humanist, wrote: "Men of good will, desirous of opening channels of communication, look back with nostalgia upon the nineteenth century when Matthew Arnold and Thomas Huxley could debate liberal education, John Tyndall explain why he was a materialist, Sir Charles Lyell write so that even clergymen could understand him, and Charles Darwin create masterpieces of literature that were also masterpieces of science." Loren Eiseley observed that the two loneliest creatures on earth are man and the porpoise: Man because he has memory, the porpoise because he wants to talk to man and cannot make himself understood. There are times when one or another sector of the academic community swims in the porpoise's element, and all of us are sometimes lonely because we, too, cannot make ourselves understood.

I believe the existence of such a sharp dichotomy between teaching the sciences and the humanities is overstated, often the product of polemic semantics. Certainly at Brandeis we did not feel compelled to choose sides. We found no incompatibility between structuring the curriculum to make available the best in the scientific tradition and the enduring legacy of the arts. Obviously, the university could not seek preeminence in every discipline. It was mandatory to be competent in all offerings, but special emphasis had to be limited to selectively chosen areas. The institution opted early, therefore, to share its resources among fields in the sciences and in the liberal arts where a unique contribution was likely, and it recruited gifted faculty who were eager to take fullest advantage of a school where what C. P. Snow called "the two cultures" could flourish side by side. In our first two years, we had too few faculty to plan a departmental structure.

Indeed, there was strong sentiment to avoid the "fragmentation" of departments altogether. We organized our disciplines into four schools—the sciences, the humanities, the creative arts, and the social sciences—each school usually headed by a senior faculty member.

Saul Cohen, whose key role in our faculty has been earlier discussed, became the first chairman of the School of Science. He shared our determination that quality must never be compromised, hence avoiding expansion into every subdivision in the bewildering diversity of modern science; but he accepted few limits in areas that he defined for major Brandeis contributions. Within five years he had gathered a nucleus of scholars and researchers with original casts of mind, some already renowned, but mostly younger people whose future distinction he confidently predicted. The time was opportune for significant progress in the areas in which such a faculty was preeminent. The dozen or so colleagues whom he recruited for chemistry became a well-integrated team, intensely loyal to their chief and proud of the university that had brought them together. The enormous needs of World War II had stimulated many research programs to develop synthetic materials, such as rubber and nylons, medical products and insecticides, and the field was wide open for the application of theory to practical chemistry.

In the sixties and seventies, Cohen turned over department management to gifted younger colleagues: Sidney Golden, Myron Rosenblum, Thomas Tuttle, Jr., Kenneth Kustin, Peter Jordan, Henry Linschitz, and Ernst Grunwald, who adhered to the same disciplined quest for excellence as did their model chief. Sidney Golden had earned his Ph.D. in physical chemistry at Harvard. He accepted the call from Brandeis and joined the chemistry faculty in 1951, becoming, after Saul Cohen, its senior member during his incumbency of more than thirty years. During his sabbaticals and other leaves, he served as visiting professor at the University of California in Berkeley, the Hebrew University, and the Weizmann Institute in Israel, and was an exchange professor at the University of Paris. He accepted consultant assignments from major professional firms such as the New England Nuclear Corporation, Technical Operations, Inc., and the Addison Wesley Publishing Company. His teaching and research at Brandeis and abroad earned him the deep respect of science scholars for his fundamental contributions to chemical theory, particularly in molecular spectroscopy, chemical reaction rates, novel computational approaches in molecular quantum mechanics, and ionic solvation. He retired in 1981 and relocated with his wife Muriel to Arizona, not simply to enjoy the milder climate but to continue his research in chemical theory.

Myron Rosenblum was a deeply respected colleague who helped guide the department from its founding years into the present. As a teacher, he prepared generations of undergraduates in the fundamentals of organic chemistry and graduate students in the chemistry of organs and transition metal complexes. In his sabbaticals, he also often accepted bids to serve as a visiting professor in foreign countries, especially in Israel.

Thomas Tuttle, Jr., was another early bird who remains active in the chemistry department. He came to us in 1960 with a Ph.D. from Washington University in St. Louis and from a three-year teaching assignment as assistant professor at Stanford. At Brandeis he had taught the theory of chemicals in solution and the application of spectroscopy to the elucidation of the composition and structure of solutions. He is widely respected for his nearly seventy researched writings in major professional journals. He was, for several years, a member of the National Institutes of Health Biophysics Review Panel, and guest professor at Katholieke University in Nijmegen in the Netherlands.

Kenneth Kustin came to the department in 1962 after he had completed his postdoctoral fellowship at the Institute for Physical Chemistry in Goettingen, West Germany. He has now spent more than thirty years at Brandeis, charged with the overall responsibility of introducing the chemistry majors to the concepts and principles of chemistry and their application to problems of science, health, and technology. He has several times served as chairman of the department. During his long tenure, he was a visiting professor of pharmacology at the Harvard Medical School, editor of volume 16 of *Fast Reactions,* dealing with enzymology, on the board of editors of the international journal *Chemical Kinetics,* and director of the National Science Foundation program.

In 1964, Kustin was joined by British-born Peter Jordan, who had been brought to this country as an infant. His undergraduate education was completed at the California Institute of Technology, and his Ph.D. was earned at Yale. He returned to England to accept a post at Cambridge as a postdoctoral research associate. The shuttle between countries continued when he joined the chemistry faculty at the University of California in San Diego. He found his permanent niche when he was called to Brandeis. He is equally at home in biophysics and chemistry and in selected topics in computational chemistry. His numerous articles in major professional journals and his definitive volume, *Chemical Kinetics and Transport,* have steadily reflected his academic diversity.

Henry Linschitz earned his doctorate from Duke University. He gave important service to President Roosevelt's scientific team in the race with the Nazis to perfect atomic power. He was a member of the staff in the Explosive Research Laboratories in Bruceton, Pennsylvania, and a section leader in the secret atomic research in the Los Alamos Laboratories. In the three years following the defeat of the Nazis, he was a research fellow in the Institute for Nuclear Studies at The University of Chicago. He then accepted a professorship at the University of Syracuse until 1957, when he came to Brandeis for the next thirty years. Like Rosenblum he was a favorite visiting scientist at the Weizmann Institute, where advanced students and faculty in his seminars explored with him, in the interest of Israel's defense, the physical mechanisms of photobiological processes and the reactions of excited molecules. In the more relaxed teaching and research climate of Brandeis, he found that one of his students, Sue Hodes, was a very talented artist, and their marriage was one of the most precious validations of the happiness that is possible in a romantic union of science and art.

Ernst Grunwald came to the United States from his native Germany just in time to escape from the encompassing Nazi repression. His basic education was completed at the University of California in Los Angeles. For a decade and more he joined the chemistry faculty at Florida State University, then briefly tried an assignment with the Bell Telephone laboratories in New Jersey as a research chemist. He returned to academic life in 1964 and spent the remainder of his professional career at Brandeis. At the peak of his incumbency, he was associate editor of the *Journal of the American Chemical Society*. The honors with which he was showered came from this country and Israel. He was, and still is, though retired, a prolific author, moving with authority in the world and sub-world of atoms, molecules, and chemical change.

By 1967, the chemistry faculty was encouraged to apply for a Center of Excellence grant from the National Science Foundation to add essential new equipment to the laboratories, to strengthen further its staffing, and to open its facilities to even larger groups of students who hoped to enter medicine, the health sciences, and public health. Though only a handful of grants was awarded, Brandeis was included among them, receiving nearly $900,000.

Meantime, the explosion of knowledge in the immediate postwar period gave biological research a dynamic quality that exhilarated all who were part of the adventure. In some, it bred a kind of arrogance. Max Perutz of Cambridge said in all seriousness, "Molecular biology is the basic science of life; it is now the only way one knows what one is talking about." James Hendrickson, who, during his tenure at Brandeis, had been invited to organize the chemistry offerings to universities in Ghana, would not agree; he reminded his presumptuous colleagues that it was the study of chemistry that made modern biology possible. The competitive chaffing over which discipline was more regenerative enlivened the luncheon breaks and added to the awe of the younger men and women, who were further prodded by the rivalry of academic pride. In such a heady climate, the biology faculty and their most advanced students worked with mounting excitement, for the dramatic developments of the previous few years were only a prelude to even more overwhelming discoveries—in enzyme research, in the role of bacteria and viruses, in the nature of complex structures and their relationship to the control of all living systems, and in the merging of animal and plant ecology.

The biologists, like all their colleagues in science, did not regard their research and teaching as mutually exclusive. In their research, they fully involved not only their graduate students but their more highly qualified undergraduates so that they, too, could enter the new world that biology was opening and charting. Students were taught the functions of the newest, most sophisticated tools: analytical ultracentrifuges, radioisotope counters, electron microscopes, chromatographic and fractionating devices of all sorts. With these skills, they moved into the eerie world of viruses, single-cell plants and animals, slime molds, chick embryos, fruit flies.

The curriculum was structured so that the students would also be exposed to the rich cargo of scientific discovery and descriptive data inherited from the past while they worked beside their faculty mentors to become part of the research in progress. "In effect," one of the biologists wrote, "many of our courses are actually two in one—the students aided in their efforts to master descriptive material by means of independent study, the lectures largely devoted to modern experimental biology."

Martin Gibbs received his Ph.D. from the University of Illinois in 1947 and began his research and teaching career at the Brookhaven National Laboratory, followed by seven years at Cornell. Not yet much beyond forty, he accepted our bid in 1965 to head the biology department. He offered innovative leadership to the department and to the university for the next quarter century until his retirement. He made the department a national center of research in photosynthesis and plant physiology. He was often asked to be a consultant for the National Science Foundation, NATO, the National Institutes of Health, and other major science bodies. He served on the Council of the International Exchange of Scholars and was chairman of the Advisory Committee for the selection of Fulbrights from Eastern Europe. On one of his leaves from Brandeis, he accepted the bid of the University of Munster in the Federal Republic of Germany to serve as adjunct professor of biology. From 1966 to about 1976 he was associate editor of *Physostagie Vegetelle* and also served for a time as editor-in-chief of *Plant Physiology*. After the publication of two definitive volumes on the structure and function of chloroplants and crop productivity, he was rated as one of the country's outstanding biologists.

Jerome Schiff came to the university in 1957, already well renowned but quite willing to risk coming to a school only just accredited. One of our first fully endowed chairs was assigned to him when he became chairman of the biology department in 1973. He opened unrealized opportunities for research in sulfur and metabolism. In 1975 he undertook the directorship of our newly established Institute of Photobiology of Cells and Organelles and served there until 1987. He served as consultant on development in biology at the National Science Foundation from 1965–1968, and consultant on metabolic biology from 1982–1986. In Israel, he was visiting professor at Tel Aviv University, the Hebrew University in 1972, and Weizmann Institute in 1977, and, for fifteen years thereafter, was a member of the grant review program of the US-Israel Binat Science Foundation. Schiff was part of the editorial board of *Development Biology* from 1971, becoming chief editor in 1981. He retired after thirty-five years, but his research continues.

Edgar Zwilling conducted experiments in vertebrate development and tissue reactions that attracted close attention. At the dedication of a whole complex of science facilities, he noted, "This is an exciting time for biology. The improvement of visualization of fine structures has gone hand in hand with the increase in information about the molecular events of various life functions." He pointed out that before World War II a magnification of two thousand times was considered close to the ideal maximum. Physicists then developed the electron microscope and magnifications of ten thousand to fifty thousand became common, opening up new worlds. Cell structures that had not even been imagined could now be described with great accuracy. Tragically, we lost Zwilling in his early middle age, and he was deprived of the time to savor the high regard of his science colleagues.

Herman Epstein, a professor of biophysics at Brandeis since 1962, had been a National Science Foundation Fellow at the University of Geneva in 1959–1960; a Commonwealth Fellow in Biochemistry at the Weizmann Institute in Israel in 1963–1964, and a Guggenheim Fellow at Tel Aviv University in 1960–1970. In 1972 he was a member of the "think tank" that created the public medicine–oriented medical school at the Ben Gurion University of the Negev. He has also taught at major European universities.

In recent years, including those after he assumed emeritus status, Epstein turned to intensive research on one of the basic problems in the development of children's learning. As most elementary schools are structured today, children are mainly assigned to elementary classes according to chronology: all five-year-olds grouped together, all six-year-olds, and so on. Epstein's research validated what some scientists before him had explored—the hypothesis that brain capacity after birth has periods of rapid growth (ages 2–4, 6–8, 10–12, 14–16) separated by periods of slow growth (ages 4–6, 12–14). This notion led to the further hypothesis that periods of rapid growth of the brain might be related to periods of more rapid learning. Epstein is persuaded that the evidence of his research and that of predecessor colleagues validates that hypothesis. He maintains that the absence of "proper input" to youngsters during the special growth periods can be shown to produce children with what may be called an "underachieving complex." He has been negotiating with government agencies to fund trial programs in primary education where children's classes are organized not by chronology alone but also by periods of growth, or slow growth, in brain capacity. Epstein is still also deep in research on the effects of cocaine and of lead on the development of the brain. He hopes that, now in his eighties, what he calls his "tennis fanaticism" will prove a reliable ally to sustain his research mission.

Andrew Szent-Györgyi, a native of Hungary, earned his M.D., *summa cum laude,* at the University of Budapest. He joined the faculty of its department of biology even as he was completing his doctoral thesis. In 1948 he was a research Fellow in the Neurophysiological Institute at the University of Copenhagen. He migrated to the United States in 1948 where he joined the Institute for Muscle Research at the Marine Biological Laboratory in Woods Hole, Massachusetts. His uncle Albert, a Nobel prize winner, headed the institution. For the next ten years, the younger Szent-Györgyi worked by the side of his uncle, deep in muscle research and in teaching physiology courses. In 1962 he joined the faculty of the Dartmouth Medical School as professor of biophysics. Four years later, he accepted an appointment as professor of biology at Brandeis, where he remained for the next quarter century. Like many members of a department brimming with eminence, he has often been asked to conduct seminars for top-rated institutions. He was an overseas Fellow at Churchill College in Cambridge, he received the American Senior Scientist Award of the Humboldt Foundation in Bonn, Germany. He was elected president of the American Biophysical Society and chairman of the International Union for Pure and Applied Biophysics.

Because of its well-reputed science program, the university had no difficulty in attracting high school students gifted in this area. Subsequently, when these students found themselves in frenetic competition to gain admission to outstanding medical and dental schools, they did very well. Indeed, in relation to its size, Brandeis generally ranked very near the top in placement. The caliber of the faculty also drew graduate students and postdoctorals from some of the most important universities. By the early 1960s, Brandeis had between sixty and seventy postdoctoral students in the sciences. The most sophisticated electronic and spectroscopic equipment was made available, not only to them, but also to freshmen and sophomores. Early in the semester, students taking introductory courses were taught to evaluate laboratory data and to present them effectively in well-structured reports.

In all of these developments the name of one modest, highly imaginative supporter must not be overlooked. Dr. Julius Rogoff, a Fellow of Brandeis, was an endocrinologist with a long teaching record at Western Reserve in Cleveland and at other midwestern colleges. He discovered the life-sustaining hormone of the adrenal gland and patented a formula, called interrenalin, that used it effectively in battling Addison's disease. He began making substantial gifts to Brandeis from the royalties, which he refused to use for personal purposes, and was the first major patron for our life science plans. At his death, he left a trust of a million dollars whose income was dedicated to strengthening the life science areas, where he hoped Brandeis would win and retain preeminence.

The almost instant national visibility of the departments of chemistry and biology was paralleled by the advanced programs in mathematics and physics that were concurrently developed. Research in mathematics had proliferated during and since World War II, and top-level faculty were much in demand. It was early determined, therefore, to concentrate graduate work on algebra and topology, so as to identify Brandeis as a major center in those areas. Vigorous recruitment enlisted a brilliant team who, though quite young, had already distinguished themselves. Though research for such a faculty was the breath of life, they did not begrudge the time spent with undergraduates, who found themselves in a rarified atmosphere where it was academically fatal to think carelessly.

Ironically, the very eminence of the gifted mathematics team created a problem for the university. The faculty knew that they were in great demand and regarded themselves as a very special group, as indeed they were. There was quick promotion for them and for their newer, younger colleagues, and salary advancement somewhat beyond the university's general guidelines; nevertheless, as they gained national recognition and as tempting offers came to them, it was natural that they would become restive. As stars, they were not seeking benefits that they did not deserve, but it was hazardous for the university to go too far beyond the limits that had been set for other outstanding faculty. The budgetary decision periods each year were quite sensitive. I often wished that I could produce a special donor angel for them, since I fully shared T. H. Huxley's wistful theorem: "What men of science want is only a fair day's wages for more than a fair day's work." Joseph Kohn, Felix Browder, and a few other luminaries were tempted away, but it was no discomfiture to lose them to such citadels of mathematics as Yale or Princeton and to distinguished foreign universities. David Buchsbaum, Edgar Brown, Teruhisa Matsusaka, Maurice Auslander, Harold Levine, and other first-rate academicians were anxious to stay if assurances were offered that every effort would be made to protect the eminence of the department. A short review of the crisis during the early sixties tells a great deal about the career conflicts of those who reluctantly left and those who gave highest priority to their continued identity with Brandeis and its mission.

Joseph Kohn, an emigrant from Czechoslovakia who came to the United States at the end of World War II, joined the Brandeis faculty in 1958 after studies at Princeton and a brief instructorship there in mathematics. He was a member of our faculty for ten years and served the last four as chairman of the department. He was receiving many attractive offers from the most prestigious universities. We wanted very much to keep him since he had become internationally eminent, but after serious consideration, he decided to accept the call from Princeton. He has remained there and has served as chairman of its mathematics department and as editor of *Annals of Mathematics*. He has contributed articles to the leading professional journals and was a member of the U.S. Pure and Applied Mathematics Delegation to the People's Republic of China.

Felix Browder had been highly recommended to our faculty in the early years of the university. When reviewing his application, we had to cope with a crucial decision. Browder, born in the Soviet Union, was the son of the chairman of the American Communist party; the country was in the grip of the McCarthy hysteria. Young Browder was a decorated war veteran and had earned a brilliant Ph.D. from Princeton. But his first career appointments were limited instructorships that did not generate visibility. Browder applied to Brandeis in 1956 to get on a tenure track. The trustees, led by Eleanor Roosevelt and Judge Joseph Proskauer, Chief Justice of the Superior Court of New York, recognizing that the action of Brandeis was a litmus test for a university in its formative period, unanimously approved the appointment. He quickly became one of the stars of our faculty. Now that he was "cleared," the major universities began seeking him out. He had an offer from Yale, a temptation for any aspiring mathematician. Browder was uneasy about accepting. He was quite aware of what Brandeis's principled action had meant. I reassured him that he had no obligation to share our adventure, and he accepted the bid from Yale. We have been very proud of his subsequent record. He received rapid tenure at Yale and became head of its department of mathematics. He was then invited to another top mathematic center at The University of Chicago and spent the next twenty-five years there, climaxed in 1987 when he was named Distinguished Service Professor. He moved to Rutgers in 1987 as vice president of the university and director of its science research.

Many of the venturesome pioneers would not be tempted: David Buchsbaum, Edgar Brown, Jr., Teruhisa Matsusaka, Maurice Auslander, and Harold Levine made every effort to remain. It was David Buchsbaum who gave leadership to the negotiations with the administration to win long-ranged assurances that mathematics, having organized a brilliant faculty in the formative years of the university, would be given priority as it continued to recruit the most gifted men and women in the field. I did not need exigent persuasion. The initiative of Buchsbaum and his colleagues was welcomed. Buchsbaum set the precedent for staying on. His teaching offered exciting topics in algebraic geometry and commutative algebra. He was in Rome during 1965–1966 to explain the innovative research forays of his colleagues, and since his visit, many Italian mathematicians have come to Brandeis for graduate and postdoctoral study. During the last fifteen years, more than half of the professorships in mathematics in Italian universities have been assigned to men and women who have studied and pursued research at Brandeis for a year or more.

In 1958, Edgar Brown came to Brandeis after short stints at Washington University in St. Louis and The University of Chicago. He earned a full professorship in six years and has remained a Brandeis stalwart for more than thirty years. To fascinated students he opened up the exciting potentialities of topology. At intervals, he accepted teaching and research assignments at key American and foreign universities—the Institute for Advanced Studies at Princeton, the British Science Research Center at University College in London, and Jesus College at Oxford. In the 1980s he accepted the chairmanship of the mathematics department. Now, though emeritus, he maintains a full schedule of teaching and research.

Teruhisa Matsusaka, before coming to Brandeis in 1961 as a full professor, had taught at Ochanomview University in Tokyo, at Northwestern, and at the Princeton Institute for Advanced Studies. At Brandeis he shared seminars in algebraic geometry and topology and guided the research of candidates for their Ph.D.'s. All of his own student academic preparation had been in Japan, and it gave him personal satisfaction to be called, at intervals, to return as visiting professor at Nagoya University and at Kyoto University where he had earned his doctorate. His long tenure at Brandeis came perilously near to turning this amiable Japanese scholar into a guardian of Jewish loyalties. One day he noticed a memorandum on the department bulletin board that announced a public lecture for a second Tuesday in October. He tore into the office of the department chairman and exclaimed, "Don't you remember that the lecture date falls on Yom Kippur?! Your expected audience would be at Kol Nidre!"

Maurice Auslander completed all of his undergraduate and doctoral work at Columbia. He joined the mathematics faculty at Brandeis in 1957 and has been with us since. On his sabbaticals he accepted visiting professorships at the University of Illinois, Virginia Tech, and Queen Mary College in London. Auslander's teaching and research, specializing in noncommunitative and monological algebra and the theory of art in algebra, has opened the door to the expansion of the role of mathematics. When he was called to European universities for seminars, his specialties enriched their curriculum.

Harold Levine, trained at MIT and Princeton, held brief junior teaching posts at MIT and the University of California in Berkeley. In 1963 he was a postdoctoral Fellow at Cambridge. He came to a tenured post at Brandeis in 1966 and was chairman of the department in 1976 and again in 1988. During his long senior status, he was graduate studies advisor and enlightened advanced students on the ever-expanding techniques of integral calculus and the versatility of its application. He was often invited for visiting teaching and research assignments at Oxford and Cambridge and was honored by the Federal Republic of Germany in 1989.

Initially, there was little expectation that Brandeis could quickly build an important Department of Physics, since eminent faculty and sophisticated facilities would require an out-of-reach investment when the financing of the total university was still precarious. Nevertheless, in a period revolutionized by the explosion of the fission and fusion bombs and the spectacular penetration of solar space, it was indisputable that emphasis on the sciences would be seriously handicapped unless at least a minimum program were launched. It was the Nobel prize winner Isidor Rabi who, when asked why he chose to be a physicist, replied: "Physics is the only basic science there is. Everything else is to the right of it and depends on it. Nothing is to the left of it." The chemistry doyens and biologists were not the only imperialists!

Apparently, however, there could be no "minimum programs" at Brandeis, for, to the astonishment of the academic world, when we invited the world-renowned physicist Leo Szilard to join the minuscule group at Brandeis as a visiting professor in 1954, he accepted without cavil and gave us one of our most exciting and productive courses—a seminar in the frontiers of science. Apart from the gratifying visibility that his presence on the faculty gave, Szilard was most generous in offering counsel on the development of the science departments.

I had held my breath when Szilard, the colleague of Einstein, Fermi, Bohr, and the pioneers of the Manhattan project, visited the campus for the first time in 1953 and was invited to inspect our first meager laboratory facilities. But Szilard was not nonplussed. He rather admired the pluck of the little David among the Goliaths of higher education. His own thinking had always been audacious, and he was eager to be helpful in what he confidently expected would place the school, in less rather than more time, in the forefront of scientific institutions.

With such encouragement, every effort was now made to procure the support that would enlist a corps of theoretical physicists and to reinforce them speedily with equally innovative experimentalists. We knew that the recruitment of faculty would be as formidable as the quest for funding. Somewhere I had read the comment of a magisterial laureate in physics: "There are only two categories of men who become theoreticians: the geniuses and the men who are merely brilliant. Those less than brilliant needn't bother to come around." Tall talk but an exacting bargaining chip.

The original permanent faculty included a dozen young men, still wet behind the ears, most of whom arrived in the fifties. They quickly fulfilled our most confident expectations. There was Jack Goldstein who came as a prodigy in 1956, the year in which the university earned its accreditation. Scarcely thirty, he was already a veteran. He had taught and carried research at the Cornell Aeronautical Laboratory, the Institute for Advanced Study at Princeton, MIT, and the Baird Atomic in Cambridge, Massachusetts. He was called to Brandeis as a visiting assistant professor, on his way, within a few years, to a full professorship in astrophysics.

Goldstein's resourceful teaching and research techniques interested many developing countries: Africa, Japan, and India. He was a visiting professor of astrophysics at the Laboratorio de Astrofisica and the University of Rome, visiting scholar at Kyoto University, and a Fulbright scholar at the Weizmann Institute in Israel. He served twice for long terms as head of his department, as faculty representative on the Board of Trustees, as Dean of the Graduate School, and as Dean of Faculty. For nine years he was director of the Astrophysics Institute at the university. In addition to scores of articles in the major professional journals of physics in this country and in Europe, he has written biographies of cherished mentors—Isidor Rabi and Jerrold Zacharias.

Goldstein's hobbies reflect a debonair personality that makes him a genial chief. Since he has traveled so widely, he has become an avid and resourceful photographer. He claims to be the innovator of many new photographic styles. He banters, "While doing a series of studies of members of my own family I came to realize that they could not say 'it doesn't look like me' if their heads were not in the picture. This is how I came to invent 'cut off their heads' photography. I was able to move close to the subjects unobserved, accomplished by first holding my hand out, then whining softly for some money for a cup of coffee." This technique, he claims, rendered him functionally invisible and explains why many of his subjects were captured wearing pained expressions. Apparently his unique portraits were compelling. They are represented in the permanent collections of the Museum of Fine Arts in Boston, the Rogers Gallery in Marblehead, the Rose Art Museum at Brandeis, and a number of private collections.

Sylvan Schweber came to this country when a boy of fourteen from

France. He earned his Ph.D. at Princeton, joining the Brandeis faculty in 1955. His teaching has centered on twentieth-century physics and its philosophical implications, an exploration of quantum mechanics and relativity, and advanced developments in contemporary physics. He was director of the Dibner Institute for the History of Science and Technology of the History of Ideas, and professor in the School of Science. He accepted visiting professorships at MIT, the Hebrew University in Israel, and Harvard. He has been faculty associate in the history of science since 1986. His definitive volume, *An Introduction to Relativistic Quantum Field Theory,* intended for graduates and postdoctorals, has become a physics classic.

At Schweber's suggestion, Brandeis conducted a series of summer institutes where some of the leading scholars discussed the status of their research. They were modeled after the Summer Institute of the University of Paris, which convened world-famous physicists for summer colloquia. Our first summer School in Physics was organized in 1958 by Schweber, with over eighty participants. It was supported in part from a grant by the Raytheon Corporation. The importance of the venture was promptly recognized, which assured continuity for the program through subsidies from the National Science Foundation and NATO. Each year the institute was attended by about seventy outstanding theoretical physicists for seven weeks of seminars and colloquia. The lecturers and resource consultants included Nobel laureates and carefully chosen graduate and postdoctoral students. The special facilities acquired by the institute were generously supported by Nathan and Rosalie Goldstein of New York.

The summer sessions in the seminars and classrooms, the discussions that centered on the most recent physics breakthroughs, the interchange during the long walks in the lovely surroundings of the campus, the table conversation during lunch and dinner hours, the bull sessions—all these made the fleeting weeks as delightful as they were productive. Since books and articles in this dynamic field are often obsolete soon after they appear, the annual publication of the lectures and discussions served as valuable reference works on current research developments. The institute became an annual summer pilgrimage to the Brandeis campus for physicists, continuing for fifteen years until, with what some of us thought was dubious concern for economy, federal budgetary cutbacks deprived the university of essential support, and the institutes had to be discontinued.

Howard Schnitzer joined the faculty in 1961 for an incumbency that has now lasted beyond thirty years. His undergraduate degree was earned at the Newark College of Engineering, his Ph.D. in physics at the University of Rochester. He has been a longtime associate editor of the *Physics Review,* a research associate at Harvard since 1976, and visiting professor at Rockefeller University. With his training in engineering and physics, he explored with his choicest students the challenges of electrostatics, magnato-statics, and boundary value problems. He was department chairman in the early eighties.

Eugene Gross, who, until his recent death, gave the university more than thirty years of scholarship and faculty leadership, dazzled his colleagues with his research in plasma physics and electrodynamics. He came to us with a Ph.D. from Princeton, earned in his early twenties. He had been deeply influenced by John Kemeny, the designer of the computer language Basic that promoted large-scale computer literacy. Gross became the interpreter of computer science activities within the physics department. His friend and colleague, Sam Schweber, who offered a eulogy at his memorial service, described what even an informal stroll with Gross could produce. "During these walks I was introduced to Piaget, Talcott Parsons, Popper, the latest developments in mathematics and in many-body physics, and much else—and came to appreciate what it meant to be an 'intellectual.' "

Peter Heller relinquished a successful research program, mainly in statistical physics, to devote himself fully to undergraduate teaching. His concern for students made him a beloved model for protégés whose careers he affected profoundly. Stanley Deser was hard at work seeking the elusive bridge that might cross the chasm between the quantum theory of fields and general relativity. Fifteen years later, he was still patiently pursuing the link that had eluded generations of his most distinguished predecessors. He often was called to Europe and the Soviet Union to share his research with their preeminent academicians.

Marcus Grisaru was another valuable colleague who introduced graduates and selected undergraduates to mathematical physics, exploring with them methods to solve complicated problems in the physical sciences. He offered special courses (enrollment by permission) in quantum theory. Hugh Pendleton taught the quantum theory of atoms, molecules, and solids. Edgar Lipworth, brought in from the radiation laboratories of the University of California, was a major recruit. After coming to Brandeis, he made some of the most sophisticated and accurate measurements of atoms, using an atomic beam apparatus that he had conceived and built himself. He won world fame for testing the fundamental principles of physics time reversal. Here, too, a brilliant scientist was lost by early death.

Stephan Berko, a young Rumanian, survived the Nazification of Europe and was one of the students spotted by the Hillel Foundation, which was seeking gifted survivors for redemption opportunities in American universities. After his doctoral training at the University of Virginia and an initial teaching post there, he rose to front rank among the younger scientists. He came to Brandeis in 1961 and was quickly identified as a brilliant researcher in experimental nuclear solid-state physics. With his colleague Edgar Lipworth, he helped plan the newly acquired science facilities that had become indispensable for teaching and for advanced research programs. He was twice chairman of the department, and in 1968, he was a member of the staff of the Solid State Physics Institute of the University of Paris. He was often on the programs of international science conferences for lectures and seminars on positronium physics. At his death in spring 1991, he was eulogized as "the department's superstar."

As the department expanded, it included not only those who followed the traditional pattern of physics but also those in other areas related to medical research. It was this outreach that encouraged the establishment of a biophysics subdivision that enlisted the cooperation of chemist Henry Linschitz and biologist Andrew Szent-Györgyi.

The physics faculty members were also intensely interested in upgrading teaching methods and materials and, with their colleagues in other scientific areas, in improving demonstration and laboratory experimentation. Many wrote textbooks, which were widely adopted in science classes. Stanley Deser took leaves for assignments in Latin America, Europe, and the Soviet Union to share his research findings and to offer counsel in teaching techniques. Our scientists served on international government and foundation commissions, and there was constant faculty interchange with institutions of higher learning in Israel.

Closer to home, the faculty provided assistance to local high schools and junior colleges. It sponsored imaginative programs at Newton High School that brought selected youngsters to the campus to work on research projects with Brandeis faculty members. The program gave the youngsters early exposure to current research in heart disease, cancer, radiation sickness, and other basic health problems. It was most successful and was gradually broadened to include several other advanced high schools in Greater Boston.

With such projects and research records, the physics faculty received impressive grants from major federal agencies. Brandeis, soon after accreditation in 1954, was cited as a Center of Excellence in physics (as it had been in chemistry) and was assigned more than a million dollars for its program. When graduate studies were evaluated every few years by the American Council on Education, Brandeis was invariably on the honor list.

Our most ambitious scientific endeavor came in the field of biochemistry. It was planned as a graduate discipline, though the considerable investment in facilities had not yet been acquired. The area was a natural one for Brandeis, whose supporting constituency was intrigued by the prospect that the university would sponsor medical research and training. Besides, biochemistry was one of the youngest of the life sciences, and Brandeis would not be at a disadvantage in seeking a respected place in so new a field. Only after World War II was biochemistry included in the departmental structure of universities (until then it was mainly limited to medical schools). The American Biochemical Society was not organized until 1908, with just thirty members, and when Brandeis was founded in 1948, the society still had only seven hundred members. It has now grown beyond three thousand.

If the program were to meet its promise, it was essential to begin with a core faculty of highest distinction. In selecting the faculty, we sought the counsel of the ever helpful Fritz Lipmann. Nobel laureate and one of our Fellows, Lipmann reviewed our own faculty's manpower suggestions, added some of his own, and then narrowed the list to five. He was doubtful that the top two on the list would wish to cast their lot with so young an institution, but he believed that any of the others, if they agreed to come, would be of almost equally high caliber. We had never been reluctant to reach out for the so-called unattainable, so the first leaders on the list were approached: Nathan Kaplan, then at Johns Hopkins, and Martin Kamen, a key member of the chemistry faculty at Washington University. Impressed by the dynamism of Brandeis and by the promise of a vigorous campaign to acquire the necessary facilities, they both accepted our invitation and formed the nucleus of what they expected would become a superb department. They recruited a group of gifted younger men and women, who, in turn, attracted the most promising graduate and postdoctoral students.

This initial faculty included William Jencks, who joined Brandeis's newly established biochemistry department in 1957. Trained as a physician, Jencks had received a medical degree from the Harvard Medical School and had performed his internship at the Peter Bent Brigham Hospital. He then continued research as a postdoctoral Fellow both at the Massachusetts General Hospital and at the Harvard Medical School. From 1953 to 1955 he served as first lieutenant in the army's Medical Corps. He inherited a large part of the responsibility for the management of the department after Kaplan was obliged, for reasons of health, to accept a post in California. Jencks was one of the pioneers in the kinetics of enzyme catalysis. His in-depth study of mechanism enzyme reactions led to the training of a large number of scientists both at Brandeis and in other universities and research centers. He was a recipient of the coveted award from the American Chemical Society. He has now completed more than thirty-five years at Brandeis and has watched the department develop into one of the great international teaching and research centers.

Lawrence Levine, who was awarded a career grant by the American Cancer Society, introduced his charges to the excitement of immunochemistry and immunology, with its many applications to medical research. His wife, Helen Van Vunakis, was his research colleague, and the two became national figures in their field, exploring problems in advanced biochemistry with Ph.D. candidates.

Lawrence Grossman was among the early researchers to investigate the enzymatic reactions involving DNA synthesis and repair. He came to Brandeis in 1962 and, with Kaplan and Kamen, helped create the university's biochemistry department. After thirteen years, he moved over to Johns Hopkins's School of Hygiene and Public Health to complete a brilliant career, studded with the highest academic and government awards.

Since one of Kaplan's early interests was in enzyme cofactors, he sought an outstanding associate to share the research with him. He offered a post to Robert Abeles, an emigrant from Vienna who had come to this country in time to avoid the Nazi takeover of Central Europe. He joined the army and served from 1944–1946 as a first lieutenant. Upon discharge, he continued his graduate education at The University of Chicago and earned his doctorate at the University of Colorado. He followed with postdoctoral research at Harvard and was named assistant professor of chemistry at Ohio State and at the University of Michigan. He accepted Kaplan's bid to come to Brandeis with tenure in biochemistry in 1963 and has been here since.

Abeles has been primarily concerned with vitamin B_{12}, and, together with Kaplan, he has continued his general interest in cofactors and applied studies on reaction mechanisms to a wide spectrum of enzymes. He served as chairman of the Department of Biochemistry from 1975 to 1987. During his long tenure, he accepted a visiting professorship in biochemistry at MIT and was a frequent seminar guest lecturer in other American and in European universities. In his teaching, he dealt primarily with graduate and postdoctoral students, concentrating on probing the significance of enzyme reactions including energetics, kinetics, and reaction mechanism.

Gerald Fasman stands out as one of our most impressive international research scholars in biophysical chemistry. Born in Canada, his undergraduate academic training was obtained at the University of Alberta. He earned his Ph.D. at the California Institute of Technology and, for about ten years thereafter, held teaching and research posts at Cambridge in England, the Technische Hochschule in Zurich, and the Weizmann Institute in Israel. He came to Boston in 1955 and, for the next ten years, conducted research at the Children's Medical Center and the Harvard Medical School, lectured in protein chemistry at Boston University, and served as assistant to the head of biophysical chemistry in the laboratories of the Cancer Research Foundation in Boston. He returned to Harvard in 1962 for a two-year stint as a tutor in biochemistry, sharing his research commitment as an established investigator at the American Heart Association.

Meanwhile, in 1961, he joined the biochemistry department at Brandeis where he has remained. His work on the prediction of protein structure was widely recognized, as were his studies on the conformation (three-dimensional shape) of biological molecules as related to their biological function. But this academic dynamo was involved in many ancillary responsibilities. He was a consultant in the African Primary Science Program in Dar es Salaam, Tanzania, a senior postdoctoral Fellow in the Protein Institute in Osaka, and in the Japan Society for the Promotion of Science. He was also a research Fellow at the Weizmann Institute in Israel, a member of the Science Steering Committee at Accra, Ghana, and part of the molecular biology advisory panel of the National Science Foundation.

A steady stream of his articles has appeared in the major professional journals. He was editor of CRC *Critical Revolutions in Biochemistry* and on the editorial board of the *International Journal of Peptide and Protein Research*. As he moved into the 1990s, the university catalogue still listed his course in Conformational Studies of Biopolymers. Apparently he does not believe in retiring; retreading better suits his animated personality.

There were many others: Mary Ellen Jones, whom we recruited from the Biochemical Research Laboratories of the Massachusetts General Hospital, whose research took her into the role of carbamyl phosphate in microbiology and mammalian systems; John Lowenstein, whose research centered on metabolic regulation of carbohydrate utilization and fat synthesis and on the regulation and jurisdiction of adenosine production in the heart; and Farahe Maloff, who was concerned with biochemical pharmacology and with radioactive iodine as a possible weapon against thyroid tumors. Such men and women were not just gifted specialists. They were animated, prodded, and goaded by a mission. They agreed with the critic who said: "Philosophers have only interpreted the world differently—the point is to change it." As they worked together, the laboratory lights burning far into the night, they turned biochemistry at Brandeis, as fellow biochemists did in a very few other select universities, into a crusade that could shape the destinies of mankind.

The leader of this impressive team, Nathan Kaplan, refused to rest on his laurels, nor did he permit his colleagues to ease off. The American Cancer Society had the fullest confidence in him, and when he began to develop a device called an automatic serum enzyme analyzer in the hope that it could detect the presence of cancer before the usual symptoms appeared, every request for grants was honored to facilitate his research. Other grants, ultimately totaling millions, came pouring in from the Public Health Service and the National Science Foundation. Every triumph became a challenge that men and women like himself and universities like Brandeis had an obligation to meet. "I would predict," he had written soon after he joined our science faculty, "that some of the most exciting aspects of biochemistry are yet to come. One such aspect is the chemical basis for development and differentiation. What chemical mechanisms are involved when one cell becomes a hear cell and another cell becomes a muscle cell during differentiation? What are the chemical changes responsible for aging? What are the changes that occur when disease strikes, and what agents will cure them? All the diseases common to man, such as cancer and heart disease, depend upon our understanding of the basic chemical problems in development and aging. A solution of these basic biochemical problems will give us an understanding of what causes abnormalities."

Tragically we lost Kaplan at the apex of his brilliant career. His personal situation had not been easy, for his wife, Goldie, was continuously ailing. He reluctantly gave up his leadership post at Brandeis and accepted the offer of a research professorship at the University of California in La Jolla. But the move to a mild climate did not help either of them, and both died all too early.

Before concluding the story of thirty-odd years in the sciences, I believe it appropriate to add a word about the special arrangements that were completed with the Carnegie Institute of Technology (now Carnegie-Mellon) and the California Institute of Technology for five-year, joint degree programs in which the students earned both their bachelor of arts and bachelor of science degrees. The arrangement, known as the 3-2 Plan, enabled students to obtain a solid grounding in the liberal arts, with science as the area of concentration, and then to go on, after the third year, for two years of specialization in the various branches of engineering. The Brandeis students enrolled at Carnegie-Mellon or CIT for their engineering program; the Carnegie-Mellon and CIT students came to Brandeis for their liberal arts. The program was maintained for several years, and it was terminated only when the technical institutes decided to bring in faculties of their own for the undergraduate work in the liberal arts. Since this type of partnership was limited to a select group of high-level liberal arts universities, it was reassuring to know that Brandeis had already earned the reputation to be among them.

During our recruitment of the faculty in all the sciences, we had promised to give every priority to obtaining the physical facilities required. A campaign involving tens of millions was undertaken in 1960. Only an institution as brash as Brandeis would have dared to plan one concentrated effort for eleven buildings, including all the astronomically expensive, sophisticated equipment. Happily, our boldness was rewarded, and the goal was over-subscribed. With the required funds pledged, construction went forward briskly for several years, and by 1965 the entire science complex was completed. It included a special library of science with a capacity of a quarter of a million volumes, which was named for the donor, Leo Gerstenzang, who had amassed a fortune from the sale of Q-tips. Many other families from various parts of the country also cooperated in the venture, each helping to underwrite one of the units. They included three physics buildings, skillfully interconnected, that came from Harry Bass of Boston, Charles Yalem of St. Louis, and the Abelson and Getz families of Chicago. A biology center, which included the most advanced equipment for teaching and research, came from a New York merchant, Charles Bassine, and his brilliant son-in-law, Arthur Cohen, who was named by *Fortune* magazine as among the most promising business entrepreneurs of the younger generation.

The dedication, set for early November 1965, was more than a university celebration. It became a major salute from the world of science. The reputation that the university had now earned was validated by the acceptance of invitations from among the most honored scientists in the United States and abroad. Hoping that our traditional good luck in convocation weather would not desert us, we planned to hold the dedication outside. The site chosen was the roof of the Gerstenzang Science Library, with the science complex rising all around us. From this vantage point, there would be a spectacular view of the campus in all directions. There *would be*! Alas, the Sunday morning dawned wet and drizzly. Dame Nature was having a fit of the sulks. A year earlier, this caprice of weather would have spelled disaster, since we would have been unable to seat all our guests in any amphitheater or lecture hall. As luck had it, the final touches had been put on the interior of the Spingold Theater Center just the previous Friday, so the center's first "onstage cast" included five Nobel laureates as well as other world-renowned scientists.

The twelve honorary-degree recipients were Carl Cori of Washington University, Nobel laureate for research in the regulation of carbohydrate metabolism; Ernest Nagel of Columbia, whose teaching and research bridged the gulf between the natural and social sciences; Oscar Zariski of Harvard, editor of major journals in mathematics; Jerome Wiesner, science adviser to President Kennedy and provost of MIT, later its president; Chaim Pekeris, Israeli geophysicist, professor of applied mathematics at the Weizmann Institute; Torjborn Caspersson, director of medicine and cell research at the Nobel Institute for Medicine in Stockholm; Severo Ochoa, chairman of the Department of Biochemistry at New York University's College of Medicine and Nobel laureate in medicine; Gerard Piel, editor and publisher of *Scientific American* and winner of the UNESCO award for service to science education; Isidor Rabi of Columbia, Nobel laureate in physics and former chairman of the Atomic Energy Commission; Albert Szent-Györgyi, Hungarian-born director of the Woods Hole Marine Biological Laboratory, who had presented his gold Nobel medal to Finland in her hour of need; and Robert B. Woodward of Harvard, who had only days before been informed he would receive the Nobel prize in chemistry for his work in synthesizing such complex substances as reserpine and chlorophyll. The dedication address was given by James E. Webb, director of the National Aeronautics and Space Administration.

A word about the honorary-degree speeches made for this occasion. They were among the most sensitive with which we ever worked. Our science faculty was generous with time and suggestions as to which achievements each recipient treasured most. I have always believed that honorary-degree citations should be something more than catalogue items, that each should contain some quotation or reference that would hold nostalgic meaning for the recipient. With the Nobelist Severo Ochoa, achieving this intent offered a special challenge. Spain had produced this remarkable man, but Spanish achievements in science had been poignantly infrequent during the last five hundred years. I had assistants scouring Spanish literature for days to uncover what would be felicitously relevant. Finally we settled on a few words from a poem by Miguel de Unamuno, the philosopher-poet-novelist whom even the Spanish dictator, Franco, had not dared to oust from the faculty at the University of Salamanca. Ochoa, a regal man with the bearing of a true hidalgo, was strikingly handsome with snow-white hair and long, dark, Spanish countenance, severe in appearance compared, for instance, with Szent-Györgyi, whose face crinkled with laugh lines. As I reached the Unamuno quotation, I glanced up at Ochoa, whose Spanish austerity lighted up for a moment with a smile like all the sunshine of Iberia. Such mini-moments were the treasured extra remembrances of our honorary-degree citations, raising them above the level of biographical detail.

In summary, the university's record in science during its first two decades carried Brandeis quickly into the front rank. The undergraduate student body was one of the most highly selected; College Board scores in the very high 700s were not uncommon, and after their undergraduate preparation, many students sought admission to the most favored medical schools. In a 1967 study by the Association of American Medical Colleges, it was noted that 83.8 percent of Brandeis applicants were successful, although they did not always receive bids to the schools of their first choice. Most of the science departments were housed in a newly completed science complex, providing over 200,000 square feet of space, furnished with modern, sophisticated equipment. There was now a special science library containing nearly fifty thousand volumes, and the Women's Committee was working at its usual dynamic pace to bring the number to a quarter million. The students were actively involved with the faculty in some of their experiments almost from their freshman days. By the early 1960s, grants for research from the major national agencies were averaging eight million dollars annually, and the character of the research in each field was winning highest acclaim from peers in each of the sciences.

To add to Brandeis's prestige in the field of science, the Rosenstiel Basic Medical Sciences Research Center is one of the leading units for research in the country, embracing biochemistry, biology, biophysics, molecular biology, immunology, and protein crystallography. For some years the center was ably directed by biologist Hugh Huxley.

Two scientists who have earned distinction for their scientific work have also capably served the university in its administration. James Lackner, professor of psychology and director of the Graybiel Lab, was provost from 1986–1989. In 1992, Irving R. Epstein, an internationally recognized chemist, accepted the post of dean of arts and sciences.

I could not end this chapter without mentioning an exciting, more recent development: the Benjamin and Mae Volen National Center for Complex Systems, scheduled for completion in 1994. Planned in the late 1980s under the direction of Brandeis President Evelyn E. Handler, the center is expected to be one of the foremost research facilities of its kind in the country. It will house researchers from the departments of biology, biochemistry, chemistry, computer science, physics, and psychology committed to research on the brain, intelligence, and advanced computation.

CHAPTER NINE

The Humanities

Immediately after World War II, no area of curriculum in university life was as much under fire as was the humanities. More than ever the pressure mounted for educational policies that would lead to practical career results. The term "relevant" kept generating public discussion, and those who sought a major place for the humanist values of language and literature, philosophy and the classics, found themselves often on the defensive. As noted earlier, Brandeis was not drawn into the contention. The university decided from the outset that, although it was very much concerned with the social and natural sciences, equal status would always be assured for the humanities and that it would seek the very best faculty to interpret them. I later summarized our view when we dedicated a major science complex. I said then: "Great as Brandeis's commitment is to accent the sciences, we will not allow the arts and humanities to be relegated to the parenthesis areas. We must encourage the future biologist to taste the salt beneath the laughter of Jonson's *Volpone,* the physicist to delight in Mozart, the chemist to place his knowledge in the perspective of history, the mathematician to see the beauty in paint and marble as in the binomial theorem."

We began building the faculty in the humanities to be as diversified in special interests as such a group could be: Ludwig Lewisohn, absorbed in translating the dramas of Gerhart Hauptmann in eight volumes and in his magnum opus on Goethe, timed for the two hundredth anniversary of the great poet's birth; Milton Hindus, shuttling between his running battles with Celine and editing a volume on Proust (which he almost titled *Remembrance of Things Proust*); James Cunningham, director of graduate programs, laboring to compress his cool, astringent poetry in such tightness that a *London Times* critic concluded "that his language is deliberately remote from speech" (in truth, no one could devastate with such effectiveness the wordy and the windy); Osborne Earle, stoutly defending the reputation of Chaucer as the first finder of our language; Allen Grossman, who went on to receive the MacArthur Foundation award in 1989, reading his own highly praised poetry in the gravelly voice that sounded like Winston Churchill; Robert Preyer, mining away on the treasures hidden in the works of the Victorians; Joseph Cheskis, whom we retained from Middlesex where he had offered the mellow charm of Spanish, French, and Italian literature, uniquely transformed by his Litvak accent. In the 1952 student yearbook, the story was spread that when the devout Cheskis said his morning prayers, he usually managed to sneak in a canto or two from the *Divine Comedy* of his revered Dante.

A major coup was achieved in 1953 with the appointment of Irving Howe, a literary critic and editor of *Dissent* who, though scarcely in his forties, already had three or four teaching posts behind him. When he disagreed— and he disagreed more often than not—his sharpness rarely cut superficially. He reserved tolerance and patience mainly for his students, and then only for the ones who demonstrated promise. He wrote always with social purpose, and his literary evaluations of Faulkner and Anderson and other modern luminaries were interspersed with volumes on current politics and international affairs. He was deeply interested in Jewish proletarian life, and he edited anthologies that brought together the classics of Yiddish literature.

These gifted scholars and others who joined or followed them revealed new dimensions in their specializations. They found a common bond in their determination to fulfill the main purpose of a humanities curriculum: to expose their students to the best that had been thought or written. They were tough individualists, quarreling, arguing, exposing, challenging, as if they enjoyed the intellectual battle for its own sake, but uniting at once against the invasions of mediocrity. I was inevitably reminded of John Stuart Mill's prayer aimed at his intellectual adversaries: "Lord, enlighten Thou our enemies, sharpen their wits, give acuteness to their perceptions and consecutiveness and clearness to their reasoning powers: we are in danger from their folly, not their wisdom; their weakness is what fills us with apprehension, not their strength."

It was Robert Preyer who wrote me when he outlined his objectives as first English and American literature department chairman: "We might not agree on morals, politics, the meaning of texts; but we did agree that our ideal aim was to put students in complete possession of all their powers. As practical classroom teachers we wanted them to have access to the productions of first-rate minds, to enable them to experience what that meant. Our negative purpose was to insure that they recognized and developed a proper disesteem for the meretricious and the third rate. Above all, we feared the inclusion of what Whitehead called 'inert ideas,' that is to say, ideas that are merely received into the mind without being utilized, or tested, or thrown into fresh combinations."

Preyer was really describing why many of our faculty had accepted the bid from a precariously supported, still unshielded Brandeis. They were in flight from institutions, many older and safer, that were filling up with people who were hostage to the mental torpor of such "inert ideas." I remembered interviewing a lively young applicant for a post in Romance languages. Cheskis was present at the interview and, after it was over, I asked him what he thought. "Ah," he chuckled, "there's the kind of colleague who will give us the excitement of tough disputes."

The department also offered hospitality, until his untimely death, to Philip Rahv, co-founder with William Phillips of *The Partisan Review.* Rahv was one of the many editor-critics who started out in the thirties when writers like Edmund Wilson and Mary McCarthy and so many others were coming into their own. Rahv had known and worked with most of the major figures of American letters. He had been, so to speak, "present at creation" of many of the works he assigned to his students. In his teaching he savored the tempestuous days when as editor he upheld Kierkegaard's conception of the master critic: "to keep the wound of the negative open."

There were others, some who even in a brief incumbency achieved national visibility. Marie Syrkin came to us from the New York high school system with few of the degrees and awards that look impressive in a vita. Apparently she needed none. She was a superb teacher and a prolific writer. Her father, Nachman Syrkin, the founder of Socialist Zionism, was a contemporary of the Zionist leaders Theodore Herzl and Max Nordau, and his home was a forum for brilliant exchange. Her *Blessed is the Match,* the moving story of the Jewish resistance movement during the Nazi terror, revealed a rare talent that was worth watching. She left Brandeis to become editor of *The Jewish Frontier.* Aileen Ward was a later arrival who had achieved national distinction when she was awarded the John Keats prize for her biography of the poet. Influenced by the psychological insights of Erik Erikson, Miss Ward took Keats through his tragic adolescence, buffeted by problems too overwhelming for the strongest spirit, and indicated how, in his finest hours, he emerged into an extraordinary poet. The compassion that she demonstrated in her interpretation of Keats shone through.

It was the presence of such initial faculty that, I believe, enabled us to draw an august roster of visiting professors and lecturers. Milton Hindus recalls how often Robert Frost returned and how thoroughly he enjoyed the refreshing beauty of the campus. "I remember showing him around the grounds and, coming upon a lovely grove of trees with their familiar-looking silver bark, 'There are some of my birches,' Frost exclaimed." Hortense Calisher, the novelist and short story writer, visited with us for a year. She was as elegant in her person as in her constantly fresh prose. There was one banner year for poetry when Pulitzer Prize-winner Stanley Kunitz came as a visiting professor and Alfred Kazin offered a mini-course in the adult education program.

The Romance language offerings were introduced with high promise. French and Spanish, and often Italian, were standard in most good high schools, and admission to Brandeis required a reading knowledge of at least one such language. In 1959 Denise Alexandre, one of the young French instructors, invited women students majoring in French to reside in a maison française, located in one of the wings of the Castle. The experiment of living in a totally French environment was at first limited to ten students. They were to dine together, speaking only in French, and occasionally entertain guests and French visitors, both in their lounge and at their dining table. The program was later extended to several other study and eating groups in the foreign languages. James Duffy, who doubled in African history and was often consulted by the State Department because of his knowledge of Portugese Africa, Denah Lida, who headed the Spanish program, and Milton Vanger, whose special field was Latin America, were enthusiastic teachers and scholars. Edward Engelberg was lured from the University of Wisconsin. He had migrated from Germany as a boy of ten at the outbreak of World War II, had earned his doctorate at Wisconsin, and had taught for eight years at the University of Michigan. He came to Brandeis in 1965 to take over the chairmanship of the program in Romance languages and comparative literature. In 1988 he hosted at Brandeis a conference of more than 250 American and foreign scholars in the area of comparative literature. He built a national reputation as the leading interpreter of William Butler Yeats and edited the volumes of the Yeats Critical and Textual Studies.

Although budgetary constraints did not allow us to plan for foreign language and literature offerings as an area for major development, we did not neglect them. In the beginning, Germanic and Slavic languages were linked in one department. In 1951 we welcomed Harry Zohn, who had escaped Hitler's Germany in the forties and then earned a doctorate at Harvard. He became a force in the uphill struggle to corral a viable department of German language and literature. The horrors of the Nazis' barbarism were too close, and he knew he was bucking the tide in trying to sustain enrollments; but Zohn persevered, even introducing into his classes the singing of traditional German folk songs. He served as executive director of the Goethe Society of New England from 1963 to 1968. His seminars on the culture of the German Republic, focusing on Berlin in the turbulent twenties, overcame student resistance. He retired in 1993, having been a member of the faculty for more than four decades.

To our surprise, there was growing interest in Yiddish. We were surprised because the children of émigrés from Yiddish-speaking lands were usually eager to shed Old World associations. Their determination to demonstrate their complete assimilation into American life often impelled them to look upon Yiddish as scrubby baggage. The third generation, however, was apparently much more secure in its American acculturation. To many of them,

Yiddish meant a reaffirmation of identity, and this feeling was strengthened when they learned that Yiddish literature was rich and robust. When Maurice Samuel wrote *The World of Sholom Aleichem* soon after World War II, it became a best-seller as the literary world discovered the precious ore in a culture too long neglected. Henry Mencken revealed that he had sat up through a whole night reading the volume "that opened a totally new world to me." Samuel and other enthusiastic interpreters began to translate the masterpieces of the nineteenth- and early twentieth-century giants. What the second generation wished to forget, the third generation strove to remember.

Yiddish became part of the university curriculum. The first instructors had to struggle to sustain enrollment, for they were old-fashioned pedagogues, the only ones then available. It was only when Robert Szulkin, an easygoing, unruffled, witty, Old World émigré who later became a popular dean of students, brought his warm personality into his teaching that the students responded with heartiness. Szulkin also doubled in Russian, which became part of the curriculum in the early sixties. Szulkin was thoroughly at home in the classics of the nineteenth- and early twentieth-century Russian literary golden age. But although there was increasing interest in Russian history and political philosophy, the students were handicapped by little knowledge of the language, which was rarely taught in the public high schools. The giants of Russian literature—Tolstoy, Dostoevsky, Turgenev, Chekhov, Gogol—therefore had to be taught in English translation.

The camaraderie of our literature faculty brought a valuable bonus in the unusual proliferation of constructive critical publications among the students. The school newspaper, *Justice,* was the conventional college gadfly, although the term "conventional" in relation to the *Justice* would have infuriated the editorial guardians of the fortress of dissidence. Conventional indeed! They seized upon every issue wherein the administration could be clobbered. They developed a genius for detraction. Editorials would drip with sarcasm and with charges that their idea of Brandeis was being compromised by growing complacency. Henry Aiken of the philosophy department was sure that nothing would satisfy such students "short of the whole university community living together in one great academic kibbutz." But their barbs were phrased meticulously, with a concern for style that their faculty had minted into their discussions. "The network of highways on campus," one wrote, "was the work of a Tibetan monk who had built mountain passes in his native land for Yaks so that two of them could never pass each other." Another wrote: "The dining hall is ideal; it is dark, damp and crowded. This creates a situation where one is unable to see the food on one's plate, thus permitting a person to eat through four years of college meals and call everything rice pudding." In fairness, the editors were as sharp with each other and with contributors as they were with the establishment. The editorial fever chart of the young critics never goaded the administration into any kind of censorship. The *Justice* remained a scolding conscience, and all the journals and yearbooks followed its tradition.

It was perhaps because we had an unusually versatile archeologist-classicist on the faculty, Cyrus Gordon, that we were influenced to establish an area called Mediterranean Studies, a combination of the classics and archeology. Gordon had been trained at the University of Pennsylvania and had filled teaching posts in Bible, archeology, and Oriental studies at Smith, Princeton, and his alma mater, Johns Hopkins, until he became professor of Assyriology and Egyptology at Dropsie College in Philadelphia. He came to Brandeis in 1956. Gordon made his courses in archeology an ongoing drama and led teams of students almost every year on digs to Crete, other Mediterranean islands, and the southern Negev in Israel. He combined the boundless enthusiasm of a Schliemann, the nineteenth-century business-cum-amateur who discovered Troy, with his own deeper and more thorough preparation for archeological research.

At the peak of his reputation, Gordon was involved in a rancorous controversy when he announced that his early archeological studies had persuaded him that the first landings on American soil had not been achieved by expeditions of Columbus, nor even by the tenth-century Vikings. He claimed that he had archeological evidence that the discovery had been achieved two millennia earlier by the Biblical Hebrews. One can imagine the scholarly imbroglio that such announcements precipitated. At its height, I was sharing a platform in Kansas City with Senator Edward Kennedy. He had just been reelected for another term in Massachusetts. With delightful banter, he thanked me for not involving myself in the Gordon dispute until after the election. As a sophisticated politician, it would have been difficult for Kennedy to express his views without alienating either the Italians, the Spaniards, or the Jews, influential voting blocs in Massachusetts. He added a speculative note that if the newcomers were indeed wandering Hebrews, remnants of the Ten Tribes, the reaction of the Indians must have been: "Good God, there goes the neighborhood!"

In the middle fifties a unique interdisciplinary program was launched, designed to give students broader understanding of the historical development of ideas and structured to lead to a doctorate for candidates who planned careers in teaching intellectual history. A listing of typical courses would perhaps best illustrate how the program operated. There was a course that dealt with the major figures in the Christian tradition, including Saint Paul, Saint Augustine, Saint Thomas Aquinas, Luther, Schleiermacher. There was another in modern religious values that examined the classic works of Kierkegaard, Buber, Tillich, Barth, Teilhard de Chardin. Still another concentrated on the Book of Job. Finally, there were courses in political thought from Machiavelli to Marx and on to Mao Tse-tung.

CHAPTER TEN

The Creative Arts

Few major universities, I imagine, have made music their first graduate program; but ours was an unusual situation. Once we had determined that the creative arts were to be required of all students, music inevitably was given a special place in the curriculum. We were encouraged further by the expectation that there would be no lack of substantial support. In disproportionate numbers, American Jews were patrons of the creative arts, particularly music. Since the days of August Belmont, Jewish names were always on the patrons' lists of symphony orchestras, museums, opera companies, theaters, and the whole range of creative arts. When Brandeis announced its objectives, it was not disappointed in the response; nor were we disappointed in the caliber of students, both undergraduate and graduate, who applied for the programs in creative arts.

Academically, we might have seemed to be bucking the prevalent tide among other liberal arts institutions. Although Boston University had, and still has, its School of Music and Institutes of Theatre and Visual Arts, this was not the accepted New England pattern. Theater, when taught, was most often incorporated as a division in schools of education, structured to produce teachers, especially at the secondary school level. In the 1920s, President Lowell of Harvard consigned creative arts activities to the limbo of the extracurricular. He all but packed off to Yale a singularly promising program in drama and playwriting, the nucleus of one of Yale's most distinguished graduate schools. Leonard Bernstein (Harvard AB *cum laude*, 1939) could not earn a single academic credit for piano. The same was true for the notable American painter Fairfield Porter and his equally gifted brother, the photographer Eliot Porter (Harvard MD, 1929). If one believes all one reads, actor Jack Lemmon (Harvard AB, 1947) all but extracurricularated himself out of college altogether.

Initially, the Brandeis School of Music comprised one unforgettable character, Erwin Bodky. He had been born in Germany and, as a youth, was one of the very few students accepted by Richard Strauss. Bodky became a world authority on the keyboard works of Bach shortly before Hitler propelled him, his wife, and his daughter on the trail of uprootings, from Holland to England and eventually to the United States. Bodky first obtained a minor position with the Longy School of Music in Cambridge, Massachusetts. There he organized a Friends of Early Music Committee, and for a number of years, he presented concerts in the Busch-Reisinger Museum of Harvard for select but distinguished groups of patrons, headed by Elizabeth Sprague Coolidge. Within three years, the membership of the committee had grown to over a thousand, and it sponsored not only concerts and recitals but gave scholarships to talented students and the use of musical instruments to those who could not afford them. Later, the committee helped in the adaption of classrooms and lecture halls for the special requirements of music.

Two families deeply interested in Brandeis, the Adolph Ullmans and the Samuel Slosbergs, had become friends of Bodky. It was on their recommendation that he came to Brandeis in 1949, and he brought with him the loyalty and commitment of the Friends of Early Music. The revered Serge Koussevitzky, conductor of the Boston Symphony Orchestra, joined the sponsoring group. In accepting his position, Bodky wrote: "Brandeis must create the very finest musical education, else it is better that we do not start." When Aaron Copland and Alfred Einstein, the musician son of the immortal Albert, joined the faculty, they set similar imperatives. Just beginning our second year, we had only a small enrollment, but this discouraged Bodky not at all. Of the 250 freshmen who were matriculating in 1950, forty had been active in their high schools as members of orchestras, chamber music groups, and school bands. These and many others flocked to Bodky, and the concerts he inaugurated drew audiences from far beyond the university family. Meanwhile, he was writing a definitive work on Bach's keyboard works. Tragically, he did not live to see it published with the Harvard University colophon. He died suddenly on holiday in Switzerland in 1958.

By 1950, when Bodky had been with us for a year and we lacked only a senior class to complete the college cycle, the time was overdue to double the faculty of one. Bodky welcomed Irving Fine, a young composer whom we winked away from Harvard. Soon Aaron Copland was added, and he gladly joined Fine in offering a joint course, The Anatomy of Twentieth-

Century Music. By 1951, when we were at last a four-year school, I was sufficiently sanguine to suggest to Fine, now the "head" of the School of Creative Arts, that we ought to dare a quantum coup. We had won the goodwill of well-wishers in many parts of the country, and among them was Leonard Bernstein. Would it be presumptuous, I asked in all innocence, for us to approach Bernstein for at least part-time service at the university? Bernstein was by then living in New York, where he was performing with the New York Philharmonic and traveling widely as a guest conductor. Fine was at first nonplussed; how could he be induced to leave New York? I suggested that we make concessions for a man of his caliber. Surely a commuting arrangement, similar to that worked out with Eleanor Roosevelt, might be persuasive. Fine conceded that there was no harm in trying.

Subsequently, Adolph Ullman and I drove up to Tanglewood for the interview with Bernstein. We made an unabashedly sentimental appeal. I emphasized to Bernstein what Brandeis meant as a symbol, how important it was for us to fulfill highest expectations in the areas we had charted as unique for our concentration, and that he would be making a pivotal contribution if he joined the music faculty in our beginning years. At that time, I did not know what has since been confirmed. It seems that Koussevitzky, himself a Russian-born Jew who had encountered difficulties in his own early career, had often urged Bernstein to Anglicize his name. Bernstein steadfastly refused. He would make it as Bernstein or not at all. Perhaps it was this quality of unintimidated pride, as well as some of the glittering unrealities I put to him, that helped to bring about his decision. We had, for example, high hopes for an annual creative arts festival, where Bernstein's direction would be given unlimited scope. When Ullman and I made it clear that he would be expected on campus only about once a month for a succession of days, that assistants would carry the supplementary assignments, his enthusiasm grew. But he wondered about our facilities. Did we have a music center? We did not. Did we have instruments for orchestra and ballet programming? We did not. Did we have a piano? "Leonard," I urged, "just let us announce that you are coming as part of our faculty and as director of our festivals. I'm sure that we shall very quickly obtain the necessary facilities, and the donors will consider it a privilege to make the gifts." Bernstein was never one to ponder important decisions. His consent was given there at Tanglewood, only moments before he went on stage to conduct.

On the long drive back to Boston, Ullman, who had been a fascinated party to the whole tableau, asked ingenuously, "What kind of facilities did you have in mind?" I had been waiting for the question. "By a strange coincidence," I replied, "I have the plans for an amphitheater in my pocket." And I passed over to him some rough sketches that had been drawn up for me before the trip. Ullman hesitated only fractionally longer than had Bernstein. Before we reached Boston, he had determined to underwrite the construction of the Adolph Ullman Amphitheater.

Bernstein's course in modern music, offered in 1951, was a tour de force. It was anything but a conventional introduction to music appreciation. Many readers will remember his *Omnibus* series that came later and that drew, at least in part, from his Brandeis teaching. His approach to students was essentially the same as he used on these immensely popular television programs: "You think you hate modern music? I cannot promise you will like it at the end of this program, but at least you will know why you hate it." Bernstein's eloquence was phenomenal. I remember his reference to "the whole Milky Way of possibilities inherent in the twelve tones of the chromatic scale; and the color and shimmer and thunder of the Romantics who nourish our sense of wonder and give us back our moon, which has been taken away by science and made into just another airport."

Bernstein and Fine joined now in stepping up recruitment for the School of Music where, they hoped, in Fine's words, "to maintain a precarious balance between scholarship and performance." They persuaded old friends to join them, and when they did, they established a department unusually strong in composition. Arthur Berger taught at Julliard before coming to us and was also music critic for both the *New York Herald Tribune* and the *Saturday Review*. He was already the chief interpreter of Aaron Copland's work and later published a definitive study on his old friend.

Bernstein's presence made it possible to plan creative arts festivals on a most ambitious scale. Our debut in this field was scheduled for our first commencement, in 1952. Work on the Ullman Amphitheater began at once, the commission going to Harrison and Abramovitz, the university's master planners. The amphitheater was designed principally for open-air affairs—convocations, commencements, and, of course, the summer creative arts festivals. Constructed on three acres with seating for two thousand, but with space on the grassy slopes for seven or eight thousand more, it was equipped with a huge stage and an orchestra pit for forty musicians. Beneath the staging area were facilities for dressing, storage, and utility, as well as a number of classrooms. Though it had seemed impossible to meet the commencement deadline, carpenters, electricians, and painters eventually walked off the stage with minutes to spare before Bernstein raised his baton for the opening.

By any standards, it was a *ne plus ultra* week for a first commencement. Every day was packed with seminars and workshops, and the evenings were given to music. The opening night audience heard the American premiere of Kurt Weill's *Threepenny Opera*. Brilliantly performed, it went from its Brandeis debut for a run of eight years in the Theater de Lys off Broadway. The next night provided a second premiere, a specially commissioned Bernstein operetta, *Trouble in Tahiti*, which, the following November, was presented by NBC on a coast-to-coast television broadcast. The new production of Stravinsky's choral ballet *Les Noces,* choreographed and danced by Merce Cunningham, was the third evening's offering. On still another night, there was a special performance of Pierre Schaeffer's *Symphonie pour un Homme Seul*. There were poetry readings by Karl Shapiro, William Carlos Williams, and Peter Viereck, a jazz festival, an afternoon of art films, and an exhibition of art works that had already been acquired. Throughout, the university was host to leading critics from around the country, and it was their consensus that Brandeis had given enduring significance to its first commencement. One critic wrote: "Not in our time, in this part of the country, had there been any such comprehensive and knowing attempt to appraise and stimulate the arts of America." And all this as the university was graduating its first 107 students.

The following year, the Creative Arts Festival was devoted to the Comic Spirit, and this theme was explored in many of its art forms. Leonard Bernstein led the planning and was easily able to persuade a unique cast of celebrities to participate. For the opening night, the Lemonade Opera Company of New York produced and Bernstein conducted the American premiere of the comic opera *Les Mamalles de Tiresias,* by Francis Poulenc. It had been internationally acclaimed upon its Paris debut. Later in the week, Morton Gould's new *Concerto for Tap Dancer and Orchestra* was given its American premiere, featuring Danny Daniels. Art exhibits, offering works concentrating on the comic spirit, were mounted in various parts of the campus. Louis Untermeyer was moderator for a group of literary figures who read and discussed light verse. Selected by a jury of movie critics, the best comic sequences were shown and discussed by Richard Griffiths of the New York Museum of Modern Art.

By 1957, the Creative Arts Festival had become an eagerly awaited part of our commencement festivities. Indeed, the 1957 festival, dedicated to an appraisal of six art forms—chamber music, dance, jazz, poetry, orchestral and *operative* music, and the fine arts—represented a kind of climax. Pearl Long and her fourteen-member dance company interpreted two new works. This was the first time that a university had commissioned composers to write original jazz music for a campus program. Three artists from the world of jazz, including Harold Shapero of our own faculty, gave their jazz premieres. Works by Irving Fine, *Fantasy for String Trio,* and Arthur Berger, *Duo for Clarinet and Piano,* performed by the Julliard String Quartet, were also given their New England debuts.

One of the largest art exhibits ever mounted on an American campus, more than two hundred carefully screened works, were displayed throughout the festival period and for a week thereafter. There were seven exhibitions by leading artists, including one-man shows by Stuart Davis and Jimmy Ernst, who had been Brandeis creative arts award winners. Works by Max Weber were also on display, and during the commencement exercises he was given an honorary degree along with former President Truman. Two Pulitzer Prize winners, Richard Wilbur and Robert Lowell, led a group of New England poets in a high-level symposium. Aaron Copland, who also received an honorary degree, conducted a concert of his own works, including *The Tender Land,* as tribute to Adolph Ullman who had died recently.

The momentum of the early exciting years never slackened. To be sure, we lost Erwin Bodky and Irving Fine by death, and the duties of the concert season in New York became too onerous for Leonard Bernstein to make regular trips to the campus. But Bernstein's devotion to Brandeis never waned. His international concerts kept him out of the country for long periods, but when he could make an appearance for us, he cooperated with commitment and affection.

Meantime Arthur Shapiro and Arthur Berger continued with their impressive teaching schedules. They reached out for an ever-expanding faculty, keeping meticulously to the standards that had now become the irreducible minimum. There was Paul Brainard, who came in 1961 and became department chairman a few years later. He had been trained in Heidelberg and Göttingen, was an internationally acknowledged Bach scholar, and was contributing to on-going editions of the works of Tarfini. He is now at the Yale Institute of Sacred Music. There was Leo Treitler, who introduced his students to the conceptual foundations of historical study in the arts. He served as dean of the college and proved as able an academic administrator as he was a scholar. He helped develop our graduate school of music and then accepted the call of Stony Brook in New York. Seymour Shifrin, one of America's most widely respected composers, was brought to our faculty from the University of California in Berkeley in 1966. We lost him by death after thirteen years of inspired teaching and composing. Then there was Robert Koff, violinist and conductor, who came to us from Julliard to direct our performance activities. Apart from his teaching assignments, he was always available for university functions. He remained as a much beloved member of the faculty until his retirement after more than a quarter of a century at Brandeis.

Caldwell Titcomb also belonged with the pioneer group, joining the university in 1954 before it had received accreditation and remaining even beyond his retirement in 1988. He introduced his students to the instruments of the orchestra and their use by major composers. He led the more advanced students to a better understanding of Beethoven. Starting in 1955, he gave the first course on Berlioz offered by any American university. In 1966 he brought ethnomusicology (nonwestern music) into the Brandeis curriculum. Beyond his teaching and research, he served as university organist for nearly twenty years until 1970 and as director of undergraduate studies in music from 1956 to 1984.

We were especially fortunate in recruiting Kenneth Levy, historian of liturgical chant and Renaissance music, who inaugurated the Ph.D. program in musicology. After a highly creative decade at the university, he accepted the call to Princeton.

Meantime, in the early spring of 1954, we launched the first of a series of annual Beaux Arts balls, and the large group drawn into the sponsorship developed a camaraderie that served the university well. The first ball, held at the old Somerset Hotel, set a precedent in its imaginative planning for those that followed. Under the general chairmanship of Mrs. Paul Smith, the hotel ballroom was transformed into a Spring Extravaganza by Alfred Duca, one of New England's most sought out decorators. Two Bostonians who were officers of the Friends of the Creative Arts undertook the production of a special souvenir art book. On each of its hundred pages was the reproduction of an advertisement done by a gifted artist, commissioned by firms who paid a thousand dollars a page. Most of the skillfully devised advertisements were original works of art, and the book itself became a collector's item. A special Costume Service Center was set up to offer counsel on the design of costumes or on how to obtain them. At a gaily planned midnight supper, the cartoonist Al Capp judged the costumes and awarded special prizes for the best. When all expenses were deducted, the university, in addition to giving its patrons one of their most enjoyable evenings, substantially augmented its art scholarship program.

Brandeis was only eight years old when it undertook to present Creative Arts Awards for distinction in the fields of music, sculpture, painting, and theater, later adding fiction and poetry. The Brandeis awards were specifically meant to pay tribute to excellence in the creative arts, and the announcement was heartily welcomed. There was no semblance of arrogance in establishing the project, for, although the university was among the nation's youngest, its reputation had few peers in the creative arts in the academic world. Besides, no similar university-sponsored awards were then in existence.

Two types of annual awards were presented: medals for artists whose career achievements were judged to have left an enduring mark upon their times, and citations and generous grants-in-aid for younger people whose present work offered promise of future eminence.

Adapting Columbia's Pulitzer Prize pattern, the Awards Commission, consisting mainly of our faculty leadership in the creative arts, received the nominations of a jury whom they had selected. We believed that the impeccable reputation of such juries would perhaps be a most important factor in lending prestige to the awards. In the first years, the funding for the project came from a few families who were persuaded to provide seed money. Later, a donor who preferred to remain anonymous underwrote the project, until his death in 1973. The program was then placed on a permanent basis by a trustee family, Jack and Lillian Poses, who had already established the Poses Institute for the Fine Arts.

The first awards went to William Schuman, in music; Stuart Davis, in painting; Hallie Flanagan Davis, in theater; and William Carlos Williams, in poetry. The caliber of such recipients set a pattern of virtuosity that gave the awards instant recognition as a very high honor. After the tenth year, another category was added to pay tribute to those whose talents ranged over all the creative arts, and medals went to such luminaries as Martha Graham, Buckminster Fuller, Meyer Schapiro, and Alfred H. Barr.

It required unusual perceptiveness for the juries to spot budding talent for the grants-in-aid that were intended to encourage younger people. The judgments were rarely disappointing; within a decade of receiving the awards, many recipients had moved into the select circle of assured preeminence. In the very first group, the grant-in-aid for musical composition went to Robert Kurka. He composed a new American opera, *Good Soldier Schweik,* which was performed by the New York Opera Company, and the reviews generally agreed with the prophetic Brandeis citation that "here was a superb talent at the threshold of greatness." Unfortunately, Kurka died of leukemia within a year, at the age of thirty-five. The 1960 grant went to Gunther Schuller, then thirty-five but already impressing his peers in music by the versatility of his compositions. Within seven years he had reached top rank and was named president of the New England Conservatory of Music.

The award presentations were always notable occasions, the audience, comprising the most loyal patrons of the arts, crowding the ballroom of one of the major New York hotels. The first such affair was held at the old Ambassador Hotel, and the awards and citations were made by Nelson Rockefeller, then chairman of the board of the Museum of Modern Art. The arrangements were under the expert supervision of Mrs. Edith Steinberg, who, for more than fifteen years until her death in 1972, directed such special events for the university in the New York area.

By 1968, the Creative Arts Awards had won a permanent place in the honors listings of American cultural life. Allen Tate, named as a medal winner for his stature as a poet, was undoubtedly speaking for many others who had been chosen when he acknowledged that, though he had an impressive array of citations, he cherished two above all, the Pulitzer prize and the Brandeis Creative Arts Award.

All this time, the music department functioned in the cramped underground space provided by Ullman, which also served the expanding theater program. The need for an adequate center became so pressing that even the most persistent critics of the bulldozer conceded that it justified a priority listing. Fortunately, by 1956, the generosity of the Slosberg family of Brookline, Massachusetts, helped solve the problem. Samuel Slosberg, a New England shoe manufacturer, had been a trustee for several years. He was involved in many philanthropic activities and was soon to be the dynamic president of the Beth Israel Hospital. He and his wife, Helen, were of the earliest music and art patrons of the university and, with Adolph Ullman, had created the Friends of the Creative Arts to give the initial impetus to its activities. A music center was underwritten by the family as a memorial to the Slosberg parents, Jacob and Bessie. Construction began at once so that it could be completed and dedicated by April 1957.

The building was designed by Harrison and Abramovitz as a two-level glass and red brick structure, matching the color and melding into the unity of the campus architectural master plan. Glass-walled offices and classrooms were constructed on the main floor; directly below were the many sound-conditioned rooms for instruction and practice. Provision was made for a projection booth for films and slides. But the heart of the building was the 250-seat recital hall, with perfect acoustics even for the most delicate chamber music. The main lobby of the recital hall became an art gallery bathed in natural light from the plastic skylight.

Even as the excavations began in the summer of 1956, we sensed that the building would be outgrown all too quickly; and, indeed, within two years it could not accommodate its audiences. The Slosbergs then provided the necessary support to double its size. The music center, however, never really outgrew its need to expand continuously. One evening, at a special concert, I discovered to my chagrin that, almost lost in the crowded audience, Sam Slosberg and his wife were standing quietly in the overflow at the rear of the recital hall listening intently to the program. I went up to them to apologize. I was stopped short in my apology when Slosberg chuckled, "Apparently the center is getting plenty of use. Let it always be that way, and we won't mind standing." And it always was.

Concerts and festivals, spectacular as they were, nevertheless did not eclipse the unique teaching contribution that Brandeis offered. The department was gratifyingly successful in integrating its academic, scholarly, and performing activities. Every effort was made to provide opportunities for music students to receive advanced instrumental or vocal instruction, even though they were not enrolled in a conservatory. To accommodate them, arrangements were made for private study with highly qualified teachers, usually drawn from the Boston Symphony Orchestra. Music M, as the course was named, kept the quality of vocal or instrumental achievement within the framework of a liberal arts college. Grants-in-aid were allocated on a competitive basis to those who, in an audition before a faculty panel, exhibited unusual talent in performance. No credit was offered for this special instruction. Within a very few years, the department had produced a considerable number of successful professional musicians along with many teacher-scholars who went on to coveted college and university positions.

A gratifying seal of approval for the quality of the music program came when Brandeis awarded William Shumann an honorary degree for his own highly rated compositions. Schumann was usually as austere in his evaluations as he was in his creations, yet he offered the judgment that Brandeis, with its superb faculty, had become in less than ten years one of the best musicological centers in the country.

Art departments, museums, and exhibitions have usually been regarded as the luxury components of a university's table of organization, even in the affluent Ivy League. It was a matter for academic astonishment when, just before the turn of the century, President Eliot endorsed the request of Charles Eliot Norton to offer fully accredited fine arts courses at Harvard, primarily in the history of art. At Brandeis, for reasons already discussed, the creative arts were listed from the outset as an integral part of the course offerings. By our third year we were ready to bring in a teaching artist-in-residence, and we encouraged him to think of his program and its needs as a basic university commitment.

Our artist pioneer was Mitchell Siporin, who had grown up in the poorer sections of Chicago during the Great Depression. Siporin had early demonstrated talent of a high order, but there were few outlets for it when hunger and despair banished consideration of "luxury" pursuits. It was Franklin Roosevelt's imaginative WPA project that first offered employment with dignity and salvaged talents such as Siporin's. His frescoes for the WPA won critical acclaim, and later, in a national competition under the auspices of the Treasury Department, he was commissioned, together with the painter Edward Milman, to execute the frescoes for the Central Post Office in St. Louis. After three years of military service in North Africa and Italy, he won a Prix de Rome in painting in 1949. Soon his forceful expressionist art found its way into the permanent collections of the most prestigious museums in the country. He accepted the Brandeis invitation in 1951, and remembering his earlier experiences as a soldier-artist in North Africa and Italy, he took in stride the makeshift facilities in which he was obliged to teach and paint. The army expression "improvisation in the field" was the order of the day, and studios and lecture halls were established first in the Castle, then in the first-floor offices of the gymnasium. Siporin served as a one-man department, teaching courses in painting and drawing as well as a survey course in the history of art, for which the slides were borrowed from the education department of the Boston Museum of Fine Arts. Borrowed, but not for long. The Brandeis collection now consists of well over a hundred thousand slides and has its own curator.

In contrast to the practice at most eastern universities in the early fifties, Brandeis placed as much emphasis on the making of a work of art as on criticism and historical research. Both studio and history courses were given in the same department, and students were exposed to and participated in the seeing, feeling, and making processes. The faculty was similarly integrated, and artists and scholars worked and planned side by side.

In 1952 a noted art historian, Leo Bronstein, was added to the faculty. He came to Brandeis from the Asia Institute, where he served as an expert in Islamic art. A student of Henri Focillon at the Sorbonne, he seemed an unworldly character, often lost in reverie but remarkably perceptive in his interpretation of the art of many countries and periods. Whether lecturing on Islamic miniature painting, Greek sculpture, or John Singleton Copley, he was an inspired lecturer. Death claimed him at the peak of his influence, but he remained a living presence. A memorial day dedicated to his legend became a university holiday, and it is celebrated with student fervor.

It said something of our determination to expose our students and faculty to every variety of art orientation that at Bronstein's side for two years as visiting professor was Arnold Hauser, a professor at the University of Leeds in England, author of *The Sociology of Art,* and one of the outstanding Marxist interpreters of the history of art. The search for diversity was further emphasized by the later appointments of the Indian scholar Walter Spink, the Sinologist Richard Edwards, the Renaissance scholars Creighton Gilbert and Ludovico Borgo, the medievalist Joachim Gaehde, and Michael Mazur, the director of the workshops in woodcutting, etching, engraving, and printmaking.

Meantime, in 1953, Peter Grippe joined the department, and we were able to add sculpture and graphics to our teaching activities. A native of Buffalo, Grippe's experiences had been similar to Siporin's with the WPA. He was at the heart of the abstract expressionist movement in New York. He had, in fact, headed Stanley Hayter's Atelier 17 at one time and was an able printmaker as well as a ceramist. Our permanent faculty was further strengthened when one of the most generous families of Cleveland, Maurice and Shirley Saltzman, sophisticated art collectors themselves, set up an endowment for the university to invite visiting artists annually for a year of teaching and art guidance.

All through these earlier years, gifts of art were being routed to the university, including valuable works of Stuart Davis, Fernand Leger, Milton Avery, George Grosz, Willem de Kooning, and others. Before we graduated our first class, more than three hundred paintings had arrived, and we hastily organized a Brandeis Art Collection Committee to evaluate the works, both for teaching and for exhibition. These works were stored in the basement of one of the residence halls, and when a raging hurricane (artlessly named Edna) flooded some of our buildings, a portion of our collection suffered water damage. Fortunately, most of the better paintings survived and were satisfactorily restored. But "the act of God" strengthened our conviction that, until we could build at least a modest museum, further gifts would have to be declined. A museum, therefore, went onto our expanding list of priorities. There were murmurs on and off campus about the imprudence of a university in hankering after an art museum when it needed so much else in terms of "basic" commitments. As often before and since, the dilemma was resolved because we followed, loosely to be sure, Thackery's sanguine guideline: "Keep one eye on heaven, and one on the main chance."

The main chance in this case turned out to be the involvement of Edward and Bertha Rose. Rose was a successful New England manufacturer of mattresses for children's cribs. His wife had studied music as a very young woman and was devoted to all the arts. I first became acquainted with Rose when a complicated lawsuit involving patent rights exacerbated the relations between his firm and the giant Simmons Company. After considerable legal fencing, Rose came up with a Solomonic solution. He wrote to the president of Simmons, "Why should we keep quarreling and piling up legal fees? Let us take the amount in dispute and divide it between a Catholic philanthropy that you will name, and a Jewish philanthropy that I will name. In this way the dispute will be amicably resolved to the advantage of causes close to our hearts." The proposal was eagerly accepted by Simmons, who designated a Catholic-sponsored hospital in Connecticut, while Rose named Brandeis.

The gift brought the extra dividend of a warm, personal friendship with the Roses. Edward soon became a trustee of Brandeis, while Bert accepted responsibility as national chairwoman for life memberships in the Women's Committee. I soon came to appreciate the art interest of the Roses and felt I could mention to them Brandeis's need for an adequate museum. Their response was immediate and enthusiastic. They agreed to make provision in their wills not only for an art museum and its complete maintenance but also for an endowment whose income would support exhibitions and scholarships. As our personal friendship deepened and the ties of the Roses to the university strengthened, it seemed appropriate to urge them not to wait for their wills to mature. The university had immediate need for the museum. Besides, I argued, the Roses were both vigorously healthy people and childless. Why should the pleasure of helping to plan the museum be left exclusively to strangers who would get all the gratification that really belonged to those who had spent a long lifetime making the resources available? Once the Roses had agreed, *they* became the impatient prodders. They served as sidewalk superintendents with what can only be described as fastidious passion.

The museum was dedicated in 1961 as part of a major community art festival. It is superbly situated on a rise, with its glass front resembling an illuminated picture after dark. The design is severe, but adaptable. A cantilevered stairway leads from the main, ground-level gallery to the lower level, where there is a decorative pool with a fountain. In the fortnight before examinations, the pool harvests hundreds of pennies thrown in by students as a good luck gesture.

Some years later, on the occasion of their sixtieth wedding anniversary, the Roses underwrote an annex to the museum that doubled its capacity for exhibition, storage, and administration. Before it was completed, Rose had not only covered all the pledges on the original building but had fully financed the additional construction. At the dedication of the annex in 1980, Rose, now eighty-six, bantered with wit and gaiety; none knew that he was to have a serious operation the next morning. When I went to see him at the hospital, he apologized that I would have to do all the talking since he now had only one lung. When I returned to the office, I ordered a five-year diary for him, only because none of the shops had any ten-year ones. Though his stamina never gave out, it could not overcome the ravages of cancer, and it was one of the saddest tasks of my life to deliver the funeral eulogy when he died soon afterward.

Meantime, several years before the museum was built and dedicated, we began recruitment for a teacher-cum-administrator with the special knowledge and skills of a curator. Our first choice was Sam Hunter who, when still in his early twenties, had been an art critic for the *New York Times* and an editor for Harry Abrams, the art publisher. He had taught at Barnard and UCLA and had held curatorial posts at the Museum of Modern Art in New York and at the museum in Minneapolis. Hunter came to us in 1960, just as our program was expanding from its modest beginnings. In developing our art collections, Hunter concentrated on both the French impressionists and avant-garde contemporary works and evaluated the hundreds of art gifts that were offered to the museum. Yet he found time and energy for a succession of critically acclaimed interpretive volumes in his own special fields: modern French painting, modern American painting and sculpture, Picasso and cubism, David Smith, Piet Mondrian, Larry Rivers, and the graphic art of Joan Miró. He brought to Brandeis other important exhibits, including one-man shows by Hans Hofmann, the most luminous of abstract painters, and Franz Kline, and a retrospective of the Belgian surrealist René Magritte. He was chosen to select the works of contemporary American artists to be shown at the Seattle World's Fair, which later came to Brandeis in a special exhibition. In 1965 Hunter could not resist a call to Princeton, and he found there even wider opportunity for his talents as professor of art and archaeology.

When Hunter left the Museum of Modern Art in New York to come to Brandeis, he was succeeded there by William Seitz, who now followed him once again, to Brandeis. Seitz, too, came with an impressive record as a teacher, critic, and art administrator. He had taught at Buffalo and Princeton, where he had been curator of the museum. He was a prodigious worker, himself a practicing artist, and he was a perceptive critic of his personal favorites—Monet, Toulouse-Lautrec, Turner, Mark Tobey, and Arshile Gorky. His volumes received wide acceptance: *The Art of Assemblage, The Art of Israel, Kinetic Art, Sculpture: Its Image in the Arts.* He was constantly asked to direct the mounting of exhibits for universities, museums, and governments. Seitz served as curator for three years and then accepted a post at the University of Virginia.

The museum reached its fullest potential under the innovative guidance of Carl Belz. His entire academic training had been received at Princeton, where he earned his Ph.D. in 1963. After a brief teaching experience at the University of Massachusetts in Amherst, he became director of the Mills College Art Gallery in Oakland, California. He was called to Brandeis for a faculty position in the fine arts department in 1968 and has been at Brandeis ever since, both as teacher and as curator of the Rose Art Museum, the directorship having been assigned to him in 1974. He has been a much respected interpreter of the fine arts through articles and essays that have appeared in the leading art magazines and journals. He has been often invited as a panelist for colloquia sponsored by the National Endowment for the Arts and the Massachusetts Council on the Arts and Humanities. Belz has been frequently sought out as consultant for universities and art museums and for juries planning exhibitions.

Ideal voluntary leadership for the museum came from the unstinting cooperation of Mrs. Lois Foster, who organized the Patrons and Friends of the Museum in 1977. The group grew within a few years to over five hundred members, who have been generous patrons but, even more, have used their influence to interest outstanding families who contribute to the fine arts. A leading staff member described her leadership most perceptively. "Mrs. Foster, as founder and head of the Museum Trustees, combines counsel short of direction with charm and friendly concern, and this elicits a loyalty that is rare." Lois, because of her own interest and that of her husband, Henry Foster, who served for six years as chairman of the Brandeis Board of Trustees, has expanded the exhibition schedule of the museum, including shows by such celebrated artists as Frank Stella and Alex Katz. The Patrons and Friends group has further broadened the museum's lecture program to include noted art authorities such as Thomas Armstrong, director of Whitney Museum, and Kenworth Moffett, curator of 20th Century Art at the Museum of Fine Arts in Boston.

The expectation that an emphasis on the fine arts would multiply its friends and patrons was amply vindicated as soon as the Rose Art Museum had been dedicated and was in full operation. No year passed without gifts of important artworks. They came from friends very close to the university and from total strangers who were impressed by what the art program at Brandeis had become. Through such generous patrons, most of the needed facilities were provided. A teaching center that included imaginatively illuminated studios and an impressive outdoor sculpture court was commissioned by the Goldman and Schwartz families of New York. Our first Canadian gift, from the Pollock family of Quebec, provided an archive for art slides and an auditorium fully equipped for art lectures. One of New York's glass manufacturers and an art collector himself, Albert Dreitzer, in honor of his wife, Mildred, underwrote the conversion of one of the main halls of the Spingold Theater Center into a beautiful art gallery.

In deciding to give a high priority to theater in the curriculum, Brandeis was instituting no revolutionary change; it was really returning to an almost forgotten tradition that linked the theater arts to student life. To be sure, in general universities had relinquished playwriting and performance to the rialto; but never completely, and several fine universities, most notably perhaps Yale, had won high honors as heirs of the old tradition. Brandeis, therefore, was in very good company and it began planning its theater program. It was also ready for the challenge since its sponsoring constituency included some of the most generous of theater patrons. They needed little prodding to join in the adventure; indeed, they took the initiative in urging Brandeis to strive for leadership and not to be unduly concerned about support. The main entrepreneurs of the theater world were quickly drawn in. The stage and screen actor Paul Muni demonstrated his high regard for theater at Brandeis by bequeathing his considerable estate for the program and for scholarship. Leo Jaffe of Columbia Pictures and Samuel Goldwyn and Louis Mayer of Metro-Goldwyn-Mayer set up scholarship and fellowship opportunities and offered their names for fund-raising affairs that generated contributions from hundreds of their colleagues. The most successful New York producer, David Merrick, assigned to our theater program a share of the profits from each of his Broadway productions. The royalties were not insubstantial when they came from such Tony Award hits as *Carousel, Becket, Luther, Hello Dolly, Travesties,* and others. The share from *Gypsy,* based on the burlesque career of Gypsy Rose Lee, was exceptional. Brandeis may have had the only college theater that was subsidized by the popular allure of a strip teaser.

The recruitment of faculty went forward vigorously with the understanding that the program was not to be structured as a theater vocational school. To be sure, there would be training—expert training it was hoped—in designing, directing, and producing. But these technical aspects of theater were to be developed within the framework of a liberal arts curriculum. The first faculty included Howard Bay, who was recruited from Broadway where he was regarded as one of the theater's best designers. He later won a coveted national award for his design of the set of *The Man of La Mancha.* John Matthews was a commuting member of the department. He had to locate his base in New York, for he had earned a solid reputation as a "play doctor." After his skillful revision of *Anastasia,* it had an extraordinarily long run on Broadway. One of his own early plays, *The Scapegoat,* based on *The Trial* by Kafka, won the Arts of the Theater Award just before we invited him to our faculty. He was invaluable to students, for he applied patience and experience to guide their talents in play composition. Martin Halpern, who came to Brandeis in 1965 from the University of Massachusetts, taught the courses in modern and contemporary drama, and he also undertook responsibility for the study of Greek and Roman playwrights. Charles Werner Moore, cited by the League of Professional Theater Schools "as one of the two best acting teachers in the country," was brought in as the anchorman for the acting courses.

A New Jersey industrialist, Irving Laurie, lost a talented daughter, Barbara, who had begun writing for the theater; in her memory, he and his wife underwrote an experimental theater, where plays by students and faculty could be given their first critical tryouts. The theater played an ever more important role in honing the talent of our most gifted students. One of these was Joshua Mostel, who titillated us all during his undergraduate years by his endearing resemblance to his father, Zero, one of the country's most entertaining wits. Joshua went from Brandeis to the innovative Proposition Theater in Cambridge. More recently, he created a cameo role in *Harry and Tonto.* Another Brandeis alumnus in the field was Michael Weller, whose play *Moonchildren* did well off Broadway and in Boston. The *Boston Globe* not only praised the play but made much of the series of "auditions" for a cat to play the major role. Meanwhile, Jeremy Larner, who began his professional career as a novelist, won an Oscar in 1973 for his screenplay of the film *The Manchurian Candidate*. Still another alumnus, Allan Fox, was given a contract in Joseph Papp's Public Theater as a director. The popular and successful cinema personality Barry Newman, as Petrocelli, quickly became a national celebrity.

The recruitment of distinguished faculty and the impressive record of students brought gratifying visibility to Brandeis. But with totally inadequate facilities, the full potential of the theater program could not be achieved. The Ullman Amphitheater served very well for open-air festivals, convocations, and commencements and provided opportunities for ventures in summer theater, enabling us to present well-known American plays. But we were always at the mercy of the capricious New England weather. During our first summer program, we came off well. There were virtually no rainouts, although I well remember otherwise exciting evenings when the temperature, ninety degrees at five or six o'clock, fell to near Siberian depths before the play had ended. In the second year, the Yankee weather gods turned petulant, not only depriving enthusiastic audiences of opportunities to see plays like Christopher Fry's *The Lady's Not for Burning* but creating havoc in box office receipts. Even more frustrating was the inadequacy of Ullman as a teaching center. It was half jocularly referred to as the Brandeis Manhattan Project, for in the early years, all theater teaching was scheduled in the basement of Ullman. To the public, who saw only the exterior, it was a handsome open-air auditorium; but during the school year, especially in the fall and winter when the rolling doors were closed, the teaching proceeded in the windowless, rectangular band shell underneath.

The grim reality remained that Ullman was too small to open to the public. The theater within Ullman saw five major productions a year, and a number of these would have attracted attention if they had been advertised, but such was hardly feasible. The American premiere of Pirandello's *Man, Beast, and Virtue,* staged at Brandeis, attracted some producers who had been informed about it and led to a production of the play in New York, but since Ullman's seating capacity was not enough to accommodate even concerned students and faculty, the public was never informed about it.

It was clear that the full potential of the theater arts could not be attained, and certainly no graduate studies begun, until adequate facilities became available. Each year the hunt for the "angel" became more urgent. At last, at the tenth anniversary of the founding of Brandeis, we could announce that Nate and Frances Spingold, a New York couple who were devoted to the theater and the arts, had become the patrons whom we had sought for so long. Spingold, a Chicagoan, had trained for the law but was early drawn into public relations, and he became a leading member of the William Morris Agency, whose clients included the stars of the cinema and the theater. An early first marriage for Frances ended in divorce; she and Nate Spingold were married in 1911, and they conducted the Madame Frances designers' salon together until it was sold in 1932.

Spingold later joined Columbia Pictures, became its executive vice-president, and helped develop the motion picture as an art form. The couple established homes in New York and in Palm Beach that were also virtual private art galleries. The collections gathered there rated among the best in the country, including French impressionists and works by artists who were experimenting with the newer art forms. In 1957 they made their first visit to Brandeis and were enchanted by its beauty and academic quality. When Spingold died the following year, his will assigned the major portion of his estate to the university, subject to a life interest for Frances, and it was designated for a theater arts center. The legacy came to more than five million dollars, and it therefore became practical to think of facilities not only for theater but also for other performing arts, including dance and film.

The commission to plan the theater was given to Max Abramovitz, and he treated it as an opportunity to provide a model for the performing arts in New England colleges. He outlined his concept in an article that was written for the dedication volume when the Spingold Theater Arts Center was completed. He identified the architectural challenge for a theater that had to combine the traditional requirements of production with teaching and workshop, where all types of performances had to be accommodated. Numerous plans for the shape of the theater had been reviewed—square, rectangular, hexagonal, circular—until the last form was decided upon. Its versatility permitted the various theater and rehearsal spaces to open off the central stage as spokes do from the hub of a wheel. The simple but sturdy materials of brick and concrete were employed throughout the building. When completed, an impressive structure emerged, dominating the west part of the campus and adjacent to the music and art centers.

The main theater was built to seat 750, with a stage that included a hydraulic lift apron. It could serve for proscenium types of production, but also for major lecture events. Special divider doors were provided to combine theater spaces to seat many hundreds more. The main floor also included a flexible theater that could seat up to 350 for arena or theater-in-the-round types of production. As noted, there was also the director's theater, named for Irving Laurie's daughter, seating about 150, for experimental use, the laboratory where graduate and undergraduate students could produce their own plays and have them appraised. A dance studio was included to provide for the possibility of dance and ballet in the expanding curriculum. It was later underwritten by Pepsi-Cola in honor of its president, the motion picture star Joan Crawford, who began her career as a dancer.

In the lower section were other facilities that were to be found only in the most modern theaters. There was a commodious production shop in which to design and construct the settings. There was a whole series of comfortable rooms for regular classroom work and graduate seminars, and there was the traditional Green Room, with facilities for entertaining guest lecturers. Six carrels were in the design as individual study units, and to reaffirm the long association of the theater with the visual arts, space was assigned for a lovely art gallery, accessible from the main entrance lobby. As an aside, it is poignant to recall that an unusual "gift-in-hand" found its way into the walls of Spingold: a section of decorative stonework from a demolished Chicago theater designed by Louis Sullivan, the Boston-born architect and "progenitor" of Frank Lloyd Wright. It is the only physical remnant of Sullivan's own genius to be found in his native Boston.

The Spingold dedication was planned to climax the 1965 commencement. It became a major festival and dramatized the commitment of the university to the creative arts. Eliot Norton, the most respected New England theater critic, wrote: "Some of the older universities are cool to the theater, or even indifferent. . . . Brandeis, aware and alert, and friendly to the arts from the beginning, has made plans to embrace the American Theater with new ardor in what well may be a significant union."

The caliber of the men and women who accepted the invitation to receive honorary degrees as part of the dedication was an index of the importance attached to the occasion. They included Alfred Lunt and Lynn Fontanne, Sir John Gielgud, Brooks Atkinson, George Balanchine, John Ford, William Schuman, Lillian Hellman, Allardyce Nicoll, Richard Rodgers, and Roger Sessions. It was appropriate for such an occasion and in such distinguished company to include Samuel Slosberg, a Brandeis trustee who had been an outstanding patron of music and the creative arts since the university was launched.

Because the dedication represented such a turning point for us, the affairs were arranged for both Friday and Saturday evenings in advance of Sunday's commencement exercises. The informal Friday night affair was held in a gaily decorated tent on campus. The Lunts began the evening, and it was they who set the tone for the whole weekend. In their reply to our invitation to come for degrees and to participate, they had written that they were "not academic people" and unaccustomed to speaking at such "august" proceedings. Might they, instead, offer a reading, perhaps a mini-scene, based on a best-selling biography of Oliver Wendell Holmes, *A Yankee from Olympus,* that had become a Broadway hit? Lunt took the role of Justice Brandeis, and Lynn Fontanne took the part of Mrs. Holmes. It almost goes without saying that their rendition all but brought the tent down. I had read the book and remembered the scene where Mrs. Holmes stands by the window of her apartment and, looking out, remarks wryly that Washington is full of brilliant men "and the women they married when they were very young." This evening, as on the stage, the line had been omitted, and I took the liberty, when Miss Fontanne resumed her place at the table, to ask why such a pungent evaluation had not been included. "Oh," she responded, "I always thought it was too bitchy."

We hardly dared to ask Sir John Gielgud to follow. His very presence had been a scheduling cliffhanger for us all week, and we imagined that he would welcome just sitting back and relaxing. He had been starring for months on Broadway in Edward Albee's *Tiny Alice.* The play's run was drawing to a close, but there was uncertainty as to the exact date of the last performance. If it ran through the Saturday of our preliminary functions, Sir John could fly up only for Sunday to receive his degree. We were in luck; *Tiny Alice* ended its run midweek, and we learned on Friday morning that Sir John could be with us that evening and would stay on through the dedication of the theater and the commencement exercises. At one point during that busy day, Marylou Buckley, who on special university occasions served as both right and left hand of my staff, wandered in and remarked that, though it was an imposition to ask a performing artist who was an honored guest to "do a turn," wouldn't it be even ruder if the immortal Sir John were allowed simply to sit there when the Lunts were offering their talent? A point well taken, but what can one ask of an artist who has just finished an exhausting assignment? But I remembered having seen Gielgud on an otherwise undistinguished holiday television special when he had simply read a poem ("recited" is an inadequate verb) by A. E. Housman, "Summertime on Bredon." I had asked that a copy be prepared so that I would have it available on Friday if it seemed appropriate to ask Gielgud to participate in the program.

When the Lunts finished their scene from *A Yankee from Olympus,* there was a slight interval after the applause died down. I took the Housman poem from my prepared packet and looked hopefully towards Sir John. Might he, perhaps? The greatest Hamlet of our time politely pushed away the typed copy. He had won his first scholarship to the Royal Academy of Dramatic Art with a reading of that poem, he said, and often had "given it to the troops" when he had appeared at far-flung British military installations during World War II. "They liked it, you know. Maybe this audience will too." And he proceeded, from memory, to give us Housman's lyrics. There was scarcely a dry eye in the house, including Gielgud's, and this time the hush came before the applause.

The upbeat mood continued on Saturday night. Brooks Atkinson and Sam Slosberg led off, each recalling that they had marched in a Harvard commencement procession forty years earlier, and Allardyce Nicoll entertained with witty anecdotes about Sir John Gielgud's early career. It was, however, George Balanchine who gave the evening its merriest moments. In his inimitable Russian accent, uncorrupted by decades of life in the United States, he confessed his bewilderment at receiving an honorary degree. What had he done to deserve it? He told us how, in his youth in Russia, ballerinas were uniformly small and pleasingly plump, both before and aft, "so that, when they walked in their tutus, they looked like two little boys fighting!" His chief contribution, he concluded, was to develop long-stemmed, decidedly unplump ballerinas, and that must be why he was getting a degree.

At his own request, we had left John Ford for the end of the program. Ford was a bluff, rough-hewn, totally independent character who wore his evening clothes as if they were a cowboy costume, his raffish appearance enhanced by the black patch that covered one eye, the elastic of which ruffled his sandy, graying hair. He held an unchallenged place in the history of the American motion picture and had been associated with Nate Spingold from the early days of the industry. None of us was prepared for what followed. "Thee-ay-ter and the Per-forming Arts!" he drawled, "formerly Show Biz and the Movies!" He picked up the remembrance of Slosberg and Atkinson and their commencement at Harvard forty years before and noted that he, too, might have participated. He had been admitted to Harvard, which he never named, calling it only "another school not far away as the crow flies," but, after only five days as a freshman, had been asked "to take his academic achievements elsewhere." Only the football coach had gone down to Porter Square in the dawn to see him off in a boxcar going west. I hope it is not anticlimactic to add that, just after the commencement exercises the next day, he teasingly chided me for inaccurate research in his honorary degree citation where he was listed with a lower admiral's rank than he had earned by the time he was mustered out of the navy after World War II. Contritely, I offered to take back the citation and have it reprinted correctly. Ford, his one good eye twinkling mischievously, hugged to his chest the citation in its leather folder and said, "Dr. Sachar, no one, but no one, is ever going to get this degree away from me." My last glimpse of him that day was of his chivalrous flirtation with enchanted junior members of the staff, asking "where a fella could hear Mass around here," and being directed to the Bethlehem Chapel. I suppose we might have considered installing a plaque saying that the man who made *The Informer* and had created a cinematic history of American naval warfare in World War II had knelt there. Ford remained a volubly loyal friend of the university, often hosting dinners for us on the West Coast and speaking with pride of his "foster alumni plumage."

The dedication over, all energies were now directed toward the inauguration of a graduate program when the new school year opened in the fall. The program leading to Master of Fine Arts degrees in acting, design, or playwriting had been approved, the faculty had been increased, classes had been scheduled, actors hired, a season of well-regarded productions promised. Only the exterior of the theater building, however, was really completed. Veterans of summer stock, two-week repertory, and Broadway openings are fanatical about meeting deadlines, and they remained unfazed by obstacles, even those that border on calamity. The department members, therefore, entered the building under showers of sparks from the welders and set to work. The construction foreman, appalled at the risks they were taking, allowed occupation of each section of the building only when sudden death seemed at least a few yards distant. The distinguished actor Morris Carnovsky, who had joined the Brandeis faculty, rounding out a brilliant performing career, was to direct the premiere production. As part of the plan to develop first-rate training, he had hand-picked a full company of seasoned, professional actors. There they stood on the main stage, calmly rehearsing *Volpone* as if for the silent screen, their voices utterly lost in the Niagara of construction noise. There was not yet place to prepare costumes, no area free in which to paint scenery, and now, because of the general chaos, no possibility of carrying through the original plan for the whole season of plays. To make matters worse, the appointed theater manager failed to materialize.

As it turned out, James Clay, one of the theater faculty's directors, took over the manager's job while teaching a full load of classes and "winged" it through the first season. Beyond the expectations of even the most hopeful optimists, the season opened on schedule, and the curtain rose on a first-night audience of more than a thousand who came to salute the new resource for the theater arts in New England. Included were John Volpe, governor of Massachusetts, John Gassner of the Yale School of Drama, and Joseph Papp, who had pioneered the popular Shakespeare Theater in New York. Donald Cragin of the *Herald* praised Carnovsky's performance as "the marvelous trouper leading the troupe." The hard-to-please critic of the *Boston Globe,* Kevin Kelly, wrote: "The production is worth its weight in Volpone's gold."

Other openings could not be announced with more confidence. Carnovsky's favorite role was *King Lear,* which he performed to perfection annually to climax the Shakespeare festival in Stratford, Connecticut. The play was billed as part of our first season's offerings at Spingold. Carnovsky preferred an audience for his dress rehearsals, more especially what he called a "schools' audience," that is, young people of high school age and even younger. This information reached my office belatedly, but members of my staff, Marylou Buckley and Larry Kane, in spite of a blizzard, conjured up a full house of high school and junior high school children and of Jesuit seminarians from nearby Weston. For many of the youngsters, this was not only a free night out at the theater but their first introduction to Shakespeare.

Jim Clay was to spend another quarter of a century "winging" matters in Spingold. He had come to us in 1960, not long out of graduate school at the University of Illinois. An actor himself, he taught at both undergraduate and graduate levels, helped to develop the M.F.A. program, wrote prodigiously, directed between forty and fifty productions, both student and professional, over the years, and along the way composed the occasional song or score. He was the heart of our theater faculty until death claimed him in the fall of 1990.

By 1967 the Spingold performances had earned such critical commendation that the newly established National Endowment for the Arts offered its coveted support. The Foundation made a grant to mount a play by Don Peterson, *Does the Tiger Wear a Necktie?* whose theme was the terrifying problem of drug addicts. Peterson had taught in a rehabilitation center for addicts in New York, and he was writing from his own life experiences. His prize-winning script had been chosen from more than two hundred that had been submitted for the Bishop Award of the American National Theater and Academy. Its premiere at Spingold was an augury of what the future held. Eliot Norton saw the play as an example of "what can be done by a combination of government, university, and the professional theater, all acting in concert." The drama critic for *Newsweek* wrote: "While the American university's contribution to theater has been as superficial as a flick of grease-paint, ... the tradition is now changing. Some change is already visible, from UCLA to Ohio State University, from Boston's Brandeis to the University of Michigan, where new drama buildings are already open or on the rise."

Michael Murray, the Blanche, Barbara and Irving Laurie Adjunct Professor of Theater Arts and director of the theater arts program, came to Brandeis in 1986. Under his direction, the program has attracted scores of talented students who have gone on to gain international reputations.

CHAPTER ELEVEN

The Social Sciences

Perhaps the liveliest faculty were in the social sciences, a reality only to be expected. The sociologists, the historians, the political scientists, and the economists were involved in the gut issues of this turbulent period, and the psychologists and anthropologists turned into very different breeds from earlier generations and joined the activists for whom the campus was a staging area.

After World War II, the sociologists were not only lively; they were explosive. Comparatively new and marginally respectable, their discipline was fighting for recognition in the academic hierarchy. The operative mode was to reexamine the sanctions of society with no sentimentality, no inhibitions, and no obligation to tradition. It inevitably attracted individuals whose temperaments and dispositions were best fulfilled when they were critical of the status quo. Any one of them could have been the anonymous author of the forgivable pun from the Cynic's Calendar, "Contentment is the smother of invention." Auden had suggested an eleventh commandment, "Thou shalt not commit Sociology." We knew very well that we were opening the doors and windows, too, to all kinds of persistent gadflies when we determined at the outset to include a sociology department in our table of organization. From the point of view of the originality and competence of the teams that we brought together, there could be no question that our choices were of a high order. David Riesman, the author of the *Lonely Crowd* and the doyen of sociologists, rated the department in the 1950s, in relation to its size, as one of the most stimulating in the country.

Our first sociologist, Lewis Coser, joined the faculty in 1951. Born in Germany and brought up just as Hitler was coming to power, he sought refuge in France and completed undergraduate studies at the Sorbonne. But he found no comfort there either: The country was already in the grip of the Nazi collaborationists. He resettled in the United States in 1941, supporting himself and a growing family with precariously held minor teaching jobs until he was naturalized in 1948. He was then offered an instructorship at the University of Chicago, which he held for two frustrating years. His outlook must have been influenced by the harassments he endured in his early years in Hitler's Europe. He concluded that only more prestigious academic titles could impress the "bureaucrats" who controlled the universities; hence, between occasional jobs in the New York area, he enrolled at Columbia where he stretched out nearly a decade to earn his doctorate.

When he came to the United States, Coser was a prolific writer and already well known as a leading interpreter of social conflicts. He was a maverick in his views of American life and its social system and became one of the editors of *Dissent*. At Brandeis, he was able to give full play to his research and writing, and a steady stream of volumes brought him much distinction. After he reached emeritus status in 1968, he mellowed considerably. His *Refugee Scholars in America*, published in 1985, placed the American haven for émigrés in an appreciative perspective. But for many years prior to his retirement from the faculty, university governance was one of his favorite targets, and he gave me and my administrative colleagues many opportunities to savor the full meaning of Shelley's ode: "I fall upon the thorns of life: I bleed." The continuing battle was not personal. Coser had no quarrel with me other than that I was an administrator. In his later volumes, he summarized his views of the rebellious intellectual's role in contemporary society: In the industrialized twentieth century, an intellectual was an alien and alienated. If he compromised, he was lost. If he fought back, he could take comfort in knowing that he was at least bloodying the enemy. He despaired of ever winning. If, to make a living, he joined government, the civil service, or a university faculty, he resignedly accepted the role of a voice crying in the wilderness. As an intellectual, therefore, Coser had to be in opposition.

During less combative moments, Coser may have admitted that abstract criticism could not solve practical problems when there was a world of building and creating to do, but this point was never conceded. It was safer for a censorious temperament to be critical within the framework of the security created by the very forces that it was his duty to excoriate. He thus stayed on; indeed, he remorsefully enjoyed one of the longest incumbencies—eighteen years. He was determined, he often said, not to give in, for conscience had a duty to defend principle. But when the tax-supported university at Stony Brook was created in the New York system and positions were offered to both him and his wife, he yielded to the fleshpots of the suburbs. His last salvos were contained in a volume *Men and Ideas,* which reflected his umbrage over the sorry plight of the incorruptible intellectual in a system that used the term free enterprise but was really a trap for honest men.

Soon we were ready for another appointment, and Coser highly recommended a young instructor, Maurice Stein, who had apparently performed satisfactorily in a junior capacity at Dartmouth and Oberlin. He was a loyal protégé of Coser, and the volumes that he wrote while at Brandeis reflected his mentor's social orientation. In 1960 he published *Eclipse of Community* and *Identity and Anxiety*. A few years later, he followed with *Blue Print for Counter Education*. The difficulties he encountered in obtaining tenure approval from his colleagues, who judged his scholarship as thin, and the blasting that his volumes received in the journals of sociology, made him wonder whether he perhaps belonged in some other area. He accepted a two-year assignment as dean of critical studies in the newly organized California Institute of the Arts in Burbank. I was amused when, after a year as dean, dealing with the problems that he encountered between the Scylla of trustees and the Charybdis of faculty, he asked to see me while I was on tour on the West Coast. There he was quite sheepish about his earlier unappreciative evaluation of Brandeis and relieved that he had not burned his bridges, for he had taken a leave of absence rather than offering his resignation. He returned to Brandeis somewhat subdued, perhaps now with a glimmer of realization that great institutions cannot be built without combining the strength of the mortar and the hatchet.

Other faculty members were added as the university expanded and as the appeal of sociology grew among the students. One of these, Kurt Wolff, also a German émigré, had spent the earlier years of Hitler in Italy. He migrated to the United States in 1939. After a number of teaching posts at Southern Methodist, Earlham, and Ohio State, he came to Brandeis in 1959. His course in the sociology of knowledge, where he drew upon his impressive erudition in German and recent American literature, was a tour de force.

In their technical tasks as teachers, these men ranked high and were often called upon for papers at their learned societies; but, almost invariably, they joined Coser, Stein, and Maurice Schwartz, a national authority in medical sociology, as institutional scolds. It was now almost impossible for an applicant to be considered who would not fit into the pattern that had been set. By 1960, though some of us had wakened to the infiltration that was taking place, it was too late to stop the process. This fact became even clearer when the department recommended Everett Hughes, former editor of the *American Sociological Review*. Hughes had been at Chicago for more than a quarter of a century, and since it was one of the most liberal institutions in the country, the sociologists under Hughes had taken fullest advantage of its hospitable climate. At Brandeis, surrounded by compatible colleagues who welcomed many of his fractious premises, Hughes looked forward to respected political and social years in a critic's paradise. After he reached the age of retirement, he gladly accepted the invitation of his former colleagues to return every few years as a visiting professor.

Anthropology was a blood brother of sociology: Indeed, in many universities the two were joined in one department. It, too, was obligated to study societies with the detachment of surgeons and usually on the principle that all forms of social organization and behavior are relative. Since there were no absolutes, no immutable social patterns, there was no shock in determining that present systems, forms, and attitudes, however deeply intertwined in the social system, were subject to critical scrutiny and to change. But when Robert Manners was invited from the University of Rochester to launch the discipline at Brandeis in 1952, he interpreted his role very differently from that of his colleagues in sociology. Manners's earlier fieldwork had been among the American Indians of northern Arizona, Utah, and eastern California and had resulted in important ethnohistorical monographs. His main research, however, concentrated on primitive African communities and on the Caribbean world. His colleagues thought highly enough of his competence to name him editor of the *North American Anthropologist,* the official anthropological journal. Manners, too, was a political activist and must have found himself very much at home amid censorious left-wingers on the faculty, but he never permitted his political views to influence his recommendations for faculty. He nominated men and women of every point of view: Elizabeth Colson, a senior colleague, and younger scholars of promise—Helen Codere, David Kaplan, George Cowgill, Benson Saler, Robert Hunt. All performed solidly and worked their way to national prominence.

We were fortunate that we could launch our economics department with a nationally distinguished incumbent, Svend Laursen. This tall, handsome, urbane, pipe-smoking Dane came with an impressive record both in writing and in public service. He had been on the staff of the United Nations International Monetary Fund in Washington and was a senior economist and economic attaché at the Office of Strategic Services in the State Department. He was valued as an expert on fiscal controls and was given leave for a year to set up the monetary system of the newly established government of Pakistan. He had been widely published on monetary problems, especially in the scholarly journals of his native Denmark, and had degrees from the University of Copenhagen and the London School of Economics. His doctorate was earned at Harvard on a Rockefeller fellowship. He began his teaching career at Williams and then came to us. He was our sole economist until we had completed the first undergraduate academic cycle. As the university grew, he began intensive recruitment, and he was able to persuade some of the ablest economists in the country to throw in their lot with us. To our sorrow, he died suddenly in early middle age.

Anne Carter came to Brandeis in 1971 and was named to the Fred C. Hecht Chair in Economics in 1976. She has written extensively on input-output analysis or techniques and served as dean of the faculty from 1981 to 1986.

Through the years, there were a number of other fine scholars, representing widely different fields, who came into the economics faculty. One of the most popular among them was the Sovietologist Joseph Berliner. He came in 1963, by which time the department had pretty well gelled. He added considerable distinction to the small but tightly knit group that included Louis Lefeber, Romney Robinson, Richard Weckstein, Trenery Dolbear, Gerald Rosenthal, Thomas Sowell, Barney Schwalberg, Robert Evans, Jr., and others. They were of a caliber that could easily have offered and directed graduate studies, but we had to wait for donors to provide adequate fellowship support and library offerings. When the International Center was constructed, I was pleased that a special wing was added through the generosity of the Bostonians, Edward and Sade Goldstein, and that the economics department could move into it.

Peter Petri, Carl Shapiro Professor of International Finance, came to Brandeis in 1972. Under his guidance, the Lemberg Program in International Economics and Finance, offering an innovative master's degree program, has become one of the finest in the country.

We began building our politics department around the appointment of Max Lerner. As earlier noted, he was more of a presence than an incumbent. Lerner could give us only a day or two each week, and usually for only one semester in each year, for he doubled as a columnist for the *New York Post* and each year traveled on foreign assignments. He could not, therefore, take on responsibilities that required sustained attendance. We always regretted that during his quarter century at the university he could not undertake the guidance of graduate students in doctoral research; nevertheless, whatever concessions were made to fit his schedule seemed worthwhile, for he was a brilliant lecturer, and his courses were invariably sought out. His wide contacts also helped immensely in recruiting faculty and in persuading world figures to visit the campus either for Education S., in whose direction he collaborated with me, or as permanent members of the faculty.

The most influential and widely known of the social scientists was Herbert Marcuse. It is virtually impossible to catalogue Marcuse, for he was a remarkably versatile scholar, equally at home in politics, sociology, and philosophy. Like so many of his colleagues, he was an émigré, fleeing Hitler's Germany in 1934. He taught at Columbia and Harvard and joined the Brandeis faculty in 1954 when the first graduate schools were established. The secret of his appeal to young people could not have been in his teaching manner or in his writing style. He spoke ponderously, the convoluted German syntax carried over into English. John Roche observed that Marcuse's platform style would more quickly empty a hall of radicals than fill one. His writing was equally turgid and prolix. One critic said that the relationship of his thought and his written English was like that of a horse to a hurdle. Yet he stimulated students everywhere, undoubtedly because his criticism of the social structure fitted so perfectly the frustration of young people in the 1960s. Marcuse dressed up all the disenchantment in Freudian and Marxian terms. He was contemptuous of free speech, treating it as a hypocritical ploy by the power group who used it as a form of repression. He became a guru for the offbeat youth movements that had set up Mao Tse-tung and Ché Guevara as idols, and his volumes were a staple for contemporary radical writers and political activists. He stayed at Brandeis for twelve years, leaving only because of mandatory retirement.

Meantime, the politics department filled up rapidly, mainly with younger people who brought vigorous teaching to their classes and a stimulating climate of social awareness to the whole university community. John Roche, whose influence has been noted earlier, was a prolific writer, but he gave considerable time to teaching and to administration as an early dean of faculty and chairman of the Faculty Senate.

I. Milton Sacks was another welcome member of the department. A rough-and-tumble character, Sacks was brought up in the Bronx in the poverty and social distress of the Depression. He took his undergraduate work at the City College of New York and his doctorate at Yale. He came to Brandeis in 1955, just as we were completing requirements for accreditation. He specialized in the problems of Southeast Asia and was to qualify more and more often as a government consultant. He made frequent visits to Asia and, on special grants, would teach both at the universities of Hue and Saigon when each was torn by civil war. Sacks was utterly devoted to Brandeis, and in the early 1960s I had enough confidence in him to ask him to take the onerous assignment of dean of students. His deanship coincided with a time when student protest arose mainly from personal issues rather than from larger humane and social concerns. The product of an environment where the necessities of life, let alone its comforts, were painfully won, Sacks had a short fuse for adolescent silliness. When some students, few if any having earned the purchase price of their secondhand automobiles, rebelled against his parking regulations, Milton simply blew up. This reaction did not diminish his popularity as a teacher, however.

Even the most easily swayed detractors among the students admitted, as one of the yearbooks acknowledged, that to "drop your pen or pencil in Sacks' class meant that you've lost a month's information before you pick it up." His short fuse, too, did not affect his standing with his colleagues. He was elected by them to serve as the faculty representative on the Board of Trustees, and he had the longest tenure of anyone as head of the Faculty Senate.

There were other carefully selected appointments in these combative years of growth, and an exceptionally strong department emerged. It included Roy Macridis, a young scholar of Greek origin with an expert knowledge of contemporary Europe and especially of French politics. His volumes on Charles de Gaulle grew out of his intimate friendship with many of the men around the general. Donald Hindley was well versed in the problems of the South Pacific, and he wrote the definitive history of the Communist party of Indonesia. Lawrence Fuchs began with general history but branched off to head a special division that we organized for American civilization, combining politics and history. He is the Meyer and Walter Jaffe Professor in American Civilization and Politics. An expert on immigration, he is serving as acting chair of the U.S. Commission on Immigration Reform and has received awards for his latest book, *The American Kaleidoscope: Race, Ethnicity and the Civic Culture.*

George Kelly covered contemporary international politics and brought home to his students the danger of adopting a dogmatic ideological stance in the post-World War II period, when it was impossible to establish an international security system. Peter Woll was concerned with the politics of American public policy and the influence of conflicting subsystems in its shaping. Kenneth Waltz combined the study of political theory, reaching back to the heritage of the ancient Greeks, with problems of national security in the crises that have faced the United States since World War II. His unusual scholarly competence and his dynamic teaching approach earned him the assignment of the Adlai Stevenson Chair. We deeply regretted his loss when he left Brandeis for a professorship at the University of California. In 1963, Ruth Schachter Morgenthau, who was assigned the vacated Stevenson Chair, came to us from Boston University with a superb reputation in African politics. She has participated in many official international organizations and served as an American representative to the U.N. I should note that when she married Henry Morgenthau III, then part of our administrative staff and manager of our communications program, the wedding was performed in the Berlin Chapel with Henry's father, the former secretary of the treasury, sitting near the ark, trying to cope with a skullcap, and with Mrs. Roosevelt smiling benignly at him and the bridal couple from her seat in a front pew.

There were a good number of young faculty to round out the department, tough individualists holding tenaciously to their ideological positions but with deep respect for the views of their colleagues. All of them were eager to be called on by the government for counsel in their specialization, and most of them were. They used their sabbaticals or were given leaves of absence to fulfill such responsibilities in Washington or in foreign lands.

There were sentimental as well as practical reasons for giving high priority to the building of a strong Department of History. My association with superb teachers at Washington University, Harvard, and Cambridge had launched me into the field professionally, and all my writing had been related to history. I knew personally many of the creative people in the field, and I was sure they would be willing to help us in recruiting able young scholars. In the beginning years, we concentrated on American history. The first major appointment went, as indicated in an earlier chapter, to Leonard Levy, whose impact not only in the Department of History but in the development of the university itself was pivotal.

Levy was soon reinforced by the appointment of a young Kansan, Merrill Peterson, who had done his undergraduate work at the University of Kansas and then gone on to Harvard for his graduate work. Peterson was a low-keyed, deliberate, circumspect, laconic personality, and he may have been a little bewildered by the intense, uninhibited type of student and faculty colleagues with whom he had to deal. When in 1955 an invitation came from Princeton for him to join the faculty there, he responded. After three years, however, he was eager to return. "It's good to be home again," he said. He was named to the recently established Harry S. Truman Chair in American history. By then he had sufficiently adjusted to the climate at Brandeis to warrant his collateral appointment as dean of students. In conformity with our policy of encouraging administrative officials who emerged from the faculty to retain some teaching assignments, Peterson continued to conduct a seminar. These were highly productive years for him and his students. His volume *The Jefferson Image in American History* won the Bancroft prize in history and the Gold Medal of the Thomas Jefferson Memorial Foundation. He remained at Brandeis until 1962 when a call came from the University of Virginia to head their Department of American History, a call he could not resist since Virginia was the nation's acknowledged center for Jeffersonian studies.

The Truman Chair then went to Marvin Meyers who came to us from the University of Chicago; within a year he was assigned the chairmanship of the department. He had earlier won the Dunning prize of the American Historical Society for his work in America's eighteenth century, and at Brandeis he found the time between teaching and other research to edit *The Sources of the American Republic*. In 1950 an invitation was extended to Henry Steele Commager whose incumbency as visiting professor meant much more than a teaching assignment, for he was an invaluable counselor for a school just setting its foundations. He gladly joined our unofficial cabinet who, at fairly regular intervals, a group of us, including Lewisohn, Cohen, Cheskis, and later Fine, Roche, and Rawidowicz, would take lunch informally, not only to discuss problems but to spin dreams.

Along with Lawrence Fuchs, another promising young scholar was added to round out the offerings in American history, David Hackett Fischer. Hackett Fischer's latest book, *Albion's Seed: Four British Folkways in America,* received awards and international attention for its unique perspective on the tie between American and British culture. Soon the courses had multiplied so substantially and the teaching of literature, economics, urban studies, and related fields had become so intertwined that it was determined to reorganize this area and make it interdisciplinary, offering graduate as well as undergraduate studies. It was given a special autonomy of its own under the general rubric of American civilization. Apart from maintaining the high caliber of its faculty, there was a later development to support graduate students concentrating on American studies. Through the generosity of Irving and Rose Crown of Chicago, a major, twenty-year trust fund was established that provided ten fully supportive graduate fellowships annually, with assurance of renewal when needed. I jubilantly wired the chairman of the board that "I had just made off with the Crown jewels," and noted that such a gift, establishing one of the best-funded graduate programs in the country, would guarantee a steady flow of talent that would probably be destined for university teaching or government service or diplomacy. At the end of the twentieth year, the Crown Fellowship Fund substantially increased and extended for another twenty-five years.

Saul Touster, another distinguished faculty member, who holds a J.D., came to Brandeis in 1979. He developed the Legal Studies Program, a popular course of study, which has attracted students who are preparing for any number of different careers, introducing them to law through a variety of perspectives. He served as councillor to Acting University President Stuart Altman, 1990–1991, and held the Joseph M. Proskauer Chair in Law and Social Welfare before his retirement in 1993. Stephen Whitfield, the Max Richter Professor of American Civilization, who received his doctorate from Brandeis in 1972, has published numerous books for which he has received awards and is greatly esteemed for his teaching skills by students who flock to his classes.

During the first two years, our offerings in European history were minimal. A highly encouraging start was made in the appointment of Frank Manuel, who had completed brilliant graduate years at Harvard but for whom only a part-time position had opened. For more than ten years thereafter, he had filled government positions but never for long, and he was eager to return to academia. He was brought to my attention by a loyal supporter of the university, attorney Paul Smith, who happened to be Manuel's brother-in-law. I agreed to meet with Manuel. The interview was most satisfying. He was obviously a very gifted man, learned, articulate, profound, and refreshingly witty. His sharp tongue and quick temper may have been the product of a severe physical disability: He had lost a leg in a war-related misfortune. The university never made a more fortunate and mutually advantageous commitment. Manuel turned out to be one of the two or three most stimulating members of the faculty and a most productive and respected scholar. His studies and biographies on the eighteenth-century mind were extraordinarily well reviewed by his peers.

During the next few years, offerings were continually added with parallel faculty augmentation. Eugene Black was brought in for the courses in Western civilization and for his own specialization, modern British history. Marie Boas, a niece of the world-famous Franz Boas and herself an authority on Robert Boyle and seventeenth-century chemistry, was added to introduce the students to the history of science and the scientists who both enriched and shook up their generations. In 1954 we welcomed Paul Alexander, a German émigré, who had taught briefly at Harvard and then for ten years at Hobart. He was a Byzantine scholar, and he strengthened our offerings considerably in medieval history. For a few years he served as chairman of the department. Almost simultaneously we invited George Fischer, a specialist in Soviet history, to come to us. Fischer's volume *Soviet Russia Today* was adopted as an authoritative text in universities across the country, and Harvard's Houghton Library assigned him to arrange, catalogue, and analyze the private papers of Leon Trotsky.

I cannot close this section without emphasizing the special role of one of our most fortunate choices of the 1960s, Morton Keller, whose earlier teaching had been done at the University of Pennsylvania. He came to us with an impressive research record, which was substantially augmented in his years at Brandeis where he gave further strength to our offerings in nineteenth- and twentieth-century American history. His formal historical research augured well for his future as a distinguished authority in his special field, but he moved beyond the confines of his department and cooperated enthusiastically in the exploration of a program in legal studies. This undergraduate program, which was part of our academic master plan, was not for students who were on their way to law school; rather it explored the role of the law in a democratic society while introducing students to the discipline of legal thinking, a prime asset for a career in many related fields. Since we already had on our faculty distinguished scholars who were offering courses that could easily be organized as a nucleus for such a program, it seemed a natural development for enriching our social sciences.

In the final months of my incumbency, I invited Professor Harry Kalven, Jr., of The University of Chicago Law School to meet with sixteen members of our faculty, drawn mainly from the social sciences, to discuss the viability of such a program. His report heartily endorsed the concept. He wrote to me in May 1968 that "the law schools, despite their intellectual strengths, do not exhaust the intellectual interest of law as a subject matter; I suspect they do not because they are professional schools. . . . The trick therefore is to somehow marry the professionalism and rigor and expertise of the professional law school world with the breadth of interest and humane concerns of the non-law-school world. For a variety of reasons, Brandeis would appear an ideal place at which to explore the possibilities of such a marriage. It is a young, vital and ambitious school in which new ideas and change are still readily available. It has a deep concern with American life and society. It appears to have a serious intellectual student body."

My incumbency ended in September 1968, and my successor Morris Abram, himself a noted lawyer, was much more interested in a professional law school that concentrated on advanced legal research. Besides, funding was a major problem during the administrative transition when two presidents served brief terms. Nevertheless, the idea of legal studies as an undergraduate concentration, within the framework of the social sciences, was not abandoned. Early in the administration of Marver Bernstein, a task force went back to the Kalven memorandum and suggested an imaginative interdisciplinary program that "would allow all interested undergraduates to study the interplay of law and society in the classic context of a liberal arts education."

After clearance with the appropriate faculty committees, the new program was modestly launched since, without assured financial support, it had to depend on faculty drawn from history, politics, philosophy, sociology, and psychology. In 1975, however, with the fortunate intercession of Jacob Goldfarb, I was able to persuade the former solicitor general of New York, Nathaniel Goldstein, and his fellow trustees of the Lester Martin Foundation to allocate a quarter of a million dollars, and the project now had a measure of security. A few specialists were added to the core faculty, mainly visiting luminaries who were intrigued by their involvement, and the program bearing the identification of Law and Society drew steadily increasing enrollment.

One of my greatest satisfactions in the presidency was the teaching assignment that I undertook for a course in contemporary history, open to advanced undergraduates. It was scheduled as a two-hour weekly session, with an assistant to take the third hour for supplementary assignments and quizzes. I knew that the responsibility would entail endless inconvenience since my travel schedule was always exceptionally heavy. I determined, however, never to cut away completely from teaching, not only because I wanted to retain a direct relationship with students but also as a welcome relief from the often tiring routines of "administrivia." I succeeded in structuring my schedule to ensure my presence during class hours, and when a commitment in the Midwest or on the West Coast had to be fulfilled the night before, I often took the night plane home so as to be on hand for the class.

Since I was teaching about personalities and events that followed World War I, I added an optional hour to the class schedule to show documentary films that dealt with the classroom assignments. A whole series of such documentaries had been developed by the major television networks. We had many devoted friends in the industry, and the films were readily made available to us. I realized that history as recorded by television technicians could not be taught with the scholarly discipline that credit courses demanded; but I believed it was important for the students to watch the great historic personalities in action, to know them better than could be possible from the best written texts or the most carefully prepared lectures. The films were not meant to substitute for historic analysis; they were supplements, to give more reality to the personalities we were dealing with. What could take the place of actually hearing Churchill in the House of Commons, defying Hitler after Dunkirk, or seeing Nehru and Jinnah as they watched the lowering of the Union Jack and the raising of the flags in India and Pakistan at the moment of their nations' independence. The experiment was successful beyond all my expectations. Very few students left when the lecture was completed, and many visitors joined their classmates for the films.

Few of us who began planning for the area of psychology, even before Brandeis had earned its accreditation, imagined that within less than a decade the curricular offerings would include the whole field of clinical, experimental, comparative, and social psychology. There were no misconceptions that such breadth of coverage, from the elementary principles of psychology to the most diverse theoretical and experimental areas of associationism, structuralism, functionalism, behaviorism, and scores of their modern derivatives, would not require massive budgets for both teaching and for the necessary facilities. These concerns rarely arose because, as in other of the Brandeis ventures, there was faith that the program would produce the support. What did create apprehension was that a faculty of strong-minded individualists, often in tough ideological disagreements with their colleagues, might not exercise sufficient discipline and cooperative resilience to work together as a team.

Much of the credit for creating a climate of amicable dissidence belongs to two men, Abraham Maslow and Ricardo Morant, who had the most to do with developing the program and who, between them, chaired it for twenty years. Maslow came in 1951 with an impressive reputation, leaving a secure post at Brooklyn College. Underlying all his interpretations of psychology, especially in dealing with motivation, was his concentration on the values that came from the best and noblest spirits, men and women who, in his words, had "wonderful possibilities and inscrutable depths." In later years, he referred to his motivation approach as the psychology of "self-esteem." His dominant approach was to study personality, searching for the most estimable motives and holding these up for guidance. He attempted to have this method applied in every field of human endeavor, hoping to evoke the finest qualities of men and women by teaching them to avoid the excuses of poor environment, wretched luck, or unfortunate decisions. Explaining, urging, encouraging wherever he could—in class, on the conference platform, or in counseling business and professional groups—he became a powerful activist force.

Maslow brought in Morant in 1952 to develop the experimental aspects of the psychology curriculum and to plan what was to become an innovative graduate program based on the premise that advanced students should be treated as colleagues and research collaborators. Morant was a young scholar of Spanish origin who had just earned his doctorate at Clark University and was deep in his studies on space perception and body orientation. His experimental approach complemented Maslow's humanistic ideas, and since each was personally devoted to the other, they formed an ideal pioneering team.

Psychology, one of the first departments to add graduate studies, soon expanded into the largest department in the university. It included many of the divisions of social psychology, child psychology and development, and educational psychology that were needed to strengthen the background of those who planned teaching careers. The faculty kept growing to keep pace with the expanded catalogue listings. An entire division in psychological counseling was set up under Eugenia Hanfmann, who came in 1952 after many years as a lecturer at Harvard and a member of its Russian Research Center, where she was in charge of the clinical studies of the Soviet Displaced Person's project. She had also been a practicing psychologist with children at the famed Judge Baker Guidance Center. How far the department progressed in less than ten years, in the esteem of peers in the field, was evident at an annual meeting of the Eastern Psychological Association: The Brandeis department, one of the smallest units in terms of outside research grants, presented six papers, more than any other college or university in the nation. In the following year, its members presented seven papers.

In 1965 we had the good fortune of adding George Kelly, who came to us from a brilliant incumbency at Ohio State. Kelly was sixty at the time and past president of both the clinical and consulting divisions of the American Psychological Association. His two-volume work, *The Psychology of Personal Constructs,* had given him a worldwide reputation and laid the foundation for a new hypothesis, the personal-construct theory. He eschewed the prevalent model of mental illness as disease and saw it rather as a problem in education that had to be approached through educational techniques.

The department was at its zenith in achievement and reputation when death claimed Kelly in 1967 and Maslow in 1970. With both gone, strains began to pull the department in conflicting directions, and many of our ablest faculty accepted other posts. The plan that had been so patiently nurtured—of a department with equal representation of humanistically oriented psychologists on the one hand and experimentalists on the other—was becoming difficult to sustain. The conflicts that had been contained at Brandeis during the first twenty years were increasingly manifesting themselves as young Ph.D.'s, themselves products of disrupted departments, joined the faculty in the late sixties and early seventies. The statesmanship of Maslow and Kelly was sorely missed. The primary task for the period ahead became one of restoring and maintaining the equilibrium that the earlier leadership had established.

It would be impossible here to outline the many new programs that have animated the social sciences at Brandeis. One of the fastest growing is the Women's Studies Program, directed by Shulamit Reinharz, professor of sociology. Using an innovative approach, the program is interdisciplinary, calling in a cadre of faculty members with expertise across the curriculum.

CHAPTER TWELVE

Social Welfare and
Public Policy

S ince Brandeis was committed not only to teaching and research but also to communal service, it was expected that, in time, it would sponsor professional schools. But it was also early agreed that any such development must not simply imitate other programs. If Brandeis were to decide upon a law school, it would be unwise to plan by the models of Harvard, Yale, Columbia, or the scores of schools whose prestige would attract the best candidates and leave the fledgling institution with those rejected for their first choice. Similar considerations had to be kept in mind if plans were suggested for schools of medicine, education, diplomacy, or business and commerce. Priority, it was agreed, ought to be given to professional school expansion only if some innovative approach were devised for which Brandeis was especially equipped.

These considerations gave not only validity but urgency to the planning for the Graduate School for Advanced Studies in Social Welfare. It was not to be a conventional training center for social work. In the Greater Boston area alone there were three such major schools that, despite their prestige, were at that time having difficulty recruiting highly qualified candidates.

The overriding need was for training in policy leadership in social welfare. The time was ripe. After World War II, every communal institution was confronted with new challenges that required a re-evaluation of objectives. There were calls for radical changes in techniques to meet burgeoning problems in community organization, social security, population planning, gerontology, deviant behavior, rampant crime, mental health, and a disturbing drug culture. There were few schools of social work that specialized primarily in training for broad-gauged policy, either in these or in more traditional areas. Hundreds of social workers, community and government

officials, and academicians required advanced training to qualify them for
tasks where their conventional schooling in social work, even when supplemented by experience, had become outdated. Here was a relevant opportunity for Brandeis. At the end of its first decade, it already had an
excellent faculty in the social and life sciences. It could work in tandem
with a core faculty of specialists who had won distinction in the frontier
fields of social welfare.

For a number of years, even as Brandeis strove to strengthen its liberal
arts offerings, intense discussions went forward with men and women
prominent in community and government service, who encouraged the university to undertake a training center for policymakers and for advanced
research in social welfare. One of the Fellows of the university, Mrs. Florence Heller of Chicago, a lay leader in the activities of the Jewish Welfare
Board and later its first woman president, was especially eager for such a
program to be mounted and indicated she would make substantial contributions to help underwrite it.

In the fall of 1957, after lengthy consultation with advisers, I submitted
to the Board of Trustees the outline of a program for a graduate school of
social welfare. I was considerably surprised by the opposition it encountered, led by Dr. Isidor Lubin, who had brought to our board the experience
of a long and brilliant career in public service. He had taught economics
in leading universities, had been secretary of commerce in the cabinet of
Governor Harriman of New York, and had served President Roosevelt as
head of the Bureau of Labor Statistics. He was supported in his dissent by
two of the more recent members of the board, Dr. Merrill Thorpe, professor of economics at Amherst, and Mrs. Adele Rosenwald Levy, the
daughter of Julius Rosenwald, one of the most generous philanthropists of
the last generation. Their misgivings were not based on concern that we
could not succeed in creating such a program, but they had always hoped
that Brandeis would remain a liberal arts and sciences university and would
avoid professional schools of any kind. Merrill Thorpe added another ca-
veat. How could a doctorate be offered in social welfare when there was
really no organized body of knowledge for guidance in earning such a degree? Would it not be wiser to enroll candidates who wished to update and
strengthen their skills in the established departments of the social sciences?
Then, argued Dr. Thorpe, the integrity of the doctoral degree would be
fully protected.

These were valid concerns, and they were put forward with persuasive
eloquence and cogency. My response was that there was urgent need for a
training center for objective policymaking in social welfare, for its research,
and for the evaluation of the complex and confusing data emerging from
the changes and dislocations of the contemporary world. The pledge was

added that the development of such an advanced professional school would in no way jeopardize the commitment to the preservation of the highest standards in the liberal arts and sciences. Indeed, the presence of distinguished authorities in this professional area would enrich the continued dialogue that characterized the intellectual climate of Brandeis. As for Dr. Thorpe's misgivings that there was no tested body of knowledge for reference, would it not be an exciting challenge for Brandeis to contribute its insights toward developing such data, formulating and evaluating it, identifying its research objectives, so that the advanced students would meet the standards that the doctorate demanded?

The discussions continued for nearly two years, since they had to be wedged in between many other academic and financial concerns. In February 1958, the board authorized the convening of a high-level advisory group to explore both the theoretical and practical implications for the immediate and the long-ranged objectives of Brandeis.

The participating counselors were an impressive group. They included Charles Schottland, the federal commissioner for social security; Katherine Kendall, the associate director of the Council on Social Work Education; Wilbur Cohen, who later served the White House as secretary of health, education and welfare; Philip Bernstein, the executive director of the Council of Jewish Federations and Welfare Funds; Fedele F. Fauri, dean of the School of Social Work at the University of Michigan; and Donald Howard, dean of the University of California School of Social Welfare. Selected members of our faculty and the Board of Trustees sat in with the advisers and, through the interchange, an imaginative concept for the school emerged, and the unanimous recommendation was made that the Graduate School for Advanced Studies in Social Welfare should be undertaken.

One of the auxiliary purposes of convening the advisory group was to spot possible leadership for the new program, if it were authorized. Charles Schottland emerged as a natural choice, both because of his long administrative and military experience and because of the prestige he commanded. Before being named by President Eisenhower to head the new Federal Social Security office, he had trained for the law, had served as the executive director of the Jewish Federation in Los Angeles, and had taught at the University of California in Los Angeles. Shortly after World War II, he was an assistant director of UNRRA for Germany, supervising the relief and relocation programs for tens of thousands of survivors in the Displaced Persons' Camps. He was decorated by the governments of France, Czechoslovakia, Greece, Holland, and Poland. After he returned to California in 1950, Governor Earl Warren of California had been sufficiently impressed with his record to appoint him director of the Department of Social Welfare. When Warren was appointed Chief Justice of the Supreme Court, he recommended Schottland to President Eisenhower for the rapidly developing federal program of social security. Schottland had been serving in this post for more than four years when he joined our advisory council. After the first sessions, where he played a leading role, I began exploring with him the possibility of his assuming the post of dean.

Schottland was very much intrigued by the challenges of the post: a new approach to social welfare problems, in a new university, in a new era. His wife, Edna, was initially not very enthusiastic about still another uprooting and even less so about exchanging the fascination of the world's most exciting capital for the quiet tempo of a college campus, in what she imagined were the dusty bowers of staid New England. After several visits to Brandeis and the welcome that she and her husband received, however, her hesitation gave way.

The board's formal decision to go ahead was made in February 1959, with the expectation that the school, under Schottland's direction, would be launched in the fall. The announcement called attention to the frontier fields that would become its major concerns: "The program recognizes the need for trained social policy workers in the newer, emerging fields of international social work, federal, state and municipal government, labor and industry, intergroup relations, the socioeconomic aspects of city planning, suburbia, and a host of new developments in our society." The students were not to be selected primarily from undergraduate or master's programs in the schools of social work. The advanced programs at Brandeis were to be designed for men and women who had already been at work for several years "in the real world."

Dean Schottland began at once to recruit faculty. Since the student body would at first be limited to fewer than twenty, only a few new faculty members were initially required. It was expected that they would be supplemented by visiting specialists and by designated members of the Brandeis faculty itself. Fears proved groundless that it might be difficult to persuade distinguished authorities to cast their professional destinies with an untested concept.

The first faculty, which identified and developed our objectives, was a most impressive group. It included Robert Morris, a widely respected authority in social planning who, like Dean Schottland, had served as a welfare officer for UNRRA in Germany and had been chief of social services for the Veterans' Administration in California. Morris had written extensively on social science theory and research in social work. After he came to Brandeis, he was joined by David French, then an editor of the *Social Work Journal,* who had taught and written on the application of social science theory in social work at the Chicago Theological Seminary and the University of Michigan. He was later called upon by the technical assistance program of the United Nations to direct the patterns of social work in Asia, mainly in India and Pakistan.

These men were reinforced by others who represented the fields where the school planned to make its early contributions. Peter Gutkind, an anthropologist who had headed research missions in East Africa, came to supervise the training for international social work. Howard Freeman's incumbency of twelve years (1960–1972) had a solid grounding in the fields of sociology and mental health and was mainly concerned with the patterns of social welfare research. In addition to his teaching, he was appointed in 1960 as director of research, sponsored by the Permanent Charity Fund of Boston. He accepted the call from the Ford Foundation to serve for two years as social science advisor to its representative staff in Mexico City, then went on to a continuing brilliant career as professor of sociology at the University of California in Los Angeles. Roland L. Warren joined the faculty in 1965. He had been professor of sociology at Alfred University and was widely known both as a theorist in the sociology of the American community and as an expert in the application of social theory and research to social welfare programs. For two years before coming to us, he represented the American Friends Service Committee in a project that sought to establish communication between leaders in East and West Berlin. In his later career at Brandeis, he became one of the most sought out scholars on problems of community planning.

Gunnar Dybwad had trained in the law in Geneva and later in social work in the United States. He served in both governmental and voluntary agencies as an authority in child development and child welfare. He was recruited for Brandeis in 1967 from the post of director of the Mental Retardation Service of the International Union of Child Welfare in Geneva. After coming to Brandeis, he was called upon as a consultant to expand the opportunities for the retarded and handicapped to achieve their maximum potential. He was also a major factor in the awakened concerns of government in protecting the legal rights of mental patients to health and education. Dybwad enjoyed an indispensable collaboration with his wife, Rosemary. From 1964 to 1967, she was co-director with her husband in the Mental Retardation Project of the International Union for Child Welfare in Geneva. In the course of their involvement, she has offered her consultant's experience to more than thirty countries around the world. From 1966 to 1978 she served the International League of Societies for Persons with Mental Handicap, first as a board member and later as first vice-president. She is the author of numerous articles and editor of the *International Directory of Mental Retardation Resources,* which was first published in 1971 and republished in 1979 and 1989.

David Gil was an expert in child welfare and conducted a pioneering study of child abuse that earned him national prestige. Child abuse has become one of the most important research areas in contemporary social welfare. Gil represented the ideal in university citizenship, and his election as chairman of the University Senate was an affectionate tribute from all of his colleagues. Norman Kurtz, teaching social theory and research methods, was a widely acclaimed specialist in problems of alcoholism and deviant behavior, including employee assistance programs. He has worked on the effectiveness of diversionary work programs for prison-bound offenders and currently is involved in assessing indicators of major urban health-related epidemics. He is the author of a popular statistics textbook, *Introduction to Social Statistics*. Robert Binstock became a national authority in the field of gerontology, his distinction recognized when he was later elected the national president of the American Gerontological Society. Violet M. Sieder had been a full professor in the Columbia School of Social Work when she joined Brandeis's first advanced social welfare student group; she later became one of our professors in administration and rehabilitation.

Finally, there was Arnold Gurin, who had obtained his academic and professional training at City College in New York and at Chicago, Columbia, and Michigan. He had a long experience with various relief agencies and with the Council of Jewish Welfare Funds and Federations of New York, where he served variously as director of budget research and of field service. His writings in the professional journals, mainly on community organization, identified him as one of the best-informed men in the field. He was teaching in the School of Social Work at Michigan State University when Dean Schottland invited him to Brandeis in 1962. He was later tapped as the dean of the school when Schottland was named president of Brandeis in 1970. He has been widely published in professional journals on the changes in theories of community organizations and their practical application. He gave leadership to the Heller School for another twenty years, until his death in 1991.

The prestige and the goodwill that the School of Social Welfare enjoyed from its very beginnings was demonstrated by the ready consent of distinguished scholars to come to us as visiting professors. They included Karl de Schweinitz, noted social work historian and former dean of social work at the University of Pennsylvania, and Richard Titmuss of the London School of Economics, one of the pioneers of British social welfare legislation. The standing that the school had won made it possible in 1964, five years after its founding, to establish a joint seminar in urban studies with MIT and a collaborative teaching program in social policy with Boston College, Boston University, and Tufts.

The public announcement of the launching of the school and the description of its objectives brought more than one hundred applications for the seventeen initial enrollment quota. They came from social workers, philanthropic foundation directors, religious and civic leaders, educators, and government officials throughout the United States and abroad. They were men and women, mainly in their thirties and forties, prepared to take leaves of absence from their professional duties to update their backgrounds and to become better equipped for more responsible policymaking positions. After careful screening, thirteen men and four women were enrolled.

The problem of seed money was considerably eased through the generosity of Mrs. Florence Heller, who by now had become a university trustee. She agreed to underwrite the deficits of the school for the first years until a steady state budget was in place. She pledged that, thereafter, she would provide endowment resources to assure realistic planning. Appeals were made to other families concerned with social welfare, and their supplementary grants sustained our prediction that the school would not have to depend for operation on the general funds of the university.

Before the first year was completed, Dean Schottland was able to announce a grant from the Ford Foundation to appraise the success of certain experimental programs that were designed to improve community services for the aged. The grant charge was to offer consultant assistance over a two- to four-year period to eight selected communities where the Ford Foundation had made an investment of $300,000 in programs for the aged. The reports from these communities were to be reviewed by a research team headed by Robert Morris, and it was expected that the evaluations that emerged would offer minimum standards for gerontological agencies.

Many more grants were to follow—some substantially larger, involving millions—but few carried the significance of this Ford grant. It came before the Heller School had even graduated its first class. It involved a field of study whose importance for American welfare could not be overemphasized. Senior citizens had become a considerable part of the nation's population, and programs for their social needs now compelled priority. The Ford Foundation had demonstrated enough confidence in Brandeis to assign this university research-based center a long-range study of key planning agencies. After the Ford grant was announced, the officers of the Young Men's Philanthropic League of New York, an influential funding agency, were persuaded to help underwrite the first chair in gerontology, which was held in the years ahead by Robert Morris. The other research grants in gerontology were undoubtedly triggered by the resourcefulness and competence with which study and research were pursued by the Heller School teams.

Soon there were other supportive grants that involved both faculty and visiting specialists. A grant from the Russell Sage Foundation was received for a broad study of the voluntary financing of health and welfare projects in the United States. General Electric made funds available for a study of corporate philanthropy and the corporation as a "concerned citizen." There were grants to study the welfare policies of private industry to promote protection for its employees; to analyze the competence of social welfare programs in selected Latin American countries; and to evaluate the effects of urban renewal upon the displacement of families and the services needed to assist them during the transition period. Even as the projects were assigned and funded, our key faculty people were called upon for consultantships by federal, state, and local bureaus. Within five years of its launching, twenty-two research grants, totaling many millions, had been assigned to the school.

The school was invariably included in the visits of foreign government commissions for briefing on their programs and for counsel in specialized areas. In the fall of 1960, the State Department routed a delegation of visiting Japanese city planners to Brandeis to scrutinize the objectives of their social welfare programs. There were commissions that came from developing countries—Indonesia, Pakistan, the Philippines—from Britain and the Netherlands, and from many of the social welfare agencies of the United Nations.

There were many satisfactions, therefore, as the university began planning for the commencement that would award doctoral degrees to the first social welfare graduates. The record of placement for them exceeded our expectations. Virtually all of them, even before commencement, had won confirmed posts in major communal, university, or government agencies, mostly in high-level policymaking roles. There was understandable gratification, too, over the complete conversion of those who had been ideologically opposed to the creation of the school. Dr. Lubin was now one of its most enthusiastic and influential interpreters. The long arguments that threshed out the need for the school had never been personalized. Once the decision to proceed had been made, Dr. Lubin had become a key member of the Board of Overseers and had made himself available in the recruitment of students, faculty, and visiting authorities. His counsel was invaluable in developing approaches to foundations for research assignments.

By now the confidence of Florence Heller in the school had been fully validated, and she was ready to make another major commitment. The negotiations with her and her attorney, Charles Aaron of Chicago, a Fellow of the university, were conducted throughout the fall, and in December the announcement was made that she was adding a million dollars to her earlier gifts. She expressed the hope that the endowment would cover the administrative costs of the school and such deficits as developed until enough chairs and fellowship support could be obtained. She was guided by the Harvard hard and fast formula for its professional schools: "Every tub on its own bottom." In appreciation for Florence Heller's generous incentives, the board gladly named the school for her and decided to dedicate the 1961 commencement as a tribute to its progress.

Accordingly, invitations for honorary degrees were offered to a prestigious group of men and women who had given long years to public service and to welfare projects and agencies. There could be no higher tribute to what the school had become than the caliber of those who cordially accepted. When all of the guests gathered for the traditional Sunday morning breakfast, the affair resembled a reunion of the stalwarts of the FDR New Deal, which had guided the country through the orderly revolution from the Hoover days of rugged individualism to the near social welfare state.

The roster was headed by Lord Beveridge, the father of modern social security and the author of the now-famous Beveridge report, which laid the groundwork for the British social insurance plan "from cradle to grave" and served as a model for the American system. His citation hailed him for "regenerating a social wasteland by infusing government with enlightened philanthropy." Beveridge was joined by Thurgood Marshall, who had been recommended by the university's senior class to give the baccalaureate address. Marshall had earned a national reputation as the legal counsel for the National Association for the Advancement of Colored People (NAACP). It was he who had directed the 1954 battle in *Brown v. Board of Education of Topeka,* which produced the unanimous decision of the Supreme Court to outlaw segregation in education "with all deliberate speed." Later he crowned his legal career when he became the first black elevated to the Supreme Court.

The suggestion to offer an honorary degree to Congressman John Fogarty of Rhode Island came from our own Dr. Sidney Farber, founder of the Children's Cancer Hospital. He reminded our trustees that no one in Congress had done more than Fogarty to extend government participation in promoting medical research. As chairman of the House Subcommittee on Appropriations for Health, Education and Welfare, he had been particularly effective in obtaining millions from the government to expand teaching facilities for retarded children and for research resources to alleviate the lot of the impecunious aged.

Special prestige was added to the roster by the inclusion of Charles P. Taft of Cincinnati, the son of the twenty-seventh president of the United States. He had served as mayor of Cincinnati, and his record there was a model of progressive administration. *Fortune* magazine had cited him as one of the most esteemed mayors in the country and Cincinnati, under him, as the best-governed city. He had become the first layman to be elected as president of the Federal Council of Churches.

From Canada came the social welfare pioneer George Davidson. During his incumbency in the Canadian cabinet, he profoundly influenced his country's policies in public welfare by shepherding to enactment an exemplary family allowance program. He represented Canada before many of the United Nations's committees responsible for health and welfare research. He offered trail-blazing counsel to the representatives of under-developed countries that had been slow to recognize government's responsibilities for the underprivileged.

An old personal friend and colleague was also included among our guests of honor. Harold Case had been plucked from an active Methodist ministry for the presidency of Boston University. His vigor and imagination had not only vastly expanded the university's facilities but had reached out to serve many newly independent African countries. He and his wife, Phyllis, were virtually roving ambassadors on the African continent, and during his incumbency the African Research Center at Boston University won an international reputation for imaginative projects that trained leaders for the newly emerging African nations.

We were also gratified that we could pay tribute to Dr. Maurice Hexter, then in his ripe seventies, the dean of Jewish social welfare executives who later became chairman of the Heller School Board of Overseers. He had been executive vice-president of the Federation of Jewish Philanthropies in New York, the world's largest and most diversified welfare fund. He was both its practical statesman and its theoretician. After retirement, he used his summer vacations for working in sculpture, and in his citation his talent was noted as a "characteristic expression of his faith that the most intractable material may be molded into beauty and significance." He titled the senior years of his autobiographical volume "My Stone Age."

At a commencement dedicated to social welfare progress, it was highly appropriate to pay tribute to Frances Perkins, the nation's first woman cabinet member. She had served with Franklin Roosevelt when he was governor of New York and was at his side when the state became a testing ground for the basic reforms of the New Deal. She served several terms in the cabinet, into the early years of the Truman incumbency. In her eighties, a witty, vivacious little lady, she was the perfect symbol of the progress America had made since the antediluvian days before the New Deal. At the Sunday breakfast, she summarized the austere work ethic of her Yankee ancestry by telling of her ninety-five-year-old father's trip to the village cobbler to have his shoes repaired. He returned a few days later, outraged by the cobbler's workmanship, storming that he could not believe that the repaired shoes would not last more than another ten years.

Abraham Feinberg, having acted as chairman of our Board of Trustees for seven years during the university's greatest physical and academic expansion, was stepping down after commencement. His business career had been one of meteoric success. Beginning in very modest circumstances, he had won control of many industrial and banking enterprises. He had demonstrated rare business acumen by linking his lingerie firm with an annual "Miss America" beauty contest. His principal causes had been the Democratic party and the State of Israel; and in Israel's wars for liberation and survival, he had used his considerable influence to obtain credits and arms for the embattled little country. He was chairman of the board of the Weizmann Institute for many years, endowed its graduate school, and led it to its preeminence as an internationally respected science research center. Abe Feinberg must surely rank as one of the authentic giants in Jewish public and philanthropic affairs.

Our commencement speaker was Hubert Humphrey, senior senator from Minnesota, who was then serving as assistant majority leader but was later vice-president in the Lyndon B. Johnson administration. He had long been the voice of the liberal wing of the Democratic party and had led the fight for progressive civil rights legislation in the party councils. He was a devoted friend of Brandeis and one of its most valued and honored trustees. This did not deter some of our roguish students, remembering his reputation for loquacity, from placing an alarm clock under the rostrum. It went off at the peak point of his peroration.

During the first few years of operation, while the Heller School was small and intimate, it was possible to operate out of the old president's house that had been inherited from the Middlesex Medical School and modestly renovated. As the faculty expanded and research grants multiplied, however, it was quickly outgrown. My search for more adequate facilities began, as usual, with Florence Heller. Very little persuasion was needed. She was quite proud of the program and the reputation it had so quickly achieved, and she shared our desire to provide dignified facilities for its housing. She offered another half a million dollars if a donor could be persuaded to match her gift.

Meantime, a warm friendship had been developed with Stephen Mugar, an Armenian immigrant who had become one of the most successful food-chain magnates of New England. He had fled as a boy from the Turkish atrocities of 1915 that decimated his people, and he had worked his way from a grocery errand boy to build the Star Market chain. He never forgot the providential circumstances of his escape from Armenia nor the role that

American opportunity had played in his subsequent success. On the fiftieth anniversary of his American citizenship, he climaxed his many years of exemplary philanthropy by offering major gifts to eight of the less substantially endowed colleges and universities in Greater Boston. I discussed with him our need for a home for our Graduate School for Advanced Studies in Social Welfare and informed him of the matching grant offer made by Florence Heller. Mugar readily agreed to match Florence Heller's generosity, but he insisted that the name of his Jewish comptroller, Benjamin Brown, who had shared the largest part of his upward struggles, be chosen for the identification. The building was therefore planned in two sections, to be located at the crest of one of the highest areas of the campus. One wing, for teaching and administration, was to bear the name of Florence Heller; the other, to house the research center, was named for Benjamin Brown.

There was a sentimental bonus for me in this gratifying development. Greater Boston has one of the country's largest Armenian settlements, centered especially in the suburb of Watertown. They are a warm, affectionate people, a good deal like the Jews in their emotional response to community service. The two groups also share a kinship of sorrow, for both were the victims of twentieth-century genocide. Their leadership had labored for many years to establish an endowed chair in Armenian studies at Harvard, and, after offering whatever counsel I could in the task of funding it, I was privileged to be the speaker when the chair was inaugurated. When I conducted a national television series on contemporary affairs and devoted a program to a discussion of the Armenian massacres of 1915, a sensitive kindling point for Armenians but well-nigh forgotten by the rest of the world, I could have been elected mayor of Watertown. In a later testimonial affair, I was identified in the citation as Abram Sacharian.

With an enlarged faculty, more adequate facilities, and the professional standing that had been achieved, the Heller School accelerated its pace of service after its first commencement. In May 1962, a new grant was assigned by the National Institute of Mental Health for training workers in its jurisdiction. The grant enabled the school to bring in five social workers for two years, fully subsidized to receive advanced graduate training in policy planning, administration, and research as applied to deviant behavior and mental illness. In May 1963, a three-year grant from the United States Public Health Service was received to broaden still further the research program in problems of the aged. This study, under Howard Freeman, was intended to learn more about what happens to the aged when they are discharged from hospitals to enter nursing homes, and it was undertaken in cooperation with the Boston College School of Nursing. The research involved a thousand aged men and women who were transferred from hospitals to nursing homes in Greater Boston, and it contrasted their welfare with five hundred men and women who returned to private homes.

A year later, in May 1964, Robert Morris joined twenty-one civic and professional leaders in a three-year study sponsored by the American Foundation for the Blind to devise means of improving the service programs for the 400,000 blind in the United States and to develop adequate national standards for the accreditation of the voluntary agencies. In the same year, the Department of Health, Education and Welfare (HEW) assigned a grant for a two-year study, in collaboration with Harvard Medical School, to appraise the educational experience of the hospital intern. Internship had been identified as "a central time span." It marked the intern's first experience as a functioning physician with responsibility for the care of patients, yet this crucial experience had never been adequately evaluated. The study was placed under the direction of Howard Freeman, in association with Everett Hughes of our sociology department and Dr. Stephen Miller of Kansas City. Dr. Miller went to great lengths to fulfill his assignment. He donned the white medical coat and lived at the Boston City Hospital with the interns on the Harvard Teaching Service. All aspects of their training were observed and recorded: their work hours, their diagnostic ability, their therapeutic skill and managerial competence. It was hoped that the recommendations of the study would set guidelines for other professional groups that were concerned with the training of apprentices.

In March 1967, within seven or eight years of the launching of the school, its reputation for research leadership in the area of aging was again recognized by a federal grant for a six-day institute on the campus to bring together leaders and executives in the field. It was organized and directed by Robert Binstock, now recognized as one of the outstanding authorities on aging. Twenty-eight state officials were invited to explore the views of ten experts, who prepared the position papers. The U.S. commissioner on aging, William D. Bechill, who participated throughout, articulated the significance of the institute. "It will help," he said, "to develop greater skill in policy analysis, translate research findings into concrete policy proposals, and deal with the complexities of local, regional, state and national organizations."

Schottland's tenure as founding dean of the Heller School was interrupted in 1970 when my successor, Morris Abram, resigned to seek the senatorial seat from New York. Schottland was called to the presidency of Brandeis for a two-year transition period until Marver Bernstein was elected president. Schottland then returned to head up the Heller School for another seven years. Edna's health had become fragile, and Schottland, then seventy-three, retired to take advantage of the climate of Arizona. He was heartily welcomed by state and federal agencies who were eager to take advantage of his determination to resume his service in the areas of social welfare. He was appointed to the faculty of the State University in Tucson as professor of social policy, joined the editorial board of *Social Policy Administration,* and accepted the presidency of the National Citizens' Law Center. In 1980, he headed the Arizona delegation for the White House Conference on Aging. He and Edna helped to validate the startling statistic that, in this generation, one out of three Americans past the age of sixty have at least one living parent.

Schottland left the responsibility for the expanding objectives of the Heller School in very good hands. Stuart Altman was invited in 1976 to assume the deanship. He brought a long, experienced past to his tasks. He had earned his Ph.D. in economics at UCLA and was named in 1966 to the faculty of Brown University. After a five-year associate professorship, he accepted the invitation of the federal government to join the Department of Health, Education and Welfare. In the last two years in this post, he headed its Cost of Living Council. It was then, in 1976, that he accepted the deanship of the Heller School to succeed Dr. Schottland. During his tenure, he was often asked to offer counsel to national and international agencies that were concerned with the funding of health care. He was an active member of the American Public Health Association and of the Institute of Medicine of the National Academy of the Sciences.

In 1990, when Evelyn Handler, who had succeeded Bernstein as the university's president, resigned, Altman was asked to assume an interim presidency until a successor could be named. He served until the appointment of Samuel Thier as Brandeis's sixth president in 1991. During that year's commencement, he was awarded an honorary degree for his achievements as a health care economist and his many years of service to our university. Following a well-deserved sabbatical, during which he served as an adviser on health reform to the newly-elected president of the United States, Bill Clinton, he returned to the faculty of the Heller School.

Meanwhile, in 1977, after considerable disputation, a master's program was introduced to serve as a conduit to the Ph.D. in social welfare. It was geared to render training in the management of banking and investments used in human services and related research activities. It was established under the direction of James Callahan, who brought a diversified experience to his tasks that quickly gave high affirmative visibility to the program. Callahan had been Massachusetts commissioner of mental health, secretary of elder affairs, commissioner of medical assistance (Medicaid), and assistant commissioner of the Health and Welfare Rate Setting Commission. He had previously served as director of the Heller School's Policy Institute, conducting long-term care research. Callahan was later called upon to serve as acting dean of the school during Altman's interim presidency and sabbatical.

In 1983, the Sol C. Chaikin Chair was established at the Heller School. The chair allows Brandeis to select an individual whose career and record of achievement in academic and public policy can serve as a central force in contributing to the development of a national health policy. The chair was named for Sol C. Chaikin, a leading figure in the labor movement, known for his lifelong concern for human rights.

A younger center established on campus in 1986 is the Gordon Public Policy Center, directed by politics professor Martin Levin. This interdisciplinary, multi-university center gathers together specialists to discuss and offer policy recommendations to government and various agencies on a variety of subjects, including health care and immigration.

CHAPTER THIRTEEN

The Jewish Component

The deep concern of Brandeis for Jewish values was demonstrated by the many special projects it undertook and, of course, by its emphasis on a strong Judaic curriculum. Yet it was clear that the Jewish component of Brandeis included an intangible—a unique atmosphere, an atmosphere that had been developed by the nature of its sponsorship and the students and faculty it attracted. One thinks of cities in this country with a special personality that distinguishes them from the hundreds of others so much like them. But New Orleans or Boston are *sui generis,* and so are St. Louis or Miami Beach, San Francisco, New York or Chicago. There are colleges as well whose history and sponsorship give them a unique personality, perhaps undefinable but pervasive. They defy catalogue description because their characters do not depend exclusively on the courses listed. They are vitally influenced by the lifestyle or the culture of the students and the faculty, the subjects that engage their interest, the causes they espouse, even the adversaries who stir their reactions.

Chemistry is chemistry, or at least its basic matter is the same wherever it is taught, as is mathematics, physics, anthropology, or modern languages. The academic difference from one school to another comes through primarily in the quality of the teaching and research. But no one will mistake Harvard for Swarthmore or Fordham or for several other equally singular universities whose academic climate is as distinctive as their history. I do not refer to the old wheeze: "You can always tell a Harvard man—but you can't tell him much." It would be more perceptive to quote John Marquand's rueful view: "If you've ever gone to Harvard, you can be sure of one thing. You will never be allowed to forget it." Behind Marquand's self-deprecating irony lurks a somewhat larger truth. Too many Harvard men have been absorbed in the public service of our country for there not to have been some mysterious stamp put on its sons, and now its daughters, by the university. Harvard today is rarely thought of as a Congregationalist stronghold; it long ago shed its Puritan image. Yet the impression of the religious commitments of Congregationalists, who brought Harvard into being and protected its welfare against many odds, still continuously surfaces. Walking quietly in its beautiful yard, studying in tradition-enveloped buildings, passing the portraits on every public wall of those who molded the patterns of American life will compel a moral responsibility, regardless of one's ultimate calling. Reading Van Wyck Brooks's *The Flowering of New England*, one begins to understand the impact of this unspoken pledge of noblesse oblige. And for all of Henry Adams's slighting remarks in his *Education* about his alma mater in the nineteenth century, the Harvard seal was left on him and on later generations of Adamses, as on the Roosevelts and Kennedys.

Then there is the phenomenal impact of the Quakers on higher education. The entire Quaker group in the United States even today has little more than 120,000 adherents, one of the smallest in the roster of denominations. Yet this group has made the building of small, quality colleges one of its major objectives, and schools like Haverford, Swarthmore, and Bryn Mawr are a crowning glory. No one can mistake their unique character. It reveals itself in more than their high academic standards, as attested to by the fact that every responsible survey of schools their size invariably places them close to the top of the list. It goes beyond such academic pioneering as the honor system, which was the brainchild of the distinguished Swarthmore president Frank Aydelotte, who lived to see this pragmatic incentive established in most of the major colleges of the land. Over and above the passion for excellence—although in roguish off-moments, students refer to themselves as Swarthmorons—is a climate of simplicity and modesty, often approaching austerity, in action and thought, a search for what Quakers call "the inner light." There is nothing ornate, neither in its instructional buildings, its residence halls, nor its unpretentious chapel. In the same vein, I remember a quiet aside made by one of our museum staff who was a graduate of Haverford: "We were called 'Mister' on the first day we arrived, seventeen and foolish. It had an effect."

Just as the Quakers are America's smallest religious group, the Catholics are the largest. They have fully met their responsibilities in the area of higher education and have created more than two hundred American colleges. They vary from the parochial school on the college level in institutions like Loyola, which combines Catholic orthodox indoctrination with secular learning, all the way to Fordham and Boston College whose Catholic identification is largely limited to official sponsorship and financial

support. Many Catholic-founded institutions have removed all course requirements in theology, and there is wide latitude for those who choose
this concentration. The level of teaching varies, of course, but their finest
schools have a commitment to learning and scholarship that makes them
prime assets in American life. Special character in such schools is quickly
sensed. Here you find deep religious reverence, a sharp restraint upon the
boundless sweep of pragmatism, a resistance to the acceptance of reason
as the sole guide to the conduct of life. The utilitarian is rarely permitted
to crowd out the sacred. Perhaps this is why there is so much respect for
pageantry and the mystical elements of faith.

When we turn to Brandeis, founded in mid-century, we may ask whether
there has been time, after only a few decades, to develop a special character.
I believe there has been, and I would say the character is built around a
sense of social consciousness, a concern for the underdog, and resistance
to any kind of discrimination. Some of it comes from the prophetic tradition, which has woven the passion for social justice into the warp and
woof of Jewish life. Some of it comes from the precarious economic stratum
out of which most first- or second-generation immigrant groups emerge.
Whatever the genealogical background, the result is plain to see. The student body is unusually activist and very much concerned with rights. The
faculty, brought together for its special skills in diverse academic areas and
with no thought of personal temperament or outlook, have somehow
quickly demonstrated a more than average concern for the protection and
advancement of progressive social values. Indeed, many of them may have
been attracted to Brandeis because it afforded a hospitable climate for such
concern. I cannot believe it is altogether accidental that the main writing
and research going forward so early at Brandeis had to do with restraints
on freedom, restraints that threaten the fullness of life. An unusual succession of articles and books still stream from faculty who are often involved
in resisting the abuse of power. There must also be some subtle relationship
between these writings and the orientation of research in the laboratories
that seeks to sustain and enrich life and attracts the support of such agencies as the National Institutes of Health and the American Cancer Society.
There is a similar relationship in the fervent concern of the young people
with racial integration, their sense of outrage with South African apartheid,
and the demonstrations against the American involvement in the Vietnam
War. As one of the student yearbook editors put it: "At Brandeis the status
is certainly not quo."

Of course, Brandeis is not alone in such concern. Fortunately, many
other universities are in the forefront of the battle to link truth with justice,
and Brandeis gravitated naturally to this doughty band. It was not always
easy for the administration to remain unperturbed when the student news-

paper, probing into every area, often far beyond normal student jurisdiction, scolded, sniped, and pontificated. It would have been much more comfortable to deal with a conforming student leadership, quietly deferential. But these were youngsters who had cut the umbilical cord of filial obedience, and they continued to question and oppose when they reached a college where the environment was favorable for challenging all credentials and sanctions. At any rate, the educational process is expected to inflict pain, to cavil, demur, and defy. The trustees have asked only that the spirit of criticism be constructive and respectful, even during the most divisive contention. All such strife is in the spirit of the reforming justice for whom the university is named. "Brandeis and Holmes dissenting" was appended to scores of majority decisions reached in the Supreme Court. The seal of the university reads *Emet* (Truth), and its motto comes from the Psalmist who demanded "the search for truth, even unto its innermost parts."

Every care was taken to make sure that what I have called the special personality of Brandeis, though intangible, did not affect our academic objectivity. This impartiality undoubtedly was misunderstood by preparatory and high school counselors who, in discussing college choices, often advised non-Jewish students not to consider Brandeis, or encouraged intensely Jewish-oriented youngsters to apply there because it was a "Jewish university." Few such advisors could know that there was no intention to develop Brandeis as a parochial school.

Nevertheless, by virtue of its sponsorship, it was appropriately expected that there would be unique strength in the Judaic curriculum (which belonged in the academic structure of any good university), in the library, and in the study of foreign countries, especially Israel. In planning for Judaic studies, high priority was assigned to the classical aspects of Bible, Jewish philosophy and literature, and Jewish history and archeology. Three outstanding scholars helped give distinction to this specialization: Nahum Glatzer, Simon Rawidowicz, and Alexander Altmann.

The first major appointment, in 1951, went to Nahum Glatzer. He was an Austro-German émigré who had come to the United States in 1938, having earlier taught at both Frankfurt and Haifa. He had established a commanding reputation in Jewish philosophy and literature and was considered an authority on the life and thought of the theologian Franz Rosenzweig and the philosopher-historian Leopold Zunz. In this country Glatzer had held a number of fill-in positions at the College of Jewish Studies in Chicago, at the Hebrew Teachers College in Boston, and at Yeshiva University in New York. But he had been engaged mainly as editor-in-chief for Schocken Books, publishers of Hebrew and German classics in English translation. He was a quiet, modest, low-keyed man. Meeting and working with him, one thought immediately of old-world dignity, but the impression never connoted pomposity. His dry humor was always surprising, because it usually emerged from such a serious façade. During his long research career, he carried on a correspondence with Judaic colleagues around the world, and, upon his passing, his invaluable papers were bequeathed to the university's archives.

One of Glatzer's early coups was to bring Simon Rawidowicz to Brandeis, a Russian-born, German-trained émigré whose erudition had earned him full honors among Jewish scholars. But before the postwar expansion of Jewish studies in American universities, positions worthy of his background were very difficult to find. When Glatzer invited him to Brandeis, he was filling a modest post in a struggling little college in the Middle West. This move to Brandeis brought him into a long, ideological controversy with the prime minister of Israel, David Ben-Gurion, who believed that there could be no creative Jewish life outside of Israel and who therefore regarded the Diaspora as vestigial. The highly publicized ideological debate with Ben-Gurion reinforced Rawidowicz's international scholarly visibility. I remember a reception at the White House in honor of the president of Israel, the late Zalman Shazar. When Thelma and I were presented to Shazar, he exclaimed, "Brandeis—that's where Rawidowicz is," and held up the receiving line to explain to President Johnson what a seminal scholar Rawidowicz was! Tragically, Rawidowicz was lost to the university and to the world of scholarship by his early death. He was barely sixty when he died in 1957. In a foreword to some of his later essays that were gathered by his son into a posthumous volume, I wrote: "Simon Rawidowicz was more, much more, than an incandescent teacher and a vigorous polemicist. He was one of the architects of Brandeis. The initial faculty was small, virtually an intimate family. The department leaders met frequently for other than their technical responsibilities. Often they had lunch together in the university dining halls, and Dr. Rawidowicz's wry wit, never malicious or mordant, his felicitous turn of phrase, his original insights made these sessions memorable. In this early period there were major policy decisions that had to be reached, with the sober understanding that they would influence the future."

Alexander Altmann was also a German-born scholar. Ordained as a rabbi, he had held one of the most distinguished pulpits in Berlin until the country was engulfed by the Nazis. He found refuge in England, where he became the chief rabbi of Manchester. When he was recruited for Brandeis, he brought with him a superb reputation for his writings in Judaeo-Arabic philosophy, rabbinical literature, Jewish mysticism, and the eighteenth-century enlightenment. As a "supplement" to his teaching, he began editing a series of classical texts and climaxed his incumbency with a definitive two-volume work on Moses Mendelssohn. In 1963, on a special grant, he made a tour of important Italian libraries and brought back, for the Gold-farb Library, microfilmed duplicates of ten thousand items, including Biblical commentaries, philosophical treatises, Kabala texts, and other documents of major historic value.

Some younger men were added to round out our offerings. In 1965, we brought British-born Nahum Sarna from the Jewish Theological Seminary where he was serving as librarian. He was later chosen by the Jewish Publication Society to edit a new multivolume translation of the Bible. He was joined by Naftalai Brandwein, a versatile Hebrew poet who had also come to us from Israel and who assumed responsibility for courses in medieval and modern Hebrew literature. Dwight Young, who might have considered himself a lion in a den of Daniels, was nevertheless very much at home among the Jewish savants in the Department of Judaic Studies. He had received a solid grounding in Hebrew and Semitic language studies at Dropsie College, and his seminars in the Aramaic portions of the Bible added depth to the courses in linguistics.

Even as the department grew in numbers and distinction, pressure mounted to supplement classical studies and research with training for contemporary Jewish affairs. It was of no small significance that it had been necessary to build our Judaic faculty almost exclusively with scholars from abroad. The American Jewish community had not yet produced many native-born savants. Until mid-century, there had been little call for them; only a few universities offered courses related to contemporary Jewish life. The upsurge of interest was undoubtedly stimulated by the enlarged role of Jews in the political and economic life of the United States and Western Europe, by their changing fate in the Soviet Union, by the tragedy of the Holocaust, and, above all, by the emergence of a sovereign Israel. Scholars with this specialization were now very much in demand. Each year there were many offers from institutions where newly established positions now promised dignity and security. But the posts went unfilled except where rabbis were tempted away from their pulpits; they were virtually the only reservoir of competence.

The time was therefore ripe to expand the curriculum in classical studies with offerings in contemporary affairs to help, among other objectives, meet the need for qualified faculty. It was also important to provide a training center for service in Jewish communal life. Of course, these areas had not been left altogether unattended. Marshall Sklare, who had written widely and authoritatively on the sociology of the American Jewish community, and Leon Jick, later to head the subdivision in contemporary Jewish affairs, formed an effective team to interpret the developments in contemporary Jewish life. But without broader financial support for faculty, fellowships, and library resources, the amplification of curricular offerings could be given no priority.

The fulfillment came in 1965 through the generosity of a New England shoe merchant, Philip Lown, whose basic communal interest had always been the training of Jewish leadership. He had played a large role in the development of the Boston Hebrew Teachers College and had served as its president for many years. Early in the life of Brandeis, he had established the chair in Jewish philosophy that was held by Altmann. Now Lown provided the seed money to launch the School for Contemporary Jewish Affairs. A major gift followed from Benjamin Hornstein and Maurice Cohen, two Boston philanthropists who helped endow the school. A whole new component was thereby added to the service the university could render. Additional faculty were brought in to give the departments full curricular and research coverage.

The honorary degree that was conferred upon Lown in his eightieth year was well earned for his role in this achievement. However, he was not so sure that a humble shoe merchant deserved such an accolade, and, at the dinner where the recipients spoke informally, he professed concern about his inclusion among the elect who were to be honored the next day. "In 1952," he revealed, "Dr. Sachar hinted that I should sponsor the first chair in Judaica at Brandeis. Who could resist his hypnotic charm? Thus my tale of woe commenced. Before committing myself, I should have remembered the story told by a wealthy society matron, who was anxious to have a family tree and history prepared. She went to an outstanding genealogist to have this done, but told him that there was one stumbling block: her family, like most, had an ancestor who had blemished a proud tradition. Indeed, his final crime was punished by the electric chair at Sing Sing. Said the genealogist, 'Don't worry, Madame, I'll take care of Uncle Charles,' and he came up with a masterpiece of equivocal ambiguity. 'C. D. occupied a chair of applied electricity in one of the government's great institutions. He died in harness, and his death came as an extreme shock.'"

The summer of 1964 included the twentieth anniversary of one of the most moving experiences in modern Jewish history, the secret flight to Sweden of the approximately seven thousand Danish Jews through the intercession of King Christian of Denmark. They were marked as certain victims of Hitler's extermination camps after the Nazi occupation of Denmark. The dangerous evacuation, with the cooperation of the Norwegian underground, was one of the few heartening episodes of the Holocaust period.

We had long dreamed of paying tribute to the royal family and people of Denmark who, almost alone of the European nations, had acted in unison to save their Jewish communities from the Nazis. Before our 1964 commencement, we approached, through appropriate diplomatic channels, the reigning monarch, King Frederick IX, the son of Christian X. The reply of the Danish embassy posed a quandary. In general, royalty does not accept honorary degrees. In this case, the king may have been persuaded to make an exception, although he believed the tribute belonged to his people. But his younger daughter was betrothed to Prince Constantine of Greece, and the wedding date fell during the weekend of the Brandeis commencement. However, an alternative was tentatively proposed. A national society of Danes and Danish-Americans held an annual festival in Rebild, in the northern province of Jutland, every Fourth of July. The American Independence Day had assumed the status of a Danish national holiday, and the royal family often attended the ceremonies in Jutland. Word came to us that, were it convenient, the king would be pleased to accept the Brandeis tribute on that day on the hillside where the celebration was always held.

Obviously we could not "hood" King Frederick. This would have been difficult in any case, even on a Brandeis platform, for the king was one of the tallest of his subjects, an authentic Viking. Fortunately, we had on hand a few of the gold medals struck by the United States Mint on the occasion of Justice Brandeis's centennial. One of these, along with the university's citation, in an artistically designed presentation case, went along with Thelma's and my luggage on the mission to Denmark.

July 4, 1964, was a beautiful day. Denmark itself looked as if it had been delivered straight from F. A. O. Schwartz's toy emporium. There were tens of thousands of celebrants on the hillside when King Frederick received and acknowledged the university's tribute. Later the king directed that the medal and citation be permanently displayed in the window of an elegant Copenhagen shop. It read: "Ours is a young university, named for Louis Dembitz Brandeis, distinguished American jurist, himself the son of refugees. We humbly claim kinship with a people whose tradition of sovereignty is 900 years old, whose respect for individual liberty was codified in 1814, whose cities have never known the shadow of a ghetto, and whose bright islands and pleasant pastures are truly 'the land of the free and the home of the brave!'"

When the American Jewish Historical Society decided in 1966 to establish its national headquarters on the Brandeis campus, it further validated the symbolic central position the university had achieved in the American Jewish community. The action was following the precedent of the Virginia Historical Society and many other cultural agencies that had linked up with college campuses. There were natural, mutual advantages. The Brandeis and the society libraries functioned virtually side by side, each amplifying the other's resources. The university's lectures and colloquia usually drew their audiences from constituencies of similar scholarly interest. Yet the action did not come easily. The headquarters of the society had bounced around for many decades in New York City, in rented or donated quarters. Successive administrations were reluctant to consider other locations both because there were no funds available and because there was no agreement on which city would best serve the interests of the society. Philadelphia disputed the claim of New York, and New York disputed the claim of any other community.

Suddenly in 1965, the funds for adequate headquarters became available in a multimillion-dollar bequest to the society from Lee M. Friedman, a well-known Boston lawyer whose devotion to the society went back half a century and who had served as its president for a number of terms. Brandeis offered a place on its campus after the proponents of New York and Philadelphia had canceled out each other's bids. The advantages offered by Brandeis appealed to some of the officers of the convention of 1966 that was held in Charleston, South Carolina, primarily to Leon Obermayer of Philadelphia, a highly respected lawyer, Dr. Abram Kanof, president of the society, a New York physician and bibliophile, and Frank Kozal, Friedman's law partner and closest to him in friendship and professional association. In a slim majority, the decision was reached at the convention. The vote was close because many of the New York delegation were convinced that the center of Jewish historical scholarship should remain in the largest Jewish populated city in the world, where there was easy access to the basic leadership in American and world Jewish life. After the vote was taken, suit was brought by some of the unreconciled dissenters. The court ruling sustained the board's action.

The move brought new life to the society, whose membership rolls increased rapidly and whose scholarly acquisitions soared. Indeed, much of the archival material on American Jewish history that had been contributed to the Brandeis library was transferred to the newly established headquarters. The arrangement was permanently validated after a seven-year trial experience.

It was to be expected that close relationships would be established between Brandeis and the universities of Israel and that every encouragement would be offered to make student and faculty exchanges. Such exchange by American universities with foreign counterparts had longstanding precedents. Already at the beginning of the twentieth century, Yale had sponsored what became a university branch in China, Yale in China. Many American universities had junior-year-abroad programs linked with selected foreign institutions. Hence Brandeis encouraged qualified students to spend a year abroad, and it was natural for large numbers to choose Israel. Faculty exchange was a keenly sought experience. At virtually every convocation or commencement, Israeli statesmen and scholars were welcomed as recipients of honorary degrees.

Many of the visiting Israelis could not resist the temptation to chide students for not emigrating to Israel. In an early convocation in June 1951, when thousands of students converged on the Brandeis campus from more than twenty-five New England colleges to greet Ben-Gurion, the prime minister scolded them for not settling in Israel. "What are you doing here," he exclaimed, "when there is a *Maase Bereshit,* a work of creation, with so much exhilaration and pioneering adventure waiting for you in a land that you can help build and fashion!" Ben-Gurion was only half serious, for, as a realist, he knew that Israel needed a strong and loyal American financial and diplomatic backstop and that Jewish cultural values would be enriched by a continuing relationship with Israel. Dr. Rawidowicz expressed the relationship graphically by the geometric symbol of the ellipse with two foci.

In 1961 a special study and research project in Israel was developed by my son, Howard, who had earned his doctorate at Harvard in Middle Eastern studies. He had begun annual visits to Israel and concentrated most of his writing on its relationship to the Middle East and the Diaspora. His proposal to Brandeis was to establish a traveling university, with its base in Jerusalem, from where the teaching and travel would be coordinated. This venture was to be no junket; the courses would be subject to the usual high standards the Brandeis faculty maintained at home. They would relate to the social, economic, and political structure of Israel and to the history and politics of the Middle East. These would be supplemented by attendance at sessions of the Knesset, the law courts, and local and rural councils. Students would visit cooperative farm settlements, agricultural research stations, newly created industrial areas, irrigation and desalinization projects, mineral drilling outposts in the Negev Desert. Observation sessions would also be arranged, by special permission, at military training centers. Under the guidance of the late Dr. Johanan Aharoni of the Hebrew University, the study of Biblical history would be reinforced by sessions at the archeological digs in the Byzantine ruins of Ramat Rachel. In an almost literal sense, all Israel would become the classroom and the seminars.

To acquire at least a working proficiency in the Hebrew language, it was planned that the students arrive early in the summer for an intensive eight-week *ulpan* training before the regular school term. It was expected that the enrollees could acquire at least a manageable conversational ability to communicate with the Israelis and to understand the Israeli press. The enrollees were not limited to Brandeis students; they were drawn from universities across the country, credit to be transferred for all work certified by the Brandeis Institute.

The funding for this ambitious program came from Jacob Hiatt of Worcester, Massachusetts, then a member of the Board of Trustees and later its chairman. Hiatt was a native of Lithuania who had completed his studies there at the national university and who had become an assistant district attorney and a circuit court judge. He emigrated to the United States in 1936 and achieved success as a paper box manufacturer. He shared his good fortune by complete involvement in Jewish and community causes, Brandeis among them.

The early days of the traveling university required persistence to cope with the physical impediments of a pioneering country. My son recalls that in the first year, 1961, on a drive to Sodom, six students were jammed into the director's tiny Ford, and the rest were crowded into a beat-up Peugot driven by an "honorary" member of the group, a Canadian who had settled with his family in Israel. The Jewish Agency had assigned him to the Hiatt program because of the excellent orientation it would give him about the land and its economic and social climate.

Pounding along the rutted road back from Sodom, the Ford suddenly coughed to a stop. The gas tank had been punctured by a boulder. The party was miles from anywhere. The Canadian was able to siphon some of his gas into the Ford, but how could he plug the leak in the tank? The problem was solved by one of the girls, an inveterate gum chewer. Her gum went into the hole, the gas went into the tank, the caravan drove off with a prayer. Miraculously, the gum held until the car reached Beersheba and a garage.

There were other adventures that were not foreseen in the original prospectus. Typical was a visit to the Bedouin camel market in Beersheba. Two of the Hiatt girls, clad in shorts, made the rounds, "oohing" and "aahing" in fascination as they watched the Arab sheikhs bidding and counterbidding. Only belatedly did they realize, with mock horror, that the leading sheikh of the district was bidding with Howard—for their purchase.

But such episodes soon faded into table conversation. Jacob Hiatt kept augmenting his support, broadening the program so that, though there were no luxuries, the food, living quarters, and travel were tolerable. Howard obtained supplementary support for the project from the State Department, which assigned annual grants of $25,000 for several years. Hiatt purchased a home in Jerusalem that became the institute's headquarters. It was remodeled and enlarged every few years as the program expanded, and, by 1970, it had become a much admired symbol of the Brandeis presence in Israel. At a special dedication ceremony, Hiatt outlined, in limpid Hebrew, his hopes for the institute. Israel was represented by the deputy prime minister, Yigal Allon, who jested in English that he would not dare compete with Hiatt by speaking in Hebrew. He hailed the institute for its original approach and for its ambassadorial service.

The Hiatt students' experience in Israel was, of course, not confined to the Jewish population. Every effort was made to bring the group into contact with Israel's Arab citizens. A three-day visit to Nazareth was planned to explore the special problems encountered by the Arab minority in the Jewish state. Hiatt students were the guests of Arab host families, and warm relationships often developed and were maintained.

Howard directed the institute for three years and then, with the program safely launched, resumed his teaching career as a professor of history at George Washington University. He was succeeded as director by Ernest Stock, who had earned his doctorate at Princeton and then settled in Israel. The popularity of the Hiatt program grew steadily, and the colleges that accepted the courses for credit included Yale, Princeton, Stanford, Wellesley, Vassar, Swarthmore, Clark, Cornell, Holy Cross, Oberlin, New York University, Rutgers, Boston University, Barnard, Pennsylvania, and many others.

Fifteen years later, there were over five hundred alumni of the institute, many of whom indicated that the direction of their lives had been changed as a result of their exposure to Israel. Several entered the rabbinate or returned to settle in Israel, and there were many romances among the participants that were climaxed by marriage. In time, the institute was expanded into a two-semester program that included the humanities as well as the social sciences. After twenty years, the institute outgrew its uniqueness. Several of the other universities in Israel introduced models of the program, and Hiatt transferred his endowment to an innovative career center at the Brandeis campus itself.

In 1969, the Benjamin Hornstein Program in Jewish Communal Service was founded to train graduate students for leadership positions in the community. The program has graduated hundreds of men and women who have gone on to work for Jewish communal organizations around the globe. The program was directed by Bernard Reisman until his retirement in 1993. Until his death in 1987, Benjamin Hornstein was a generous benefactor to the university. The Maurice and Marilyn Cohen Center for Modern Jewish Studies, directed by Gary Tobin, has added to our knowledge of the trends within the Jewish community through the many studies it has conducted.

A few years after I became chancellor, a major expansion in the development of our science curriculum and a research institute devoted to the study of Nazi desolation were planned and developed. They were brought to fruition by the action of Dr. Laszlo Tauber, a distinguished neurosurgeon who had survived the atrocities. He had arrived penniless in the United States in 1945 and had built a remarkably successful career in medicine and in real estate investments. In August 1977, he set up a million-dollar endowment at Brandeis for chairs and fellowships in science and, soon after through another major gift, funded a research institute to probe the background and to seek understanding of the tragedy of Hitler's "Final Solution."

Behind the grants was a dramatic story that predated the creation of Brandeis. When the Nazi terror was overcome, the fate of those who survived became a priority concern for Albert Einstein who had lost many of his science colleagues. He had come to the United States in 1934 to accept a post at the Institute for Advanced Studies at Princeton after the Nazi government had deprived him of German citizenship. I was then national director of the Hillel Foundations and had earned Dr. Einstein's friendship in the early years of his incumbency at Princeton. He wrote to me in 1945, "Can't we do something to rescue and give new significance to the lives of some of the children who were hopelessly trapped in Europe?"

I had already been involved in a program to bring students and faculty to this country. My Hillel post had established working relationships with scores of universities. I had been helpful in obtaining an offer of admission to some of them: The offer qualified them to receive the precious visas to emigrate. Many of the university administrators cooperated further by offering tuition remission; campus fraternities and sororities provided housing and board, and the Joint Distribution Committee underwrote travel expenses. I had also located some faculty posts for well-qualified scholars who had been encysted in Displaced Person's camps in Central Europe. With Dr. Einstein's cooperation, this intermittent effort turned into a major organized emigration program under Hillel auspices. Within two years, more than 120 youngsters had been brought to American universities, and twelve scholars had been invited to accept faculty posts.

Laszlo Tauber, an uprooted Hungarian, was among these selected scholars. His parents and most of his family had died in the extermination camps. He had escaped at the end of the war and settled in Sweden, having obtained a state fellowship for neurosurgery research. But he was desperate to turn his back on the nightmare Europe had become. The Hillel-based program secured a faculty position for him at the University of North Dakota. He remained in the West only briefly, relocating to establish a highly successful medical practice in Washington. His side ventures in real estate investment made him a multimillionaire. During the next thirty years, he reached out to subsidize surviving relatives, teachers, and science colleagues.

In 1979, some years after I had become chancellor, Dr. Tauber arranged for a personal meeting with me. It was an emotional reunion and was climaxed with a million-dollar gift to the university that established two endowed chairs in biochemistry, supplemented by a fellowship fund. They were to be identified as memorials to his parents, other members of his family, and his martyred teachers. He explained that he was making this "initial . . . gift through my respected benefactor, Dr. Sachar, who brought me to America, and to acknowledge the special debt I owe to this beloved land."

As noted in the section on the sciences at Brandeis, the chairs were assigned to two internationally respected scientists. The chair in biochemistry and molecular pharmacodynamics went to Professor William Jencks who had come to Brandeis in 1957. The other in biochemistry and molecular pharmacology was assigned to Dr. Robert Abeles, who had joined the faculty in 1964. As fate would have it, Dr. Abeles shared a common bond with the émigré who had endowed his chair. He and his family had escaped the Nazis in 1939 by fleeing their native Austria.

A warm personal friendship had now been established with Dr. Tauber, and, inevitably, his interest in the university itself was steadily deepening. It reached beyond the superb research work that came from the laboratories of Dr. Jencks and Dr. Abeles. I began sharing with Dr. Tauber the university's plan to establish an institute whose research would relate the Jewish genocide to the forces that contributed to it. Dr. Tauber was impressed with the university's plan for such research. He offered to add $1.6 million to his earlier contributions for the launching of the institute. He hoped that the institute could be named for his parents.

No time was lost in organizing an advisory conference, drawn from a broad range of institutions, to offer guidance in identifying the special role the institute could undertake. Those who gathered in April 1979 for the three-day sessions included our own faculty specialists and scholars and academic administrators, Jewish and non-Jewish, from the western world and Israel.

The consensus of our conferees was that Brandeis would be helping to fulfill a historic mission if it cooperated with the Jerusalem-based *Yad Vashem*, organized by a sovereign Israel in 1953 for just such a serious academic undertaking. Its leadership were key figures at our conference, and they heartily welcomed such a collegial relationship. Indeed, Professor Yehuda Bauer, who was associated with *Yad Vashem*, agreed to offer our institute copies of its vast duplicate material.

The institute, its objectives now heartily endorsed, was formally announced in the late summer of 1980, and its director, Professor Bernard Wasserstein, a native of Great Britain, assumed his post in September. He came to his pioneering duties with a superb background. He had received his undergraduate and doctoral degrees from Oxford and had been named as a Fellow of the Royal Historical Society of Britain. He had taught at the University of Sheffield, at Oxford, and at the Hebrew University. He had written a well-acclaimed volume on *Britain and the Jews of Europe*.

One of the director's first decisions was not to use the phrase "holocaust studies" in the title of the institute. He declared, "The word 'holocaust' is inappropriate as applied to the mass murder of European Jewry. The literal meaning of the word is 'a wholly burnt offering.' The notion of a 'Jewish holocaust' is alien to Jewish tradition, which is opposed to human sacrifice. The term is not only offensive to religious tradition; it is also inaccurate. For the Jews of Europe did not perish as part of a sacrificial rite." Wasserstein also noted that "the phrase conveys much too narrow an impression of what must be our mandate if the institute is to undertake serious work. Its focus should not be restricted to the process of destruction. A real understanding of what happened in Europe between 1933 and 1945 must be based on an appreciation of the general historical context. Without a constant stress on such a broad approach to our tasks, the research would run the risk of degenerating into the mere chronicling of tragedy."

In 1983 Wasserstein became chairman of the history department, and soon thereafter the directorship of the Tauber Institute was placed in the able hands of Jehuda Reinharz, an Israeli sabra who had come to the United States at the age of seventeen. Reinharz did his undergraduate work at Columbia and at the Jewish Theological Seminary. He earned a master's degree from Harvard and, in 1972, his doctorate from Brandeis. Following ten years as a professor of modern Jewish history at the University of Michigan, he joined the Brandeis faculty in 1982 as the Richard Koret Professor of Modern Jewish History. In 1992 he became the university's provost and senior vice-president for academic affairs.

Since coming to Brandeis, Reinharz has completed a series of volumes, chief among them a definitive biography of the Israeli statesman, Chaim Weizmann, published by Oxford University Press. The first volume of the biography, published in 1985, won The Present Tense Literary Award, the Kenneth Smillen Literary Award, the National Jewish Book Award, and the Shazar Prize in History from the Israel Historical Society. The second volume of the biography was published in 1993. Among his many other distinctions, Reinharz was the first recipient of the President of Israel Prize, awarded by the Knesset for his work on the history of Zionism. He has also served as editor of several studies of contemporary affairs, notably *Israel in the Middle East* and *Living with Antisemitism*.

When he became director of the Tauber Institute, Reinharz reconstituted the Board of Overseers to provide ongoing supervision. Its prestigious membership, headed by the British scholar, Professor Walter Laqueur, added confidence in its mission. The institute was renamed "The Tauber Institute for the Study of European Jewry" to confirm its broadest objectives.

Reinharz undertook as a priority the expansion of the conferences that had been launched by Wasserstein in May 1982 on "Terror in the Modern Ages," followed, in 1983, by another on "The Jews in Modern France."

In April 1986, "The Jews of Poland Between Two World Wars" was organized by Reinharz with an eye toward a reexamination of this most dynamic period in Polish-Jewish history, unencumbered by the mythologies that had emerged in the postwar period. The revised analyses were continued in the conference of February 1988, co-sponsored with the Jerusalem Center for Research on the History and Cultures of Polish Jewish Studies. The papers delivered and the discussions they generated made it ever clearer that the massacres perpetrated by the Nazi invaders of Poland had destroyed not only millions of Jews but a rich historic culture. The proceedings of the conferences, published in the spring of 1989 and issued in paperback in 1991, provided new assessments of the nature of Christian-Jewish political and cultural relations.

Another major conference was held in April 1990 in collaboration with the Historical Society of Israel and the Zalman Shazar Center for Jewish History (Israel) on "Zionism and Religion." The history of the Jewish national renaissance movement is inextricably bound with a complex relationship to the Jewish religious tradition. The conference examined this historical legacy in a series of ten sessions, with the participation of scholars from Israel and the United States. The year-long symposium on "Modern European Jewish Literature," 1990–1991, reviewed the breadth and scope of Jewish literary creativity, especially in Yiddish and Hebrew, and its place among the literatures of modern Europe.

The institute also organized a publication series not only to include conference proceedings but to commission volumes undertaken by leading scholars in twentieth-century Jewish history. Many of the publications have become standard for courses in colleges and universities in the United States and beyond. Above all, central to the institute's mission was the training of a new cadre of Jewish scholars. The institute provided graduate students the opportunity to work alongside visiting scholars, while fellowships to promising young graduate and postdoctoral students encouraged them to pursue careers in the field of Jewish studies.

The institute, in less than fifteen years, had gone far beyond, in program and influence, the expectations of the launching period. Dr. Reinharz proved to be a resourceful interpreter of the impact the institute was having. "Seeking support for a vital cause," he jested, dead-pan, "is not mendicancy. I enjoy helping a donor to give richer meaning to his good fortune." He generated major grants from foundations and philanthropic families. One of the largest endowments, to underwrite the international conferences and symposia, came from Max Ratner, a Cleveland industrialist and realtor, whose devotion to the university reached back to its founding years. His whole family had been involved; he as a Fellow, two of his children as alumni, and his wife, Betty, as a member of the Women's Committee.

In 1956 I was approached by Erwin Griswold, dean of the Harvard Law School, who informed me that the state of Israel was eager to launch a major project for the codification of Israeli law. The newly created state had to cope with a multiplicity of legal systems and practices that were hopelessly snarled. There was Talmudic law, American law, British law, Arabic law, Turkish law, and the law practices that had evolved in an ad hoc way during the influx of immigrants from nations around the world.

An Israeli commission had been appointed to study the inevitable social and cultural changes that had taken place in recent centuries and to recommend a legal system that could then be submitted for enactment to the Israeli legal authorities and to the Knesset. It was hoped the project could be as sweeping in its scope as the Justinian Code of ancient days and the Napoleonic Code of the last century. The Harvard Law School was quite willing to cooperate with the state of Israel and to place its faculty resources at the disposal of the commission. What was needed was the research money, an initial grant of $100,000, and Dean Griswold hoped that Brandeis, with its access to imaginative and generous supporters, could approach some of them in the interest of a Harvard-Brandeis-Israel legal codification enterprise. It could become a significant model not only for the development of a consistent and efficient legal code for Israel but for many of the developing Third World countries.

I responded cordially to Dean Griswold's proposal, for it seemed especially appropriate for Brandeis to cooperate. The university was named for the justice who was a son of Harvard, one of the two or three most outstanding alumni, and whose interest in the development of Palestine had been climaxed by leadership in the Palestine Economic Corporation. I promised to approach a few of our donors and to have some of our faculty join in a consultant's role with whoever was appointed by the state of Israel to direct the research.

Within the next few months, I obtained the assistance of Judge Joseph Proskauer, one of our board members who had been a justice of the Supreme Court of New York, and James Rosenberg, who had had a long and successful career as a New York lawyer and was deeply interested in the university. They in turn brought into the project a number of their friends. The funding assured, a research director was appointed, Joseph Leifer, an Israeli with an excellent legal background. By the end of three years, draft codes were ready in several areas. The data was sent on to the authorities in Israel, who submitted the drafts to Knesset committees, leading to enactment.

Another instance of useful cooperation came in 1960 after several years of strained relations between Israel and the American State Department that grew out of the Suez War of 1956. It was deemed critical for Prime

Minister Ben-Gurion to meet with President Eisenhower on a man-to-man basis to seek better understanding, but there was no initiative from the White House. The Israeli ambassador, Avraham Harman, approached me in the hope of using a ceremonial occasion at Brandeis to provide Ben-Gurion the opportunity to visit the United States for a special mission. Diplomatic courtesy would then dictate that, as a visiting prime minister, he be received by the president. Using university occasions as the instrument for accomplishing diplomatic missions was not unprecedented; the Marshall Plan had been announced at a Harvard commencement in 1947. Brandeis was a natural intermediary for Ben-Gurion's purpose, and its good offices were quickly made available. In March 1960, a special convocation was planned. The invitation from the White House was extended to Ben-Gurion as soon as it was announced that he was to receive an honorary degree. The meeting between Ben-Gurion and Eisenhower was cordial and effective.

Apparently, Ben-Gurion also had confidence that the university could offer guidance in an educational project that was close to his heart. After he had completed his incumbency as prime minister, he became deeply interested in establishing a university in the Negev, building upon the nucleus that already existed in Beersheba. Early in 1967, he asked me to set up a conference with academicians and administrators to discuss some of the problems that a desert university would have to face and ways of coping with them. I welcomed the opportunity to have him return to the campus. I asked some of the most knowledgeable men in the area to join the prime minister for lunch at the Faculty Center. There was our own trustee, Milton Katz, head of international legal studies at Harvard, James Killian, president of MIT and science advisor to President Johnson, Jerome Wiesner, provost and later also president of MIT, and senior members of our faculty and administrative staff. It was fascinating to watch Ben-Gurion as he interpreted his dream of a university that would join with other great institutions in bringing fertility to the deserts. Only about one-third of the world was blessed with fertility. The rest was desert or barren mountain rock or ocean salt water. Ben-Gurion hoped that specialists in desert ecology who applied themselves to the desalinization of brackish and sea water could convert the Negev into what the Bible termed, "a place of springs." And the Sinai and the Sahara and the deserts of the rest of the world?

As the dreamer talked on, all practical problems seemed trivial. Milton Katz, one of the behind-the-scenes architects of the Marshall Plan, broke the spell. Gently, he asked what table of organization Ben-Gurion had in mind, the scope of the university's faculty and research personnel, the necessary facilities, the sources of funds—all practical questions. Ben-Gurion looked startled. What table of organization? What funds? What blueprint?

"Do you think," he asked, "that there would have been an Israel if we had worried about such matters before moving into action?"

Yet, miraculously, the University of the Negev came into being, although, it must be added, it required some hard-nosed administrators to give it shape and form. They were sensible enough, however, in their procedures never to allow the dream to be eclipsed. They remembered that dreams often produce substantive support but that support alone is never enough to sustain a dream. And they remembered, too, that when Ben-Gurion moved into the desert and settled with his Paula in the village of Sde Boker, his farewell speech was just one word: "Follow." Thelma and I visited the university in 1969. Though the facilities for study and research were then still nominal, the esprit de corps of the pioneering faculty and the grim determination of the students were clear evidence that Ben-Gurion's spirit had enveloped the project. Twenty years after its launching, the university already had an international reputation, especially for its pioneering desert ecology.

Sometimes, because of the respect that Brandeis evoked in the academic world, much more was expected of it than could possibly be delivered; thus, in 1965, I was again approached by Avraham Harman, who expressed grave concern at the increasing unfriendliness of the government of India toward Israel. India had never recognized the sovereignty of Israel, and there were no diplomatic relations between the two countries. There was widespread admiration for Israel's democratic institutions, its service to the underdeveloped countries of Africa and Asia, but, with eighty million Moslems in its population, India's diplomatic dilemma was understandable. In Nehru's last years and during the incumbency of his successor, Shastri, the diplomatic coolness had turned into outright hostility. Israelis were now continuously denied visas to attend international scientific and cultural conferences in India, even when they were specifically invited by their Indian colleagues.

Harman knew that Brandeis's contacts with Indian academic and political figures had been cordial. At the fifteenth anniversary convocation ceremony in 1963, Nehru's sister, Madame Pandit, had been the featured speaker and had received an honorary degree. There had been a good opportunity to review with her not only the frustrating relations between Israel and India but also the growing anti-American influence there. When Nehru died in the fall of 1964, the memorial to him, in cooperation with the Indian Students' Association of Greater Boston, was planned at Brandeis, and the Indian ambassador, B. K. Gandhi, flew in for it. His visit was dramatized when he landed in the Three Chapels area in a chartered helicopter that brought him from the Boston airport. With such excellent rapport, strengthened further by the continuous stream of Wien students from India, it seemed practical to explore ways in which the university could mitigate the alienation between India and Israel. I consulted with John Kenneth Galbraith, who had returned to Harvard after his post as American ambassador to India. He indicated that one of India's most influential diplomats, M. J. Desai, who had directed the foreign office under Nehru, had now retired and was eager to write a volume on the foreign policy of India during the first decades of Indian independence. He could do much of his research and writing if he were attached to a university, and Galbraith offered to be the intermediary if Brandeis invited Desai to accept a visiting professorship. This seemed like an excellent approach, and the invitation for a Ziskind Visiting Professorship was extended and promptly accepted.

Desai spent the 1965–1966 school year on the Brandeis campus, teaching several advanced courses in the history and politics of contemporary India and the Southeast Pacific and pursuing his own research. When Israeli officials visited the campus, they conferred with Desai, who offered confidential advice. Unfortunately, the times were not propitious for any diplomatic progress. The continued exacerbation of relations between Israel and the Arab states led to the Six-Day War in 1967 and arrayed the entire Arab and Moslem world against Israel. Though the intellectual community of India and many of its leaders remained personally friendly, there was no diplomatic improvement with Israel.

It was primarily in promoting academic exchange with Israeli institutions that Brandeis was most influential. When I retired as president in the fall of 1968 to become chancellor, the trustees established in Thelma's name and mine a special fund for sending selected Brandeis students and faculty to other parts of the world, and each year a number fulfilled their objective through study and research in Israel. We also invited advanced graduate students and faculty to come to us. We offered fellowship support to a young Israeli Arab, Sami Geraisi, who received technical training in public polling at our Heller School so that the views and the reactions of the Arab communities in Israel could be better understood and evaluated. He became one of the department directors in the Israeli Ministry of Social Welfare. Among our visiting professors on the Tribute Fund were the outstanding Jewish historian Shemaryah Talmon and Benjamin Mazar, the former president of the Hebrew University and world-famous archeologist, each of whom taught at Brandeis for a year. Another special fund was created by Joseph Foster of Leominster, a plastics manufacturer, who early in the history of the university established an endowed chair in Mediterranean studies, held by Cyrus Gordon. Foster agreed to create another million-dollar trust whose income would provide an exchange so that our students and faculty could go to Israel to fulfill educational objectives and their students and faculty could come to us.

The special relationship with Israel was continuously strengthened, and I was glad to serve on the board of governors of the Hebrew University, the board of the University of Haifa, and the board of the University of the Negev, now renamed Ben-Gurion University. Some of our trustees were urged to share their generosity with Israeli institutions, and a number of exchange programs were instituted in addition to those already described. Joseph and Abraham Mailman of New York and Florida commissioned me to develop a major fellowship program for the Technion, which they established with a grant of half a million dollars. This sum was matched by the Israeli government's budget for higher education, and it provided for about twenty fellowships each year to help in the training of engineers for the growing technological needs of Israel. Before one of our trustees, Edward Rose, died, I worked out with him and his wife Bertha a very generous bequest to Ben-Gurion University to further its research in desert ecology.

The promise had been given at the inaugural exercises in 1948 that Brandeis would always remain a school of opportunity, that there would never be any restrictions on the basis of creed or color or ethnic origin. This pledge was meant as more than a commitment to avoid quotas in enrollment or employment. It was meant to emphasize that Brandeis was created for learning and scholarship, not for indoctrination. In reviewing the special emphasis and activities that gave the university its "Jewish character," I hope it is fair to conclude that the pledge was never in jeopardy. The Jewishness of Brandeis was in its climate, not its orientation. In the classrooms and laboratories, it functioned in the highest tradition of other denominationally supported universities that protected and encouraged the components that linked them with ancestral traditions without impinging on the completely nonsectarian quality of their academic contribution. It was by meticulously maintaining this sensitive balance that it was possible for Brandeis to earn a reputation for excellence in its studies and research, while it also was sought out as an influential center of Jewish learning and communal responsibility.

CHAPTER FOURTEEN

Religious Diversity:
The Three Chapels

From the outset, Brandeis had been set squarely in the framework of the nonsectarian schools and had meticulously striven for complete impartiality in the choice of faculty and staff, in the enrollment of students, and in the development of curriculum. Yet it did not follow that the religious experience, so basic in our lives, should be ignored. It was believed that young people on a college campus should have some opportunity to confirm their faith, to link themselves with the enduring values of their tradition.

There were many historic models for religious expression on privately sponsored campuses. The most common was to build the chapel in the image of the host group. At my own school, Washington University in St. Louis, the Graham Memorial Chapel reflected the Episcopal tradition of the founding and supporting groups. Hospitality was gladly offered to students and faculty of any denomination who wished to use the chapel for their own religious purposes, but there was never any doubt that Graham was an Episcopalian chapel. Since worship is largely intertwined with mood and sentiment, it was difficult for other than Episcopalians to evoke the ethos of their own tradition, however gracious the hosts. A Jew, away from home, could not enter fully into the mystique of the sacred Yom Kippur liturgy when he worshiped at Graham amid the Christological symbols that mellowed the Episcopal ritual. Fordham's Catholic chapel was at the disposal of all groups, but though its austere symbolism breathed reverence, an alien quality clung to the worship of students reared in other traditions. The model, therefore, of creating a Jewish chapel and offering its use to all other groups, was not followed at Brandeis.

Some attention was given to the concept of the chapel at Cornell, a gift to the university from Myron Taylor, a distinguished Quaker diplomat who had spent many years as the ambassador of the United States to the Vatican. Behind the altar wall, each denominational group arranged its own symbols for worship. The chapel was equipped with special electronic controls that spun these symbols into place as they were needed. When the Jews gathered for worship, a button was pressed, and an Oren Kodesh and its Torahs hove into view. When Protestant communicants came for worship, they could command the appropriate religious symbolism by the touch of another appropriate button. Catholics rarely use facilities that are shared by other religious groups; hence at Cornell, as elsewhere, they attended the Catholic churches in Ithaca itself. The Cornell pattern held little inducement for us.

There was an adaptation of the Cornell pattern by the Air Force Academy, newly established in Colorado to complement West Point for the army and Annapolis for the navy. There was but one chapel building, a stunning and commodious edifice. The entrance led into a beautifully designed sanctuary that could seat more than one thousand worshippers, intended primarily for the Protestant cadets and officers. One flight down was a smaller allocated area, designed in the Catholic tradition. Since the Jewish cadets numbered only a few hundred, about 3 percent of the total enrollment, a small chapel on this lower floor, in one of its corners, was constructed for them and their visitors. Each denomination therefore had its own facility, its size and position determined by the approximate proportion of the enrollment. Though some of the shortcomings of the Cornell pattern were not present here, the general concept offered little appeal in the planning stages for the Brandeis religious needs.

It seemed more appropriate for the first Jewish-sponsored university to be especially sensitive hosts. The architects Harrison and Abramovitz were commissioned to develop a plan that would include three separate chapels, one for each of the great western faiths, to stand side by side, none to cast shadows upon the others, all linked within an interdenominational area that could be used when general university purposes were to be served. Each group was to have its own chapel, designed to fulfill its own tradition, with no need for electronic devices, space allocations, or time schedules. What went into the chapel would be there permanently to sustain the religious climate each group counted uniquely as its own.

It was also determined that the costs for construction were not to come from the general funds of the university. Each group would seek support from its own co-religionists for its chapel, and its officials and student leaders would remain in charge of their own affairs. Since the campaigns to finance all three chapels might stretch out inordinately, it was at first suggested that the Jewish chapel be built forthwith, with the others to follow as soon as their funding was assured. Here the student leadership inter-posed. There were protests in the Student Council and in the columns of *Justice*. The students expressed concern that the Jewish chapel might stand by itself for a long period. It was better to wait until all the funding had been assured, then the three chapels could rise on their sites together. The students' arguments prevailed, and the architects were instructed to draw the plans according to their original assignment. The appeal for construc-tion and supporting funds proceeded simultaneously.

As expected, the campaign for the Jewish chapel was completed first. It took the form of a tribute to one of New England's most beloved surgeons, Dr. David Berlin, a thyroid specialist. Scores of his grateful patients under-took to finance the construction of the Jewish chapel to celebrate Dr. Ber-lin's fiftieth birthday by honoring the memory of his parents, Leah and Mendel Berlin.

For the design of the chapel and its equipment, the architects studied the plans of some first-century synagogues that had recently been discov-ered by the Israeli archeologist Elizzer Sukenik and his son, Yigael Yadin. The design that emerged won the coveted Award of Merit of 1956 of the American Institute of Architects. The eternal light and the menorah were modeled on those that had been unearthed in the dig in Israel. The window curtains took the form of a *tallit* (a prayer shawl), the ark was a replica of the tabernacle that was carried by the Israelites in the desert. An espe-cially woven cover was created for it by Mitchell Siporin of the Brandeis art department, who studied the directions for the *parochet* (the orna-mental cover for the ark) described in the Second Book of Chronicles. Sev-eral Torahs were contributed for the ark. One had been retrieved from a burning synagogue in Germany during the Black Thursday of November 1938, when Hitler launched one of his first pogroms. Another was pur-chased in Israel as the gift of Nate and Frances Spingold, who later funded the Spingold Theater. Other families competed for the privilege of contrib-uting the facilities to be used in the chapel—furnishings for the chaplain's study, an organ for the services, an alternate outdoor altar. A symbolic sculpture by Elbert Weinberg, representing the Biblical Jacob wrestling with an angel, was commissioned by a devoted patron of the university, Mrs. Harry Cline. It was placed at the entrance to the chapel.

Simultaneously, campaign plans were launched to obtain the funds for the Catholic chapel. The former governor of Massachusetts, Paul Dever, gladly accepted the honorary chairmanship. Louis Perini, one of New England's most respected building contractors, took the active chairman-ship, and many of the Catholic lay leaders of New England were brought into the campaign committee. The architecture and the symbolism in the sanctuary were planned with the cooperation of the highest Catholic authorities. The vestments were the personal gift of Archbishop, later Cardinal, Cushing. The organ was a memorial tribute from the family of William Callahan, a courageous young man who had given his life during World War II. Archbishop Cushing compared the architectural restraint and unpretentiousness of the chapel to the one in Assisi where the Franciscan Order was born. With fine sensitivity, he named the Catholic chapel Bethlehem, to link the traditions of the Old and New Testament.

Some early problems developed, even before the dedication, because of the opposition of some fanatic dissidents. A fundamentalist group in Boston, the Feeney sect, disavowed by the Catholic Church, was greatly disturbed that there should be a Catholic chapel on our campus. How could Catholics permit the Savior to be captive to the Jews whose ancestors had crucified Him! There were many ominous warnings that there would be an "invasion" of the campus to disrupt the dedication. The threats were not treated as the zealotry of fundamentalists. The Fenians, founded in the mid-nineteenth century to fight pontifical control of Ireland, were a well-organized brotherhood, with branches in many parts of the world. More recently, it had become part of the Irish Republican Army, and its major weapon was terrorism. That its threats did not materialize was due almost entirely to the instant action of Archbishop Cushing. The projected Fenian invasion was, he assured me, *his* problem. He announced that he would himself bless the chapel and conduct its first mass. So he did, and the united service was held in peace and dignity.

The Protestant chapel, like each of the others, was built in the form of a Bible, an open Bible, as eloquent a sermon in stone as the imagination of the architects could devise. Its symbolism reached back to the noblest models of the Protestant tradition. Its funding was made possible by the goodwill of Protestant families in every part of the country, whose generosity was spearheaded by the leadership of C. Allen Harlan, a Detroit communal leader. He was a kinsman of Justice John Marshall Harlan, whose grandfather had sat on the Supreme Court of the United States in the late nineteenth century. The elder Harlan, in the case of *Plessy v. Ferguson* in 1896, was the lone dissenter from the decision to establish separate facilities in public educational institutions for blacks and whites; "separate but equal," the writ had decreed. His grandson had the satisfaction, sixty years later, of sitting on the Warren court, which, in *Brown v. Board of Education of Topeka,* unanimously overturned *Plessy v. Ferguson* and mandated integration "with all deliberate speed." Allen Harlan agreed to take the chairmanship of the campaign for the erection of the Protestant chapel, which was to be named for his distinguished forebear.

As the construction of the three chapels was nearing completion, offerings poured in from families everywhere, not only altarcloths, candlesticks, prayerbooks, skullcaps, chalices, and flowers, but major gifts such as organs, a communion table, and furnishings for the lounges and chaplains' offices.

Leading from the three chapels that stood in a circle, an interfaith area was developed, its many acres of immaculately tended lawn stretching a quarter mile across the inner campus up to the science cluster. It had an outside altar that was to be used for occasions when all groups came together, usually for baccalaureate services, convocations for international visitors, or similar all-university functions such as Thanksgiving Day. Its construction and maintenance became the project of the alumni of a New York high school fraternity, Mu Sigma, through the persuasion of General Bernard Barron, who had served with distinction in World War I and World War II. He was joined in leadership by fellow officers he had met in wartime and by the Kriendler family, who were the proprietors of the renowned "21" Club of New York.

The relationship with Mu Sigma was a fortunate one beyond the interfaith project. The friendships that emerged from the reunions resulted in major future gifts when the lawyers, the accountants, and the tax specialists in the group served as friendly interpreters to their clients of the university's concept. Many of the members came for visits to the campus, especially those whose children had enrolled as students. Invariably, they made their pilgrimage to the interfaith area of the three chapels to be reminded again of the unusual way in which a high school fraternity's reunion was made to serve the long-range interests of the university where they had all become foster alumni.

Several years before the interfaith area was funded and developed, a combined dedication of all three chapels was held. It took place on a beautiful fall day in 1955, and it was much more than a Brandeis event. It stirred national interest, for the three chapels had become a dramatic symbol of practical interfaith amity. The *Boston Herald*'s lead editorial eloquently summarized the significance of the occasion: "The magnificent thing we seem to have partly achieved here is a comfortable coexistence of diverse faiths, cultures and individualities. There have been a lot of failures and there will be more. But the ideal we mostly practice, the ideal that is embodied in the protection of the Constitution, is the ideal of a communion of diversities. . . . We have not the strength of conformity on which the totalitarian nations rely. We ought not to put our trust in any attempt to match it. Our strength is the far greater strength of accepted diversity."

We invited Justice Harlan and three internationally distinguished religious leaders representing the Jewish, Catholic, and Protestant faiths to receive honorary degrees at the dedication. Rabbi Leo Baeck, who had been the chief rabbi of Germany all through the Hitler period and had refused to flee the country, sharing concentration camp horror with his people until the collapse of the Nazi regime, was invited to bless the Jewish chapel. Unfortunately, he became seriously ill on the eve of the convocation and died soon afterward. Jacques Maritain was invited to honor the consecration of the Catholic chapel. He was considered the profoundest interpreter of the scholastic system of St. Thomas Aquinas and had been former ambassador of France to the Vatican, teaching at Princeton since his arrival in the United States. Paul Tillich, the erudite theologian, represented the Protestant tradition. He had taught in the great universities of Europe and was now in a joint appointment at Union Theological Seminary and Harvard.

In the dedicatory address, I summarized the rationale for our chapels: "Our concept was developed after patient introspection and exploration. It came out of the consciousness that a campus experience must be a preparation for the tasks of life. Our world is tragically fragmented, disrupted by bitter ideological disputes, nationalist rivalries, racial antipathies, religious bigotry. When we say that the world is crazy we are using the word in its very literal sense, for crazy stems from the French root, *ecrasé*— broken, shattered. And the illness of our world comes from the fact that it has been so broken and shattered. The great task of the religious experience is to help restore cohesiveness by rechanneling the forces which break and shatter. . . . Here at Brandeis we shall each respect our own faith, draw strength and meaning from its survival values, and carry this respect with pride in the presence of each other."

Through the years, the chapels served the Brandeis family in their worship, their glad days and their sad ones, their weddings, confirmations, and funerals, their study groups, and their conferences. We were especially pleased with the large number of student romances whose weddings were often planned for the college chapels. There was scarcely a week without such a joyous occasion, and on some weeks, all three chapels were exuberantly busy. They became a model for other universities that were ready to abandon the tradition of a single denominational chapel. Hardly a year passed without a visiting committee that came to explore the Brandeis example. LaGuardia Airport and the West Point and Annapolis academies adopted the Brandeis three chapels pattern. In recent years, Brandeis has enrolled a significant number of students from lands with large Islamic populations—Pakistan, Indonesia, Turkey, India, Israel, and others. Are our visionaries already beginning to plan a chapel concept that will include a mosque?

The programmatic influence of the chapels depended in great measure, of course, on the caliber and personalities of the individual chaplains. In the main, I believe, we were fortunate in the perceptiveness of our representatives. Most were young men, often not long ordained and almost as often involved in doctoral or advanced-degree study at Brandeis or some nearby seminary. Whether their predominant youth was a deciding factor or not, in general our chaplains identified themselves in each college generation with prevailing student interests. I think particularly of the combined involvement of students and chaplains in the civil rights movement of the 1960s and of the adverse reactions to the Vietnam War and South African apartheid.

A later Hillel chaplain, Rabbi Albert Axelrad, beginning in the sixties, directed many community projects most resourcefully. He organized teams of students to visit the Hebrew Rehabilitation Center for the Aged once a week in a kind of "adopt a grandparent" program. Another program organized visits at hospitals, mental institutions, and prisons. Still another involved students as assistants to the part-time Jewish chaplain at Massachusetts General Hospital. Some of the students began corresponding with handicapped youngsters at the residential Alyn Orthopedic Center for Crippled Children in Jerusalem. Others conducted Jewish holiday parties and services at the pediatric and adolescent wards of mental institutions and hospitals, as well as at the Perkins School for the Blind. Clusters of students and the Hillel Singing Group paid Jewish holiday visits to nursing homes in the area. Students and faculty came together for weekly letter-writing sessions to Soviet Jewish activists ("Refusniks") and their families. They reached out to befriend and assist Soviet Jews who had been resettled in the Greater Boston area. Rabbi Axelrad has made the Brandeis Hillel a model of its type.

There were many other experiences, some related to me by others, that I have cherished over the years: The Sunday morning when the Protestant chaplain, a tall, commanding young man, rushed around the pond shouting, as the wings of his gown flapped wildly, "Father, Father, can we borrow your organist? Ours didn't show." Or the day a distraught student burst into my outer office with the alarming report that the menorah was gone from Berlin Chapel. My assistant, Larry Kane, himself a Catholic alumnus of one of our earlier classes, strolled in and said, "It's all right, Dr. Sachar, Rabbi loaned it to Father until Friday for the Advent Wreath in Bethlehem." There was the Jewish graduate student in our Department of Music who composed a Catholic liturgy as part of her doctoral studies, which was given its premiere performance in Bethlehem chapel.

Two memories remain most vivid. One was the chapels' tenth anniversary rededication in the autumn of 1965. There was a reunion of former chaplains, and the program included panels and symposia involving our faculty and distinguished visitors drawn from various fields. The day-long affair culminated in a major banquet that was so well attended it had to

be held in the Athletic Center. The speakers were men of international repute. I cannot remember any of their remarks now. Neither, I am sure, can
they. But none will forget what was to be one of the last appearances of
Cardinal Cushing at Brandeis, when he agreed to help us climax our celebration. He arrived quite late, and we could all see the ravages of the cruel
disease that would erode all but the courage of his faith. He was both unusually subdued and apparently extremely tired. He merely played with his
food, for he had already begun to experience difficulty in swallowing.
Nevertheless, he listened patiently to the three internationally prominent
speakers. At last, he rose to deliver the briefest speech any of us could
remember. He professed an admiration for the previous speakers and their
theological insights. His own theology, he insisted, had barely gone beyond
that taught to children via the catechism. "And what," he asked, "have I
been doing all day?" Dramatic pause. "I've been giving away *fish*." There
had been a strike that had left tons of fish in danger of rotting on the
wharves. Someone had called the cardinal's residence and said he might
have the fish for his poor if he could find ways of giving it away. He had
attended to this mission and then come, exhausted but eager, to participate
in the interfaith reunion.

The other remembrance is of the tragic afternoon when young President
Kennedy was assassinated. That crisp November day had begun pleasantly,
outwardly at least. I still recall, incongruously, how green the playing fields
were across the road from the president's office, how unusually mild it was.
I had a particularly difficult faculty meeting scheduled for three o'clock,
however, which I was not anticipating with any delight. I was at lunch when
news was brought me of the shots in Dallas, and I immediately hurried
back to my office. There I found my staff in various stages of bewilderment.
Crowds congregated around radios. When we heard through the static that
the priests had left the hospital, one of my assistants said, "Then he's gone,
sir," got up, and walked away weeping, bumping into the furniture on the
way.

Somewhere in the ensuing confusion I directed that someone get in
touch with all three chaplains. I need not have done so. All were at their
posts. As the word spread, students, faculty, and staff began stumbling and
streaming up the hill toward the chapels. Hastily we prepared an order of
service. The chapels were not only filled to overflowing with sorrowing
members of the Brandeis community—groundsmen, students, kitchen
helpers, and faculty—but with neighborhood folk who came, clotting in
grief-stricken groups on the lawns and pathways leading up to the chapels.
As all, in their hundreds, went reluctantly on their way, I reflected how, in
such moments of unspoken grief—now for a fallen president, but equally
for a stricken faculty member or a youngster scarcely past his teens—it

seemed so natural to make one's way to the chapels, where only hearts need speak.

To add to the spirit of diversity on campus, in 1991 Myra and Robert Kraft and Jacob Hiatt donated funds for a professorship at Brandeis and Holy Cross. The program is designed to heighten the awareness of shared values among students of diverse backgrounds. It provides for the appointment of a scholar of Christian studies at Brandeis and a scholar of Jewish studies at Holy Cross. The first appointment at Brandeis for this professorship was Krister Stendahl, dean of the Harvard Divinity School and former bishop of the Church of Sweden. Stendahl is a noted biblical scholar and authority on relations between Christians and Jews.

CHAPTER FIFTEEN

An International Emphasis

It was natural for Brandeis, in identifying its academic goals, to include an emphasis on international studies. This commitment was reflected in the curricular offerings in history, politics, economics, anthropology, sociology, comparative literature, the history of ideas, and related areas. It was further pointed up in the recruitment of visiting scholars from abroad and in the support program that encouraged our faculty to apply for Guggenheims, Fulbrights, Marshalls, and other fellowships that underwrite teaching and research in foreign lands. Above all, it was clear that our objective would be substantially advanced if we could ensure a steady flow of foreign students to our campus to study, to be introduced to the patterns of American life, to exchange views with their American classmates and each other, and to return to their homelands as more knowledgeable interpreters of American life. To mount such an ambitious program would, however, require a substantial endowment to provide the scholarships and fellowships for assignment to the ablest and most promising foreign students. The man I hoped could help us obtain such major support was Lawrence Wien, who had joined the Brandeis board in 1957 and become one of its most committed members.

Wien was an extraordinarily able and attractive person. He was the son of a middle-class New Jersey family and had taken his undergraduate and his law degrees with high honors at Columbia. While practicing law in New York, he pioneered a technique in real estate investment known as syndication, the acquisition of very large holdings by dividing the cost into units to be offered for purchase to many participants. Wien's holdings became ever more substantial and included major hotels, equities, and office buildings in many parts of the country, including the Rockefeller Center and the Empire State Building. The Wiens lived well, with lovely apartments in New York and Palm Beach and an eighty-acre country estate in Weston, Connecticut. They traveled widely, using as their base an elegant apartment in London. They were sophisticated connoisseurs of art and patrons of music, ballet, and theater. Having achieved a most gracious lifestyle and having fulfilled all family responsibility, Wien concluded early in his career that there was little else money could give him in personal satisfaction. This decision led him to adopt what he called a philosophy of "reasoned philanthropy." He became a generous contributor to Columbia and the Lincoln Center, the Institute for International Education, and a long roll call of communal causes. He gave dynamic leadership to the causes that he supported and headed many of their campaigns. It was in this period of expanding philanthropic service that he was first introduced to Brandeis University.

I had been scheduled to address a group of potential supporters in Westport, Connecticut. My hosts, Jack and Lillian Poses, invited Larry Wien, their neighbor in Weston, to attend the interpretive affair. Wien was having second thoughts about too many communal involvements, which might have an adverse effect on his priorities, and he asked to be excused. He offered a pledge of ten thousand dollars to the university "if I do not have to come for still another speech." Poses told me later that he had adroitly turned down the "bribe." It became the largest sum that had ever been offered to avoid listening to me. Wien finally attended the function where, in discussing the obligation of Jews to make a corporate contribution to American higher education, I must have touched a responsive nerve. He came up to the lectern and asked if we could have lunch together in New York within the next few days. The luncheon clinched his identification with the university, and, as he often said with affectionate ruefulness, it turned out to be the most expensive meal of his life. I was reminded of the mock contrition of Meyer Weisgal, who garnered tens of millions for the Weizmann Institute in Israel. "To have lunch with me can be a most enriching experience," he said, "but it can also be very impoverishing."

In the years that followed, Wien served as chairman of the Board of Trustees, and hardly a season passed without some major underwriting from his family for facilities and programs. But his most valuable gift was of himself, his initiative, his eloquence on a platform, and the leverage he had with scores of influential families.

In 1958, when we gave the highest priority to the launching of a foreign student scholarship program, Wien believed that he could interest Henry Crown of Chicago, one of the country's most public spirited industrialists, as a possible patron. Crown had already been sufficiently impressed with the concept of Brandeis to have established, several years earlier, a science laboratory complex in memory of his parents.

The appointment with Henry Crown was readily arranged, and Wien and I flew out to Chicago. It was agreed that the proposal would be made by Wien. It was a fascinating experience for me; I had rarely listened to such a persuasive presentation. Apparently, our timing was not propitious. Crown explained that he was deeply impressed by the project, but he was in the midst of discharging major commitments that he had assumed for a number of universities in this country and in Israel. He promised that Brandeis was on the family list for another gift, which did indeed materialize a few years later when a multimillion-dollar endowment was established, named for Irving and Rose Crown, to subsidize fellowships in American studies.

In the early part of our return flight, Wien was unusually reticent. I attributed the mood to disappointment, and I tried to make the point that, in presentations for major objectives, it was inevitable that only a fraction of the attempts would come to fruition. I, too, was disappointed, but not discouraged. Surely many other families could be approached. I soon realized that Wien was hardly listening. It was not comfort that he needed. He was turning over in his mind his capacity to make room for the program in his own long roster of philanthropic commitments. He had presented the case for international scholarships with such eloquence and effectiveness that he had persuaded himself that this was a project he should undertake! I don't remember whether we were over Kokomo, Indiana, or Akron, Ohio, when he turned to me and said quietly, "We won't wait for Crown or for anyone else. Mae and I will do the job ourselves." It was a commitment that involved an immediate annual expenditure of $300,000, which was to rise to $420,000 annually for 112 students, fully supported, and ultimately to grow into an endowment providing more than $1 million annually.

Wien did not feel that he had fulfilled his responsibility, however, if he did not simultaneously add another contribution to his alma mater. Within the week, therefore, he called up the dean of the Columbia Law School and introduced himself as an alumnus. He said that he planned to establish a scholarship program for foreign students at Brandeis. "But I have a compelling obligation to the Columbia Law School, and I would like to contribute a million dollars for scholarship purposes there." The dean afterward admitted that he nearly suffered a heart attack. What university official had ever had a telephone call that announced an unsolicited gift of a million dollars from an alumnus with whom he was not personally acquainted? Later I described the incident to Erwin Griswold, then dean of the Harvard Law School. He noted with affectionate envy that he would gladly risk such consequences if one of his alumni called him for a similar announcement.

In preparation for launching the program, I set up an appointment with Dr. Earl Dennis, director of the International Exchange Service Office under the State Department. I was eager to explore how to use the experience of our American cultural attachés so as to be assured that we were giving the scholarships to students who would later be of service in their own countries. The program was meant to be much more than a resource by which foreign youngsters could advance their own careers. Dr. Dennis was most enthusiastic. He noted that the usual foreign scholarship was limited to one year; a Wien scholarship offered several years of full support for tuition, room, board, and personal expenses related to academic needs. And the number of annual scholarships meant that the program could become truly international in scope. A Rhodes to Oxford is limited to scholarships for English-speaking countries, a Fulbright, to graduate students who may choose any American college for their advanced studies. Dr. Dennis instructed the cultural attachés and the information officers in every American embassy to offer the fullest cooperation.

An advisory council was then appointed that included academic and public figures with valuable experience in international exchange: David Henry, the director of the foreign student service at Harvard, Henry Kissinger, then on the Harvard faculty, Mrs. Karl Compton, wife of the late president of MIT, Leonard Bernstein, Benjamin V. Cohen, one of Franklin Roosevelt's first policy advisers, and a number of other advocates of international cultural exchange. Several members of our faculty were included, not only because of their own experience but also to interpret the program to their colleagues. There was a tendency among some of them to resist "service" programs, however attractive, as long as committed needs for faculty salaries and fringe benefits were still not fully protected. I hoped that the expected criticism would be diluted if key faculty members were part of the administrative council. We also took precautions to dissipate possible resentment among our American students. If scholarship funds for their own needs proved inadequate, they might wonder why foreign students were being treated with such hospitality. Student government leaders were therefore carefully briefed so that the message would get back to their classmates that the Wien funds represented a special grant and that no general scholarship resources would be diverted for the program.

A special convocation was set for October 1958 to inaugurate the program and welcome the first contingent of students. The convocation address was delivered by George F. Kennan, former American ambassador to the Soviet Union. Kennan had been a major molder of policy for the State Department and had written widely on foreign policy issues. The two Massachusetts senators were also invited to receive honorary degrees—Leverett Saltonstall who, before election to the Senate, had been a three-time governor of Massachusetts, and John F. Kennedy, who was then serving his first term in the Senate.

From the outset, the Wien director worked closely with the Institute for International Education (IIE). The IIE was an efficiently managed clearing house, with headquarters in New York, that received recommendations from its personnel in countries around the world and then sought out universities in the United States for placement of its most promising candidates. Its files were always at the disposal of the Wien staff, and each year a number of applicants were channeled to the university. But the majority of the Wien students were recruited directly through the special committees that were set up in many of the foreign countries.

We had the advantage of easy access to faculty members who were living abroad, either on sabbatical or on leave, and they were only too glad to accept assignments to establish such committees for us. Thelma and I spent several weeks in university centers in Europe, Asia, Latin America, and Africa and left behind working committees in twelve countries. There was little problem in obtaining the cooperation of the American ambassadors and their staffs, the heads of universities and their key officers, the ministries of education, the directors of binational commissions. The offices of the cultural attachés distributed the application forms; the committees screened and evaluated the returns, conducted personal interviews, and made their recommendations to the director of the Wien program at Brandeis. Within a few years, Wien agreed to add another sixty thousand dollars in annual income so that graduate students could be included. As the availability of the Wien scholarships became widely known, applications poured in, and the pool for selection was large enough to ensure a steady stream of students of the highest caliber.

The counsel of the foreign committees was indispensable in coping with specialized problems. The representative of the ministry of education in East Pakistan (later Bangladesh) noted that the most brilliant applicants were not necessarily the ones who could be of greatest national service when they returned. If they achieved their degrees with honors in biochemistry or physics, there were neither facilities nor opportunities in their homeland to utilize their training fully. Would it not be better to learn from government officials what national services were most urgent and then select the students interested in these areas? General Carlos Romulo, then president of the University of the Philippines and later foreign minister, was deeply concerned that Filipino youngsters were often staying on in the United States because career opportunities there were so overpoweringly alluring. He suggested that contracts be drawn up that would assure return to the Philippines for at least a few years, with the additional inducement of guaranteed positions there.

Such counsel, and growing experience with the problems of the students themselves, brought considerable flexibility in structuring the program. Orientation sessions were set up in advance of the opening of the school year that included the participation of Wien scholars. The curriculum was modified for some of them so that they could make fuller use of the precious, limited time they had at Brandeis. Every attempt was made to introduce them to the realities of American life. Families in the environs of the university gladly offered frequent hospitality, and the foreign students enjoyed the informality of American home life. In the early years, when the Wien students were virtually the only foreign youngsters on campus, it was possible to send them on university-sponsored tours so that they could become acquainted with other areas of American culture. During recess periods, they would visit Washington for interviews with government officials under the guidance of faculty couples. In New York, they would tour newspaper plants, television and radio stations, and universities and meet with media personalities and political and educational figures.

The operation of the program has had an impact on more than just Wien students. They brought a delightfully diverse quality to the campus and to all extracurricular activities. They were not isolated as foreign students had been in the early years of the Rockefeller International Houses at the University of Chicago and at Columbia. They lived and ate with the American students, attended classes and social functions with them, and were frequent visitors in their homes. Brandeis fielded a soccer team quite early, and the formidable array of Finns and Swedes, Italians and Greeks, Israelis and Kenyans, brought impressive victories and high standings in intercollegiate competition.

It should be noted, too, that very soon after the Wien program was instituted the university steward planned regular international nights for the dining halls. Foreign chefs in the community from the major hotels or restaurants enthusiastically cooperated, and each month students and faculty entered the dining hall, decorated to create the atmosphere of the host country, and were delighted by a menu that featured choice native dishes. The earliest international evenings were planned by the students from France, Germany, Spain, and Israel, but as the diversification of the Wien students multiplied and their friends from other universities joined them, there were also evenings dedicated to the countries of Asia, Africa, and Latin America.

The program won the hearty support of governmental and educational officials around the world. The university was eager to create ambassadors for the democratic ideals of American life, not through propaganda but through education, and to prepare the students for crucially needed service in their homelands. Within two years of its inauguration, the application pool reached one thousand, of whom 350 were eminently qualified. Jean-Pierre Barricelli of our Romance language faculty, the first Wien program director, reported, after a long tour in 1959, "The countless talks I had with local government officers, university representatives, and cultural attachés, during my recent visit to ten Asian and African countries, provided ample support for the belief that cultural and educational exchanges are not just a matter of educational philanthropy. . . . When the youngsters come back they are swamped with requests to interpret their experiences, sometimes in as many as a hundred talks, to be frequently on the radio, and to write or to be the subject of many feature newspaper stories. . . . In the aggregate, it is evident that those who spend some time at an American institution can foster an appreciation of our country, of its achievements, and of the democratic ideals it aspires to realize." One of the Kenyan legislators told Barricelli that the Wien program was "the most energetic and encouraging contribution made by any American university to the growth of my country."

Inevitably, some proportion of the Wien students did not return to their homelands. The problem of the "brain drain" that troubled General Romulo was not limited to the Philippines; it included students who came from many of the underdeveloped countries. Some were undoubtedly glamorized by American life and its standard of living. Some could not return home because of changed political conditions. Some of the men married American women; a larger number of women married American men. Three Turkish women in successive years became Americans through marriage to American men, one of them the son of a trustee. At the ceremony, I gave the bride away in place of her absent father. Wien was elated over a romance that was so happily consummated. When I told Larry of our experience with the Turkish women, he bantered that it might be wise thereafter to bring over only ugly Turkish women. But where were we to find them? . . . At one of our commencements, when an honorary degree was conferred upon Barbara Ward, editor of the *London Economist,* whose husband was Lord Jackson, a British government official in Ghana, I introduced her to one of our Ghanian Wiens, and she expressed concern that such potentially valuable leaders for Ghana might be tempted to stay on in America. But the majority of the Wien scholarship students did return. In the first few years of the program, it was not to be expected that their impact would be significant, but there were gratifying results when they had adjusted to relocation and had taken advantage of their special opportunities.

One of the photographs in this volume recalls the inauguration of the

Wien program, and it includes a Japanese student, Wakako Kimoto (Hironaka). She enjoyed a full four-year experience at Brandeis, married a Japanese Harvard graduate fellow, returned with him to Kyoto, became a distinguished novelist, and, in 1989, was elected as the first woman in Japanese history to sit in the Diet.

Subhi Abu-Gosh was a young Arab who came from the village of Abu Gosh on the outskirts of Jerusalem, whose inhabitants had opted to remain when Israel was established. The little village had never emerged from its semiprimitive agricultural status. No one had reached out for advanced education. Subhi's family rejoiced that he was offered an opportunity at Brandeis through the Wien program. He studied at Brandeis for three years and was then assisted to continue with graduate studies at Princeton. During one of the summer recess periods, Thelma and I visited the village where Subhi's uncle was the mukhtar, and we were received with overwhelming hospitality. We did not meet the women of the family who were still tied to the medieval tradition where mixed company was forbidden, but their culinary art, simple but more than ample, was a delight. When Subhi returned to Israel, he joined the faculty of the University of Tel Aviv, teaching Arab subjects there, cherishing the ambition that someday he might sit in the Knesset and serve as a link between the Arab and Israeli peoples for a future of reconciliation and peace. Some years later, he became the head of the Moslem Courts in Israel.

Age Kristoffersen was a young pianist from Norway who came to Brandeis in 1959. In his several years at Brandeis, he supplemented his program in the liberal arts with special training that the university provided in its music courses, conducted in cooperation with members of the Boston Symphony Orchestra. When he returned to Norway, he performed often as a solo pianist with Norwegian symphony orchestras and gave recitals not only in his native land but in Germany, Holland, Belgium, and in the United States. In 1973 he was appointed director of culture for one of the communities near Oslo and continued to direct opera for the Norwegian Broadcasting Company. Meanwhile, he had married Anna Borg, the prima ballerina and artistic director of the Norwegian National Ballet Company.

Adriano Arcelo came from the Philippines in 1960 and took advantage of every course in economics that he could crowbar into his schedule. He graduated with the class of 1963, and a place was waiting for him in the economics department of the University of the Philippines. Three years later, the president of the Philippines took him into his office as an assistant for economic affairs, and he continued to teach as professor of economics and environmental planning. When the government established a fund for assistance to private education, Adriano was named project director. Meanwhile, he was writing extensively on problems of school planning, and his series of monographs on institutional management and development became a key textbook for the educational system of the Philippines.

Elsa Valdes had chosen a career of social work in her native Panama. The little country, with only one school of social work, was in desperate need of personnel. When the Florence Heller Graduate School at Brandeis was launched, it met her needs for policymaking training, and she was one of the first Wien students chosen for graduate study. She received her doctorate with honors and returned to become the director of the School of Social Work at the University of Panama.

Osman Faruk Logoglu, who had come to us from Turkey in the early 1960s, went on for a doctorate at Princeton. He entered the diplomatic service of Turkey when he returned and became one of the officials in the Turkish Ministry of Foreign Affairs. After Yakabu Lot, a Nigerian who graduated in 1963, went through a rigid apprenticeship in the Consulate General's office in New York, he became the planning director for economic development in the Ministry of Finance in one of the Nigerian provinces.

Mohammed Nawaawi of the class of 1963 taught at Wellesley College before returning to the Far East as a visiting professor at Silliman University in the Philippines, then resettled in his native Malaysia to teach political science at the University of Sains and also to serve as the dean of the School of Comparative Social Sciences. Raoul Kneucker of the class of 1959 married his classmate Linda Brailove, earned a doctorate at Graz University, and became the secretary general of the Austrian Rector's Conference, a standing commission that represents and coordinates all Austrian universities. He joined the faculty of the Diplomatic Academy in Vienna, where he taught comparative government. When Thelma and I visited the University of Vienna during the celebration of its eight hundredth anniversary, we were greeted by the Kneuckers and two other former Wien students who were members of the faculty. And there were scores of others who brought distinction to the Wien program and their alma mater.

Oluwatope Mabogunje came to Brandeis in 1960 from Nigeria, where he majored in biology and graduated cum laude with Phi Beta Kappa honors. He went on to the Harvard Medical School and qualified for his M.D. in 1967. Then, after a succession of medical schools, training extensively in surgery, he returned to Nigeria and held a number of faculty posts, rising to full professorship and head of the department of the Amadu Bello University in Zaria, Nigeria. His research, lectures, and writings, linked to his surgical skills, gave him international visibility. He was showered with honors, culminating in election to the presidency of the Nigerian Surgical Research Society in 1987. Brandeis brought him back to the campus for an honorary degree at its 1991 commencement.

Even most of those who remained in the United States after their training years at Brandeis vindicated the judgment of the international commissions who chose them for a Wien opportunity. Olaf Olafsson became a prime example. He came out of Iceland from a distinguished family. His father was a novelist, and Olaf started early to emulate his father's creative career. In his early twenties, he had written two fine novels that became best-sellers in Scandinavian countries. He was recommended by the Scandinavian Wien Commission for undergraduate years at Brandeis. Here he showed great promise in physics and was encouraged to go deeply into its research by a senior member of our physics department, Professor Stephan Berko, himself a Hungarian Holocaust survivor. Berko quickly recognized Olaf's potential. "This kid is absolutely brilliant." He was recommended to Michael Schulhof, who had earned his doctorate at Brandeis in 1970 and went on to an extraordinary career in electronics, climaxing it when he became president and CEO of the Sony Corporation of America. Schulhof, now in his early fifties and a Brandeis trustee, encouraged Olaf, who himself became president of Sony's New York division, not yet out of his twenties. Both Schulhof and Olafsson have become cover story subjects for their spectacular resourcefulness in penetrating the consumer electronics market.

Meanwhile, we had become interested in a combined degree program. We encouraged students to arrange a portion of their concentration in their own university and then to supplement their research studies in a university abroad, where they might find more ample resources in their specializations. Upon satisfactory completion, they would receive full credit for their studies in both universities. In effect, it would be as if two universities, though oceans apart, had pooled their offerings in a field, permitting the student to choose the best from each, receiving the degree from one or the other or, in some special instances, from both. I had broached the plan to Philip Coombs of the State Department several years earlier. He was quite impressed and urged us to experiment with it. We were able to plan such combined programs as pilot experiments with one of the new British universities, Sussex, whose president, Asa Briggs, was an academic maverick. We found that Brandeis offered opportunities in the sciences that did not exist at Sussex, while the offerings at Sussex in the humanities opened areas that were not yet adequately covered in our curriculum. We established similar relationships with the University of the Andes in Bogota, Colombia, and for a number of years their students took science and social science courses at Brandeis and our students took Latin American history, economics, and anthropology at Bogota.

But mainly, I believe, because of the conservatism of our faculty and its Educational Policies Committee, we never really got far beyond the experimental combined degree ventures. Our faculty had set up study groups, spent time on statistical comparisons to equate credits, and made its way through all the bureaucracy that kept delaying the expansion of the programs. If there had been genuine confidence in the usefulness of such exchange, the technical obstacles could have been overcome.

Soon, it no longer mattered. When my incumbency as president was over, the program was quietly dropped. I imagine I could have fought the issue through, especially since it was fully funded through the Wien program, and many of the foreign universities, especially in England, Germany, and Latin America, were quite ready to cooperate. But there are always innumerable issues in dispute between faculty and administration in a lively university, so there must be an order of priority in what to battle about if one is not to be bogged down. Curriculum in practice belongs within the jurisdiction of the faculty and its Educational Policies Committee, and there were more crucial issues in the early 1960s that demanded considerable time and energy. I learned once more that, however young a university may be, it is in the nature of the average faculty member to remain conservative and to give the benefit of the doubt to routine. It is easier to let sleeping courses lie. To this day, however, I regret that a program so full of promise for international education and for linking universities across frontiers could not have been brought to continuity.

Another venture involved us for several years with the training of Peace Corps volunteers who were to be posted to Bolivia and Colombia. The Peace Corps was one of President Kennedy's most cherished undertakings. Soon after his inauguration in 1961, he had sent a message to Congress calling for the establishment of a permanent Peace Corps, "a pool of trained American men and women sent overseas by the U.S. government, or through private organizations and institutions, to help foreign countries meet their urgent needs for skilled manpower." In September, Congress had approved the project with an initial grant of $30 million and had placed the enterprise under the direction of the president's brother-in-law, Sargent Shriver.

Bureaucratic delays were cut through, and, within a year, more than two thousand mainly younger men and women had enlisted. Contracts were given to many American and foreign universities and to private educational organizations to help with training preparation. Those who enlisted were expected to serve for two years. By the end of the first year, five hundred Peace Corps workers were at their tasks overseas—teachers in Ghana, Nigeria, and the Philippines, rural development workers in Chile and Colombia, surveyors and geologists in Tanganyika, nurses in Pakistan, agricultural extension workers in India. In our 1962 commencement, we included Sargent Shriver among the honorary degree recipients, and the citation was not exaggerated when it noted his achievement: "Director of the Peace Corps, he rejects the discredited motivations of 'the white man's burden,' harnessing instead the traditional idealism of young America to help the emerging nations to help themselves." We discussed with him during his stay the possibility of bringing a training unit to Brandeis, and he encouraged it.

In the fall of 1964, on a grant of $138,000 from the State Department, fifty volunteers for a Bolivian Peace Corps came to Brandeis for their three months of special training. They were required to submit to a grueling schedule of fifteen hours daily, living in conditions that simulated what they could expect to find in Bolivia. Pierre Gonon, head of our career planning office who coordinated the project, wrote: "The Center will prepare volunteers in a health project to teach nutrition, install sanitary facilities and train citizens in their use, conduct inoculation campaigns, and treat diseases. In addition, the education project will train volunteers to become instructors and teaching assistants in Bolivian universities."

The Peace Corps curriculum at Brandeis included the study of Bolivian and American international history and politics, technical studies for one assigned task, health and medical training, physical education and recreation typical of both the United States and the host country. After three months, sixteen of the volunteers left for Puerto Rico for a few final weeks, mainly for language practice. The others remained on campus and then joined their classmates in Bolivia. The grant was repeated in 1965 for similar training with a slightly larger group. Another Peace Corps training program, in the summer of 1966, was organized for service in Colombia. What the Colombian government most desired was specialized assistance in strengthening the competence of its primary and secondary school teachers in mathematics, biology, chemistry, physics, and elementary science. The 1966 Peace Corps brought together sixty volunteers to prepare them for university teaching and secondary school teacher training in some of Colombia's urban areas. An important innovation in this mathematics-science component of the program was the institution of a laboratory school that was developed in cooperation with the nearby Lexington school system, which invited Peace Corps trainees to participate in planning, teaching, and evaluating a special mathematics-science curriculum. It should be added that, in addition to the formal training programs that were centered at Brandeis, a substantial number of our students signed up each year to serve in many parts of the world as Peace Corps volunteers.

Campus life was much enriched during the fall in the three years of Peace Corps training by the presence of the volunteers and the seriousness with which they went about their preparation. We were gratified that members of our staff and faculty later became important national leaders—Joseph

Kauffman, our dean of students, became coordinator of training programs; Lawrence Fuchs of our American civilization concentration, heading up the largest Peace Corps unit in the Philippines; and Joseph Murphy, who came out of our politics department, as director of the unit in Ethiopia. Kauffman later became president of Rhode Island College, and Murphy, chancellor of the City University of New York. Fuchs returned to Brandeis as chairman of the American civilization program.

Because of my own concern for the international program, it was natural that, when a tribute designation was offered me at the conclusion of my incumbency, I chose fellowship support for our most gifted students who wished to study abroad and a center where such programs could be adequately housed. The site chosen was in one of the newer parts of the campus, looking out on the woods, and it lent itself to most imaginative treatment. I was especially pleased with the chancellor's suite and its adjacent patio office, where, on lovely days, my work could go forward as if in the heart of the woods. On the facade of the building, metal plates of all the flags of the United Nations were mounted. The roof (which became a colorful plaza for open-air gatherings) carried twelve flagpoles, and on special occasions, selected flags were flown to welcome visiting foreign dignitaries. Apart from housing the administrative headquarters for all the international programs, the center was planned to include a lounge and study hall for our foreign students. Their activities on campus would be completely interwoven with the routines of their classmates, but they would have an attractively appointed center for their leisure hours. The library lounge was underwritten by Jack and Helen Lazar of New York, who had made the Kimberly name a symbol for exquisitely styled women's clothes. An intimate auditorium, seating about three hundred, was included as the gift of Mrs. Evelyn Silver of Texas, in memory of her husband, Harold. An entire wing was set apart for the economics department, underwritten in full by Edward and Sade Goldstein of Boston. Goldstein was a Fellow responsible for much of our fund-raising success in Palm Beach. The spacious lobby was made possible by the gift of the Malkin family of New York. The Malkin son had married one of the Wien daughters, and the lobby led into the Wien international program wing.

Several years after the International Center was dedicated, Viola Addison, a close personal friend and a most generous patron of the university, died. She left virtually all of a $700,000 estate to Brandeis, stipulating that she wanted a designation for the bequest that would serve both the Goldfarb Library and the International Center. Half the bequest therefore went for a new level in the library. The plaza on the International Center roof was also designated in the names of Viola Addison and her late husband and parents. Since the roof area had been included when the center was built, this portion of the Addison bequest was turned into a trust fund, whose income would provide the maintenance costs of the center. I had always hoped that the day would come when our physical facilities would be protected with endowment funds for maintenance. In the earliest years, the university could not insist upon such provisions when donors provided essential facilities. Therefore I felt special satisfaction that a start could be made toward this objective.

After the International Center had been constructed, there was still enough capital to provide income for what became known as the Sachar Foreign Fellowship Program. Each year a faculty committee, appointed by the president, screened the applications from students and faculty, who used their fellowship grants for study abroad in one of the institutions of their choice.

The various tribute projects helped to complete the vicennial campaign goal, then in progress. As I looked over the substantial acreage that was salvaged for future growth or watched the comings and goings in the international center as students and faculty came back from their study and research trips abroad, aglow with their experience, I was gratified that my incumbency as president could be wound up so productively.

CHAPTER SIXTEEN

University Governance

Brandeis was created soon after the end of World War II, before problems of university governance became as public and emotionally charged as they became in the sixties. The colleges were crowded with veterans, faculty and students, who had survived Guadalcanal and Anzio and Omaha Beach, and to whom the embattled concerns of academe seemed trivial or irrelevant. The returning military had unproductive years to make up, newly stirred ambitions to fulfill. The editors of the *Harvard Crimson* kept their peace during James Conant's long absences while serving as American High Commissioner for postwar Germany. A later generation of student editors would keep a running tally of the days Nathan Pusey spent out of town in fund-raising efforts (usually to stimulate scholarship and fellowship support). Students were expected to sign up for their courses, usually with limitations that related to their core curriculum, to attend their classes, to be tested at the end of the semester, and to accumulate the required number of credits to earn graduation, with or without honors. The admonition of a Columbia professor, on first meeting his class, may have been extreme, but there was enough authority in it to set the climate of behavior. "I am here," he announced, "to teach. You are here to listen. And if you finish before I do, please raise your hand." But such teaching and academic duties comprised the limits of faculty clout. Their role was advisory and not supervisory. At this stage, the mechanics of internal university government, even the issue of participatory decision-making responsibility, triggered board resistance as intrusive.

Adding to critical restraint was the fear that political pressures from without would erode the hard-won right to teach and write freely. This was the period when Joseph McCarthy, the junior senator from Wisconsin, and a cocksure congressman from California, to paraphrase Alistair Cooke, "placed a generation on trial." Both tax-supported institutions and those underwritten by private philanthropy were often subject to coercion, forced to hedge on commitments to professional independence, since support could crumble if those with the power of the purse were offended. McCarthy used his demagogic skills unabashedly for blackmail. Eminent Sinologists and long-honored political scientists were often forced into resignation and obscurity. It was not an easy period for a free-acting president of a university to protect the campus as a citadel of conscience while appealing for support from often intimidated constituencies.

Through all this ordeal, Brandeis came off well. Problems of freedom and independence were taken in stride. The Board of Trustees regarded faculty with what was close to awe, an attitude rooted in the traditional Jewish respect for the teacher and the learned. I had come to the presidency out of a long university experience and fully appreciated the importance of protecting faculty and student independence.

The university was still a very small family. Until accreditation, six years after founding, there was no Faculty Senate, not only because of the very limited size of the school but because we still had no critical mass with a career commitment to Brandeis. Governance meant informed consensus. A small group of faculty and administrative officers met frequently with me at the president's house, in my office, or, most often, at lunch for casual off-the-record discussions. The conversations ranged over the expansion of faculty as the classes grew, changing strategies of recruitment, the reforms that were everywhere under scrutiny in educational orientation. Our main planning, of course, came from some of the younger faculty who had decided that Brandeis was to be their career—Leonard Levy, Saul Cohen, John Roche, and a few others who worked their students into overanxiety by their tough academic demands. They were usually thanked afterward for their coercive perfectionism. When visiting professors came for a season, they added yeast and ferment to our discussion. Since we were soon seriously concerned about graduate studies, a library, and the labyrinthine diplomacy necessary to garner research funds from national agencies, it was fortunate that we had Henry Steele Commager's counsel. Our testing point, therefore, did not come in issues that involved freedom of expression. It came in recruitment of faculty, where it would have been less threatening to steer clear of controversial appointments. Two episodes, both occurring in the McCarthy period, may point up the mettle of the trustees and the administration.

In 1952, as the university was preparing for its first commencement, I addressed a fund-raising conference in Miami and appealed for help in the development of our physical plant. A partner in a major paperback firm indicated that he would be glad to underwrite the facilities for our undergraduate Department of Economics. "Would you tell me, however," he added, "whether it would be possible for me to know, in advance, of faculty appointments to the department, who they would be, and something about their background?" There was a hush in the room, for obviously this was more than a perfunctory question about the designation of a building or the academic competence of a faculty appointee. "Joe," I responded, "if we gave any donor even implied veto power over faculty appointments, I don't believe you would have sufficient respect for the school to want to offer it any support." The potential donor quickly retreated, "I wanted to be sure about the spirit of this young school. Had you given any other kind of response, you would get no contribution from me or my firm." There was nothing heroic about my reply; any school of quality would be expected to stand by the principle of complete freedom in the choice of faculty. The test only came for Brandeis because these were its founding years and the need for physical facilities compelled an almost desperate quest.

Another test came soon after, in 1956. At the recommendation of the mathematics department, I had brought the name of Felix Browder to the trustees for final confirmation. As noted earlier, Browder was the son of the head of the Communist party in the United States. He had served with distinction in the military forces during World War II and was a highly regarded mathematician; but with the sinister shadow of McCarthy hanging over every university, several of the most important ones had bypassed Browder's application. I wondered if some of our trustees would feel a similar concern. The discussion, of course, recognized the public relations problem. Mrs. Roosevelt was present, and she spoke up at once. She noted that Brandeis had been established in a climate of great national tension, when the forces of repression were striving for mastery in the political, business, and academic worlds. There was indeed no obligation to bring in Browder; there were many other excellent candidates. But the appointment would test the university's courage in a time of trial. Her statement was quickly seconded by Joseph Proskauer, a former justice of the Supreme Court of New York. He indicated that, exactly because Brandeis was so young and was now fashioning its precedents, it was essential to announce to the academic world that there would be no buckling under to threat or intimidation, real or fancied. The board, basically a conservative group, unanimously endorsed these sentiments. When the new faculty appointments were announced the next day, a *Christian Science Monitor* reporter, who had spotted the name in our routine release, called me for a statement. I indicated that Browder's father was not under consideration any more than Benjamin Cardozo's father, a Tammany Hall hack, had any bearing on the choice of his gifted son for a vacancy on the Supreme Court. I added that the rationale for our action had already been voiced twenty-five hundred centuries earlier by Ezekiel, when he declared that each man must be judged on his own: "If the father hath eaten sour grapes shall the teeth of the children be set on edge?" Old Ezekiel and young Browder both made the front page.

Any review of governance in the first two decades of the university's history must include a tribute to the staff people at my side who worked tirelessly to achieve the results that brought so much gratification. The relatively smooth functioning of the university, with all its complicated academic planning, funding, promotion, and administration, was made possible because behind the decision-makers were their loyal, patient assistants, their aides, and their secretaries. Only a few can be named here, but they are typical of the scores of conscientious workers to whom their service at the university was more than a job.

No catalog of our early administrators would be complete without at least a few lines about Gertrude Carnovsky. Gertrude came to Brandeis as a competent secretary and retired many years later as the highly esteemed associate dean of faculty. She was a member of a multitalented St. Louis family that included her brother Morris, the distinguished Shakespearean actor. One of her most important contributions in the Office of the Dean was continuity. This constancy was achieved in an office that was something of a revolving door. She was virtually unflappable; all of her deans held her in high esteem. She could be crisp. Once a new staffer, terrified after having been taken over the coals verbally by Leonard Levy, went to her in tears. "It's not that bad," observed Gertrude, "at least he knows your name." On another occasion, she let down with consummate gentleness a timid freshman girl who had tiptoed in to ask, in a whisper, if such-and-such a young faculty member was married. (He was.) When one of her deans was asked what he planned to do if Gertrude decided to retire, he replied, "Oh, that's easy. I'll just go out and commit suicide." Gertrude lived out her remaining years in Connecticut, as a beloved legend.

There was a long period of service from Joseph Kauffman, and it was an indication of his versatility that he could function with resourcefulness successively as fund-raiser, as assistant to the president for special missions, and as dean of students. When he left Brandeis after ten years, he became one of Sargent Shriver's right-hand men in organizing and directing the Peace Corps, and he went on from there to become president of Rhode Island University. He soon learned some of the frustrations of managing a tax-supported university in a sharply divided state and accepted a professorship in education at the University of Wisconsin. His letter to me radiated the cheer and relief of being free to devote himself to teaching, research, and writing.

Another pioneering member of our administration was Philip Driscoll, who might be described as a vivid contrast to many of his colleagues. Driscoll, a Williams College graduate, was a patrician of speech, able to recite reams of William Butler Yeats at the slightest suggestion. His dark Irish good looks were complemented by the Titian comeliness of his wife, Eileen, who taught in the Romance languages department until the rising tide of small Driscolls rose above her knees, so to speak. Driscoll, as dean of admissions and a devout Roman Catholic, was an effective ambassador for the university to the academic world that did not yet know Brandeis.

I gave Driscoll a single directive when he became dean of admissions. "Get the best prospects, the ones who are prepared to take tough assignments." In this, he can be said to have succeeded quite well. Outright academic failure among students recruited by him and his bright staff was extremely rare. Indeed, those few who came a-cropper academically were most often discovered to have been affected by other factors, scarcely any by academic incompetence. A small number of students requested transfers to other colleges and universities. Curiously, this tiny group turned out to consist largely of young ladies who, in the perhaps apocryphal words of one, were "sick and tired of having our prettiest party dresses hanging in the closet, unworn for weeks on end." Brandeis was not a "dress for dinner" school, and, I suppose, we were short on proms.

Driscoll succeeded Kermit Morrissey as dean of students and, in that capacity, proved as effective as he had been in admissions, certainly for the remainder of my incumbency. What we, none of us, could know was that an era of restlessness in the early seventies was on the horizon that would tax the talents of even as urbane an individual as Driscoll. Student strikes, disruption, sit-ins, and, on the part of a few, self-destructive behavior would invade the groves of academe. In time, Driscoll became a casualty of changes in administration. He spent a few years helping to form a consortium of colleges in western Massachusetts and then moved on to the Midwest as an educational consultant. Sadly, he suffered a crippling stroke in his early fifties. (Thelma and I were to share the Driscoll family's anguish a few years later when the same tragic illness struck down our second son, Edward, then in his forties and chairman of psychiatry at Columbia's College of Physicians and Surgeons. We were to lose Edward before his fiftieth birthday.)

The wholesale appointments of faculty went forward all through the early years. When graduate areas were opened, often two or three in one year, staffing was similarly recruited in multiples. There were inevitably strong differences of opinion as senior faculty members discussed candidates and recommendations. Disagreements usually involved academic considerations—teaching ability, research and writing productivity, concern for students, capacity for growth. Some of the individuals who were gladly welcomed revealed they had been unable to make headway in their applications elsewhere, so Brandeis was a haven as well as a professional career.

Early incumbents at Brandeis included Herbert Marcuse, the maverick in philosophy and politics who had achieved national prominence as a radical guru. Marcuse's appreciation for the hospitality with which he was received at Brandeis deserves relating, since he became perhaps the most relevant symbol in my experience of the cynical radical who demands independence as a right for himself but considers it "hypocrisy" when it is expected of him. Marcuse was appointed to the faculty in 1954, when the first graduate programs were established. His views, highly critical of capitalism and moderate socialism, and his association with extremist radical movements had brought him into difficult confrontations with government agencies and with the institutes he served at Harvard and Columbia.

He was a man who apparently equated effrontery with boldness, but he nevertheless worried continuously that his past association might create problems of security for him. For example, there was the instance when the spy Soblen was brought back to this country to stand trial for possible treason. Marcuse came to see me in great agitation. He noted that the government records would undoubtedly reveal his association with Soblen, and he was fearful that, when this relationship became public, the university might not be willing to stand by him. I asked him if any of his activity had been subversive, and he assured me that this was not so. He had indeed been an intellectual mentor in the movements Soblen had manipulated, but he had never participated in any activity that could be legally judged subversive. I assured him that he had nothing to fear if he had indeed restricted his activity to the exposition of his views. Soblen committed suicide before his trial began, and his case became moot.

As Marcuse grew older, his corrosive style became more biting. He baited academia unmercifully, as he did national government and the economic and social system. He criticized the effectiveness of the principle of free speech, which he called "repressive tolerance," treating it as a ploy by the power groups who exercised their control in more subtle ways. He became one of the rallying points in the offbeat youth movements, along with Ché Guevara and Mao Tse-tung. I was often placed on the defensive by our more conservative supporters who wondered how the university could continue to tolerate Marcuse as an objective teacher. But in the twelve years of his stay at Brandeis, no attempt was ever made to censor him.

In the spring of 1965, approaching his sixty-eighth year and following general academic practice, Marcuse came in to see me to discuss the university's rule for retirement. The Faculty Handbook prescribed retirement at age sixty-eight, but there could be extensions to sixty-nine and seventy if recommended by the president to the Board of Trustees. At seventy, retirement was mandatory, a provision that the faculty itself had set up to make way for the promotion and tenure of younger men and women. Marcuse said that he had been offered a three-year appointment at the newly created University of California branch at San Diego, and he asked if he could have a matching three-year extension at Brandeis, through his seventy-first year. I indicated that I would be glad to recommend his reappointment to age sixty-nine and then to age seventy, after a physical examination. But a three-year contract would not be possible. This procedure was the practice at Harvard and at other elite colleges, and it was strictly enforced by the Brandeis faculty. He would, therefore, have to make his own decision; he could stay on with us for two more years, until seventy, or he could be assured of an extra year of active teaching at San Diego. Marcuse chose the longer contract of San Diego. After the interview and the announcement of his decision, the word went out through the Students for a Democratic Society (SDS) that Marcuse had been "fired" for his radical views. This distortion was uncritically repeated as student editors of the *Justice* kept going back into its files, and it congealed into an anti-administration record known as the Marcuse case. Marcuse remained silent through the years that followed, making no effort to set the record straight. We had views that were poles apart; we had clashed often on political and philosophical issues; but no man at the university had been treated with such impeccable fairness through his long years at Brandeis, and Marcuse knew it.

There was only one case during my twenty-year tenure where the administration's record on the principle of faculty freedom of expression was challenged. It came in 1962 during the Cuban missile crisis. Davie Aberle and his wife, Katherine Gough, a British citizen, were both members of the anthropology department, Aberle serving as chairman. The headlines were dominated by the problems the Kennedy administration was having with Fidel Castro when the confrontation brought the world perilously close to a nuclear war. On the campus, the climate was not unlike that in the last act of Bernard Shaw's *Heartbreak House,* where all the characters prepare to go out into the garden to watch for the bombers. The director of our international services was besieged with lines of foreign students inquiring anxiously whether or not they should go home. In this near-panic atmosphere, a public meeting was held in Ford Hall, and several left-wing faculty speakers vigorously upheld the Khrushchev-Castro policy as a legitimate response to "American imperialism." Katherine Gough was on the program, and, before a wildly excited audience of youngsters, she exclaimed that, if she were back in London where anti-American rallies were taking place before the American embassy, she would join the demonstrators in their cry: "Viva Fidel, Kennedy to hell." She added the hope that, if war broke out, the United States would be defeated so that its imperialism would be repudiated before the world.

When the report of the meeting reached me, along with indignant protests from the community that Miss Gough had spoken with such irresponsibility, I called her in to learn first hand what she had said. She repeated her statements and stood firmly by them. I made it clear that I did not quarrel with her right to denounce American foreign policy. Three other speakers, including Herbert Marcuse, had been just as forthright in their denunciation. But they had spoken with the discipline and self-control that was to be expected on a university platform. I told Miss Gough that freedom of the platform gave her no warrant for an irresponsible attack. Her husband, as head of the department, came to protest my reprimand. I asked him why he considered it perfectly legitimate for his wife to lash out, consigning the president of the United States to hell, but for my remonstrance to elicit immediate protest. "Apparently," I remarked, "freedom of speech means to you and Katherine that you can dish it out, but you cannot take it." Aberle responded that a faculty member has every right to speak without restraint, but when a president ventures a reprimand, it becomes "intimidation." This incident gradually tapered off into casual campus conversation, but it was revived when budgets for the next school year were under consideration. Aberle had submitted a salary schedule for his department, listing his wife's name with the others who were recommended for special merit increases. I discussed the recommendation with the dean of the graduate school, Leonard Levy, who had always staunchly defended faculty rights and standards. We agreed that Miss Gough's contract, of course, would be renewed and that she would have the normal faculty increase, but that there was no reason to reward her conduct with the special merit increase submitted by her husband.

The Aberles had already been in negotiation for other positions. Soon after the budgets were approved, they announced that they had accepted posts at the University of Oregon. Inevitably, the media got wind of the controversy. The Aberles allowed themselves to be photographed walking together through the snow-covered landscape, arm in arm. A picture that appeared on the front page of a Boston newspaper was captioned: "The last walk across campus." That their contractual obligations to the university ran through June was ignored. It was only after this misleading story appeared that the Aberles revealed their acceptance of the Oregon appointments. But before leaving the campus, Miss Gough brought her grievance of "unfair treatment" to the national American Association of University Professors (AAUP), the Brandeis faculty, and the Massachusetts American

Civil Liberties Union (ACLU). The national AAUP declined jurisdiction since the case had become moot with the Aberle resignations. The faculty debated whether academic freedom had been involved and concluded that, although there may have been mistaken judgment on the part of the president in the procedures of the reprimand and in the salary decision, his record in protecting academic freedom had been outstanding and his action warranted no rebuke.

I was rather bewildered a few weeks later when the Massachusetts ACLU's judgment was announced that I had "blemished the reputation of a highly respected institution" and a good record of protecting academic freedom by an unwarranted reprimand of Miss Gough and a "discriminatory denial of a merit salary increase for her." My bewilderment came because the executive committee of the Massachusetts ACLU had reached its decision in my absence abroad, without offering me any opportunity to present my interpretation of the circumstances or to defend my action. Further, I was the president of a university whose dedication to academic freedom had never been questioned, and I played no small part in creating this climate of freedom. One of the projects that had brought me great pride was the establishment of an institute, fully subsidized by the Mary Lasker family, for a semester of updated study that would strengthen the background of carefully selected people from every part of the country whose professional careers were linked with the protection of civil rights and civil liberties. Miss Gough had been permitted a full hearing before the union officers, but I had not been given the courtesy of a personal call. Kermit Morrissey, my assistant, had been reached by phone and asked a few questions to which he replied, not knowing that what he said was to be "the evidence" after which the executive committee rendered its judgment.

Later, I learned that one of the members of the executive committee had, a few years earlier, applied for a position in our Department of Economics. Her credentials had been submitted to Svend Laursen, the chairman, who concluded that she did not meet the required standards. She had appealed for intercession to a number of university contributors, who were sensible enough to refuse to be involved. She had apparently nursed her resentment through the years, and, when the Aberle case came up, she had pressed the ACLU for an immediate judgment. It might have been reached anyway, but it would have been more seemly had she disqualified herself.

When the ACLU publicized its statement, it brought a flood of protests and a number of resignations from the Massachusetts union's executive committee, which had not been consulted. Mark Howe of the Harvard Law School wrote to Dean Levy: "Too many of today's libertarians seem to me to be looking for a crusading fight and it sounds to me as if the local chapter had revealed its tendency on this occasion. . . . I don't suppose it's in the cards that either an apology or a retraction will be forthcoming. You may have succeeded, however, in giving the eager warriors a useful fright. I hope so." Henry Steele Commager, a longtime member of the ACLU advisory committee, wrote an even more scathing note: "I have read the material which you were good enough to send me about the reprimand to President Sachar by the ACLU of Massachusetts. I regret to say that I find the argument unconvincing, and persist in thinking the action of the Executive Committee ill-advised. As there is no point in being a member of an 'advisory committee' whose advice is not sought on matters of this kind, I must ask you to accept my resignation from this committee."

Dean Levy presented a personal reaction, but he spoke for many in the community who, quite apart from the judgment on Brandeis, resented the kangaroo procedures that had been followed. He wrote to the state chairman of the Civil Liberties Union: "I would not have thought it possible that the Civil Liberties Union of Massachusetts on the basis of exparte evidence would gratuitously chastise Dr. Sachar and Brandeis University without first affording a hearing or inquiry in which we might have the opportunity of defending ourselves before you and your Executive Committee passed judgment. Due process or fair hearing, I should not have to remind you, as well as common courtesy, required that you at least give us notice of your interest in the case. By us I refer not only to the President, but to the faculty and its instrumentalities, principally the Faculty Senate. I should have thought too that you would have been keenly sensitive to the obligation of securing all the facts before forming an opinion. Your statement, which is improperly founded, turns out to be an irresponsible distortion interlaced with insulting and false innuendoes. . . . The President of this University—I note again—has been praised by this faculty for his courageous fifteen-year record in defense of academic freedom. There is no doubt whatever of this President's or this University's commitment to free inquiry and free speech, despite the misinformed judgment of your committee. Nor is there any doubt of the right of our students to assemble, select speakers, and discuss issues of their choice. Gus Hall, Herbert Aptheker, and Malcolm X have been denied the right to speak on other campuses; all three, as well as other leaders of extremist groups, spoke to student organizations at this University during this academic year. There has never been any censorship at this University."

The chairman of the ACLU fell back on legalities in his response and reminded Dean Levy that the union "never conducts hearings." He did not indicate that Katherine Gough was given her full say before the union officers who passed and publicized the judgment. Dean Levy rejected the chairman's explanation. "You feel free," he wrote, "to condemn an honored and honorable institution and its President; you feel free to publish your condemnation; you feel free to do all this without at any time writing or calling the President himself or any of the several deans of this University or the Chairman of its Faculty Senate; and, yet, you can state, reference to academic due process in this matter is wholly beside the point."

As I look back upon the episode, I am inclined to agree that it was a mistake to take upon myself the full responsibility for the reprimand of Miss Gough. The issues of academic freedom are so sensitive that, since the times were tense and emotions ran high, I should have protected myself by having the dean of faculty or a faculty committee undertake the responsibility. Fortunately, however, several useful consequences followed the tempest raised by the Aberle case. The faculty statement was the best refutation to the concern that independent faculty action, even in criticism of the president, had to be avoided because of the fear of reprisal. And I was reassured when a leading liberal of the faculty community expressed himself so forthrightly throughout the controversy. Except for the faculty-supported refusal to recommend the reappointed service of Marcuse into his seventy-first year and the reprimand and bypassing of a special merit bonus for Kathleen Gough, there were no other major problems of freedom. However deeply emotions ran, the statement on the plaque at the entrance of the auditorium in the American Civilization Center offered the inviolate pledge of the university: "To speak freely: to question openly: to differ without fear."

There were more frequent disagreements over the issue of shared decisions in the appointment of senior members of the faculty and of deans and administrative officers. By now, no president could be an unqualified, authoritarian figure. Gone were the days when he could follow the counsel of Jowett, the autocratic master of Balliol at Oxford, whose rule was simple: "Never retract, never explain, get it done, and let them howl!" The pendulum had now swung to the other extreme. There were many faculty activists who regarded administrative officials as bureaucratic annoyances who could serve best when they concentrated on fund-raising, public relations, and circuit-riding for speeches to alumni. They insisted that decisions that affected academia belonged exclusively to the faculty.

I agreed that the substance for the curriculum, the standards of student admission, the rules of tenure, and similar concerns should be left to the faculty for final judgment. But I could not agree that a president had to go along automatically with a senior faculty appointment that a department recommended. I respected the high motivation of most faculty, their devotion to their students, and their deep commitment to their scholarly disciplines. But to me, the profession was no saintly fellowship. It also included occasional opportunists who were as much concerned with the pursuit of the dollar as their counterparts in other professions and in business. When the pursuit became too blatant and seemed to threaten the integrity of the university's commitments, I felt it necessary to exercise the presidential prerogative of the veto. Fortunately, such circumstances arose rarely.

In the spring of 1963, the head of one of our departments submitted the appointment of a well-recommended candidate who was then at a neighboring university. He had been carefully screened and had met all academic standards. I always made it a point to meet the applicants for senior positions, and he had therefore also been interviewed by me. I, too, was quite favorably impressed, and I informed him that I would confirm the recommendation of the department chairman and bring it to the board for its technical approval. To my surprise, he hesitated and indicated that he was not quite ready for a decision. He wanted a written offer from the university, which he would consider carefully for several days. I already had had a number of experiences when bona fide offers were similarly delayed, after which the candidates had decided to remain where they were but at increased salaries. Confronted now with what again seemed like a ploy to parlay a salary increase from his own university, I indicated that our oral offer had been given in good faith and that it would have to be accepted or rejected, that we had no interest in improving his bargaining position.

The applicant, as I later learned, went back to his own university, explained that he had an attractive offer but that he would remain if the offer were met. The provost was apparently as repelled as I had been, and the applicant was advised that he was welcome to leave. Quite chagrined, he returned to the Brandeis chairman and expressed his willingness to transfer. It was then that I stopped the appointment, determined that we would not encourage the spreading practice of pitting universities against each other to hike up salaries. The senior members of the department argued that the action of the applicant was no disqualification, that our sole criterion for the appointment had to be his professional competence. I stood my ground, making the further point that senior faculty could scarcely be counted on to give priority to the ongoing welfare of our young university if they were as tolerant as they seemed to be of such rip-offs by their colleagues.

Then there was the case of a senior member of the French department who contrived a call from a Canadian university. He was quite emphatic that, unless his terms for remaining at Brandeis were met, regardless of budgetary considerations that involved the rest of his colleagues, he would resign and transfer. The dean and I conferred and decided that he was quite dispensable. A few days later, he sheepishly informed the dean that he had decided that the move to a foreign country, the uprooting of his family, and the dislocation in the schooling of his children made it impractical for him to go through with the change.

There are, of course, occasions when the ablest faculty inevitably are sought out, and they must weigh what they have against what they may expect if they decide upon a change. There is then legitimate reason for negotiation, and the university, too, must consider how far it can afford to go to encourage an incumbent to remain. But the bargaining practice is much more dubious when the incumbent has no intention of leaving but arranges for an induced bid that is spurious. Sometimes the stratagem comes off, but it has rarely been successful at Brandeis. We were not desperate for good people. We had many more outstanding applications than we could absorb.

Perhaps the closest the administration came to a direct confrontation with the Faculty Senate was near the end of my incumbency. It revolved around the issue of where the final authority was vested in the appointment of a dean. The incumbent had resigned as dean of the graduate school because of failing health, which led to his early death. I invited recommendations for succession from colleagues and academic trustees. One of them, Milton Katz, head of the School of International Legal Studies at Harvard, had just completed a consultant's task that had merged Western Reserve University and Case Institute in Cleveland. His aide had been Lawrence Finkelstein, a brilliant student of institutional problems of organization, and Katz warmly recommended him. The appointment was challenged by the senior faculty leaders. The ostensible objection was that Finkelstein had no doctorate, but this criticism was obviously irrelevant since some of our ablest faculty—Irving Howe, Philip Rahv, Howard Bay, Charles Schottland—also had no earned doctorate. The issue really came down to whether the faculty had veto power in the appointment of deans. I still followed the traditional line that, in the final decision, the appointment was for the president to make.

The confrontation lasted several weeks, drawn out primarily because Thelma and I were abroad in the interest of our foreign student exchange program. When we returned, it was clear that some kind of compromise would have to be reached. I realized that a dean, however well qualified, forced upon the graduate faculty would find the going extremely rough. The faculty leaders understood that I could not yield without abandoning the principle that the final decision must lie with the president. When I suggested that we name Finkelstein as acting dean, the situation to be reviewed after a year, the faculty leadership accepted the compromise. The issue no longer mattered by then because I had completed my incumbency and had been named chancellor. My successor had too many other problems to keep this issue alive. He yielded to the Faculty Senate, released the graduate acting dean, and named the senate's choice. Finkelstein went on to Harvard, where he quickly completed his doctorate and became secretary of its Center for International Affairs and consultant to the State Department on defense analysis.

The issue did not disappear, however. It came to life several times in the incumbencies of my successors. I am still convinced that the progress of a university depends on a cabinet form of government, where the deans, though necessarily sensitive to the needs and objectives of the Faculty Senate, must be presidential appointees. I cannot forget the near paralysis that overtook the progress of the Hebrew University after a solid core of German refugee professors established the European system of governance there. The president was little more than a symbol and a traveling fundraiser. The rector carried most of the academic responsibility, and he was a spokesman for the faculty, who elected him for short terms so that he would be sure to remain a temporary official with very little authority.

I believed further, as I watched the developments in our own university world, that though it was wise to involve the faculty and students in decision-making, the shift in the fulcrum of responsibility for academic administration and the erosion of the authority of the president have seriously weakened the innovative opportunities of the university. Most of the service projects I had proposed to expand the role of the university—the foreign student Wien International Scholarship Program, the Florence Heller Graduate School of Advanced Studies in Social Welfare, the Center for the Study of Violence—had been invariably initially opposed by the faculty. Their virtual reflex response was that any new resources the administration uncovered should go for faculty salaries and fringe benefits. And in many instances, those who fought hardest to center control of academic policy within the faculty, as the appropriate arbiters of the destiny of the university, left for other positions where they seemed to be offered better personal opportunities. None could blame them for such mobility. But, as noted in an AAUP address that I gave in 1963, the primary loyalty of a faculty member is to his discipline rather than to the university that sponsors it. I noted that when Harlan Cleveland was dean of the Maxwell Graduate School at Syracuse, he wrote, "The dynamics of a university are inevitably centrifugal. This is simply because the career of the faculty member does not depend primarily on his position within the power structure of his own institution, but on his reputation in his own field of specialization. The basis for a professor's self-esteem, the mirror of the esteem of others he admires, comes from outside the formal structure that hires and pays—but often cannot fire him. . . . It is the friendship and professional regard of his colleagues in his own department and in similar departments across the nation that the professor covets most—because it is hard to come by. For it is they who have some reason for an opinion: they can be presumed to see his journal articles and read his books. Even the professor's position inside his own academic structure depends ultimately on his regional or national repute in his professional field."

Pursuing this line of thought, I added: "My own view is that faculty should be given *every leeway* where the welfare of their own discipline is involved. And since they have both a personal and an academic stake in the institution which they serve, however temporarily, they should be called upon for counsel in the planning and the development of the totality of the University. . . . Matthew Arnold's *Scholar Gypsy* calls up no heroic image for today's faculty, here at Brandeis or elsewhere. Granted, the academician is a pretty special sort of bird, but as a former member of the aviary I would be embarrassed to regard the scholar as a peacock in a terraced garden: 'Look, but don't touch. Admire, but do not fraternize.' Collaboration, with mutual respect and with mutual understanding, is a primary condition in the pursuit of excellence."

"But where the total welfare of the University is concerned," I continued, "the faculty ought not to be the final decision makers. To begin with, they have an innate conservatism, a natural dislike of change and innovation. David Riesman refers to faculty as 'intellectual veto-groups.' A university whose welfare can be influenced by faculty veto power would thus not only soon resemble Chaucer's 'Parliament of Fowles,' but would shortly cease to be a university, since dedicated scholars would soon return to their own work and leave policies and committees to others." I therefore appealed for a continuous exploration of methods to widen the avenues of consultation; but because of the nature of the university, its legal structure and its many constituencies, the "consent area" had to have specific limitations.

Of course, in determining such limitations, there must have been times when my actions were considered paternalistic. I make no claim to omniscience. Undoubtedly, especially in the early days when decisions had to be reached quickly, I did bypass procedures that later could be judged as disregard of normal handbook regulations. Doubtless, I lost patience when it would take faculty committees and subcommittees endless argument to reach a decision, and then—fortunately, not often—I would have to cut through the argument with action. This behavior could be accepted only because we were a young school in the process of tooling up. When our country was being built, even our most sensitive statesmen were not always models of procedural restraint. I take refuge in remembering the protest of very pious Israelis who complained that the workers in the war-ravaged country often desecrated the Sabbath during their military leaves. The wise old chief rabbi reminded them that, when the Holy of Holies was being built in the ancient Temple of Solomon, it was understood that, when completed, only the high priest would be permitted to enter it, and then only on the Day of Atonement. But during the building period, it was necessary for the laborers to use it as a workroom and to walk in and out to perform their appointed duties. The procedures of emergency activities in a building period must be judged differently in relation to regulations that are wise and valid when times are normal.

Apparently, most of the faculty who had gone through the pioneering period with me agreed with this judgment. After I ended my twenty-year incumbency, Abraham Maslow told a magazine interviewer: "When we're all dead, when the personalities are forgotten, nobody will know whether Sachar was lovable or not lovable. All they'll see are the consequences, what happened here."

CHAPTER SEVENTEEN

Honoris Causa

It is a coveted distinction in American life to be honored by a university. Although the citations and plaques and "Man or Woman of the Year" awards of philanthropic and community service organizations are gratifying salutes, they rarely carry exceptional prestige. But the honorary degree of a highly ranked university is a tribute greatly cherished in a country that has no titled nobility. Thomas Jefferson helped to set the evaluation pattern by preparing his own epitaph. He did not list the fact that he had been president of the United States, or secretary of state, or ambassador to France. He included no political or diplomatic achievements. He limited himself to but three identifications: He had written the Declaration of Independence, he was the author of the statute of religious liberty for the state of Virginia, and he had founded the University of Virginia. To be thus identified as the founder of the university was, to him, more enduring identification than having been the president of the United States.

Unfortunately, the practice of awarding honorary degrees has been too often abused. Under the pressure of overwhelming financial need, many universities have succumbed to the temptation of dangling the degree as an incentive to a wealthy patron, with the implication that a liberal gift would be welcomed. Some institutions have allowed their overenthusiastic public relations departments to lead them into absurd gaucheries. The University of Idaho bestowed an honorary doctorate on a New York restauranteur for "promoting better health in the world with the genuine Idaho baked potato." Charlie McCarthy, Edgar Bergen's brash and flippant ventriloquist's dummy, was given an honorary master's degree for "the finesse that he used in the art of innuendo and snappy comeback," eliciting the comment that this was not the first time that a blockhead had received a university citation.

Because the honor was often blemished by misjudgment, it was an easy butt of satire. When Mark Twain was offered an honorary degree by Oxford, he hesitated because he had vowed that, in his advancing years, he would make no more transatlantic trips. "But since the degree was unearned," he wrote, "I decided that I could take as much joy in it as an Indian would in an unexpected scalp or as anyone would who found coins that were not his. I rejoiced again, when Missouri University made me a Doctor of Laws, because it was all clear profit, I not knowing anything about laws except how to evade them and not get caught."

Brandeis tried from the outset to emulate the impeccable standards of its elite neighbors. The screening of recommendations for honorary degrees always called for long and careful consideration. It did not, of course, exclude men and women whose munificence helped to fulfill the university's long-range objectives, but, to qualify, such service to the university had to be part of more generalized philanthropy or public service. Lawrence Wien, later to be chairman of the Board of Trustees, contributed many millions to Brandeis; but, beyond Brandeis, he headed the Jewish Federation of Philanthropies in New York, he led the Columbia Alumni Association to its most productive year of university support, and he was in the forefront of the campaigns for Lincoln Center and the Institute for International Education. A national magazine listed him as one of the three men who had most influenced the economic life of New York City. His honorary degree from Brandeis was followed by similar honors from his own alma mater.

Robert Benjamin, vice-chairman of the Board of Trustees and later its chairman, was exemplary in his philanthropic contributions to Brandeis, but his career in public service matched his professional success both as a distinguished lawyer and as chairman of the Board of the United Artists. He served successively as senior advisor of the United States Mission to the United Nations and as ambassador-designate to the Twenty-second United Nations General Assembly. He succeeded Eleanor Roosevelt as chairman of the American Association for the United Nations, Chief Justice Earl Warren as chairman of the United Nations Association, and Adlai Stevenson as chairman of the Eleanor Roosevelt Memorial Foundation.

Jack Poses, with the enthusiastic support of his wife, Lillian, took the creative arts program of Brandeis under his wing. He established the Institute for the Fine Arts that sponsored major exhibitions, and he underwrote the annual Creative Arts awards that paid tribute to masters and promising apprentices in music, theater, and the fine arts. For many years,

Poses wrestled, as chairman of the investment committee, with the complicated problems of the young university's fiscal policies.

Hence, it was clear from the outset that, though our young university, with virtually no endowment, very appropriately expressed appreciation to donors who made its academic reputation possible, the honorary degree itself was a tribute to be reserved for more than a major gift to Brandeis.

The university first began awarding such degrees after it had received full accreditation in 1953. Only three were awarded that year, since it would have been ill-advised to overshadow a very small graduating class by too large a representation of national celebrities. Hence, besides the founding chairman of the board, George Alpert, who was hailed for his tenacity in warding off dangerous pioneering challenges, degrees went only to the outstanding liberal in the United States Senate, Paul Douglas, and to one of the nation's most erudite Jewish scholars, Louis Ginzberg.

At succeeding commencements, special consideration, thoroughly earned, was given to the founding trustees. To be sure, they had few credentials for spectacular national achievement; but none could doubt that their faith in the concept of Brandeis, their unhesitating willingness to write a blank check to ensure support for the highly precarious pioneering years, and above all, their undeviating tenacity that saw their fragile little project through every early crisis entitled them to the highest form of gratitude within the power of the university. The citation of Morris Shapiro could apply to each of them—"moving with patience and courage through the beginning years of flint and thistle, impelled always by pride in his people and a passion for education." It would have been awkward to honor them all at one time. It was thus decided to add one or two to the roster of degree recipients in scheduled commencements. There were no prouder men anywhere when the turn of each came and the hood was placed over their shoulders.

Senator Herbert Lehman, chairman of our Brandeis Fellows, headed the roster at the commencement of 1954. He was one of Franklin Roosevelt's most loyal colleagues, four times governor of New York, director of UNRRA in its most challenging period, and winding up a spectacular career as senator from New York. That same year, Eleanor Roosevelt again graced the commencement platform, and the university was given the opportunity to say thank you to one of its most dedicated friends. We needed no elaborate citation for the First Lady of the World, and the salute simply quoted the Biblical definition of the woman of valor "whose price is above rubies and upon whose tongue is the law of kindness."

The audience erupted in an emotional ovation for Alvin Johnson, who had brought to safety hundreds of scholars from the Nazi frenzy and given them the opportunity to continue creative lives as teachers and writers in the University in Exile that he organized and directed. None would forget the scene as the freedom warrior, still youthful in spirit and action, stood erect in his eighty-fifth year to receive the honorary degree. The roster was completed with a tribute to Dr. Selman Waksman, the Nobel laureate in medicine who brought healing to millions through his discovery of the antibiotic streptomycin.

The convocation of 1955 again brought a group of illustrious national figures to climax the exercises. The roster included Christian Herter, the former governor of Massachusetts, who earlier in his career had administered the American relief program for the shattered countries in Europe in the aftermath of the first World War. After several terms as governor, he had become secretary of state under President Eisenhower. Then there was Paul Hoffman, who was rounding out a versatile career of international public service. As president of the Ford Foundation, his guidelines had influenced its philanthropic objectives in a period when traditional standards required complete reevaluation. After World War II, he had directed the implementation of the Marshall Plan, to which the United States contributed billions of dollars to shore up the economies of the impoverished western allies.

The roster was completed with salutes to the oldest of our trustees, Judge Joseph Proskauer and Joseph Ford. Proskauer, now in his eighties, had earned so many honorary degrees that he was sure a crazy quilt made out of all his hoods would keep him warm by degrees. Ford could not understand the deference paid to him by all the celebrities who were campus guests, for he took for granted that his service to universities and other cultural agencies were natural duties and warranted no special attention.

Nineteen fifty-six marked the hundredth anniversary of the birth of Justice Louis D. Brandeis, and commemorative exercises were planned in many parts of the country and in Israel. It was appropriate for the university bearing his name to provide leadership in the tribute offerings. Surely no one would consider it presumptuous to celebrate such a centennial in the eighth year of the university, for a rather impressive achievement had been telescoped into less than a decade. The university offered honorary degrees to leaders in American life who were associated in some meaningful way with the career of the justice: Federal Judge Calvert Magruder, his first law clerk; Dean Acheson, former secretary of state and another of Brandeis's law clerks; Felix Frankfurter of the Supreme Court, who cooperated with Brandeis in drafting and obtaining Woodrow Wilson's support for the Balfour Declaration; Erwin Griswold, dean of Harvard Law School where Brandeis had compiled his superlative academic record; Judge Charles E. Wyzanski, Jr., chairman of the Board of Overseers of Harvard; Robert Szold, president of the Palestine Economic Corporation, which had been created by Justice Brandeis to help place Palestine on a firm economic base; and Irving Dilliard, editor of the *St. Louis Post-Dispatch* and the interpreter of Justice Brandeis's liberal tradition and his definitive biographies.

It was at this birthday weekend that we began a tradition of informality that made it possible for our honorary degree recipients to be seen and heard away from the more stylized protocol of commencement. Since the exercises initially were held on Sunday afternoons, we usually preceded them with an informal brunch at the president's house. The spacious grounds made it possible to invite the inner family of trustees and Fellows and several hundred friends of the university. Just before we sat down, Thelma whispered to me that it might be a refreshing experience to call on each of the honored guests to speak, not too seriously, for a few minutes. Men of the caliber of Dean Acheson, Felix Frankfurter, and Charles Wyzanski, who were justly noted as brilliant conversationalists, assuredly needed no preparation. Their display of wit, each taking his cue from what the others had said, was offered with gay spontaneity. At one of the later functions, Pierre Mendès-France, former French premier, said, in mock terror, "*Mon Dieu,* bantering can be a very serious business!"

The practice was followed during the next few years; it was continued even when the number of guests outgrew the facilities of the president's house and the brunch had to be transferred to the campus, where it was held under a huge tent. In time, even the tent on the campus could no longer accommodate all who clamored for invitations, and regretfully the affair was shifted to Saturday night and into the banquet halls of Boston hotels.

The centennial events continued into the fall of 1956 and were climaxed by a convocation on Justice Brandeis's natal day in mid-November. To signalize the centennial, Congress approved the striking of a medallion by the United States Mint. Lawrence Wien had offered to commission a statue of the justice, which would be mounted on a knoll in the very heart of the campus. He had been very much impressed with the work of a young sculptor, Robert Berks, who was given the commission. Within the year, Berks had created the statue, with flipping robes, that symbolized the courageous dissenter defying the forces of precedent and tradition.

In the summer of 1956, I flew to Washington to invite Chief Justice Earl Warren to the special convocation when the Brandeis statue would be dedicated. Justice Warren was the soul of courtesy and cooperation, and he readily agreed. Warren ranked Brandeis with Holmes as the two most creative members of the early twentieth-century Court. During our interview, he provided a fascinating footnote. He recalled that, when he was named chief justice in 1953 by President Eisenhower, he learned to his surprised dismay that Oliver Wendell Holmes's bequest of his estate to the government of the United States had been transferred to the treasury and that it was on deposit there, apparently unused and unremembered. Justice Holmes had not been a very wealthy man, as wealth was judged in his generation, but the bequest came to about $300,000, which represented his lifetime savings and investments. The Holmeses were a childless couple, and the justice had willed the entire estate to his homeland in gratitude for the opportunities it opened to all free men. Eighteen years had now passed, and the bequest had still not been designated for service.

As Warren recalled the lax stewardship of the officials in charge, all of his original indignation was rekindled. He had set up an immediate appointment with President Eisenhower, to whom he expressed his chagrin and disappointment that the memory of one of America's titanic legal figures had been so abominably neglected. Eisenhower, too, had not known about the bequest, and he acted at once. An advisory committee, including Justice Warren, decided to convert the Holmes bequest into a memorial trust fund that would sponsor a history of the Supreme Court. Paul Freund of the Harvard Law School was named as editor-in-chief, and, under his scholarly guidance, the multivolume history was launched. Warren concluded our interview by observing, "We so often have short memories when we deal with nonpolitical figures who shun the limelight. But your people never forget. Brandeis has been gone only a few years, and there are creative remembrances of him in this country, in Israel, and in many other parts of the world. And you already have a great university named for him."

The special convocation was held on November 8, 1956. We had no facility large enough to accommodate the huge assemblage that gathered and decided to risk an open-air ceremony. It turned out to be so cold that it was necessary to distribute several thousand blankets for the crowd that shivered on the hill where the statue stood. But the presence of the chief justice, his moving address, the spirit of the occasion itself—all provided the warmth that the inhospitable weather denied. No one present would forget the testament of faith that Chief Justice Warren uttered at a time when nuclear threat was creating a paralyzing mood of despair: "If he were alive today Brandeis would act according to the belief that, over the long haul, universities such as this would have more power than the H bomb, and that disciplined minds will eventually have more penetrating effect than guided missiles."

When we invited former President Truman to participate in our commencement in 1957, we were delighted that he decided to attend an informal tribute dinner the night before. Truman was at his homespun best. He confided that his daughter, Margaret, had reminded him that she had spent long, taxing years to earn her college degree, and here was her father, without even a college education, being awarded a doctorate. How could she go on believing in the American credo of hard work and fair play!

Turning serious, Truman paid a glowing tribute to one of the most loyal aides of his presidential administrations, our own trustee, the late David Niles. Noting that Brandeis was a very young school, functioning in the midst of some of the world's most distinguished universities, he counseled ambitious planning, prosecuted with confidence and self-reliance. "Don't get bogged down," he asserted, "by petty objectives. They have a way of muffling and stifling major achievement." It was stirring advice for a nine-year-old university where every innovative venture was a battle between audacity and prudence.

Another special guest of honor at the 1957 commencement was Arthur Compton, a Nobel laureate in physics at the age of thirty-five whose scientific genius had helped in the race against the Nazis to develop the atomic bomb. There was a sentimental satisfaction in his participation, for, when I was inducted as president nine years before, he had been chancellor of Washington University, my alma mater. Compton had a commitment in St. Louis the night before the commencement, but he had flown through the night so that he could be the speaker at the inaugural ceremonies the next morning at Symphony Hall. At the commencement brunch, Thelma commented on what seemed to have become a family tradition: Two of Compton's brothers were also college presidents, one of Massachusetts Institute of Technology, the other of the University of Washington. She wondered whether there were enough satisfactions to compensate for the inevitable frustrations. Dr. Compton chuckled and noted that his sister, too, was married to the president of Berea College in Kentucky. So all four of the Compton children had gone the route. He left Thelma's question unanswered but noted that he went back to scientific research much before the retirement age of college presidents!

Albert Guerard returned to the campus as a cherished old friend. He had been among our first faculty, offered another teaching harvest after his retirement from Stanford. During the time he was on our faculty, we took advantage of his mellow counsel, and I had assured him that I shared his views on gradualism in educational reform. But as he toured the campus and noted what had happened in just the few years since his second "retirement," he chaffed, "This does not look like gradualism to me." We also attempted to demonstrate our appreciation to Aaron Copland who had worked with enthusiasm at the side of Leonard Bernstein in the first years of our creative arts festivals. Surprising as it may seem, the honorary degree for Max Weber was the first offered to him by an American university, and he could not contain his appreciation. He had been the link to the revolutionary art forms of Picasso, Rousseau, and Matisse and the development of modern art in this country. He was a proud and sensitive Jew and spearheaded the reawakening of interest in Jewish themes.

The presence of Detlev Bronk served to summarize the versatility of talents that commencement brought. Bronk had been, in succession, president of Johns Hopkins, director of the Institute of Neurology, and president of the Rockefeller Institute for Modern Research. During World War II, he had been coordinator of research in the Air Surgeon's office and chairman of the Regional Research Council. He was equally at home in the mysteries of biophysics, physiology, neurology, medical physics, and aviation medicine. No man to whom we had offered the university's tribute better exemplified the ideal synthesis of the scholar and the administrator.

Nineteen fifty-eight marked Brandeis's tenth anniversary, and it seemed appropriate to choose as the theme for commencement the place of the small, privately supported, quality college. We therefore invited the heads of Goucher, Swarthmore, William and Mary, Le Moyne, MIT, Georgetown, and Vanderbilt. We saluted a number of other college presidents who were our guests, expressing the hope that the great Midwest and western state universities that now enrolled fifty and sixty thousand students, important as their programs were for the masses to whom they opened cherished opportunities, would never eclipse the institutions where faculty and student could remain on intimate terms and where innovative ventures in education could be encouraged.

We added four other honorees to round out the roster of distinction. There was Harry Wolfson of Harvard, for whom an endowed chair had been named at Brandeis. As I read the citation that referred to his monumental studies in the sources of Jewish and Christian thought, I could have sworn that he did not hear a single word and that his mind was on one of the ancient manuscripts that was at the moment under his scrutiny.

It was now the turn of Norman Rabb, the youngest of our founding fathers. From the earliest turbulent days of Brandeis, he had served as secretary of the board, and later, when Abraham Feinberg's incumbency ended, he was to become his successor as chairman. The informal cooperative relationships between a board chairman and a president were, at least to my way of thinking, ideally fulfilled. Rabb's home was only a few short blocks from the president's house, and before every board meeting, I would meet with him to go carefully over the agenda and to seek a meeting of minds. The years of "back porch" conferences marked the period of greatest expansion for the university, and, since Rabb brought prudence to my adventuresomeness, we each could influence the other and come up with recommendations to the board that had the advantage of the pooled thinking of the academician and the experienced business executive.

The commencement weekend of 1959 brought as impressive a roster of distinction as any university could muster: Leonard Bernstein, who by now had demonstrated even to doubting critics that he was no flashing meteor but an abiding star; Pierre Mendès-France, whose incumbency in 1954 as premier during the French Fourth Republic had gone a very long way to free his country from the exhausting hemorrhage of colonialism; Fritz Lipmann, the Nobel laureate in biochemistry who had broadened the understanding of the life processes that unfold in the human cell; General Yigael Yadin of Israel, who had utilized his brilliant scholarly research into the archeological remains of Biblical days for some of the most dramatic military victories in Israel's War of Independence; Ernest Gruening, governor of the territory of Alaska and its persistent advocate for admission as a state in the Union, then elected as its first senator; General Alfred Gruenther, chief of staff in World War II, commander in chief of the North Atlantic Treaty Organization (NATO), and president of the American Red Cross; Elmer McCollum of Johns Hopkins, one of the country's most respected biochemists; Jacques Lipschitz, the world-renowned sculptor and pioneer in cubism who vastly extended the horizons of modern art; Julius Stratton, president of MIT, who prepared engineers for unprecedented tasks in World War II with his pioneering volumes on electromagnetic radiation and electronics; and Edward R. Murrow, the gifted war correspondent and radio and television interpreter, whose news broadcasts from besieged Britain during the darkest days of World War II bound the democratic peoples in a communion of faith.

During the weekend, Lipschitz, enamored with the intellectual ferment of the campus, offered to transfer the models of all his sculpture to Brandeis if we could house them permanently, as the Rodin masterpieces were housed in Paris. Unfortunately, the university, at this stage, could not command the resources to undertake a commitment that would overwhelm even the best-endowed institutions. But it was a touching and flattering offer. At the commencement breakfast, Murrow revealed that, blessed with such a resonant voice, he had been initially destined by his parents for the clergy, but he was certain that, with his views, he would quickly have been unfrocked. I comforted him by commenting that he had really been in no danger, since he was obviously unsuited.

The visit to the campus of Mendès-France opened a valuable friendship for the university. He was sufficiently impressed to accept our invitation to return in the next school year for a series of lectures on contemporary Europe. He also agreed to accompany me to some of the major U.S. cities to serve as a guest speaker for a number of interpretive functions. His lectures attracted both a popular audience and leading academic and government figures. It was a measure of the deep interest in him and his views that McGeorge Bundy, later a defense policy adviser for Presidents Kennedy and Johnson, sat in the seminar taking notes.

During one of our flights, Mendès-France detailed an experience that pointed up how difficult it was for Jews to shake off the onus of alienism, no matter where they lived, even in the advanced countries of the western world. In 1954, as premier of France, he succeeded in extricating his country from the quagmire of blood in Indochina and, afterward, in Tunis and Morocco. He would have carried out similar peace missions in Algeria, where the costly colonial wars had begun to threaten the social fabric of France itself, but he was thwarted by the opposition of De Gaulle, who later, as premier, went far beyond the concessions Mendès-France had been willing to make in the interest of peace. One of his closest friends in the Chamber of Deputies said to him, after the peace settlements in Asia and Africa, "It was fortunate for France, Pierre, that *you* were the premier when the amputation of French territory had become inevitable; a *real* Frenchman could never have gone through with it." Mendès-France's family had lived in France for more than six centuries; it had produced personalities of great capacity in every generation. But he was neither peasant in ancestral stock, nor Gallic, nor Catholic, and it was difficult, therefore, for him to be accepted as "genuinely" French.

Another of his experiences touched a lighter note. When France fell to the Nazis in 1940, Mendès-France fled with other Resistance leaders to North Africa, where he was captured and imprisoned by the Vichy leadership. He managed a dramatic hacksaw, bedsheet escape, dropping from his window to a ledge about ten feet from the ground. However, he had to remain hidden on the ledge because, on the grass below, a young couple was going through the preliminaries of a romantic consummation. But the girl kept resisting the final stage, and the persuading process dragged out for what seemed an eternity. Mendès-France said that he had never prayed so hard for a girl to lose her virtue. At last the girl yielded and gave the boy his triumph. The couple departed, and Mendès-France made his escape. He reached safety in England, where he joined De Gaulle and flew bombing missions in the Free French air force until the Nazis were driven out of France. When I published *The Course of Our Times,* I omitted this episode, believing that it was meant as a confidence. I was delighted when Mendès-France later told the full story in a documentary film, *The Sorrow and the Pity.*

Nineteen sixty represented the fifteenth anniversary of the founding of the United Nations, and the commencement weekend was planned as an appraisal of efforts to achieve broader international understanding. The honorary degree guests were mainly men and women whose careers had been identified with the search for peace. They included, among others, Marian Anderson, whose magnificent contralto voice carried the music of goodwill to the ends of the earth and made her an international amity movement all in herself; Eugene Rabinovitch, the editor of the *Bulletin for*

Atomic Scientists, in whose columns he served as a tireless crusader for the peaceful uses of nuclear power; Brock Chisholm, the Canadian scientist who had pioneered the research that led to the curbing of the scourge of malaria and who headed the World Health Organizations (WHO) of the United Nations; and Clarence Pickett, the head of the Friends Service Committee who had brought his Quaker passion for peace to the mediation tables in the dangerous conflicts of North and South Korea, the Arab-Israeli wars, and the problems of apartheid in South Africa.

Marian Anderson stayed on for the sessions of the Brandeis University National Women's Committee. It had not been too many years since the Daughters of the American Revolution had denied her access to a concert in Constitution Hall in Washington. Her address, given in a rich, gentle voice without a note of rancor or resentment for all the tribulations she had suffered as a black, made this speech one of the most moving experiences for the delegates.

I felt a strong kinship with another degree recipient, Joseph Schwartz, head of the Joint Distribution Committee, who could not accept the offer to become president of the Hebrew University when he was persuaded that the overwhelming refugee crisis of Israel had more urgent claims upon his talents. The scholar had proved he could also be a superb administrator and a most effective interpreter of causes that called for sacrificial compassion. But as we renewed our friendship, I sensed the wistful note of regret that he could not have returned to academics and its more serene lifestyle.

The invitation to Ralph Bunche recalled our earlier frustration when he came for our first convocation in 1949. We had gone through a whole series of embarrassments in reserving hotel accommodations for him. In those days, southern governors stood in school doorways to prevent the entrance of black children. Bunche had just been awarded the Nobel Peace prize for his diplomatic skill in bringing about a truce in the Arab-Israeli disputes of 1947 and 1948. But when the reservation was sought for a suite in one of Boston's hotels, the assistant manager, dismayed by the prospect of a black in his elite establishment, reluctantly agreed to make the reservation on condition that Bunche take his meals in his room. Bunche was to be widely entertained, so there was no problem about his meals. It was with satisfaction that our public affairs officer told the assistant manager to go to hell. A little more than a decade had now passed, and Bunche could speak with restrained satisfaction of the interracial progress that had since been made. But in his luncheon remarks, his banter still carried a not too subtle verbal thrust. He related some early experiences of discrimination when he was a student at the University of California. He became much more acceptable there when he demonstrated expertise on the football field.

As he ran toward the goal with the ball, the cheering was almost as deafening as if he had been white, "and the faster I ran, the whiter I got."

It was especially gratifying to welcome Marc Chagall, who came with his wife, Vava, and remained for nearly a week. They apparently savored their stay, identifying with the students, with whom they spent a great deal of time, joining with them at breakfasts, luncheons, and assigned bull sessions. I have very vivid memories of the scene where Chagall, sitting on the floor in the living room of the president's house, answered the eager questions of his young admirers, his reminiscences and observations flowing with uninhibited enthusiasm. He hit it off well when he told them, "When I was young, I wanted to learn from older men. Now I only want to learn from the young." At an informal dinner party at our home, we showed him one of his own early sketches of his father's grave. Nearly seventy years had passed since it was done, and he had had no information about its acquisition. When he saw it, he wept, and then added that the sketch represented the only peace his father had ever known in his wretched Russian village.

Chagall was intrigued by our plans for the Goldfarb Library and the spacious lobby wall that was to be a part of it. What a perfect setting, he said, for an all-encompassing mural! Then, with impetuous enthusiasm, he promised that, as a gift, he would come back to do such a mural, a study of the Creation itself. We were exultant. But when Chagall returned to France and other substantial commissions arrived, his business-minded wife kept postponing the fulfillment of the promise until it faded as a reality. One of Vava's letters began with the gloomy announcement that her husband had slipped on an icy walk and therefore could not proceed just then with his design. I was genuinely concerned, of course, and not for some weeks did I wonder where Chagall had found the ice to slip on in the south of France in spring! However, we had no claim on Chagall and were grateful for the heartwarming experiences that were ours, shared so fully by the student body. But a mural of the Creation on the main library wall by Chagall—ah!

We planned for a special convocation in the fall to celebrate Phi Beta Kappa accreditation. The honorary degree roster included Laurence Gould, national president of the Phi Beta Kappa society and one of America's leading geographers and explorers who had headed Carleton College in Minnesota; Adlai Stevenson, twice Democratic candidate for the presidency of the United States; Barbara Ward, Lady Jackson, the brilliant editor of the *London Economist*; Luis Muñoz Marin, the father of Puerto Rican autonomy within an American framework; Ralph Lowell, the genial head of the Lowell family that had played, and continued to play, a productive role in New England history and letters; Nils Wessel, president of Tufts University, who had been chairman of the New England body that had passed our accreditation; Nelson Glueck, a world-famous archeologist who combined his digs in the Sinai with an effective presidency of the Hebrew Union College; Leo Szilard, one of the creators of the atomic bomb who led the battle to convert its lethal power to uses of peace once the menace of Hitler had been destroyed; and the peerless Shakespearean actor, Maurice Evans.

The program was held in a climate of mixed anxiety and gaiety. The anxiety was induced because the presence of Luis Muñoz-Marin brought bomb threats that were taken seriously since, not long before, fervent Puerto Rican nationalists had attempted to assassinate President Truman and had actually invaded the House of Representatives. Our own security staff and those sent by the government were everywhere about the campus, safeguarding for possible danger, but, upon the insistence of Muñoz Marin, it was decided to risk the threats and not disrupt the commencement brunch. Fortunately the threats proved to be a hoax, although the tension for those who had the responsibility for the safety of the audience never lifted throughout the long morning and afternoon.

When Adlai Stevenson was called to the dais, he related how he had missed an important assignment in New York where he was to be the guest of honor. He had been caught in a gigantic traffic jam occasioned because General De Gaulle was then on a visit to the United States and was leading a parade that paralyzed the traffic of inner New York. He noted ruefully, "My schedule has apparently always been disrupted because I keep running into national heroes." The statesman's gallantry was apparently instinctive. After his remarks, I recalled another gracious act of self denigration when he had lost out in the primaries for the 1960 election to young John Kennedy. He congratulated a Los Angeles audience the next day on how prescient the American electorate really was. He compared himself to Cicero and Kennedy to Demosthenes. When Cicero finished an address, there were responsive shouts, "how eloquent, how felicitous." When Demosthenes finished an address, the crowd roared, "let's march."

A poignant note in the gaiety of the morning was the appearance of Leo Szilard. He was now so far advanced in the illness that was to kill him, it was clear to most of us that this was a goodbye session. We recalled his semester at the university in its very earliest years and the prestige that it brought to our fledgling school to have him associated with it. He spoke gently to the hushed audience, and we could understand why he could not enter into the bantering spirit of the occasion.

Perhaps the largest audience we ever had for a convocation crowded the Ullman hillside for the afternoon ceremonies. The weather cooperated fully, and we enjoyed one of the rarest of New England's beautiful, crisp fall days. Adlai Stevenson and Barbara Ward shared the program and spoke in much soberer tones than during the morning, although it was impossible for them to avoid the stiletto keenness of wit with which they punctuated their addresses. Their tone and mood were influenced by the nuclear threat that hung over the world. This period was that of John Foster Dulles's most dangerous brinkmanship. Stevenson made no partisan attack, but, facing the threats of that hazardous moment, he emphasized again how important it was to avoid impetuousness in the conduct of national affairs. Ward almost upstaged the eloquent Stevenson. She spoke of our planet as a fragile spaceship, precariously sustained and beset by the dangers of pollution and overpopulation. Meanwhile, the rich, white world, a privileged minority, and the poor and the disadvantaged, the vast majority, were moving towards collision as frustration and hatred mounted and threatened nuclear warfare that inevitably would end in apocalyptic annihilation.

Our theme for the 1962 commencement was "International Perspectives," and the emphasis was on the role of higher education in international affairs. Our honorary degree recipients included Lawrence Wien, Philip Coombs, Sargent Shriver, Theodore Hesburgh, Mordecai Kaplan, Jean Piaget, and Mario Laserna.

It was an ideal occasion on which to express appreciation to Wien, the chairman of the board, who had, with the rarest generosity, established one of the most important privately sponsored and financed program of foreign student scholarship aid in the country. His role in this unique venture is elsewhere described. We owed a great deal to the helpful intercession of the assistant secretary of state, Philip Coombs, the commencement speaker, who was chief executive officer of the Ford Foundation when the Wien program was established some years before. Coombs had long experience in developing projects for economic welfare and education in countries as far apart as Turkey and India. When Thelma and I were preparing for visits to foreign lands to establish committees to recruit and select nominees for study at Brandeis, Coombs' counsel and assistance had been invaluable. He had alerted his diplomatic staff, wherever we were to visit, to make sure there was cooperation to help us fulfill our mission.

At a commencement dedicated to international amity, it was most appropriate to honor Sargent Shriver, who had helped discredit the old pretensions of the "white man's burden" concept. Sargent Shriver arrived late at the commencement exercises, harried and apologetic. Only that morning he had received word of the first death by accident of a Peace Corps volunteer, and Shriver had been trying to get in touch with the youngster's parents. He had been a valued adviser in the presidential campaign of John F. Kennedy, whose sister, Eunice, he had married. In 1961, Kennedy named him organizer and director of the Peace Corps. President Johnson later added to his responsibilities by appointing him to direct the Office of Economic Opportunity (OEO). He also became the running mate of

George McGovern in the unsuccessful 1972 Democratic bid for the presidency.

For a number of years we had been trying to persuade Jean Piaget to come for an honorary degree, and there was immense satisfaction, especially among our psychologists, when he finally consented to make the long trip in 1962. He was perhaps the most representative of all the guests whose careers were bound up with international problems, for he was an indefatigable trail blazer in the inner world of childhood, which recognizes neither boundaries nor frontiers.

It had been difficult for Father Theodore Hesburgh to find some open time to fit into a commencement period, for he seemed forever to be commuting between Notre Dame and the rest of the world. At our dinner, there was no need to catalogue his record, for his name was as well known in Kinshasa, the capital of Zaire, as it was in South Bend and Washington. I felt, however, that his citation should include a lesser-known example of perceptive sensitivity; for example, when, some years before, he had given refuge to the Yugoslavian sculptor, Ivan Mestrovic, by naming him, in that rebel titan's old age, Notre Dame's artist-in-residence.

The Jewish sage, Mordecai Kaplan, defying chronology, came to us on his eightieth birthday, accompanied by a charming bride. Inevitably, I referred to him as an "octogeranium." Declining the arm of his faculty escort when he was called to the lectern, he came forward briskly to receive his hood. Immersed in the twin-running streams of traditional Judaism and modern western thought, drawing from each its life-giving quality, he had been an eloquent revisionist force in American Jewish life for more than half a century. A movement, rather awkwardly termed Reconstructionism, took form from his teachings, dedicated to the principle that Judaism was not merely a faith, a ritual, or an ethical discipline but an evolving religious civilization. I met him a decade later in Israel, still vigorous, still optimistic, justifiably proud that elements of his philosophy had now mellowed all branches of Jewish religious and cultural life.

The high hopes of 1962 had undergone various trials by dangerous crises when we reached the commencement of 1963. The Cuban confrontation, which had taken place in the fall term of the academic year, had been a convulsive experience, especially for the foreign students. There was genuine danger of a nuclear war. We did our best, albeit with inner reservations, to reassure the Wien youngsters, many of whom had personal experience of the terror of incendiary nationalist confrontation. They kept trooping into the faculty administrative offices to ask if they might or should try to get back to their homelands, for to them, it was not fantastic to believe that parachute troops might soon be landing on the fields of

Brandeis. It was a tribute to the discipline and experience of our staff that our ragged nerves did not unsettle the planning for the commencement routine.

We invited Eliahu Elath, now president of the Hebrew University, who had been the first Israeli ambassador to the United States. There was timely symbolism in his participation, for the sovereignty of Israel and the founding of Brandeis had come to pass in the same week of 1948. Alfred Knopf, aristocrat of publishers, joined our roster, and the audience must have included scores of "his authors." Knopf has been my publisher for half a century, and his relationship to Brandeis is discussed in chapter 4.

John Gardner, whose contributions to the country go on and on and on, was with us, too, a special favorite of the students. There was a world of wisdom in his observation that "unlike the great pyramids, the monuments of the spirit will never stand untended." Then there was the peer of choreographers, Martha Graham, in all her graceful elegance, who had taught the world that the rhythm of the dance was the diversion of the angels. We were honored to welcome the senior Arthur Schlesinger who, with Dixon Ryan Fox and others, had brought the writing of American history into hard-edged honesty, wherein neither women nor any contributory ethnic group were disregarded. Senator Margaret Chase Smith, whose Declaration of Conscience had ripped off the mantle of pseudo-patriotism that cloaked the four horsemen of calumny—fear, ignorance, bigotry, and smear—came as much to pay tribute to her colleagues on the platform as to be honored herself.

Finally, there was Dr. Sidney Farber, later to become a Brandeis trustee. Dr. Farber was one of the remarkable men of medical science, a pathologist, who had, in his own words, "gotten fed up" with being unable to explain to young parents back in the 1930s why their children had died from unknown circumstances. From this frustration had come his Children's Cancer Research Hospital and the Jimmy Fund, which he served not only as research director and administrator but as the physician who walked the wards and corridors every evening, comforting each child and parent, even as he strove for cures.

In the fall of 1963, there was a special convocation to celebrate the fifteenth anniversary of the founding of Brandeis. The crises that had seemed so portentous in the summer had yielded to a brief interlude of international accommodation. Kennedy was still in the White House, dreaming his dreams of Camelot. Pope John XXIII was in the Vatican, bracing the human spirit with his healing ecumenism. Colonialism was being challenged ever more successfully, and peoples in Africa and Asia who had lived in darkness for centuries were now tasting the first fruits of independence. It was a period, all too brief as it turned out, when young people could get off the mourner's bench and believe again that they had some control over their fate.

It was appropriate at such a time to link the theme of our convocation to the prophetic injunction, "to seek peace and to pursue it." This theme brought us an eminent group of honorary degree recipients, including the president of the United Nations General Assembly, Madame Vijaya Lakshmi Pandit. We were privileged to receive Dr. George Beadle, the recently named president of the University of Chicago who had won a Nobel prize for his research in biomedical genetics. We also welcomed another distinguished Chicagoan, Newton Minow, the chairman of the Federal Communications Commission. Minow had early recognized the power of the sleeping giant known as television. As chairman of the commission, he challenged the "wasteland" that he had found there, and he labored endlessly to improve its standards. There was also Ralph McGill, the militant editor of the *Atlanta Constitution,* John Kenneth Galbraith, the iconoclast Harvard economist, just back from his service as ambassador to India; and Father Michael Walsh, president of Boston College, the vigorous and courageous promoter of Pope John's ecumenical policies in this country. It was an opportune occasion to pay tribute to the daughter of Justice Brandeis, Susan Brandeis Gilbert, a gifted New York attorney who had always been one of the university's most enthusiastic emissaries. Finally, there was Jack Goldfarb, one of our own trustees, whose generosity had made our library possible.

The preconvocation banquet proved to be an enthralling evening. Galbraith, trenchant critic of the affluent society, was at his best. He swept away Carlyle's canard that economics was "the dismal science." Father Walsh, tongue in cheek, took the audience into his confidence by referring to the problems that the iconoclasm of Pope John XXIII was creating. He related the dilemma of the village priest who received a present from one of his parishioners: six towels designated "His," and six designated "Hers." What was the conflicted priest to do with them? He was advised to hold onto them: "With this Pope in the Vatican you can never tell what he is likely to decree next." Susan Brandeis told some stories about her father's consideration and sensitivity. What she did not know as she spoke was an incident that revalidated how consideration ran in the family, for this very weekend had originally been chosen by her daughter Alice and her fiancé for their wedding. The young couple agreed in camera that the marriage date must be postponed so that the commencement day could be Alice's mother's own.

Sunday morning dawned bright and clear. The featured speaker was Madame Pandit. Her plea for a better understanding of India's determination to remain a liberal democracy left a deep impression, not least on Kenneth

Galbraith. Later, as I walked back with her to our luncheon, I asked her how India, which she had described as very close in spirit to the United States, could permit Krishna Menon, as foreign minister, to flaunt openly his violent anti-American bias. Madame Pandit replied mischievously that Krishna Menon was the Indian John Foster Dulles. When I recalled the sanctimonious pontification of the late secretary of state, who had earned the reputation of a "card-carrying Christian," I had to admire Madame Pandit's apt Roland for an Oliver. To say that Madame Pandit shared the platform with Hastings Banda, prime minister of the newly liberated Nyassaland, is an overstatement. Dr. Banda's allotted fifteen minutes became twenty, became forty. . . . He had had his medical education at Meharry University in Tennessee. It was his American experience, he told us, that had schooled him in anticolonialist rebellion.

The hooding went smoothly until we called Galbraith to the lectern. I had considerable trouble getting the hood over his shoulders, for he towered nearly seven feet tall. He recognized my problem, and his bow to me, to bring his shoulders down to my level, must have been deeper than the one he offered when he presented his ambassador's credentials in New Delhi.

Two college presidents added to the impressiveness of the honorary degree roster. They were men of rare scholarly distinction, as well as highly successful educational administrators. Dr. Beadle had spent a lifetime probing the mysteries of genetics and had won a Nobel prize for his revelations of its infinite mutability. Our citation wondered whether, from such research, might not come the answer to Emerson's question: "How shall a man escape from his ancestors?" Father Walsh had also come to the presidency of his college from the biology laboratories. The night before, he had bantered about Pope John's religious flexibility. The citation stressed the serious side of his contribution and noted that "he dissects enigmas of heredity as skillfully as he synthesizes the humanist heritage of his faith, thus wedding Loyola's zeal to Lacordaire's heart of fire for charity."

Although all the degree recipients were enthusiastically received, the most heartwarming ovation was reserved for Jacob Goldfarb, who had made a career of enlightened philanthropy. The library that he gave to Brandeis was only one of his many gifts to causes that touched his heart. When he stood to be hooded, I was reading the citation and therefore could not see the tears trickling down his face. But the audience could, and they not only offered applause but cheered without restraint. After the ceremonies, a new member of the economics faculty, as brash as she was brilliant, and by no means reticent in her acidulous appraisal of administrators, remarked, "Mr. Goldfarb is wonderful. You tell the administration to give honorary degrees to more people like him."

The commencement of 1964 was intended as a tribute to international leaders in education, religion, the arts, and medicine. We approached it with a measure of dread, for the national climate was beginning to heat up again, leading to the confrontations that demoralized almost every aspect of American life and, above all, the universities. We could hardly expect that our Saturday night session would sparkle with its usual gaiety. But halfway through the evening, the mood changed due to the arrival of Cardinal Cushing. He was very much outside the pattern of the prelates who had been assigned to New England. Indeed, he fitted no one's preconception of a Catholic prelate. As Phyllis McGinley wrote of Simon Stylites, "I think he puzzled the good Lord, rather." He prided himself on coming up from the poorest neighborhood. "I am not lace-curtain Irish," he would say, "and I am not comfortable with them." His wry sense of humor and his public-speaking style was a startling melange of primitive English filtered through an accent that carried no connotation of a prince of the church. He was close in spirit to Pope John XXIII and shared his iconoclasm. With a twinkle in his eye, he used to say that "Pope John is the only Pope who really understands me." Who could forget Cardinal Cushing's contribution at the ecumenical council, Vatican II, during the debate to remove the ancient canard of Jewish guilt for the Crucifixion. No scholar, his prepared remarks had been translated into Latin, but in the midst of his plea, he abandoned the formal statement and lapsed into his own South Boston Irish-English. The "bishops near the door," which is to say, the younger prelates present, burst into spontaneous and prolonged applause. He was a genius at fund-raising for Catholic education and welfare projects. I remember also how he used to twit me about our bizarre adventures in the tasks of philanthropic mendicancy. "Dr. Abe," he teased, "why don't you turn Catholic, and then the two of us can conquer the world."

When he was invited for the commencement, he alerted us that he could stay only for a moment. A long evening had been prohibited by his physician, for he was already under treatment for a terminal cancer: "I must be home by ten," he said. We had told him that he could come after the dinner, that he would be called upon early, and that it was our tradition for speakers to limit themselves to five or ten minutes. He arrived when the program was underway and, when called upon, launched into a lively biographical odyssey, with comments about his sister who had married a "wonderful, considerate Jewish businessman who, like all Jews, knew how to cherish a wife. . . . It was a tragedy," he said, "that Lou died so early," and he only hoped that his sister would be fortunate enough to marry another Jew! He mocked the Catholic establishment and its sonorous ecclesiastical rhetoric. He wandered all over Jewish history. He spoke for an hour and had the audience howling with laughter throughout. When he concluded, fresher than when he had started, he looked at his watch and exclaimed in mock horror: "I thought you had promised me a short evening."

We worried a good deal about what would happen at the exercises the next morning, not only because the weather had been threatening but because it was the 1960s, and scores of recent major college commencements had been quickly taken over by militants who turned the exercises into pandemonium. We were greatly relieved that, though the student speaker outdid himself in vituperative indignation, the graduates, many of them restless and sullen, stayed well within the limits of civility. Perhaps it was the choice of the honorary degree recipients, whose statesmanship and compassion could not be questioned by even the most rebellious, that turned what might have been mutinous bedlam into an impressive occasion. Even Clark Kerr was received with respect, though as president of the "Multiversity" in California he later received some of the roughest treatment that any college head has endured. Indeed, Kerr was sometimes described as the only tsar who had written the revolutionaries' manifesto for them.

The honorary degree list included Dr. George Packer Berry, the retiring dean of Harvard Medical School. When I came into the robing room, he was looking about almost distractedly, intent above all to meet Helen Hayes. "My daughter," he said, to explain his search, "went to school with her daughter, Mary MacArthur." As a young medical researcher, he had worked with psittacosis, parrot fever, and his hazardous research had affected the tissues of his spinal column. He had come painfully trussed up in a steel brace to accept our degree, but he insisted upon marching with the other honorees.

From Israel came General Yaakov Dori, president of Technion, who was rapidly converting the young, unendowed school into a world-famous technological center. The versatility of the man, shy, and quiet-spoken, was demonstrated during the Suez War of 1956 when the schoolmaster carried out his duties as chief of staff for the Israeli forces and helped win the war.

I rejoiced in the opportunity to convey the university's tribute to Maurice Samuel. In a succession of more than twenty volumes, he had literally resurrected the old European Jewish world, now virtually extinct after the obscene horror of the Holocaust.

Then there was lovely Helen Hayes, who had already had her enchanting reunion with Dr. Berry. In her citation, I alluded to the very first remark made to her by her adoring Charles MacArthur when he passed her a handful of peanuts, saying, "I wish they were emeralds." Miss Hayes's eyes were suspiciously moist at that stage in the reading. After the hooding, I had just finished congratulating her when, to the surprise of everyone, Miss

Hayes, who was by no means an ingénue, turned and gracefully knelt to kiss Cardinal Cushing's ring. She had, however, to wait a moment or two for the completely dumbfounded cardinal to extricate his hand from his voluminous robes. It was an old-fashioned reverence and undoubtedly a memorable moment for the cardinal and the actress.

We brought back an old friend of the arts by inviting August Heckscher to share the honors of the day. Heckscher had started out as a journalist, and a very good one, becoming chief editorial writer for the old *New York Herald Tribune*. Intrigued by the basic research projects that were being undertaken by the Twentieth Century Fund, he joined the staff and soon became its director. But the avocation of an art lover drew him into the career of an art administrator. Under President Kennedy, he became his special consultant in the arts, then art commissioner for the city of New York and chairman of the board of the international council of the Museum of Modern Art. He never abandoned his writing, however, and a stream of books and articles came from him, within which he moved with equal competence between his twin concern for art and for social policies.

The list also included Leo Sharfman, the Michigan economist and a longtime Brandeis trustee, chairman of its academic policy committee. Sharfman had come out of the Jewish neighborhood of Worcester near the turn of the century and had sold newspapers in Boston's Scollay Square until he could afford to go to college. He had produced the classic work on the railroads of the United States, which was influential in changing thought and action in the field of mass transportation. But his greatest achievement lay in his teaching career at Ann Arbor, where, for better than two generations, he trained scores of students for crucial governmental positions throughout the world.

There was a special sentimental gratification for me in that the commencement speaker was James "Scotty" Reston, perhaps the ablest of my students at Illinois, who had now risen to the highest editorial position at the *New York Times*. None of us realized to what lengths Reston had gone to join us on that June Sunday. One of his sons had graduated from college in the Washington area only the day before, and our public relations people had the curious experience of watching a world-famous newsman finishing his commencement address in one of their offices, using the only manual typewriter to be found in the building. Because his wife wished to stay on in Washington for the remainder of their son's festivities, Scotty brought his mother, a lively little lady who must have been in her eighties and whose Scotts' burr was a joy to hear. In drawing on material for the Reston citation, I was struck by the frequency of his allusions to the Scottish Presbyterian catechism, especially to the "chief end of man." We included the quotation, and Reston began his own address with the very words. He made no attempt to evade, with the platitudes of conventional commencement oratory, the problems that sorely troubled young people. He told the graduates bluntly that he had no intention of suggesting that they, in their unruliness, take over the world. His generation, with all its mistakes, had not managed badly. By and large, our democratic system had proved itself; it had survived two world wars, a major depression, and the evils of McCarthyism without sacrificing its heritage of freedom. He urged the students to stop feeling sorry for themselves, to get off their butts, and to do their part to change what they found to be wrong.

By 1966, the universities of the country—and, for that matter, of most European countries—were in the throes of disruption. The militants among the students, abetted by many of the faculty, were apparently determined to effect radical changes in university governance or to bring down the institutions themselves. Brandeis was comparatively quiet in comparison to the physical and administrative havoc that other schools suffered. All the same, a commencement program was an ideal opportunity to obtain visibility for protest. As we planned the 1966 commencement, therefore, we expected attempts at disruption, but we hoped that the bizarre dress of the dissidents, the language of the posters, the displays themselves, could be kept to manageable limits. We had established the tradition that the commencement program include a student speaker chosen by the seniors themselves. We made no attempt to censor what the student would say, but in discussing procedures, we made the point that the occasion was not a political rally, that parents and other relatives had waited many anxious years to see their children graduate, and that to mar the festive mood of commencement to protest conditions over which the university had no control would be very much like carrying on a political rally at a wedding ceremony. Perhaps this logic had some moderate influence in holding the exercises within bounds.

It was fortunate that the honorary degree recipients on this occasion were mainly unaffiliated with these emotionally charged issues. There was Andrew Cordier, the beloved dean (imagine a dean beloved!) of Columbia University, who later, though past retirement age, was called back as acting president when Grayson Kirk was forced out of office by the turbulence of the times. He had devoted a long lifetime to the amelioration of knotty diplomatic and political problems in every part of the world, serving every president of the United Nations with uncanny conciliatory skill. Henry Heald, former chancellor of New York University and now president of the Ford Foundation, may have broken precedent by coming for an honorary degree, since the invitation might have been interpreted as a bid for preferential treatment in an appeal for grants. Apparently, Heald harbored no such suspicions, and his response indicated the respect in which Brandeis was held. An invitation also went to Francis Keppel, former dean of faculty at Harvard and United States commissioner of education, now the president of a newly created general learning corporation. As a latter day Horace Mann, he inspired a whole new breed of superintendents of schools, commissioners of education in major cities, college presidents, and much sought-after classroom mentors.

In Greater Boston, we knew Erwin Canham as the equable moderator of a television panel that starred New England editors in a peppery colloquium. Throughout the nation he was known as the editor of the influential church-sponsored newspaper, *The Christian Science Monitor.* We welcomed back Avraham Harman, Israeli ambassador to the United States, representing an infant republic surrounded by hostile Arab states. Not since Federalist John Quincy Adams represented our own young republic in imperial European courts did an emissary carry more vulnerable mandates in his portfolio.

Our neighbor from Brown, Barnaby Kenney, its twelfth president, was trained as a historian, an authority on the thirteenth century, but in his administration he had all the sophistication of the twentieth. As first chairman of the National Foundation for the Humanities, he championed traditional scholarship in a predominantly scientific age. The honorary degree for David Dubinsky, noted in an earlier chapter, came as he was stepping down from the presidency of the International Ladies' Garment Workers Union, one of the strongest in the country, built to its strength primarily by his conciliatory acumen. Co-founder of the American Labor party, he had exorcised communism from the councils.

Two of our most committed trustees were included in this fifteenth commencement. Isidor Lubin had served his country well from the days of Franklin Roosevelt to Lyndon Johnson. He was commissioner of labor statistics in the New Deal days, Averell Harriman's secretary of commerce for New York, ambassador to the Councils of UNESCO, and economic consultant to Israel. He was winding up a most productive career as one of the directors of the Twentieth Century Fund. Brandeis had been fortunate to have him almost from its earliest years as chairman of the education committee of the board, where he tenaciously exacted factual validation for every new enterprise. The other trustee was Benjamin Swig, who had left Boston many years before, his family resources not only strained but his father's business ventures having left a mountain of debt. Swig had vowed that the family would not rely on legalities to evade its responsibilities. He paid every creditor down to the last penny and, in California, became its leading philanthropist. It was a unique personal tribute when Catholic-founded Santa Clara College elected him as the chairman of its board of trustees, and he taught his colleagues how to keep the ever-impecunious college out of debt. His concerns reached far beyond his adopted city and encompassed congregations and convents, medical schools, theological seminaries, and the welfare of American Indians.

With such a roster, we felt that we could probably weather the stormy demonstrations that had disrupted so many other commencements. The one possibly vulnerable figure was Arthur Goldberg, the commencement speaker. His rise in American life had been spectacular: from a poor boy in Chicago to the head of the legal staff for the United Steel Workers, secretary of labor for President Kennedy, and a justice of the Supreme Court. He was now the head of the American delegation at the United Nations. There was the rub. It would not have mattered what his political or governmental affiliation had been. The fact that he was a spokesman for American foreign policy in Vietnam made him a natural target, and the militants had planned carefully to put the bead on him. To take some of the danger of disruption out of the exercises, I suggested to the leaders among the graduates that it might be useful to invite Goldberg to meet with the senior class at an early breakfast, just before the ceremonies. There they would have the opportunity to question him fully instead of being obliged to sit as a captive audience, as most commencement audiences do. The seniors were impressed, and I at once called Justice Goldberg to give him the background of our dilemma. He readily agreed to cooperate. He knew he was not the most persuasive of platform speakers, but he was in his element in the give-and-take of discussion. The breakfast was arranged, and virtually all the seniors rose at the crack of dawn—no mean sacrifice—to come out for it.

It was an experience that few would forget. Goldberg reminded the students that he was himself the father of the sit-down strike. He had planned it when he represented the United Steel Workers, and he had justified it only because he could not get management to listen; "all other alternatives failed." But here was a university that always gave students every opportunity not only to voice their points of view but, in most instances, shared them. Whom were they fighting? Disruption at their own commencement would be meaningless and would undoubtedly be counterproductive. The questions, though not disrespectful, were blunt and forthright. Goldberg treated every inquiry or argument as if it came from the representative of a major national power. He was considerate, patient, and completely aboveboard. At the conclusion of the breakfast dialogue, the young people gave him a standing ovation. When he was called upon to speak at commencement, about three-quarters of the graduating class, wearing special armbands, rose in their seats and stood throughout the address to express their protest against American policy. But there was no heckling, and when Goldberg finished, the dissidents sat down and then generally rose with the rest of the huge audience to applaud heartily. It was a personal tribute to Goldberg's persuasiveness, and also to the good sense of a mature student body.

The 1967 commencement was planned as the demonstrations on college campuses reached their noisy and disruptive climax. But, as in the previous year, the theme that linked the degree recipients was the quest for international peace and understanding, and only the extreme militants remained surly, and even they created no disturbance.

We were glad to welcome Kenneth Holland, the president of the Institute of International Education. Holland had been mainly responsible for translating the concept of Fulbright fellowships into the practical reality that had opened opportunities for exchange to thousands of gifted students and faculty. After the abortive uprising of the Hungarians in 1956 to shake off the incubus of Soviet control, he had found places in American universities for more than seven hundred young freedom fighters, saving them from the terror that followed the crushing of the revolt.

One of the most stimulating of our guests was the erudite Sir Isaiah Berlin, who came to us from All Souls' College at Oxford. He combined profundity in analysis with lucidity in expression. During World War II, with assignments in both the United States and the Soviet Union, his dispatches were models of style and wisdom. They won an accolade from Winston Churchill, himself a master of prose. Our citation read: "Whether philosophically debating free will, examining Tolstoy's view of history, or proving concepts of liberty and political theory, his gaiety is as irrepressible as his erudition is austere. The least superficial of men, he cannot swim with the tide without being drawn irresistibly beneath the surface to investigate the darker depths below."

We had invited Ambassador Averell Harriman months before to give the commencement address, and he accepted, warning us, however, that there was always the possibility that President Johnson might send him out of the country on an emergency mission. We therefore decided to be prepared with a second speaker, and we invited the former ambassador to Japan, Edwin O. Reischauer, who had returned to his teaching duties at Harvard. Harriman spoke first, and, though he gave no emphasis to a defense of American foreign policy, he urged students to bring fairness to all of their judgments.

Reischauer turned to what he believed was responsible for the blunders of our Asian policies. He had been born in Japan while his parents were missionaries there, and his interpretive skill both there and at Harvard and other American universities had helped bring the two nations together after their long trauma of hostility and war. He deplored the parochialism of American teaching, which centered so completely on the western world, with little attention paid to the Far East. He believed that the failures of American foreign policy in postwar China, Japan, and Southeast Asia were largely the failures of ignorance. He emphasized the imperative need for revision of the curriculum in American schools to create a better understanding of the Far Eastern world and its cultural and social institutions. Ambassador Harriman allowed no expression of disagreement to cross his face. He did, however, turn off his hearing aid.

When we called up John Volpe, governor of the commonwealth, we were welcoming one of the oldest friends of the university. The son of Italian immigrants, he had risen in the classic American tradition from the humblest apprenticeship to the presidency of a major construction company, which had, on the Brandeis campus and on many others, brought daring architecture to fulfillment. Returned to office for the first four-year governorship in the state's history, he had championed enlightened programs for equity in taxation, increased opportunities in higher education, comprehensive medical care for the elderly, and a realistic minimum wage law. It was a heartwarming fulfillment for him to be named America's ambassador to Italy.

Stephen Brademas, Indiana congressman and disciple of Adlai Stevenson, joined the commencement party. He was the spearhead of the Peace Corps bill and the International Education Act of 1966, both of which he had shepherded through the legislative mazes of Congress. Douglas Cater, professor of public affairs at Princeton and president of Washington College in Maryland, had been one of President Johnson's counselors and consultant to cabinet members on governmental responsibilities in education. The costs of higher education had become a major impediment for even upper middle-class families, and Cater was welcomed for his efforts to bring amelioration. There was a warm reception, too, for David Henry. He had pioneered an imaginative international program at Harvard after long experience with foreign students in many parts of the world. As a volunteer to analyze the school system of Nigeria, he poked and prodded and wheedled into shape the first cohesive programs for African undergraduates, whose own universities had not yet evolved viable policies. After commencement, he joined our Wien Board of Overseers, and few members proved more valuable in casting a sure line (he was an ardent fisherman) over the restless waters of international education.

The commencement was appropriately climaxed by the tribute of an honorary degree for Samuel Lemberg, one of our own board's most beloved colleagues. Lemberg was that rare phenomenon who was embarrassed by compliments and eschewed all honors. Often he was besieged to accept a tribute dinner, offered because of the respect he commanded and also because we knew that any affair that was built around him would be unusually productive in gifts for the university. His widely diversified relationships in the real estate world helped us find leaders for our major functions, for who could say no to this man. But he had steadfastly refused testimonials, although he made the exception for the Brandeis honorary degree. His citation brought an ovation, and the students led in the spontaneous salute: "Neither the poverty of his childhood within the pale of settlement, nor his decades in the marketplace of American business, have coarsened the fiber of his humanity or quenched the flame of his compassion."

I cannot close this review of our honorary degrees without referring to an ambitious plan for a reunion of all the recipients. The occasion had been scheduled for early December 1963, to coincide with the fifteenth year of the university. There were now more than a hundred recipients of our hood. Within a few weeks, acceptances had been received from the great majority of them. Tragically, only a month before the affair would have taken place, President Kennedy was assassinated, and of course the gathering had to be canceled. We did not, however, give up our plans for such a reunion, although eight years passed before it could be implemented. By then, a new harvest of testimonialees had been added, although the reconstituted affair was interlaced with sadness because we had, by then, also lost through death some of our most cherished foster alumni.

The reunion was held in 1971, during the administration of my successor Morris Abram. It recalled the White House dinner to which President Kennedy had invited all the Nobel prize winners who could arrange their schedules to be in the United States at that time. The president's matchless toast stated that "no more brilliance had ever been gathered at one time under the roof of the White House since the evening Thomas Jefferson had dined there alone." For us at Brandeis, the reunion, apart from the sentimental journey it made possible, spelled out an important message about the sense of values of the university, and I referred to it during the program.

I recalled a long debate in Israel when, soon after the War of Liberation in 1948, recommendations came to the prime minister, David Ben-Gurion, to authorize medals for outstanding courage and valor. Ben-Gurion at first resisted. He saw no reason for special honors to go to those who were fulfilling the obligations of service to their country, even when the service was rendered far beyond the call of duty. But he was overruled, and the main thrust of the rebuttal was that the medals were not primarily meant to honor the recipients; they were intended as a message to the nation and to the world about the values most deeply cherished in Israel. The choices for the awards answered the question that lies at the heart of national life: Who are your heroes? To be sure, the honorary degrees were tributes to outstanding men and women who enriched the life of their generation. Undoubtedly, the awards were personally appreciated for the honor that was involved and for the fact that they came from Brandeis. But in the final analysis, the choice of recipients was an alert to the academic world that, by the quality of those who were honored, the university was committed to their highest traditions of integrity.

CHAPTER EIGHTEEN

Athletics

The mythical president of a midwestern university who appealed in frustration to the state legislature, "Give us a library worthy of our football team," was not very successful. He did not get a new library; the university got a new president. The apocryphal episode was set in the garish days before World War II, when intercollegiate athletics in mammoth stadiums often drew fifty, sixty, and seventy thousand spectators and affected the reputation of university life. Red Grange of Illinois and Benny Friedman of Michigan were better known than most Nobel laureates. The Four Horsemen of the Fighting Irish of Notre Dame were national heroes. In recruiting student athletes, every blandishment was held out to build gridiron strength, and the rules that governed amateur athletics were interpreted with such subterfuge that a Philadelphia lawyer would have been impressed. I had Red Grange in my history course at Illinois, and he was a competent student; he probably would have earned more than the qualifying C if so much of his waking time had not been spent in football practice. But Frosty Peters, who unwittingly registered for my course, sat like a zombie and, on the advice of Coach Zuppke, transferred to some more lenient course when the word got through to him that Sachar was a tough grader.

By the time Brandeis was launched, after World War II, intercollegiate football was being eclipsed by the highly professional competition. The national leagues recruited their best players from the colleges, but their choices were now narrowed to major universities that could afford to field impressive teams. We knew at Brandeis that, while physical education was indispensable, we would have to be quite prudent about intercollegiate competitive sports. Most reluctantly, we included football; the decision was influenced by special problems Brandeis encountered in attracting a student body that ultimately was to become diversified in its regional and ethnic composition. It could not concentrate exclusively on hard-driving intellectuals who remained encysted among their books and in their laboratories. Persuasive also was the importunity of many of the alumni and of our most generous supporters to make sure that Brandeis, in addition to its intellectual standards and its national service, also project the traditional American image of college as a center for wholesome physical fitness. They had no doubt that modestly organized athletic squads, whose schedules were limited to the smaller schools where intercollegiate athletics did not dominate, could provide the intangible asset of "school spirit" and give visibility to the pattern Brandeis aimed to achieve.

A great deal depended on the resourcefulness of the director of athletics. I approached Benny Friedman, the Michigan All-American, whom I remembered with respect from the days when he was the rival of Illinois's Red Grange. He had since opened a summer camp for boys and had lectured widely on physical fitness. Since he had avid admirers in every community, he could be a most useful drawing card in our interpretive affairs throughout the country. Our interview took place in the early part of the university's second year, when our student body was still limited to two classes, freshmen and sophomores, numbering approximately 350. He was intrigued by the challenge that Brandeis offered as a quality institution but was not so sure about its ability to promote a viable program of intercollegiate sports. "How large is the student body?" he asked. "Almost three hundred and fifty," I replied bravely. "Does that include girls?" "Of course!" (This with a touch of defiance.) "Do you have an adequate playing field?" "Not yet," I said. "I am quite sure that we will acquire one fairly soon after we announce our sports program and can say that Benny Friedman is its director." His look seemed to be equally bewildered and amused. "Do you have a football?" Anyway, he joined the Brandeis family with the understanding that his summers would be as free as those of any of the faculty so that he could still manage his camp.

Fortunately, the Shapiro Athletic Center was approaching completion, and Benny could get under way. It was easy enough for him to organize the program of physical education, despite some trouble with a small group of doctrinaire libertarians who were opposed to compulsory nonacademic activity. Benny got around the hurdle with surprising dialectic skill by reminding his critics that the ancient classical authors had always advocated sound minds in sound bodies. *"Mens sans in corpore sano."* This was probably all the Latin Benny knew, but he had it down so pat that the defenders of individual choice beat a hasty retreat.

To create even a freshman football squad in the beginning of our third year challenged all of Benny's resourcefulness. He was given access to the application pool, but the pickings there seemed bleak. He called upon his coaching friends in high school athletics and asked them to cooperate. He traveled widely, especially in the Midwest that he knew best, and interviewed scores of youngsters who had never heard of Brandeis. All the while, he kept doggedly after colleges in the area to include Brandeis in their freshman schedules. The goodwill of many of our neighbors was encouraging. Even Harvard made room, and the schedule that emerged was quite impressive. It was now necessary to meet my promise to acquire a playing field. Thirty-six acres just across from the original campus was available for purchase. In those early days, before the proximity of Brandeis had sent costs through the stratosphere, we could acquire land at one thousand dollars an acre. We gave the assignment to raise the funds for the field to a group of Brandeis friends in Memphis. At the interpretive affair there, I suddenly became an enthusiast for college athletics but promised no climactic objective for a game between Brandeis and Notre Dame. The required sum was quickly raised, and the first major augmentation of the original campus was designated the Memphis tract.

Meanwhile, we began actively seeking friends of the university who might be attracted by our sports program. The donor sought after was in our own backyard, Frank Gordon, a successful Boston industrialist who was very much interested in competitive sports. There were two or three Sunday morning breakfasts at his home, and the deal was completed for a combination football field and an encircling track. The underwriting included the preparation of the field, stands for seventy-five hundred spectators (!), and even an elevated press box for our budding journalists, our enthusiastic radio broadcasters, and perhaps some of the metropolitan sportswriters who might find occasional human-interest stories in the challenge the Brandeis Davids offered the widely touted Goliaths.

The 1950 season opened on one of the Harvard playing fields, and our stalwarts faced the Harvard freshmen, encouraged by pretty cheerleaders decked out in new blue and white costumes. Thelma and I had been joined by Adolph and Mary Ullman. Ullman was a German immigrant whose major interest was in art and music; he knew nothing about football but had come because the game represented a first in Brandeis history. He wondered who the little blue and white clad moppets were who shouted and gesticulated in upbeat rhythm. I informed him that they were there to alert the crowd when to get enthusiastic. Our total student body was now about four hundred, and apparently most of them had turned out to cheer our warriors. Benny had coached the team with all the intricacies of his Hall of Fame days, and one of the early Brandeis miracles came to pass. Brandeis beat Harvard, though narrowly.

At no time during the next few years could the thrill of the opening game be duplicated, even when the university fielded full-fledged football teams and played against rather formidable rivals. But under Benny's skillful coaching, the teams did well, and though no championships were won, the Judges, as the teams were inevitably labeled, gave good accounts of themselves. A basic purpose was also fulfilled as the team lineups were detailed in newspaper summaries. There were, of course, Goldfaders and Steins and Shapiros, but there were also Baldaccis and Hemingways and Napolis. The message reached the nation's student applicants and their counselors that, though Brandeis was Jewish-founded, it was an interdenominational institution.

The "golden age" of Brandeis intercollegiate football lasted only nine years. But when it was suspended, the reasons were not those that compelled similar action in hundreds of other universities, the exorbitant cost of recruitment. Brandeis had never attempted to buy its players. The farthest it went in recruitment competition was to offer scholarship assistance to those who needed it to afford a college career. The problem for Brandeis arose when applications far exceeded the capacity of a small university to offer enrollment. In the first years, virtually all qualified applicants could be accepted. But after the university received accreditation and its graduates were quickly accepted in professional schools across the country, applications poured in. There was some expansion in the size of freshman classes, but there was a strong determination that Brandeis would not become a mass-enrollment school. When only one out of three fully qualified applicants could be taken, those who were recruited so that they could participate in the intercollegiate football program were at a grave disadvantage academically. They may have been qualified to survive the rigorous standards that Brandeis had set, but it would have been grossly unfair to give them the precious few places and reject better-qualified applicants who were well above them in their testing scores and their high school records. The difficult decision to drop intercollegiate football had to be made, and, though it was strenuously resisted by Benny, by outstanding alumni, and by many loyal supporters of the university, the decision stood.

The suspension of intercollegiate football did not mean the elimination of all intercollegiate sports. There were many outlets for those who had other athletic talents and for the stimulation of school spirit. Brandeis was especially well equipped to sponsor soccer, still too much regarded as basically European to have achieved popularity in American colleges but growing fast in interest and participation. Many of the Wien students, particularly those from the Scandinavian countries, Greece, Italy, Spain, and many parts of Africa and Latin America, turned out for soccer and played with superior power and skill. The 1960 team, trained by a British coach, Glenn Howells, went through its season as undefeated champions against formidable opponents. The sportswriters of 1961 found it newsworthy to report the Brandeis games when the teams included Dinos Sinioris, Dimitri Procos, and Evangelos Djimopoulos of Greece, James Chen of Jamaica, Anthony Lorraine of Scotland, Faruk Logoglu of Turkey, Reno Schiavo-Campo of Italy, Sylvester Awuye of Ghana, Peter Nagy of Hungary, Daniel Obasun of Nigeria, Saha Amarasingham of Ceylon, and Ernst Van den Boogaart of Holland.

Brandeis's supremacy in women's fencing was basically a tribute to its resourceful coach, Lisel Judge, an Olympic fencing star who brought her skill and her teaching magnetism to the university early in its history. Her squads kept winning regional honors and, in some years, went on to the highest national competition. When I attributed her success to her teaching talent, she modestly demurred and offered an interesting rationale for the university's record. "Fencing," she said, "more so than most other sports, seems to have a special appeal to the intellectually oriented Brandeis student. It is a sport of skill and dexterity, demanding the keenest of intellectual acumen for those who master its techniques. It is not a game of brute force—for 'jocks' only." There may have been some validity in her analysis; but that her finesse and her extraordinary patience counted most of all was demonstrated one year when she took charge of an almost blind girl. By skillfully evoking all the sensory potentials beyond normal vision, Lisel interested her in fencing and helped train her for teaching in a school for the blind. No one was more happily surprised than the girl's mother who remarked, with jesting affection, "How could this be? Physically she was such a *klotz!*"

Basketball was the game where Brandeis could create the largest interest and do extremely well in competition. Many of the high schools in New York with a large Jewish enrollment had won preeminence in the sport. We brought one of their coaches, Harry Stein, to take charge, and his own competence, as well as his influence with former colleagues who were glad to recommend their best prospects to him, gave Brandeis an advantage that it maintained steadily. In 1953, minuscule Brandeis, with a very small pool to draw upon, found a star in Rudy Finderson, an honors student, who racked up seventeen hundred points in intercollegiate competition and won a place on the New England all-star basketball team. Stein died in early middle age, one of the most deeply loved of all the faculty at Brandeis.

Then, in 1966, Brandeis again reached for the top and recruited K. C. Jones, one of the Boston Celtics who had helped bring the team continuous national professional basketball championships. There was a special significance in his appointment, for it made Brandeis the first college in the country to name a black head coach of a major sport. K. C.'s reputation became an important recruiting asset. Both his extraordinary ability and the youngsters whom he persuaded to enroll at Brandeis gave the university a new golden age for a leading intercollegiate sport. K. C. remained as head coach for three years. Then the call from the University of California could not be denied, and it led soon after to an appointment at Harvard. K. C. never lost his devotion to Brandeis, and the affection was heartily reciprocated. Brandeis also discovered in the 1960s that it could field superb track teams. The sports world was agog as records fell. For several years a versatile youngster, Ed Gastonguay, a Dean's List scholar and president of the Catholic Newman Club, headed the track teams, which competed with the best New England colleges.

Though intercollegiate activities had to be confined to a few sports, there was always an athletic outlet in intramural competition between dormitories, or classes, or specially organized teams. Such sports included not only soccer, basketball, tennis, and fencing, but swimming, tennis, track, golf, bowling, and wrestling. There were endless opportunities for the women, too, who, in addition to fencing, enjoyed major participation in most of the regular sports and added others, such as volleyball and archery. A major expansion of athletic opportunities came when Mrs. Charles Revson, emulating her husband—the Revlon cosmetics magnate who contributed a million dollars for graduate fellowships in science—set up a special fund to encourage sports for women, not only at Brandeis but at other colleges in the area.

In 1967, following the resignation of K. C. Jones, the university was fortunate to recruit another stellar head coach, Nick Rodis, a Harvard man who had made athletics his professional career. He had demonstrated his versatility in the positions he had held in a number of New England universities. Then, for five years he was identified with the Bureau of Educational and Cultural Affairs of the State Department and developed its international athletic programs around the world. From this post, he came to Brandeis, and it was simultaneously announced that he had become president of the United States Collegiate Sports Council. It was comforting, in the last year of my incumbency, to know that a wholesome, sensibly proportioned program in athletics was in good hands.

The major sports patron of Brandeis was the highly popular liquor magnate and race track proprietor Joseph Linsey, who had come up the hard way to become one of the major philanthropic leaders of Greater Boston. He led two of the campaigns for the Combined Jewish Philanthropies in one of the blackest and most dangerous periods of the Israeli struggle for survival. He took over the presidency of the Jewish Memorial Hospital when it had little standing and its financial woes threatened its continuance.

He led it to security and a coveted relationship as one of the teaching hospitals of Boston University. His dog track interests brought him into advantageous personal relations with leading figures in the sports world, and they readily consented, when he asked for their cooperation, to approach donors and to place stories in the press and other media.

Linsey accepted the chairmanship of the Brandeis Athletic Association and joined the Board of Trustees. He quickly demonstrated that, though he interpreted it as his responsibility to encourage and protect the sports activities of the university, its general financial welfare was an even greater concern. He launched the national and regional dinners that interpreted the university to special trade and industry groups, eliciting annual support. He began with liquor, and soon the technique was expanded to food products, shoes and rubber goods, jewelry, cosmetics, discount houses, soft goods, real estate, and banking. At the liquor dinners, held usually in New York, Linsey could produce the most sought-after public figures to serve as guests of honor. Senator John Kennedy, in the year before he won the presidency, greeted the huge audience as old family friends. After all, he bantered, his father belonged to this group, and he was glad to be welcomed back into its fold.

Meanwhile, Linsey, while publicizing the needs of the athletic program, made a major conquest in reaching his friend and colleague Louis Smith, the enterprising owner of the Rockingham Race Track. By the time Linsey had drawn up the bill of particulars for his Brandeis sports ambitions, Smith felt that he had come off fairly cheaply with his gift of more than $300,000. In the light of Linsey's undeviating concern for Brandeis and its sports program, when it was planned to construct a swimming pool and sports center to be named for him, it was most appropriate that the campaign be structured as a tribute to him. The effort could scarcely be called a campaign. To begin with, Linsey himself contributed more than half the cost. The committee in Boston, New York, and in other areas where Linsey's contacts were most numerous and influential went about their tasks with more determination than if they were promoting some personal enterprise. Within less than a year, the Linsey Center was completed, with a pool, saunas, squash courts, lockers, and administrative offices. Students, faculty, and staff would no longer be obliged to journey to the ends of Waltham and to rely on the goodwill of the Boys' Club and the other agencies that had offered hospitality during the long wait for our facilities.

The dedication brought out many colleagues from the industries in which Linsey was a key figure as well as representatives from the philanthropies he had served so well. Lewis Rosenstiel, the Schenley tycoon, though in frail health, flew in to pay his tribute. When the announcement was made that unforeseen costs had sent the construction bill about

$165,000 beyond the estimate, Rosenstiel came to the lectern for a brief statement. He asked the various committees to stop their penny-ante appeals; "I shall pick up the tab."

In succeeding years and administrations, the athletics program was conducted with prudent concern that brought a sensible balance between physical education and appropriate intermural and modest intercollegiate competition. When the university had grown to nearly four thousand students and the alumni of early classes had achieved enough personal business and professional success to become enthusiastic donors, a major athletic center was built in 1992, triggered by major gifts from the estate of one of our founding trustees, Joseph Ford, and another from Boston entrepreneur and businessman Abraham Gosman.

Today the massive Joseph F. and Clara Ford Athletic and Recreation Complex, which includes the Gosman Sports and Convocation Center, offers students one of the largest and best equipped multi-purpose, indoor athletic facilities in the East. The Gosman Sports and Convocation Center includes a fieldhouse and an indoor track ensemble that features the Red Auerbach Arena. The building can hold the whole Brandeis community for commencements and accommodate major conferences. To add to the popularity of the building, the Celtics have chosen it as their practice center.

CHAPTER NINETEEN

Special Projects

The Papers of Justice Brandeis and Other Projects

In 1956, as the centennial of the birth of Justice Brandeis was reached, some of my faculty colleagues and I began discussing the appropriateness of sponsoring a project for the gathering, editing, and publishing of his voluminous papers. Justice Brandeis had deeply influenced not only twentieth-century American legal philosophy but the country's social and political life as well. He had been a trusted advisor of President Wilson; President Roosevelt regarded him as an inspiring prophetic symbol, indeed, he usually referred to him as Isaiah. He had also been a major force in Jewish life, especially in the diplomacy that led to the establishment of a Jewish homeland in Palestine. Only five books dealing with the justice and his role (two of them long out of print) had been published, and these contained only a small section of his correspondence. Of 528 Supreme Court decisions that Justice Brandeis wrote, only thirty had been published under his name. Since the few selected documents that were published did not go beyond 1934, there was little record of his role in the court where he served until 1939. His five final years were among his most productive and included the landmark decision that upheld the TVA, in which he concurred, but where his deviations from the arguments of his colleagues were considered classic examples of legal sagacity. Clearly, a definitive edition of his opinions and writings was long overdue, and it was most appropriate for the university that bore his name to undertake the responsibility.

Of course, nothing as elaborate as the Jefferson Papers was contemplated, whose editing in a hundred volumes had been undertaken by the University of Virginia. But a ten- or twelve-volume edition of Brandeis Papers, containing his judicial opinions, especially his dissents, his correspondence on public issues, and his articles and addresses, had long been warranted for scholarly access.

It was first necessary to obtain the cooperation of the Brandeis family, and this was quickly, indeed gratefully, granted. Two daughters had survived the justice, who died in 1941 at the age of eighty-five. Elizabeth Rauschenbusch lived in Madison, Wisconsin, the wife of a professor of economics. Susan Gilbert lived in New York, the wife of an attorney, Jacob Gilbert. Elizabeth had not been keen over the launching of the university in her father's name, worried at the outset that those who were first involved might not be able to fulfill her father's austere standards. Susan had heartily welcomed the venture and had lent her name to all the early pioneering efforts. But both sisters were enthusiastic over a project that would assemble the dispersed documentary material for a definitive edition of their father's papers, and they agreed that the university was the ideal sponsor for such an undertaking. Since the death of the justice, Jack and Susan Gilbert had tried to gather as much of his correspondence as they could trace. But the materials they obtained and placed at the disposal of the university were only a fraction of what remained in private hands and in libraries throughout the country and abroad. In 1958, a bibliography was published by the Yale Law Library, the patient work of Roy Mersky, professor of law at the University of Texas. It proved to be a valuable guide in tracking down basic source material. It identified 179 briefs, articles, and speeches written by Brandeis and 333 books and articles written about him by other scholars.

To obtain advice on the parameters of the undertaking, I requested an appointment with Supreme Court Justice Felix Frankfurter in his offices in Washington. Frankfurter had been a younger colleague and protégé of Brandeis. He had collaborated with him in the negotiations with President Wilson to obtain American cooperation in the issuance of what became the Balfour Declaration, endorsing the establishment of a Jewish homeland in Palestine. He was gratified to learn that Brandeis University was exploring the possibility of sponsoring the publication of the Brandeis Papers.

He agreed that it was necessary to have an overall editor to direct the project, to organize the acquisition of the widely scattered documentation, and to clarify objectives. But, he added, such an editor would need rare perspective and background, for Brandeis had been a broad-gauged man and one of the most distinguished jurists in American history. He had been an activist, pioneering such reforms as women's working hours and savings banks' life insurance; but even more, he had conceived of the law as a developing instrument, influenced as much by social needs as by precedent. In this sense, he belonged among the conceptual fathers of the New Deal. Finally, Brandeis had been a seminal factor in twentieth-century Jewish life.

To be sure, here he was a late comer; he had very little identification in his earlier years with Jewish concerns. It is generally believed that his interest was awakened, and then became a full-fledged fascination, when he arbitrated a labor dispute in the clothing industry of New York and came to appreciate the cultural richness and the passionate idealism of many of the Jewish labor leaders and their immigrant employers. Brandeis always mastered the background of problems that he wrestled with, and, the more he studied the economic situation of the Jews, the more intrigued he became. Zionism was still a struggling movement, drawing to it negligible numbers of American Jews, and these mainly of recent East European immigrant stock. But to Brandeis, it became a shining ideal, a possible solution to the problem of homelessness for Jews in lands where the most elemental rights were denied to them. Within a few years, Brandeis had become a leading influence in American Zionism.

From the general discussion of the organization of the project, we turned to possible assignments. Frankfurter named two men. One was Judge Charles Wyzanski, Jr., United States district judge for Massachusetts, whose scholarship and grasp of the law were impeccable but whose duties, in one of the busiest federal jurisdictions in the country, made it highly unlikely that he could accept, even if the assignment appealed to him. The other was Paul Freund, who had been Frankfurter's young colleague in the law school at Harvard and later served as one of Justice Brandeis's clerks. Frankfurter believed Freund could bring to the task not only a sound and far-ranging approach to the law but a deep sympathy for the Brandeis legal philosophy. The prescience of Frankfurter's judgment was later validated when President Eisenhower appointed a commission to edit a history of the Supreme Court of the United States and named Paul Freund as the editor-in-chief.

As it turned out, the editorial choices had to be postponed. The needs of the university kept escalating as its reputation grew, and they had to receive priority. The editorial project had to be placed on a back burner. But it was never out of mind, and it was revived in the mid-sixties when the twenty-fifth anniversary of Brandeis's death became the occasion for widespread evaluation of his place in American history.

It was determined, therefore, to establish a commission that would review all the preliminary planning, offer further guidance in organizing the project, and supervise the editorial and publishing tasks. It was gratifying that everyone who was approached quickly accepted. The commission included Judge Wyzanski and Harvard professor Paul Freund. From our own Board of Trustees we had access to Professor Milton Katz, who had collaborated with Dean Acheson as one of the architects of the Marshall Plan and who was professor of law at Harvard and director of its program of international legal studies. Others included Yale law professor Alexander Bickel, who had been one of Justice Frankfurter's law clerks and had written *Unpublished Opinions of Justice Brandeis*; Benjamin V. Cohen, who had served many American presidents since World War I as a valued counselor; Professor J. Willard Hurst of the University of Wisconsin Law School, who had been another of Justice Brandeis's law clerks; and Alpheus Mason, professor of jurisprudence at Princeton, the definitive biographer of Justice Brandeis. Charles Schottland joined the commission as well; he was now dean of our Florence Heller Graduate School for Advanced Studies in Social Welfare and was later to be the third president of Brandeis. The liaison with the old Brandeis law firm was supplied by the inclusion of Benjamin Trustman, now senior member of the Boston firm and one of New England's most distinguished attorneys. The family interest was represented by the inclusion of Justice Brandeis's daughter, Susan Gilbert.

At the organizational meeting of the commission, it was agreed that first priority be given to the public documents of the justice. The private correspondence would be limited to material that clarified Brandeis's public views and actions. Several young scholars were already far advanced in their work on the private correspondence, and four volumes had been published in the early 1970s, edited by Melvin I. Urofsky and David W. Levy. As for the public documents, a beginning nucleus had been secured. For many years, both the Brandeis family and friends of the university had been forwarding original material for permanent location in our archives. Nevertheless, what the library owned at this stage was a fraction of what remained in other jurisdictions. The great bulk was still widely scattered— in the law library of the University of Louisville, at the Harvard Law Library, in the Zionist organization archives, in the vaults of the Savings Bank Life Insurance headquarters, in the files of Brandeis's old law firm, and in the possession of hundreds of families with whom Brandeis had conducted correspondence on public issues, reaching back to the early years of the century. But the project could not even move off the launching pad until the funding had been assured for assembling this data and publishing it.

I approached Judge Joseph Proskauer, then in his middle eighties, remembering that he was a widely esteemed member of the board of the Cromwell Foundation that often encouraged such enterprises. But the foundation had recently undertaken support for the publication of the papers of Alexander Hamilton, Daniel Webster, and Learned Hand, and its income was committed for some years to come. Fortunately, Benjamin Trustman of our own commission, and a leading trustee for the Lincoln and Theresa Filene Foundation of Boston, came to the rescue. Brandeis had been attorney for Filene, and Trustman was confident that such a project would have excited him, both for itself and because of his admiration for

Justice Brandeis. Hence, with Trustman's unqualified recommendation, the seed money expenses for the employment of a project director for the first two years, during which the primary effort would focus on gathering the data, were pledged by the foundation, and the venture was at last underway.

A young member of the American civilization department, William Goldsmith, who was teaching in the field of governmental problems in the Brandeis era and had pushed for the project, was given the assignment to assemble the papers. He spent the next two years, in between his academic duties at the university, traveling to many parts of the country, ferreting out the materials that were much more widely dispersed than we had anticipated. He made many trips to the University of Louisville, where Brandeis had received his undergraduate training and where both he and his wife had been buried under the steps of the law school. The justice had willed all of his official papers and personal correspondence to his alma mater. Goldsmith spent weeks among them and, through photocopying and microfilming, assembled what seemed most valuable. He followed other trails to libraries in Washington, New York, and Harvard and to the collections held by families who had carried on active correspondence with Justice Brandeis. He ferreted out articles in long-discontinued magazines and memoranda that had been retained by some of his law clerks. He rummaged the files of the Social Law Library and the state archives in Boston, as well as other local libraries and the archives of the Savings Bank Life Insurance organization. He copied documents that were mixed in with hundreds of others in the Zionist headquarters of New York. He pieced together materials Brandeis had used for one of the two courses he taught, Business Law at MIT in 1896–1897.

Goldsmith's perseverance now made it possible to study virtually every detail of Brandeis's public life, reaching back to his earliest days in Boston. There his success as a lawyer had made him independently wealthy and allowed him the freedom to turn his attention to public service—investigating, analyzing, and ultimately trying to solve neglected municipal, state, and national problems. During this period, he frequently went to court or before a legislative or regulatory commission as the people's advocate. "It was during this period," Goldsmith noted, "that he developed the famous *Brandeis Brief,* a razor sharp compilation of factual and frequently highly technical economic and social data to support the general argument he was advocating." Out of these many known briefs, only a few had been printed, one privately. The other seven had not been published, nor were the hundreds of pages of argument and testimony that Brandeis prepared for legislative committees, commissions, and other bodies before which he appeared in defense of the public interest.

Goldsmith resurrected the numerous speeches Brandeis had made, most of them buried in such publications as the *Journal of Accounting, Municipal Affairs, The American Cloak and Suit Review,* the *Cambridge Chronicle,* and other not easily available sources. He excerpted the relevant material in nationally important cases where Brandeis had been fully involved: his briefs in *Mueller v. Oregon* and numerous related cases, his role in creating the Board of Arbitration in the women's garment industry, his defense of state laws that limited and set minimum wages for work, his involvement in the Bollinger case and the railroad freight rate case, and his continuing efforts to investigate and expose the root evils of monopoly, interlocking directorates in the giant corporations, and control of the money market. When the task of assembly had been completed and deposited in the university library, separated topically and chronologically and indexed, the basic Brandeis materials, from his earliest days in Boston to his appointment on the Supreme Court, were at last available in one place.

Unfortunately, so much time had passed since the project was initiated that the cost of even a ten-volume edition frightened off the most adventurous publishers. Obviously, the original plans would have to be modified. It was during a social evening with an old friend, Marc Friedlander, who was directing the publication of the Adams Papers, that a practical solution to our problem was suggested. The voluminous Adams Papers had been planned to comprise about one hundred volumes; as the research went forward, it became evident that it would take several generations to complete a project whose scale was awesome and whose costs would become prohibitive. Meanwhile, scholars were clamoring for access to the original material to fulfill their research objectives, and they could not be endlessly put off. Friedlander therefore persuaded his commission to limit the enterprise to make the material accessible, without editorial interpretation, to be quickly accomplished by microfilming all the papers. Wouldn't it be practical for us to issue the Brandeis Papers in a microfilm edition? Editing and publishing could be postponed for a later period.

Friedlander's counsel provided the key to our dilemma. We had accomplished the most difficult part of our project by gathering the papers and depositing them in the library. Goldsmith now prepared the material for a microfilm edition of Brandeis public papers (including briefs, testimony, articles, speeches, etc.). This material covered the period from the 1890s when Brandeis began his public career until 1915 when President Wilson appointed him to the Supreme Court. The Filene funds had been exhausted, but the microfilm costs were immediately undertaken by the ever reliable Samuel Lemberg.

The microfilm edition was completed in less than three months. It represented only a partial fulfillment of our original plans, but the main objective had been achieved. The legacy of one of the legal giants of the twentieth century at last had a permanent home at the university. A guide to the microfilm edition was prepared by Goldsmith, and we jointly prefaced it with a background genealogical table, obtained by Jacob de Haasq of Boston, a close personal friend, when he visited Prague. I also included an extended essay that offered an evaluation of Brandeis's place in contemporary American history.

Although it is impossible here to highlight the many other projects linked to journalism, the most recent is a good example of Brandeis's interest in this area. A donation from Milton and Shirley Gralla has enabled Brandeis to launch a series of panels and speakers to debate key issues concerning the media. Brandeis has also introduced journalism into the curriculum as an interdisciplinary program.

Lemberg Institute for the Study of Violence

Within a few weeks of the issuance in 1964 of the Warren Commission Report on the assassination of President Kennedy, I was called by a New York manufacturer, Frank Cohen, head of the Biflex Corporation, who indicated that a group of his business associates, deeply concerned about the escalation of violence throughout the country, wondered whether the university would be willing to undertake a scientific study of the causes of such violence. A number of his business friends were prepared to provide the seed money for a preliminary exploration that might lead to useful recommendations. They realized that such research, if pursued under controlled conditions, would require a major investment; but they were hopeful that, if a series of preliminary conferences were held under the auspices of Brandeis, support for the research itself might then be secured through one of the major foundations.

There was no doubt that the whole area of social violence required earnest study. Though the Warren Commission had concluded that the assassination of President Kennedy was the act of one disturbed loner, there was no doubt that the country was threatened by extremely dangerous corrosive forces spawned by racial tensions, deplorable conditions in the black urban ghettos, mounting opposition to American involvement in Southeast Asia, and campus disorders that were linked to such opposition and to dissatisfaction with university governance. Remedial action in communities and on the national level was piecemeal and hopelessly snarled in self-serving politics and demagoguery.

Brandeis was in an excellent position to undertake the necessary exploration. It had a core of faculty in sociology, psychology, politics, and social welfare who could bring helpful insights to the problem. It was located in an area where the faculties of some of the best universities in the country offered further resources. And the university could command the cooperation of some of the ablest specialists who had been long concerned with the centrifugal bitterness that threatened American social stability. The offer of Frank Cohen and his colleagues was therefore accepted, and a series of three national conferences on the campus was held under the direction of Louis Cowan, the director of our Morse Communications Center, and Norton Long, professor of politics.

The first conference was convened in December 1964; it attempted to define the problem. The participants, along with our faculty representatives, were drawn from many of the professions—psychiatry, medicine, government, and law. They included J. Lee Rankin, chief counsel to the Warren Commission and solicitor general of the United States during the Eisenhower administration; Judge David Bazelon, chief justice of the U.S. Court of Appeals in Washington who had pioneered the relationship between psychiatry and the law; Milton Katz, one of our trustees and head of the International Legal Studies program at Harvard Law School; Frank Freidel, chairman of the American Civilization Committee at Harvard; Karl Menninger, president of the famed clinic and mental center in Kansas; and Gresham Sykes, executive director of the American Sociological Society. There was a wide-ranging discussion that covered "senseless" individual action by loners and "wierdos" as well as the conspiratorial violence of large groups who planned the disruptions and explosions that shook our society in the 1960s. Ralph McGill, editor of the *Atlanta Constitution,* hailed the deliberations of the conference, commenting, "Brandeis has moved; now imitators and followers are needed."

A second conference was convened in April 1965. It concentrated on the economic problems whose frustrations and disappointments often triggered violence and riot. Many labor leaders and corporation executives attended, and they presented their opposing views with utmost candor. Problems of housing, mass unemployment, inadequate educational opportunities, the often intransigent power of labor unions, the overwhelming compulsion of giant industrial and commercial enterprises to create profits, all came under review.

A third conference was held in July and brought together leaders in the communications field. Attention was focused on the reporting of violence and the influence of such reports as a factor in its escalation. Many thoughtful observations were made on the dilemma posed by the need for complete and uninhibited reporting to illumine the problems that stimulate the response of violence. Participants asked, are not difficult situations exacerbated when the reporting focuses on sensationalism, when it takes episodes and reactions completely out of context, when it gives major visibility to unrepresentative and irresponsible elements? All the conferences encouraged the establishment of an institute for continuing discussions and research so that the recommendations of the Brandeis sessions would not trail off into ineffectual rhetoric.

Within a few months, the problem of adequate funding had been solved. As so often happened before, it was the generosity of one of our trustees, Sam Lemberg, that was responsible. Lemberg was an authentic genius in real estate operations and their intricacies. He had equal success, and even more gratification, in winning support for communal causes. He had already underwritten the Brandeis Psychology Center for a nursery school to take care of the tots of Brandeis working faculty and staff members. His incentive contribution of a million dollars helped create one of the most impressive student union facilities of New England colleges. Every time a special academic need was announced at a trustee's meeting, Lemberg's name was part of the list of those who responded. He now became a fellow conspirator with me in the task of finding a donor for an institute for the study of violence. A very likely prospect was one of his oldest friends, a New York manufacturer and philanthropic leader who had recently contributed half a million dollars to Brandeis for a dormitory complex. I was standing with them at a university reception when Lemberg began his low-key persuasion. "We need a million dollars to do all that has to be done," he said amiably, as if he were asking for some modest membership dues. His friend replied that he was already vastly overcommitted to other philanthropies. Lemberg gently warned him that he was missing a historic mission. He added, "If you do not take it, I will!" The reply was, with a chuckle, "So take it, Sam, and you'll have my blessing." Lemberg turned to me and said, "You are a witness that I offered it to him first. Now, go ahead with the project, and I'll pledge the trust fund whose income you will need to set it up."

The invitation to head the institute went to Dr. John Spiegel, associate clinical professor of psychiatry at Harvard Medical School and lecturer in the Department of Social Relations at Harvard. He had been chief of psychiatric service at the Army Air Force Convalescent Hospital in Spokane, Washington, during World War II and later served as director of the psychiatric clinic of the Michael Reese Hospital in Chicago. He had been engaged in numerous research enterprises, among them, the response of various populations to acute disaster. Several of his volumes, *War Neuroses* and *Men Under Stress,* were based on his service to patients who had cracked under the pressures of combat. Spiegel added teaching duties to the directorship of the institute when he was named professor of social psychiatry in the Florence Heller School. He quickly organized a national board of overseers under the chairmanship of Philip Klutznick, who had been housing commissioner for President Truman and a former U.S. representative to the United Nations. Simultaneously, recruitment went forward to build a research staff for the institute, and by the spring of 1967, its activities were well under way.

The initial research assignment was virtually dictated by the national concern with social disruption. The incidence of urban ghetto violence had risen alarmingly in many parts of the country. In 1964, there had been fourteen serious disturbances in major cities; in 1965, the civic violence was repeated, including a seven-day riot in Watts, California. By 1966, the whole country was engulfed, and there were more than fifty riots with serious loss of life and property. Spiegel and his staff, supported by a major grant from the Ford Foundation, undertook a study of six major cities, three that had been torn by riot—Cleveland, Dayton, and San Francisco—and three that had thus far escaped such disturbance—Pittsburgh, Akron, and Boston. The Roper Associates was given the contract to interview five hundred blacks and five hundred whites in each of the cities; black interviewers for blacks, white interviewers for whites. There were long and detailed interviews with the city officials, police officers, school authorities, church and labor leaders, militants, moderates, as many segments of the community profile as could be reached. The social and economic structure of each community was analyzed. Political and educational officials and business and labor leaders were closely questioned on the strategy that had been followed to affect social change. The data that emerged was fed into computers for statistical analysis and discussed with authorities in carefully structured seminars to ascertain the grievance levels, how they were reached, and how they were met or not met. The research process was later followed in detail by the President's Commission on Civil Rights when it undertook an expanded analysis of fifteen cities where major disruptions had occurred.

In 1966, the institute undertook a six-city study to explore the grievances rooted in the high levels of black unemployment, in the maldistribution of educational opportunities, in the housing restrictions that condemned tens of thousands to the degradation of the slums. What emerged, with startling clarity, as the major grievance was that *"no one listens."* The report noted that hardship could be endured, but when there seemed to be complete indifference on the part of the governing officials, the detonation level was dangerously close. The most trivial incident could set it off with consequences to life and limb and property that made a mockery of fancy rhetoric and the platitudes of compassion. In Cleveland, the hatreds, fed by humiliation and hopelessness, had been festering for years. There were reassuring phrases uttered, only to put off action. Apparently, it was always "business as usual." Hence, when a black youth was refused a drink of water by a white man in a Cleveland bar, the explosion of arson, pillage, and killing had a trigger relationship to the incident that set it off.

Through 1967, the rioting escalated and in many cities raged out of control. The studies at Brandeis drew national attention and concern. A substantial grant was now assigned by the National Institutes of Mental Health so that the six-city study could be expanded to ten cities. Data was now sought in four additional key communities, Birmingham, Nashville, Atlanta, and New Orleans. The institute now offered "early alert guidelines," spotting symptoms that could be more readily interpreted as a warning to community leaders that a crisis was dangerously close to catastrophe. The early alert became a community fever thermometer; there might still be time for negotiation and adjustment.

Among the most serious problems that contributed to lack of communication was a misapprehension of the hold the black militants had on their people. Because of their unbridled language and their disruptive action, they were labeled subversives, thugs, terrorists, outlaws. Not only were the white liberals repelled by them, they were also repudiated by the black moderates. The ten-city study made it clear that the militants were not to be so easily dismissed. They were folk heroes to their people, who had given up hope that conventional negotiating tactics would ever accomplish anything more than cosmetic changes. Dr. Spiegel and his associates spotted early the ominous significance of their "gladiator response," their determination to make their needs felt and to fight for their solution even if it meant perishing in the attempt. "We are not afraid to die" was their defiant message, and Spiegel warned that this brag was not to be interpreted as grandiloquent rhetoric.

It was therefore considered essential to convene a major conference in May 1967 to which representative militants would be invited, where the issues would be considered candidly, with no preconditions. It was co-sponsored by the National Conference on Community Values and Conflict and by the New York Commission on Human Rights. It had the full cooperation of the Department of Justice, and it was held in Brotherhood House in New York City. Three hundred participants came from forty cities, and they included mayors, white and black civic leaders, social workers, law enforcement officials, and, above all, advocates of black nationalism and the proponents of root and branch radicalism.

It was a stormy conference, with unabashed insult and student confrontations. The civil wars within groups often surfaced: white liberals assailed by white extremists; black moderates representing the traditional social welfare organizations, the Urban League, and the NAACP denounced by the black militants as obsequious, ineffective Uncle Toms. The issues cut too deeply for any consensus, and the recommendations that were formulated at the end of the conference were excoriated by the militants as the usual liberal phony gobbledygook. One New Jersey observer remarked cynically that the only thing resulting from all the luncheons and dinners that dealt with disorders was obesity.

Yet the conference was not futile. The impassioned confrontations must have shaken the men and women who commanded a measure of influence. They must have been sufficiently sobered by the experience to realize that new approaches, cutting into new territory in law and education and social welfare, would have to be ventured. Only three or four years had passed since President Johnson had hammered through the landmark Civil Rights bill, but, in the light of the volcanic changes that had occurred, it now seemed as unfulfilled as the Emancipation Proclamation. Lawrence Landry, president of ACT of Chicago, warned bluntly that "ghettos are jails and the blacks are determined to break out, with or without the law." In a New Brunswick conference in 1968, Robert Curvin said, "To be black and powerless in American society is to live in a state of rage. . . . And tragically the decisions are being made by neocolonial masters who hide in the suburbs or luxury mainstreet apartments in the city." Ernest Chambers of Omaha addressed the challenge directly to the white establishment: "You are the problem. You have to find out and figure out what you can do to help solve this."

Publicizing the confrontations of the conference was not left to the official report. It was decided to turn them into a film directed by John Marshall, who had already established a reputation for imaginative documentation. He developed a film based on the gut issues of the conference, "You Are Our Problem," jointly sponsored by the Lemberg Institute and National Educational Television, and it received extensive network coverage.

Meanwhile, as tensions mounted and disruptions multiplied in many parts of the country through 1967 and well into 1968, there were calls for counsel from harassed and beleaguered officials. Spiegel and his staff met with the governors of Michigan, Massachusetts, and Pennsylvania while cities in these states seethed with violence. They testified at length before Connecticut's Senator Ribicoff's committee on the crises in the cities and before the Senate Judiciary Committee as it considered legislation to cope with the escalating disorders. They were called in by Robert Kennedy and Ramsey Clark as the problems of racial tension reached the offices of the attorney general. They were advisers to the federal Civil Rights Commission and participated in television and radio panels on violence and crime. The *Riot Data Review,* published by the Lemberg Institute, analyzed the data developed by the Brandeis conferences and received wide distribution.

By 1970, the main work of the institute had been incorporated into other national programs. The federal government had established a series of similar commissions to study violence and to offer recommendations that might cope with it. Some of the foundations allocated major grants for specific undertakings in cities that had been victims of disruption. Hence the Brandeis institute was gradually phased out. Dr. Spiegel returned to full-time teaching in the Florence Heller School as professor of social psychiatry. He completed a number of volumes that had been shunted aside during his years of intense leadership in the institute on violence, and he was elected president of the American Psychiatric Society.

The six-year operation of the institute had made a major contribution during a critical period in American life. The problems of racial tension and the militancy they spawned were studied by well-qualified specialists with laboratory objectivity. Scores of troubled cities had used the resources of the institute in their periods of deepest trouble. The university had become a respected clearinghouse for data that was indispensable in dealing rationally and practically with the problems of urban disruption. Above all, the Lemberg Institute served as a model for utilizing the expertise of a university in rendering service to the country in a time of grave crisis. And since virtually all of the research activities had been funded by foundation or federal grants, the trust Sam Lemberg had established was still virtually intact. It could now be assigned for other university purposes. It later became the funding base in the economics department for the Lemberg Program in International Economics and Finance. It was further strengthened by the establishment in 1984 of an endowed chair, which was created from the gifts offered in a testimonial marking my appointment as chancellor emeritus.

Communication and Education

When Brandeis came into being in 1948, educational television was still in its infancy, and its impact on the cultural life of American communities was still minimal. There were only a few functioning stations, precariously financed, viewed as threatening competitors by the commercial networks. But their progress, though slow, could not be arrested. The broadening of interest in adult education, the pressure for programming beyond the level favored by Main Street America, the cooperation of colleges and universities, museums, symphony orchestras, and other cultural agencies, won ever more viewers.

Untrammeled by tradition, Brandeis gave early support for the broader use of educational television. It already had a number of eloquent faculty members, experts in many fields, who were at ease before microphone and camera and eager to be there. From the outset, Brandeis brought distinguished personalities to the campus, whose messages usually had considerable public interest. Moreover, a near neighbor in Cambridge, WGBH, was then and now one of the most imaginative of the educational television channels. Its support and programming were participated in by most of the universities and cultural agencies of the area, whose representatives sat on the station's advisory council. The founding father of WGBH was Ralph Lowell, scion of one of the oldest New England families, who early attracted the interest and backing of the Ford Foundation, the State Department, and other government agencies. Many of them readily provided seed money for television projects to the universities that were part of the Lowell Broadcasting Council.

Brandeis therefore gave every encouragement to faculty members who were interested in television as a teaching medium. Max Lerner, whose course "America as a Civilization" had been edited for a volume that became a best-seller, taped his lectures for the educational channels. The courses of Robert Koff, who had come to the music department of Brandeis from Julliard, were much in demand. By 1959, two of the twelve programs adopted by WGBH for national distribution were the work of Brandeis faculty—the lectures of Max Lerner, and the biweekly colloquium, "Prospects of Mankind," presided over by Eleanor Roosevelt, then a Brandeis visiting faculty member. The theme for Mrs. Roosevelt's colloquium program of 1960 was the survival of democracy. The participants were Adlai Stevenson, Henry Kissinger, and the Yugoslav dissident, Dedijer, who had just broken with Tito and had fled his homeland. The three years of "Prospects of Mankind," 1960–1963, represented one of the early high points in national educational television programming, and they enabled the university to render a major service to hundreds of thousands of families. Such programs made it clear that an institute, related to a university and relying upon its faculty and invited specialists, could offer influential guidance to the fast-developing, worldwide communications field.

For the three years of Mrs. Roosevelt's program, many of the newsmakers of the nation were welcomed to Brandeis where the program was televised. Mrs. Roosevelt was meticulous in fulfilling her assignment, and she never missed a session. Her "guests," as we regarded them, included Nelson Rockefeller; Ralph Bunche; Adlai Stevenson; Luis Muñoz Marin, governor of Puerto Rico; Barbara Ward (Lady Jackson), editor of the *London Economist*; John Kenneth Galbraith of Harvard; Julius Nyerere, a young African nationalist, soon to be the first prime minister of Tanganyika; Erwin D. Canham, editor of the *Christian Science Monitor*; and John

Kennedy, then senator from Massachusetts. Kennedy used the occasion to hold a news conference just prior to announcing his availability for the Democratic nomination for president.

Beginning in 1959, a series of seminars was held to chart the areas for effective programming. Participants included R. Gordon Arneson, director of the U.S. Office of Cultural Exchange, Henry Morgenthau III, Louis Lyons, curator of the Neiman Fellows at Harvard, Henry Kissinger, and Louis Cowan, who had been president of the CBS television network and was on the faculty of the Columbia University School of Journalism.

One of the seminars was built around Edward R. Murrow, the dean of commentators. His immensely popular program "Person to Person" indicated that Americans wanted more from the "boob tube" than escapist entertainment. He advised that the projected communications institute at Brandeis avoid emphasis on the technology of broadcasting. "Leave techniques to the practitioners," he said. "The objective must be the target and not the missile." It was sound counsel, and when two New England philanthropists, Alfred and Lester Morse, offered seed money to establish the institute, it was decided that it would concentrate on educational radio and television. It could make its most significant contribution by sponsoring special research projects, by counseling the directors of communications, especially in the developing countries, and by studying the purposes and effects of major changes in communications methods. Louis Cowan, who had been outstanding in the preliminary exploratory sessions, was now invited to take over the directorship of the Morse Institute. During the war, he had been a senior official in the Office of War Information, and in 1959 he had been in charge of the communications section of the famed Salzburg Seminars in Austria. As president of CBS, he not only had been exposed to all the reefs and shoals of commercial broadcasting but he had also established important relationships with government agencies and foundations concerned with communications, so he knew his way around Washington and its complex bureaucracies. He at once brought over Henry Morgenthau from WGBH to serve as his associate.

Within weeks of Cowan's assumption of responsibility, he had negotiated a $130,000 grant from the State Department to conduct a 120-day, Multi-National Communications Specialists' Seminar. The plan was to invite those who were in charge of communications in Asia, Africa, Latin America, and in the main centers of Europe to spend about four months in the United States, mainly on the Brandeis campus, to familiarize themselves with the uses of radio, television, and other media for policymaking purposes in government and education.

Morgenthau spent many months through 1961 and early 1962 traveling to clarify for governments and broadcasting officials what the institute hoped to provide and to screen the participants. Fourteen countries agreed to send delegates, and, in June 1962, thirty-five men and women assembled at Brandeis. They came from Britain, Sweden, Cyprus, and Italy in democratic Europe, and from Poland and Yugoslavia in the Communist bloc. The Africans came from Ghana, Nigeria, Kenya, and Southern Rhodesia; the Asians, from India, Japan, and Singapore.

The only Middle Eastern country represented was Israel. Television had held no charm for Prime Minister Ben-Gurion and his government. Ben-Gurion had, as always, expressed himself with colorful vigor: "We need no idiotic stories on cowboys and Indians while we are surrounded by one hundred million Arabs!" Now more sober evaluation of the problems of administration and cultural integration in a land that drew its Jews from seventy countries and that had more than a million Arabs brought changes in his thinking. The government concluded that Israel had better take fullest advantage of the powerful new medium. The Israeli officials were now among its most eager participants.

The stay on campus of the international visitors was made extremely comfortable. A magnificent seven-acre estate that included a Tudor-style mansion had recently been donated to the university by the family of Mrs. Babette Gross, a longtime resident of nearby Weston, who was planning to move to California. Themis House, as it was called (after the Greek goddess of law and justice), was set amid beautiful woodland and a small lake. It had eighteen bedrooms, spacious reception and living rooms, a library, two kitchens, two dining halls, and many small studios. The university had accepted the gift for use in the tradition of MIT's Endicott House and Columbia's Arden House. The communications institute was its first large-scale event.

For the first six weeks, participants attended classes, visited neighboring colleges and universities, interviewed specialists, and concentrated on required reading. A strong battery of Brandeis faculty gave lectures and led discussions. They included John Roche, chairman of political science, Leonard Levy, dean of the graduate school and constitutional historian, and Max Lerner, who not only explored problems of democracy but brought to bear his own considerable experience with media. They concentrated on the American experience—its history and politics, social complexities, and approach to diplomacy policies. The faculty members were reinforced by Henry Kissinger and David McClelland of Harvard, Ithiel de Sola Pool of MIT, James Hagerty, former press aide to President Eisenhower and then vice-president of the National Educational Television and Radio Center, and Theodore Conant of the Ford Foundation. Several sessions of "The Prospects of Mankind" were being taped while the institute was in session. This provided opportunities for the delegates to confer with

Mrs. Roosevelt and her guest panelists. Commencement, which was scheduled during this period, enabled them to meet and interview some of the influential honorary degree recipients.

After the sessions at Brandeis, the participants fanned out over the country for two months of observation and study, visiting the main radio and broadcasting stations, newspaper plants, book and magazine offices, public relations firms, colleges, and universities. The participants were given access to whomever and whatever they wished to see and the policies they wished to probe. In all instances, the way for the interviews was cleared by State Department officials, who made it clear that the visitors were under the sponsorship of the American government.

In scheduling a final fortnight at Brandeis, Cowan and Morgenthau were sensitive to several factors that, when neglected, had vitiated the usefulness of other exchange programs. Not least of these was the need for a "decompression chamber" for easily offended visitors who had become involved in an unusually sensitive program and who required a period of reflection and mature analysis before returning to their homelands. Some of the Africans and Asians would have encountered experiences of prejudice that could poison all the good results that had been achieved. These debriefing sessions were found indispensable for the purposes of both the institute and the sponsoring State Department. Then, as a climax, the participants were routed to Washington for a long, productive session with Newton Minow and his staff at the Federal Communications Commission.

When the program was completed, perhaps the highest tribute to its effectiveness was the request from the State Department for Brandeis to plan a similar program for the next year, in the fall of 1963. Though the time was shortened to three months, the base of sponsorship was broadened: Seventeen of the participants came under the auspices of the State Department, seven came through the Agency for International Development (AID), and two each through the Asia Foundation and the Ford Foundation. This second round involved twenty-eight new participants from twenty-eight countries, some of which had not been previously represented.

There were instances of almost immediate impact in foreign lands. The Japanese were apparently particularly impressed. Television and radio had been expanding sensationally in postwar Japan and had become virtually a way of life. It was therefore arranged, again through the good offices of the State Department and another generous subvention, to have twenty of the leading communications specialists of Japan come to the Brandeis campus for an institute program similar to earlier ones for the more diversified groups. Similarly, the Nigerians carried glowing reports of their experiences to their homeland. They brought back a much deepened respect for the power of radio and television and the determination to make it available for their countrymen. Soon after their return, the University of Ife in West Nigeria, in conjunction with the African American Institute, moved to set up a national school of communications. Staff members from our Morse Communications Center were invited to serve as consultants, and they cooperated fully as West Nigeria launched its program. Television in Israel, too, now received major impetus as the earlier misgivings were dispelled, and the Brandeis consultants proved invaluable in the planning. Meanwhile, the United States Information Agency commissioned the institute to make a study of the publications that influenced the methodology of the Voice of America.

The State Department also sponsored a special two-week seminar on American politics and economics in the fall of 1964. Fourteen student leaders, from this country and abroad, came for intensive discussions at Brandeis and followed them up with visits to the campaign headquarters of political candidates, union meetings, settlement houses, and urban and suburban communities. The second week was spent in New York during one of its hard-fought election campaigns and, on the night of the election, the students visited network and wire service headquarters to watch the American experts tabulating and analyzing the returns. While at Brandeis, the participants were housed in campus dormitories, each with a student host, and they were invited to observe regular undergraduate extracurricular activities.

One of the most important projects that grew out of the seminars was the conference, subsidized by a $44,000 grant from the Department of Health, Education, and Welfare, to appraise the economics of educational television. It was sponsored jointly with the American Academy of Arts and Sciences and the United States Office of Education. A distinguished panel was brought together on campus and at Themis House for a long May weekend in 1963. It was ten years since the first educational television station had gone on the air; now there were eighty, and new ones were being launched almost weekly. There was significant growth also in Britain and Canada, and their representatives joined the seminars, whose sixty participants included broadcast specialists, teachers, business and labor leaders, scientists, government officials, lawyers, and foundation heads. There was little time for entertainment: The discussions proceeded all day and evening. Prior to the conference, sixteen background papers had been prepared that dealt with instructional television research and systems analysis, audience evaluation, general broadcasting, talents, services and materials, production, and distribution. Financial data had also been gathered so that the participants would be able to deal with practical realities.

The object of the conference was to explore the social objectives of and the community stake in educational television and to evaluate how high

standards and imaginative use would affect costs. There was agreement
that educational television had now become a major force in the English-
speaking world, and it would inevitably play an increasing role in government and education. The dangers of irresponsible censorship and political
manipulation were clear, and the sessions devoted considerable time and
thought to these problems. Jerome Bruner, director of the Center for Cog-
nitive Studies at Harvard, warned against cramming too much material
into instructional programs. Kenneth Cox and Frederick Ford of the Federal Communications Council discussed the need for subventions of tax
money to sustain and expand the progress of educational television. One
of the most timely recommendations was that every priority be given to
assure enough channels for educational television. The conference also
made clear the urgent need for further exploration and stimulated at least
two more national conferences that were held in Washington by the National Education Association. Following the conference, several of the participants met in Washington to respond to FCC-proposed criteria for
ultrahigh-frequency channel allocations. A volume based on the conference
proceedings and recommendations, with updated financial material, was
published by the U.S. Office of Education.

Meanwhile, other significant research projects had been undertaken. In
conjunction with the American Academy of Arts and Sciences, a study was
made of a typical week of educational television. Such a study was deemed
necessary because educational television meant different things to different
people. It was controlled locally, and its purpose and content varied widely
from station to station. The only commonality the eighty-odd stations had
was that they were noncommercial. It seemed logical, then, in studying
them, to bring together in one place information on what all these loosely
connected stations were broadcasting. No agency had yet undertaken such
a survey.

Every public broadcast was monitored in the week of May 21–27, 1961,
and the tabulated results indicated that science and technology had now
become the most important program material, comprising more than 21
percent. There was a sharp drop to 1.377 percent in programs dealing with
religious topics. The news programs, which had been steady fare in the
early days of television and had provided sophisticated analysis, had apparently been taken over completely by the well-informed, perceptive commentators on the major commercial networks, for such programs now
comprised only .61 percent of educational television.

When the report was published, the demand for copies of it exceeded
the Morse Communications Center's expectations. Since the service that
it rendered was clearly important, a study of another typical week, this time
March 18–24, 1962, was undertaken. Requests for the studies continued

for many years from educators, broadcasters, government offices, libraries, critics, foundations, businesses, and advertising institutions. Impressed with the studies, National Educational Television asked to cooperate with the Morse Center for a third survey and took responsibility for monitoring the much-increased number of educational stations. A third report, with additional information on station ownership and program sources, was prepared in 1964 to include all the programs that had been monitored during the week of April 19–26. A small book on WNYC-TV, the country's first municipal television station, was published by the Morse Center with a foreword by Commissioner Robert Lee of the Federal Communications Commission. The booklet outlined the station's history from its earliest inception as WUHF—an experiment in ultrahigh-frequency broadcasting—to its status as WNYC-TV, with a basic audience of 350,000.

Another valuable project was initiated in November 1964 to study crisis decision-making. The actions of the broadcasters in the dramatic hours and days that followed the assassination of President Kennedy were considered indispensable data for such a study. It became clear at the end of one day of coverage that the broadcasters had been undergoing one of the severest tests they had ever faced. The problems were manifold, and the decisions were of extreme importance. There was little question that television and radio were the prime source of news, that the broadcasters were being placed in a series of familiar but new roles, roles that kept shifting during the four days covered. It was thought that important data could be secured that might have multiple uses in years to come. To be effective, it was essential that no time be lost. The Morse Center worked with Paul Lazarsfeld, Robert Merton, and Herta Herzog of Columbia University in structuring the question guides, the periods to be analyzed, and the methodology. A phalanx of the best-trained sociologist-interviewers was assembled and put into the field to select the taped material that related to the four broadcast days during and after the assassination coverage. The center ultimately gathered nearly half a million words of raw interview material from thirty states and related broadcast materials from England and France. This was made available to the Warren Commission and to scholars from many disciplines. Almost everything in the project's archives was obtained without cost from the three networks, many stations, and political candidates. A small grant from the Hearst Foundation was all that was needed to cover the supplementary costs for the creation of the archive, now housed in the Brandeis library. It should be added that the archives also include the Kennedy-Nixon debates that preceded the election of 1960. The fidelity of the recording was superb, and the tapes became a precious historic asset.

By the end of 1965, the number of educational channels had risen well beyond one hundred; nearly every large city was now actively involved.

Such progress inevitably stimulated immense interest in developing their most effective use. There was now a government-sponsored Committee on Economic Development whose research agenda gave high priority to communications problems. It was felt, therefore, that our own research program in communications had fulfilled its purpose, and the Morse Fund was transferred to become the base of an endowed chair in urban studies.

The four-year record had been gratifying, especially for its service to many of the developing countries. Quite apart from the research results, the cooperation of the State Department, the Department of Health, Education, and Welfare, the American Academy of Arts and Sciences, and the Ford Foundation and the participation of national and international celebrities had gained new and influential friendships for the university.

It was during the seminars of the Morse Institute that references were made to the techniques of oral history, then being developed by the distinguished American historian Allen Nevins of Columbia. Under his supervision, interviews had been taped with personalities who had deeply influenced their times. In a twenty-year period, more than three hundred people had participated, discussing their areas of interest, the turning points in their lives, their appraisals of the events and the men and women whom they had come to know. The conversations, especially when guided by skillful interviewers, recorded considerable original data to supplement the conventional documentation used in writing history and biography. Some of the interviews had been excerpted to become valuable volumes. One such book, *Frankfurter Speaks,* summarized many hours of interviews with one of the most perceptive members of the Supreme Court, whose long tenure stretched through many presidencies.

It occurred to some of us that such a program could be amplified by adding a visual dimension, the camera. All the lineaments of personality would then come into focus more convincingly and significantly, without losing any of the vitality of the conversation; indeed, it would enrich it by the magic of the camera's unerring eye. If only such a technique had been perfected and available for interviews with Woodrow Wilson, Lloyd George, Mahatma Gandhi, Chaim Weizmann, or Justice Brandeis. How much clearer our insights would be in appraising and understanding temperament and motivation. Such considerations sent Brandeis into the project that we labeled "Living Biographies." And, fortunately, a donor was secured to give it full support without encroaching upon the general funds of the university.

The donor was Samuel Dretzin, the head of the World Wide Automobile Corporation. He had participated in many of the major philanthropies of Greater New York and had become deeply interested in educational television and its potential for broader adult education. Dretzin was intrigued by the possibility of improving on the Nevins oral history project, and, after several conferences, he agreed to contribute $36,000 annually, for a twenty-year period, to underwrite what became known as the Dretzin Living Biography Program.

At first the program was centered at Brandeis itself. Half a dozen audio-visual programs were taped. David Ben-Gurion, past eighty but as vital and ebullient as ever, readily submitted to many hours of interviews on the Brandeis campus, as he ranged over the great turning points of his dramatic career. The last living disciple of Sigmund Freud, Dr. Grete Bibring, associated with the mental health service of Harvard, discussed Freud's influence on his students and the significance of the differences that resulted in conflicting schools of thought in psychiatry. General Carlos Romulo, president of the University of the Philippines and later foreign secretary, covered the earlier period of his life, carrying the story through World War II. Dr. David Seegal, an almost forgotten pioneer in the problems of chronic illness and one of the best-loved teachers at Columbia, discussed the obstacles that had to be overcome in coping with the conservatism of the medical profession. These interviews were all deposited in the Brandeis archives for future research.

During our negotiations for interviewees in the Living Biography series, we sustained one most regrettable disappointment. We had planned to include the president of the Irish Free State, Eamon de Valera. His interview was to be taped in Dublin, and I journeyed there to conduct it. The old rebel who had led the Irish uprising, now nearly ninety, had never yielded to such requests. But educational television, as a medium to tell his story to the young people of the new world and of the future, apparently intrigued him, and he consented. Our preliminary conversations with the almost legendary figure, sharp as ever, brimming with memories of the long struggle for independence and sovereignty, made the discussions an unforgettable experience.

Unfortunately, at the last moment, as the taping was to begin, a dangerous attack of bronchitis compelled de Valera's physician to eliminate the television aspect. It was too risky to expose the gallant nonagenarian to many hours under powerful lights. But the interview was held, and it was memorable. De Valera expressed wistful envy of his much-admired friend, David Ben-Gurion, "who knew so much about philosophy, including the wisdom of the Orient." He declared that he regarded Ben-Gurion one of the most remarkable of the world's contemporary statesmen. "Think of the achievement," he said. "Into his newly created state poured the Jewish immigrants from seventy nations, all with different languages. Ben-Gurion knew well that there never could be a visceral national consciousness unless a common language united such diverse components. And it had to be

Hebrew, not just classical Biblical Hebrew, but the colloquial language of daily life. Through universal military service and the school system, such a language emerged within a generation." Then he added, "We failed to accomplish this in Ireland. Our native language is Gaelic, but it could be spoken and read only by select scholars and writers—Shaw and Yeats and Joyce and Hyde and the lovely Lady Gregory. We are obliged to communicate in English, the language of our oppressors!"

Several years later, when my incumbency as president was over, I returned to Dublin for a telecast on the career of de Valera, who had died at ninety, within a year of our interview. I linked the program with site visits to the crucial events in the career of the courageous revolutionary—the Black Rock College where his career began, the street where the Easter Uprising of 1916 was launched, the prison to which de Valera was sent when the rebellion failed, the tiny cell from where his orders were obeyed by an aroused nation, the execution ground where his companions were shot, the museum that housed so many of the Gaelic treasures that were precious to Irish pride, and the headquarters in the Glenvary House where the prime minister functioned as the head of a free and independent Ireland. It was appropriate to wind up the telecast with the lines from the most beloved of the plays of Yeats, where the Countess Kathleen, the traditional symbol of ancient Ireland, saunters into an Irish village in the guise of an old woman and expresses the hope that someday, with the help of friends, it may be possible to drive out the invaders. A little later, one of the villagers is approached and asked, "Did you see an old lady walk down the road?" "An old lady? Oh no, but I saw a beautiful young girl, and she had the walk of a queen!"

Many other interviews were planned in our Dretzin program, but it now became clear that, if they were to be more than research data and widely distributed, they needed a relationship with a well-established television station that would take such responsibility. When the project, fully underwritten, was suggested to WGBH, a partnership was quickly established.

The scope and format of the interviews were immediately transformed. With the consent of the Dretzins, we decided that the university would annually offer an award to an outstanding public figure whose career had beneficently affected our times. The recipient, to be chosen by a distinguished national jury, would also be invited to take part in an extensive interview on television, during which the turning points of a decisive career could be discussed and evaluated.

There was little difficulty in reaching a consensus for the first recipient. The jury, which included educators as well as the program directors of the best in educational television, unanimously agreed it should be offered to Earl Warren, whose sixteen-year incumbency as chief justice of the United States decisively altered the course of American life. Justice Warren had never granted a television interview. For that matter, he had never wished to discuss his Court experiences, since what he had to say might become political static during a Nixon presidency. Apparently, however, Warren was satisfied by the pledge of meticulous respect for his position, and he therefore consented to return to campus. I was privileged to conduct the interview.

Justice Warren, then eighty-one, was astonishing in his vitality. He sat under the harsh television lights for hours, relaxed, poised, incisive in his responses, now teasing and bantering, again serious and reflective. I began by asking him about the psychological demands made on him when he was called on by President Eisenhower to shift suddenly from a world of political warfare to that of judicial objectivity. He confessed that his first day on the Court was the loneliest and most difficult of his life. Eisenhower's summons had left him with little time to wind up his eleven-year governorship of California, and none to prepare for the huge backlog of controversial cases waiting for final disposition by the Court. He added that life on the Court compelled immense restraint, for "a justice cannot respond to criticism, he cannot explain anything he does, . . . and that's the reason why the courts are so much traduced in this country; they can be so easily used as the whipping boy." I remarked that this silence must have been hard on Mrs. Warren. He chuckled and revealed that she could not for years abide the signboards on the highways that caterwauled, "Impeach Earl Warren," but that she had ultimately learned to smile resignedly.

Soon the discussion turned to the 1954 landmark Court decision in *Brown v. The Board of Education of Topeka*. I asked how he was able to persuade a Court made up of such rugged individualists to reach a unanimous decision. In Warren's opinion, this result was no personal accomplishment, and he refused to take credit for it. The arguments in the case had begun in November 1953, and in the weekly review, the members of the Court were encouraged to bring up debatable points. He let the discussion go on informally so that no polarization would take place that would prevent a unanimous judgment. Not until the following February did Warren ask if the justices were ready to vote. He seemed to be saying that the months of reflection had brought each man to assess the awesome responsibility of his decision, apart from purely legal precedents. It had become a compelling social responsibility for the decision to be unanimous. And it was. Warren went on to speak compassionately of several of the justices. He noted that Hugo Black was not welcomed in his home state of Alabama for many years, that Tom Clark was rejected by East Texans, "and Stanley Reed, the Kentuckian, gentle soul that he is, I know that it was a great strain on him to determine the case as he did. . . ."

I asked, too, for the sake of the historical record, if the phrase "all deliberate speed" that qualified the mandate for integration had been the creation of the Warren Court and if it had been hard to come by. He explained that the term was a centuries-old term from British Admiralty law, and it had been used by Justice Holmes in *Virginia v. West Virginia*. It was ideally appropriate here since the Court was looking for "a progression of action, a progression I may say, with which we still live. . . ."

Justice Warren's visceral conviction that the American people could be trusted to decide their destiny by basic democratic procedures emerged in his evaluation of *Baker v. Carr*. He considered this case, unequivocally, the most important decided during his sixteen years on the Court. He called it "the parent case of the one man-one vote doctrine, which guarantees to every American citizen participating in government an equal value of his vote to that of any other vote that is cast." The politics of the right to vote had been murky for years, and there had been no way for people to obtain justice in a state that was malapportioned. The Court finally cut the Gordian knot and separated what was political from what was *sub judice*.

Inevitably, we came to the presidentially-appointed Warren Commission, which was to examine the circumstances of President Kennedy's assassination. Warren affirmed his initial resistance to the president's request that he assume the chairmanship of the commission or even to join it. He had cited the unfortunate consequences of the involvement of earlier justices in such matters as the Tilden-Hayes election, the Pearl Harbor investigation, and the Nuremburg trials. He was oppressed by the fear of a possible nuclear war, since there were ugly rumors afloat that there may have been complicity by Castro and Khrushchev in an assassination conspiracy. But when Johnson asked him to remember that the request to serve came from the commander in chief, Warren yielded.

The commission, he said, found no evidence to support any conspiratorial theory. It published not only a one-volume, condensed report, but twenty-six volumes of testimony, which recorded the words of hundreds of witnesses and tracked down every shred of purported evidence. The Justice Department at that time was presided over by Robert Kennedy. The commission had the fullest cooperation of the CIA, the FBI, and the Secret Service and its resources. Every shade of political opinion was represented on the commission, which also employed fifteen independent lawyers, some of the highest in the profession, including Lee Rankin, former solicitor general. Warren noted that he had stayed briefed on all material published in the intervening years, and not one iota of proven evidence had appeared to challenge the determination of the *Report* that Oswald was acting alone. Warren characterized him as a Dostoyevskian nobody, looking for a place in history. In this aberration, he concluded, Oswald had models in the assassins of Garfield and McKinley and the psychopath who had killed Mayor Cermak of Chicago in the attempt to shoot Franklin Roosevelt.

It so happened that the interview took place on the very day that a volume by the chief justice had been published, and I had a copy at hand for the interview. The title, *A Republic, If You Can Keep It,* was based on a riposte of Benjamin Franklin to an elderly lady who addressed him as he left a meeting of the Continental Congress in 1787: "What kind of a government are we to have?" she asked. "A Republic—if you can keep it," replied Franklin. Warren believed the admonition to be even more apposite in our own time, with all the complexities of our society. He noted, "A Republic is not an easy kind of government to keep, because it depends upon the continuous concern of all the people. It is because I believe the responsibility to keep it must be equated with the rights it bestows, that I used Benjamin Franklin's phrase."

On the day after the interview, we held an informal ceremony in the Brandeis three chapels area, where Warren was asked to plant what we hoped would be the first of many maple trees that succeeding Dretzin Prize visitors would plant. The ceremony took place near the Protestant Harlan Chapel. The chief justice lightened the proceedings by expressing his gratitude for the availability of a left-handed shovel. Privately, he returned the cash award to the university.

Not only was this first Dretzin program aired as a special throughout the public television network, it was often a rerun. There was editorial comment by the *New York Times* and other influential newspapers, and the entire transcript was reprinted in the *Law Review Journal*. On the night of Warren's death two years later, it was shown again on network prime time. Once the tradition of the Dretzin Prize had been set with the award to Justice Warren, it was not difficult to persuade other men and women of international stature to follow. The next interview was arranged with Averell Harriman, and negotiations for others were well under way.

Meanwhile, I had become integrally involved in educational television with a program of my own, and it was to become one of my chief activities when I completed my incumbency. I had been teaching a course in contemporary affairs, History 36, and Hartford Gunn, Jr., the director of WGBH, the Boston public service station, suggested that the "classroom" would be substantially extended if the course were televised. The temptation to reach an impressively diverse viewing audience was irresistible. I agreed to experiment with a series that would begin chronologically with the period immediately after World War I, then to evaluate its public reception. It turned out surprisingly well, and the telecasts grew into five series of thirteen half-hour lectures that involved an ever-increasing number of channels, until the telecasts were being viewed, at different times, on different days, in more than a hundred cities. Often, when the series had been completed, it was scheduled for reruns, and it continued nationally for several years.

CHAPTER TWENTY

From President to Chancellor

In November 1967, soon after the beginning of my twentieth year as president, I notified several close friends on our Board of Trustees that I wished to relinquish my post and asked the chairman to begin the procedures that would lead to the selection of a successor. I made it clear that I was at the peak of health and vitality but that, approaching my sixty-ninth year, I believed it was time to assign leadership to a younger educator, one who would be a more integral part of the postwar world and its very much changed conceptions about our society and its problems.

I felt that transition in leadership at this stage carried no danger: The ship was safely in port. Its new adventures and destinations could be undertaken with infinitely more confidence than when it was launched nearly twenty years before. Virtually the entire physical plant of ninety buildings—supplied and furnished with the most sophisticated equipment, representing a fully paid or pledged investment of $70 million in mid-twentieth-century dollars—had been completed, so that the new president could give much more time and energy to the substantive problems of the educational process. An endowment fund had not been stressed, since immediate needs had more pressing priority than the quest for future security; but, at $40 million, with no founding bequest, it offered assurance that a committed supporting constituency was growing steadily. We had no way of knowing what sums had been reserved for us in wills that would mature in later years. Smaller bequests were usually not discussed with us by their donors, but when the intended legacies were substantial, there had often been conferences with key board members and with me to make sure that what was planned would serve the university to best advantage. In twenty years, such conferences had been frequent, and, at the completion of my incumbency, we could guess with a measure of realism that about $50 million, intended for diverse purposes, had been planned as bequests.

The method by which maintenance funds were raised by the university offered an additional cushion of safety for the future. Many donors made pledges that could be paid over a period of time, usually averaging about five years. By 1968, such pledges on our books totaled $63 million, and even if there were an inevitable falloff because of unforeseen contingencies, there must be at least $50 million that could be counted on. These funds later became a vital factor in tiding the university over recession and war periods, when the cash flow tapered off, and they were acceptable collateral for even conservative banks when application was made for short-term credit. The longer-term loans that subsidized the construction of dormitories were payable over a forty-year period, and since both interest and amortization were expected to come from student room rentals, this was less a debt than a self-liquidating investment. In summary, the pledges that had been raised over the years for every purpose totaled about $200 million, of which $40 million had been reserved as endowment, $70 million had gone into plant, and $63 million remained in pledges. About $27 million had been disbursed over the twenty-year period to cover the excess in expenditures beyond tuition and other charged income. We therefore were able to end every year in the black.

On the academic side, the reputation of the university no longer was laced with the patronizing sentimentality accorded the prodigy, running breathlessly to keep up with bigger and older brothers. It was now solidly anchored in achievement: Accreditation included twenty-four graduate departments, many of them listed as outstanding in the evaluation of the American Council on Education. A Phi Beta Kappa chapter had been authorized in record time. Our graduates secured admission in disproportionate numbers to the best professional and graduate schools; many offered highly coveted fellowships and awards. When the university was launched, I had paraphrased the early colonial Governor Winthrop's exclamation, "we too are pilgrims." After two decades, we were still pilgrims, but we could journey with more assurance.

My friends among the trustees were not surprised by my resignation request. I had been discussing such action, off and on, for several years. They knew how eager I had become to enjoy with Thelma the benefits of travel and to complete several volumes that I had kept postponing because of the responsibilities of academic administration and fund-raising. The trustees had a measure of anxiety about my plans for retirement. They felt that the university was too young to count upon its small body of alumni for basic support, as most private universities do. The board urged some kind of continuing relationship for me that could preserve the "leverage" they attested was far from exhausted in winning friendships and support for the university. Surely a service formula could be devised that would still make room for the writing that would be my major objective. The new president would be completely responsible for the administration of the university. Would I remain on the active list in a specially created post, as chancellor? I would be freed from the tyranny of clock and calendar. My basic obligation would be to interpret the university's needs to selected families where I had the advantage of lifelong relationships and to offer counsel when it was sought. The inducements were attractive, and I consented to the arrangement.

The search committee included representatives from every sphere of the university. Recommendations poured in, and there were many interviews, a few in depth. But the choice gravitated very quickly to one of the most gifted men in American Jewish life, Morris Abram, a New York attorney, born and reared in the South, who had been actively identified with many civic and Jewish causes, including the presidency of the American Jewish Committee. He was just turning fifty. The decision was not long drawn out: Indeed, it was accelerated because of a deadline that Abram set if he was to be considered. By the end of March 1968, all names for nomination to a vacant United States Senate seat from New York had to be filed, and Abram had expressed interest in candidacy. When the search committee's recommendations had been informally circulated and approved, Abram withdrew from the political race in New York and was invited to meet all the trustees.

Abram's formal election to the presidency, to take effect at the opening of the next college year, was unanimous. He was to begin working by my side during the final months of the school year, and I would use the summer to clear up unfinished business and to offer such transitional briefing as would be requested.

I was not to be let off easily, however. Two years before, a campaign had been undertaken for $20 million for special building needs, and it was now well past the half-way mark. Why not now wind up that effort by offering a salute to the retiring president, thereby fulfilling objectives that had always been a priority for him? Five million dollars raised as a tribute fund would permit the acquisition of acreage to protect the future expansion of the university; it would make possible the construction of a center to house all the international activities; and it would establish a special fellowship fund to subsidize faculty and student research abroad.

As it happened, just about the time I had asked to be relieved, we had learned that twenty-seven acres directly opposite the entrance to the campus were available for purchase. Only seven acres were occupied by the plant of Judson Thompson, a manufacturing firm that had suffered severe reverses and had sold out to the Rockefeller interests. Larry Wien enjoyed a friendship with David Rockefeller and was informed by him that the purchasing combine, IBEC, planned to close the plant and transfer its operations elsewhere.

Wien began negotiations for the university to take over the IBEC investment, plant and acreage, at a purchase price of $2.32 million. Our intention was to sublease the plant so that its operations, with two hundred employees, could continue, and we would still have available twenty unencumbered acres, contiguous to the university. The land would probably not be used up for decades, but it would be comforting to have the assurance that the front of the campus, down to the Charles River, would not be hemmed in by future industrial or commercial developments. All the negotiations were successfully completed, and we had been given a year to raise the necessary funds. Our 1968 annual Palm Beach affair was only a few months away. Wien suggested that there could be no more productive way to begin our testimonial in Palm Beach than by raising the money for the purchase. Wien then prepared to approach the Palm Beach group with an ingenious adaptation of his syndication technique. He set the goal at one hundred units of $23,000 each, with the understanding that a pledge could be paid out over a period of years. There would be no restriction on the number of units that a benefactor could take; and, for those to whom a unit was beyond philanthropic capacity at the moment, parts of a unit would also be available. How better to demonstrate to the president that his virtual obsession with land to protect the future of the university was fully respected and supported?

There were about two hundred men and women at the Palm Beach luncheon in February 1968. Larry Wien explained his program. Probably few who were there ever had experienced what followed his presentation. He himself subscribed ten units, and his example triggered other major pledges. Half the goal was reached in the first few minutes; the rest took nearly fifteen minutes longer. At one point, there were more than thirty hands waving at the chairman, signaling the desire to get in on the commitment to units before they were all gone. Some of the purchasers must have thought that they were at an art auction at Parke-Bernet or Sotheby's. And it should be remembered that those who gave with such generosity were not, as a result, reducing their contributions to other causes. These were among the men and women who had offered unstinting leadership to the emergency campaigns that had been mounted to shield Israel in the critical months that followed the Six Day War of 1967. Through the rest of 1968, the campaign for the other parts of the tribute program was continued, and it went beyond its goals.

Despite the many manifestations of respect and affection, I approached with some trepidation the 1968 commencement weekend. By the late spring, campus protests against American foreign policy in Southeast Asia and the ongoing struggle for civil rights, culminating in the assassinations of Martin Luther King and Robert Kennedy, had spread from Berkeley and San Francisco State to many other universities, including such Ivy League citadels as Columbia. The anger and frustration that were at first directed against the government swept on to threaten other visible symbols of authority.

Brandeis had been largely spared the uglier incidents, but not because our students were less concerned or involved in what Justice Holmes had called "the actions and passions" of our times; rather, it was because the majority believed in following the tradition of free discussion and free access to all points of view, and they had always received full cooperation from the administration in their efforts to make their views felt. But the climate of student life was changing at Brandeis, too, during my last year, and the summer of 1968 was an emotionally combustible period in which no one could predict what would happen.

My misgivings began to dissipate when the president of the Student Council came to my office at the opening of the weekend, bringing with him an inscribed platter, which he presented on behalf of the student body, conveying its high regard for my incumbency. On commencement day itself, the student speaker, though he followed the practice that had become routine—blasting our social system—announced that the senior class had created a tribute fund that would be set up for scholarships in Thelma's and my name.

The honorary degree list for the commencement was impressive. The roster included two of our most highly regarded trustees, Senator William Benton, president of the Encyclopedia Britannica, and Jack Poses, a trusted adviser throughout my incumbency who had built a cosmetics empire and then shared its proceeds for significant contributions to art and education. It also included Dr. Grete Bibring, one of Sigmund Freud's last students, who, having fled from Hitler's Austria, had organized a nationally famous psychiatric workshop and had crowned her career as the first woman clinical professor at the Harvard Medical School. She was joined by Wilbur Cohen, secretary of HEW, who had served under five presidents of the United States and, as father of Medicare and Medicaid, had freed the country from the rigors of "rugged individualism." There was Judge Henry Friendly, who had been one of Justice Brandeis's law clerks and whose record in the Harvard Law School had surpassed that of his mentor, a record that had stood unchallenged since the law school was founded.

There were also tributes to several educators who were, in their separate ways, attempting to structure their institutional programs to cope with the alienation of the new generation of restless youngsters. There was Asa Knowles, the president of Northeastern University in Boston; William Saltonstall, president of the Massachusetts Board of Education and former principal of Exeter Academy; and Sister Jacqueline Grennan, the young president of Webster College in Webster Grove, Missouri, who was later released from her canonical vows as a nun to go on to a brilliant career as president of Hunter College in New York.

The roster also included Edward Levi, president of the University of Chicago. Jews had occasionally been chosen as college presidents during the past generation, but such choices were limited to small schools, none of them with the academic reputation of Chicago. Levi's father, Gerson Levi, and his grandfather, Emil G. Hirsch, had been two of the most illustrious rabbis of the twentieth century. It would have been unthinkable twenty years earlier that this scion of a long rabbinical line would some day take over the leadership of an institution founded with the millions of John D. Rockefeller, who had meant for his endowment to create an influential Baptist intellectual center in the Midwest.

We welcomed the Israeli ambassador to the United States, Yitzhak Rabin, who was later to succeed Golda Meir as prime minister. Rabin was the son of Americans who had settled in Palestine when it was still under the British mandate. Essentially a man of peace, trained for diplomacy, he had achieved decisive military victories in each of Israel's wars. Quiet spoken, modest, a team leader, he represented the new generation of native-born Israelis. He had taken up his diplomatic post in Washington after his stunning military victories in the Six Day War of 1967. The citation was both tribute and hope as it read: "Eschewing the soldier's role, preferring to seek peace and pursue it, he suggested that the lightning triumph be named the Six-Day War, paralleling the span of Creation, hopeful that the Sabbath of reconciliation would follow."

After the degrees had been conferred on our guests, my turn came to deliver my farewell. Yet I had to begin my valedictory address in sorrow. I was talking to a class that came to us out of the raw wound left by the assassination of President Kennedy, a class that had tried to carry on its studies during the violent explosions and revolutions on every continent, that had witnessed the civil rights battles in their own country, with the murder of many of its leaders and participants. The spirit of hatred, vengeance, and frustration was abroad in the land. It recalled Horace Walpole's judgment on another turbulent age: "The world is a comedy to those who

think, a tragedy to those who feel." This was not a time to offer a valedictory as a review of the founding years of our university. I spoke instead
of the travail of this generation, "children of the dusk," as the Hebrew poet
Bialik had designated those who had to live their lives in an interregnum,
between a world that was passing and a world that was a-borning. I expressed the hope that the mood of disillusionment and defeatism would
not harden into a permanent philosophy of repudiation and despair, calling
for a root-and-branch destruction of what was all too glibly called a sick
society.

"I am honestly convinced," I said, "that the crises which dislocate and
disrupt the world are not the crises of disintegration. This is no Spenglerian
apocalypse. The crises come because we are in the midst of the greatest
and most promising revolution in human history. They come from the release of hope in once darkened continents, so long chained by the old slav-
eries of ignorance, poverty and desperation. They come because hundreds
of millions of people are at last reaching for the sun. They come because
in every part of the world colonialism is being uprooted and, in our own
country, millions who had for so long been submerged and humiliated, are
on their way to dignity and opportunity. . . . How can we expect such cata-
clysmic changes to occur without disturbance? An old order does not quietly fold its tents and steal away. When revolutions come they inevitably
tear into the valuable, the precious, and the sanctified, as well as into the
obsolete. What is astonishing then is not that there is so *much* violence,
but that there is so little. . . . On what is my valedictory Commencement,
I would emphasize that however deep the sense of frustration in this sor-
rowful hour, you must get off the mourner's bench, you must not cloak
yourselves in the mantle of a wailing Cassandra. You are participants in a
great revolution—indeed you are the very heart of it—and the pains of
birth must not be confused with the agonies of death."

CHAPTER TWENTY-ONE

Valedictory

The end of August fell on one of the most beautiful days of the New England summer. All my books and personal papers had been transferred either to my home or the small suite in the faculty club that I would occupy as an office until the International Center had been completed and the chancellor's wing had become available. I had not gone through formal goodbyes with anyone because I was not really leaving Brandeis. I expected to be seeing and occasionally conferring with the personnel that remained in the Administration Center. I stood at the window of the president's office in the Irving Enclave, which had been the center of all the planning and action of the last decade. The copper beech on the far side of South Street overlooking the playing fields had grown, I thought fancifully, into a noble tree in all too short a time. Inevitably as I looked out, more thoughts came tumbling over each other, following no sequence, pointing to no one objective. I knew that I was turning another important corner in my career, but there had been no attempt yet to clarify its import. Perhaps this was because I was not one in a succession of presidents who came, did their job, and left; I had been here from the outset. I was to be a continuing predecessor.

So much came back in the weeks of relaxed interlude on walks to the Rose Art Museum, to the library, in the lovely woods that bordered the campus: the baccalaureate processions winding ahead of me over the green field to the chapels' area, where the iris stood sentinel and a young family of mallards always quacked garrulously through the ceremonies; the time when the students declared Gentle Thursday and tied balloons to the hand of Justice Brandeis's statue—and the morning I requested someone to remove the pumpkin sitting on his head; the Nobel laureate who dozed off during someone's very long speech and was propped up discreetly on either side by equally distinguished colleagues; Adlai Stevenson's name being called for an honorary degree, and the appearance on the platform of Cholmondley, a badly overstuffed sausage of a dog belonging to Ralph Norman, our school photographer, Cholmondley amiably walking across the stage and positioning himself gravely beside Stevenson as if he, too, expected a degree; back through other great days of festival to the first graduation in 1952, held during the frustrations of the Korean War, when Eleanor Roosevelt, the commencement speaker, heard about graduate Gus Ranis's gloomy valedictory, put aside her written speech, and spoke with youthful determination of the effects of playing it safe. Ranis went on to Yale where he is now Frank Altschul Professor of International Economics. Elected to the Board of Trustees in 1968, he became Trustee Emeritus in 1993.

Other vivid remembrances: Marianne Moore in her tricornered hat, coming to read poetry of a spring evening; the philodendron or aspidistra or whatever it was in my secretaries' precincts, which could not be discouraged from growing along the ceiling even after it was festooned with toy monkeys; the Arab Israeli Subhi, in the first Wien class, presenting me with an elaborately headed cane that had been in his Abu-gosh family for generations and that I hung in my office under a portrait of Ben-Gurion; the alumnus who had been an especially disruptive malcontent in his student days returning for a fifteenth reunion, after many chastening experiences in a world where action supersedes rhetoric, moving shyly up to the dais after the dinner, shaking hands quickly, saying only "Thank you," and fleeing; remembrances of our alumni and staff members who were now in college presidential positions or in influential media berths, who as students or faculty had been pretty thorny problems, causing me to wonder how they felt and acted when they sat on the other side of the table.

Winter, and my reliance on the snowplow and its driver, Walter Mahoney, who doubled as groundsman and baseball coach; the morning when Joanna and David presented Thelma with our first grandson and no work got done because everyone had a favorite name to suggest; the Japanese landscape in motion, of students wending uphill through the snow; the squirrels and wild rabbits in the president's office garden, who got handouts against all advice; and further back, when we all walked webfooted on treacherous duckboards between the snowbank and the muddy ditch to get from one half-finished facility to the other, and hardly anyone grumbled.

Above all, the autumns, when year after year the change of season flung a Joseph's coat over the campus; the annual wonder of the freshman class lining up to board the buses to drive to the president's house for the get-acquainted tea, having been admonished by our dean of women to be sure to wear hats and gloves, and the years of the next generation when we paid no attention to what the students wore as long as they came with shoes; the faculty receptions at our home, beginning with the pioneering thirteen in the first year, with the entire group and their wives greeted in the living room, and winding up with hundreds after twenty years under the spacious, gaily decorated tent on the two-acre lawn, with children and neighbors lined up outside until Thelma beckoned them to come in to dispose of the delicacies that the diet-conscious guests had reluctantly waived; all the autumns back to that first October morning of my inauguration in Symphony Hall, when my father, once a poor immigrant from Lithuania whose courage had made possible everything good that came to his family in this country, was unable to attend the greatest triumph of his perseverance because he lay dying in a St. Louis hospital, waiting only for word that his son was now officially inducted as president of the university that had made the American Jewish community a host at last.

Index

UNIVERSITY PRESS OF NEW ENGLAND publishes books under its own imprint and is the publisher for Brandeis University Press, Dartmouth College, Middlebury College Press, University of New Hampshire, University of Rhode Island, Tufts University, University of Vermont, Wesleyan University Press, and Salzburg Seminar.

Library of Congress Cataloging-in-Publication Data
Sachar, Abram Leon, 1899–
    Brandeis University, a host at last / Abram L. Sachar. — Rev. ed.
      p. cm.
    Rev. ed. of: A host at last. c1976.
    Includes index.
    ISBN 0–87451–581–5. — ISBN 0–87451–585–8 (pbk.)
    1. Brandeis University—History.　I. Sachar, Abram Leon, 1899–
Host at last.　II. Title.
LD571.B42S22　1995
378.744'4—dc20   91–50821